About This Book

On these pages you'll find everything you need to use Netscape Navigator to successfully publish on the World Wide Web. You get instruction on every aspect of Web page composition—from what you want to say and how to make it look good, to strategic, working hyperlinks and multimedia.

Who Should Read This Book?

This book is for you if

- [ ] You've been exploring the World Wide Web for a while and you want to create your own Web site.
- [ ] You already operate a Web site, but want to update it to support all the latest features and capabilities offered by Navigator 2.0.
- [ ] Your boss told you that the company wants to "get onto the Internet" and you thought he was talking about some new exercise program.
- [ ] You've heard a bit about Live Objects, JavaScript, Java, or plug-ins, but really have no idea how they can be used on your existing Web site.

How This Book Is Structured

This book has been laid out as a seven-day teach-yourself training course, complete with exercises, chapter quizzes, and examples that you can try out on your own. To get the most benefit out of the book, you should first attempt to keep to the pace set by the daily structure, and you should also attempt to complete all the exercises.

Conventions

 Note: A note box presents interesting pieces of information related to the surrounding discussion.

 Tip: A tip box offers advice or teaches an easier way to do something.

 Caution: A caution box advises you about potential problems and helps you steer clear of disaster.

 An input icon identifies some new HTML code that you can type in yourself.

 An output icon highlights what the same HTML code looks like when viewed by either Navigator 2.0.

 A CD-ROM icon lets you know that the CD-ROM included with this book contains the information you're reading about.

Teach
Yourself
Netscape Web

Publishing
in a Week

Teach Yourself
Netscape Web
Publishing
in a Week

Wes Tatters

201 West 103rd Street
Indianapolis, Indiana 46290

This book is dedicated to my brother Philip and sister Julie-Anne.

Copyright © 1996 by Sams.net Publishing

FIRST EDITION

International Standard Book Number: 1-57521-068-1

Library of Congress Catalog Card Number: 95-72580

99 98 97 96   4   3   2   1

Interpretation of the printing code: The rightmost double-digit number is the year of the book's printing; the rightmost single-digit, the number of the book's printing. For example, a printing code of 96-1 shows that the first printing of the book occurred in 1996.

Composed in AGaramond and MCPdigital by Macmillan Computer Publishing

Printed in the United States of America

Trademarks

President, Sams Publishing	Richard K. Swadley
Publisher, Sams.net Publishing	George Bond
Publishing Manager	Mark Taber
Managing Editor	Cindy Morrow
Marketing Manager	John Pierce

Acquisitions Editor
Mark Taber

Development Editor
Fran Hatton

Software Development Specialist
Merle Newlon

Production Editor
Kitty Wilson

Copy Editor
Cheri Clark

Technical Reviewer
Susan Charlesworth

Editorial Coordinator
Bill Whitmer

Technical Edit Coordinator
Lynette Quinn

Formatter
Frank Sinclair

Editorial Assistant
Carol Ackerman

Cover Designer
Tim Amrhein

Book Designer
Alyssa Yesh

Production Team Supervisor
Brad Chinn

Production
Mary Ann Abramson,
Georgiana Briggs,
Gina Brown, Mona Brown,
Michael Brumitt, Tom Dinse,
Jason Hand, Sonja Hart,
Mike Henry, Aleata Howard,
Ayanna Lacey, Paula Lowell,
Donna Martin, Steph Mineart
Casey Price, Laura Robbins
Bobbi Satterfield. Craig Small
Laura A. Smith, SA Springer
Josette Starks, Andrew Stone,
Tim Taylor, Colleen Williams
Susan D. Van Ness

Overview

Contents

Acknowledgments

Where I have directly quoted from additional sources throughout this book, you will find that I have attributed the quote to the appropriate person. However, because much of the information in this book comes from personal knowledge gained over a period of years, it has been impossible to directly attribute all sources of information.

To this end I would like to express my appreciation to all the people I have corresponded with in the past few years, many of whom have provided me with valuable insights into the workings of the Internet and the World Wide Web.

Appreciation also goes to Laura Lemay for her ground-breaking book *Teach Yourself Web Publishing with HTML in a Week* and to Netscape Communications and Sun Microsystems for the online documentation, which they make so readily available to the Internet community.

I would also like to acknowledge the work of the many hundreds of people responsible for the creation and collation of the thousands of Request for Comment, For Your Information, and Standards documents maintained by InterNIC, the historical and informational articles compiled by the Internet Society, and the Frequently Asked Questions documents produced so regularly and tirelessly by people whose sole interest is in promoting and developing the Internet.

It also goes without saying that no book on the World Wide Web could ever really go to print without acknowledging the work of Tim Berners-Lee in developing the World Wide Web; the W3 Consortium for its ongoing coordination of the future developments of the World Wide Web; and again, Netscape Communications, for the amazing computer program this book is devoted to.

And finally, thank you to all the people who helped make this book a reality:

- ☐ My girlfriend, Cait Spreadborough, for reading and editing the original manuscript.
- ☐ Susan Charlesworth, for her work in checking all the information, sites, services, and technical aspects of this book.
- ☐ The staff at Sams who helped guide this project to its completion, especially Mark Taber, Fran Hatton, and Kitty Wilson.

About the Author

Wes Tatters has worked in the computer industry since 1984 as a computer programmer and systems designer. During this time he has worked on a number of computer platforms using a variety of computer languages and communications tools. Currently, he operates a video production company while regularly writing articles for a number of Australian computer magazines and the Internet Daily News at `http://tvp.com/`. These articles deal with a diverse range of topics including the Internet, CompuServe, Amiga computers, Windows 95, and database technology. He is also the author of *Navigating the Internet with CompuServe* and *Navigating the Internet with America Online,* also by Sams.net, and can be reached on the Internet at `wtatters@world.net` or `taketwo@webcom.com`.

Introduction

Over the course of the past few years, the World Wide Web has become the most visible and possibly the most well-known feature of the Internet. Whenever you see a story about the Internet in the newspapers or on television, you can bet that there will be at least one screen shot of a computer connected to the World Wide Web somewhere in the piece.

For the most part, it is the graphical, user-friendly nature of the World Wide Web that has made it such a popular tool. But at the same time, the very fact that just about anybody can become a Web publisher also makes the World Wide Web very attractive. If you had not already guessed from the title on the front cover, Web publishing is the main subject of the this book, and more specifically Web publishing for Netscape Navigator Version 2.0.

Who Should Read This Book?

Everyone—it should be on the international required reading list—the more copies sold the better. But seriously folks, if you fall into one of the following categories, this book is for you:

- ☐ You've been exploring the World Wide Web for a while and you want to create your own Web site.
- ☐ You already operate a Web site, but want to update it to support all of the latest features and capabilities offered by Navigator 2.0.
- ☐ Your boss told you that the company wants to "get onto the Internet" and you thought he was talking about some new exercise program.
- ☐ You've heard a bit about Live Objects, JavaScript, Java, or plug-ins, but really have no idea how they can be used on your existing Web site.

On the other hand, if you fall into one of the following categories, maybe you have the wrong book for your needs:

- ☐ You're new to the Internet and want to learn how to use a Web browser. There is a chapter on the Navigator 2.0 Web browser on Day 1, but maybe you should take a look at a more general book like *Navigating the Internet*, also by Sams.net.
- ☐ You want to learn how to send and receive electronic mail. Yep, *Navigating the Internet* is probably the book for you.
- ☐ You live in a commune that does not even have electricity, let alone a computer system. (Although if you plan to move back to the big smoke sometime in the future, Web publishing could offer some viable job prospects.) What the heck! Buy the book anyway—if nothing else you can used it to plug that hole in the roof.
- ☐ You hate computers, abhor technology, and think we should all go back to living in trees.

How This Book Is Organized

This book has been laid out as a seven-day teach-yourself training course, complete with exercises, chapter quizzes, and examples that you can try out on your own. To get the most benefit out of the book, you should first attempt to keep to the pace set by the daily structure, and you should also attempt to complete all the exercises.

Creating and publishing Web pages on the World Wide Web is not a difficult task, but there are a number of different commands and instructions required to do so. By working through all the exercises and examples yourself, these commands will rapidly become second nature to you. After all, any teacher will tell you that the best way to learn about something is to put it into practical use.

Day 1: Introducing the World Wide Web, Hypertext, and Netscape

On the first day you'll learn about what the World Wide Web is and how it came into being. In addition, you will learn something about Netscape Navigator 2.0—the Web browser that much of the information in this book relates to—and some of the many Web publishing tools and utilities that are currently available.

Day 2: Creating Simple Web Documents

On Day 2, get ready to jump headlong into the world of Web publishing. You'll explore some practical tips and planning steps, which should be the hallmark of any Web publishing project, and you'll also learn how to create your first Web page. In addition, you'll learn about one of the most important concepts in Web publishing—the hyperlink.

Day 3: Building on the Basics

The third day builds on what you learned on Day 2 by first exploring many of the more advanced formatting options available when creating Web pages targeted at the Navigator 2.0 Web browser. You will also learn how to add tables to your Web pages and incorporate hyperlinks that point to Internet services and resources other than a Web page.

Day 4: Enhancing Your Web Page's Visual Appearance

With all the main formatting and layout functions now behind you, on Day 4 you will learn how to enhance the visual appearance of Web pages by adding inline images, external multimedia, and Live Objects—or plug-ins. And as an added bonus, Day 4 also explores one of the latest Navigator 2.0 features, called *frames*.

Day 5: Going Online

On Day 5, all the efforts of the previous four days are brought to a culmination. On this day you will learn how to take the Web pages you have created previously and publish them on the World Wide Web. First, you'll learn all about Web servers and why you need them, and then you'll explore some of the many techniques available online to tell the world about the existence of your new Web site. In addition, the last chapter of Day 5 takes a step back from the mechanics of Web publishing by examining some practical considerations for developing effective Web sites.

Day 6: Developing Interactive Web Pages

Apart from being a good system for publishing information, the World Wide Web is also ideally suited to more interactive tasks such as online shopping, data collection, and feedback forms. On Day 6, you will learn how to develop Web pages a user can interact with. This is achieved through a technique called *CGI scripting* and through the use of *forms*. In addition, you will learn how to create *image maps* and dynamic Web pages.

Day 7: Programming with Java and JavaScript

With the introduction of Navigator 2.0, two new advanced programming options have been made available to Web publishing: JavaScript and Java. On the final day of this book you will learn how to use JavaScript and Java to further enhance the look and feel of your Web pages.

Note: Several chapters in this book have been adapted from Laura Lemay's *Teach Yourself Web Publishing with HTML in 14 Days, Premier Edition*—still the best general introduction to Web publishing anywhere. Chapters 3, 11, 13, and 15 through 18 all contain material that has been updated, revised, and added to specifically for this book and the Netscape Web publishing environment.

About the CD-ROM

At the back of this book you will find a CD-ROM. Included on this CD are a number of helper applications and utilities, image/graphics editors and converters, a collection of HTML document editors and processors, some Navigator 2.0 plug-ins, the current documentation for the Java language, and the source code for all the exercises and examples used in the book.

If you don't have access to a CD drive, many of the files included on the CD can also be obtained online from the book's home page at `http://www.mcp.com/samsnet/books/tynwp/` or from the various FTP and World Wide Web sites listed throughout the book. In addition, copies of all the exercises and examples can be obtained from my Web site at `http://www.webcom.com/taketwo/samstyn.shtml`.

What You Need to Get Started

Apart from some previous experience with the Internet and more specifically the World Wide Web, all you really need to become a Web publisher is a computer and a bit of spare time.

Naturally, you will also need an Internet connection and a copy of Navigator 2.0 to get the most benefit out of this book, but unlike in many other areas of the computing world, you don't need a degree in computer science to become a proficient Web publisher.

With that said, sit back and turn to Day 1 to teach yourself Netscape Web publishing in a week.

Note: Although you don't really need to have any previous experience with the World Wide Web to become a Web publisher (although it will help) the best way to learn about the capabilities offered by the World Wide Web is to get online and explore them for yourself.

DAY 1

Introducing the World Wide Web, Hypertext, and Netscape

1

Welcome to the World Wide Web

As you turn to this, the first chapter of *Teach Yourself Netscape Web Publishing in a Week*, you are about to embark on a journey that will, over the next seven days, guide you through the process of publishing Netscape-aware Web pages or Web documents.

However, before jumping headlong into the publishing process, it is important that you have some understanding of the principles behind the World Wide Web and Netscape Navigator 2.0.

To get you started, this chapter takes a look at what the World Wide Web is and how it operates. If you are already familiar with the World Wide Web, you might want to skip ahead to Chapter 2, "Getting to Know the Netscape Navigator," which examines the Netscape Navigator 2.0 Web browser itself. However, you may find that a quick refresher course now will be helpful as you delve further into the world of Web publishing.

For everyone else, this chapter examines the following topics:

- [ ] What is the World Wide Web?
- [ ] Who runs the World Wide Web?
- [ ] Web browsers
- [ ] HTML—the language of the World Wide Web
- [ ] Web servers
- [ ] Uniform resource locators
- [ ] Home pages

Note: Since its inception, the World Wide Web has become known by a number of different names and titles. These include the Web, WWW, W3, and naturally, the World Wide Web. For consistency, however, the term World Wide Web is used throughout this book when referring to the World Wide Web itself, and the abbreviation Web is used when referring to particular elements such as Web servers, Web browsers, Web pages, and Web production.

What Is the World Wide Web?

Trying to define the World Wide Web is not as easy a task as might first be anticipated. According to Tim Berners-Lee—the father of the World Wide Web—it is a "distributed heterogeneous collaborative multimedia information system." The problem, however, is that unless you sleep with a dictionary under your pillow, such definitions make about as much sense as a Martian road map.

> **Note:** In 1989 and 1990, while working at the European Laboratory for Particle Physics near Geneva, Switzerland—known more commonly as CERN—Tim Berners-Lee developed the concept of the World Wide Web and created the first Web browser on a NeXT workstation. It was called—not too imaginatively—the NeXT browser.

While Tim Berners-Lee's definition may use language that for the most part is probably best suited to the confines of a laboratory, it does indicate one very important point about the World Wide Web. Basically, it is impossible to define it using a single word, although for many people the term *cyberspace* does spring immediately to mind.

So what is the World Wide Web? To put it in a nutshell, the World Wide Web is a graphical *hypertext*-based information system that provides access to a multitude of Internet resources. Or to put it in even more common terms it is an easy way to access the interconnected web of computers and information that can be accessed by just about anyone with an Internet connection.

However, even this definition still fails to do the subject justice. To get a better understanding, you really need to look at the various elements or attributes that make up the World Wide Web. These attributes include

- ☐ Multiple protocol support
- ☐ Hypertext-based information access
- ☐ Distributed information
- ☐ Graphical interface
- ☐ Multimedia capabilities
- ☐ Interactive access
- ☐ Dynamic updating
- ☐ Cross-platform support

What Is Multiple Protocol Support?

Before the World Wide Web was developed, researchers at CERN who wanted to locate specific information on their Internet-based network were forced to work with a number of different applications whose operation and usability often varied greatly. For example, if a person wanted to read an article posted to a Usenet newsgroup, he or she needed to run a newsreader program. To download a file mentioned in one of these articles, another program called an *FTP client* was required, and then if the downloaded file was a photograph, yet another program was needed to display the image on the user's computer screen.

 **Note:** The various types of services available on the Internet are accessed using what are called *communications protocols*. Each different service has its own protocol, which must be used when communicating with the service. For example, to retrieve a file from an FTP server you must use the File Transfer Protocol.

For those people who were used to the vagaries of the Internet, such actions were considered to be just a minor distraction compared to the overwhelming benefits the Internet brought. But for the growing number of scientists and researchers who began to take advantage of the facilities offered by CERN, the complexities involved in finding and accessing information were often the cause of considerable aggravation. What was needed was a single tool that gave people access to all the resources provided by the Internet.

In developing the World Wide Web, Tim Berners-Lee created such a service. Instead of running separate programs to download files, read articles, or view images, all that was needed was a single program called a *Web browser*. (See Figure 1.1.) Using such a program and the concepts Tim Berners-Lee developed, it is now possible to explore almost every part of the Internet without ever needing to worry about changing programs.

 Note: Chapter 2 examines the Netscape Navigator Web browser and looks at many of the features it provides.

Figure 1.1.
Using a Web browser like Netscape Navigator, you can explore almost every part of the Internet.

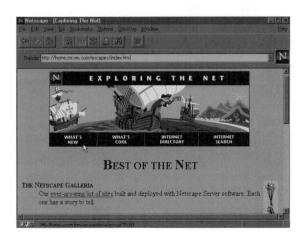

What Is Hypertext-Based Information Access?

Dealing with the many programs required to explore the Internet was not the only problem the people working at CERN faced. Even when they did come to grips with the complexities of Internet access, there was yet another bridge to cross.

The Internet, as its name suggests, is a network of millions of interconnected computer systems. To access information on any of these computers, you need to first know the *address* of the specific computer you want to communicate with. As a result, using programs such as the FTP client discussed previously meant keying in computer addresses, and then directory paths, and finally filenames, before any information could be downloaded. The researcher who simply wanted to read the contents of a paper written by a fellow scientist was often less than excited by the amount of work required to obtain a copy of the file.

To rectify this situation, Tim Berners-Lee decided to adopt the hypertext concept made popular by the developers of the Apple Macintosh in their HyperCard application. If you are not familiar with HyperCard, but have used any of the online help systems provided by Microsoft Windows or Sun Microsystems' AnswerBook, then you have already seen the concept of hypertext at work.

Hypertext is a process that allows special connections called *hotlinks* or *hyperlinks* to be embedded in what have become known as *Web pages* or *HTML documents*. (See Figure 1.2.) Clicking on one of these links tells the browser to automatically load the file represented by the link. In Web terminology, a hyperlink is said to *point to* a new file or resource. With these hyperlinks, you can very easily move from page to page without ever needing to know the physical name of the file or even the address of the computer where it is stored. You simply click on the link and your Web browser knows where to go to locate the new information.

Tip: Traditionally, on a Web page hyperlinks are represented by underlined text and are highlighted in the color blue or purple.

Note: For those of you who are new to the World Wide Web, hyperlinks use an addressing system called a universal resource locator (URL) to indicate the location of Web pages and other resources. For example, the main URL for the Netscape Communications Web site looks something like this:

```
http://www.netscape.com/
```

In addition to pointing to other Web pages, hyperlinks can also point to Usenet newsgroups, files stored on anonymous FTP servers, Gopher holes, and just about every other type of Internet resource.

Figure 1.2.
Clicking on a hyperlink tells the Web browser you want to look at the information the hyperlink points to.

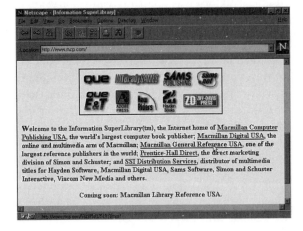

Note: The basis for most of the information displayed by a Web browser is a special type of file called a *hypertext markup language document,* or HTML document for short. Such documents are used to describe the contents of pages displayed by Web browsers and the location of hyperlinks within a page. The section "HTML—The Language of the World Wide Web" later in this chapter explains in more detail exactly what an HTML document is.

What Is Distributed Information?

The Web browser's ability to move at will around the Internet, traveling from computer to computer, with little more effort than the click of a button, leads to one of the most important concepts you need to grasp when dealing with the World Wide Web.

There is no physical location or computer system anywhere on the Internet that can be pointed to and described as the World Wide Web. In other words, there is no central location where all the Web pages that can be displayed by the World Wide Web are stored. Instead, parts of the World Wide Web are stored on computers all over the Internet.

This effectively means that the amount of information which can be stored on the World Wide Web is limited only by the number of computers connected to the Internet and the collective storage space these computers contain. This, for all practical purposes, means that the World Wide Web has an infinite storage capacity.

What Is a Graphical Interface?

Until the appearance of the World Wide Web, the greater percentage of the Internet could best be described as text oriented. There are a number of reasons for this, the most predominant of which is the fact that historically most connections to the Internet came from UNIX and mainframe computers whose terminals were strictly text-only affairs. As a result, when services such as FTP, telnet, Gopher, and Usenet were developed their creators saw no need to allow for the possibility of anything but straight text.

The World Wide Web, on the other hand, is very much a graphical application, although some people will argue that text-only Web browsers such a Lynx (see Figure 1.3) operate very nicely without any graphics whatsoever. The simple reality is, however, that to get the most out of the World Wide Web you need a computer with a graphical user interface, or *GUI*. Figure 1.4 shows how the Web page displayed in Figure 1.3 looks when viewed using the Netscape Navigator Web browser.

Figure 1.3.

Text-based Web browsers such as Lynx give people with terminal-based access the ability to explore the World Wide Web.

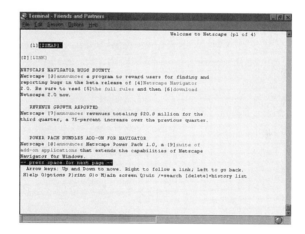

Figure 1.4.

With the increased use of image maps and image-based hyperlinks, a graphical interface is now a necessity for Web exploration.

Many images displayed by Web browsers are not just there for visual effect. Take the large Welcome to Netscape image displayed at the top of Figure 1.4, for example. This image is actually a special type of hyperlink called an image map. Clicking on different parts of this image will cause the Web browser to load Web pages that discuss the topics indicated by the image.

Note: There is a considerable amount of debate surrounding the use of the term hypertext to describe the way the World Wide Web operates. Some people argue that because hyperlinks can be images as well as text, the term used should really be *hypermedia*. However, the fact still remains that the initial design for the World Wide Web was based on the concept of Hypertext.

What Are Multimedia Capabilities?

The World Wide Web is not limited to displaying text and images. With the advent of fast Internet connections, many Web browsers can now play sound clips and even realtime audio using systems like *RealAudio*—`http://www.realaudio.com/`. By taking advantage of such features, the World Wide Web has become not only a source of text-based information and pictures, but also a radio network. Figure 1.5 shows one such *Web site,* which is operated by AudioNet at `http://www.audionet.com/`.

Note: The term Web site is used throughout this book to refer to collections of Web pages that have been grouped together on a single computer system.

Figure 1.5.
AudioNet brings realtime news, interviews, talkback radio, and live sports broadcasts to the Internet.

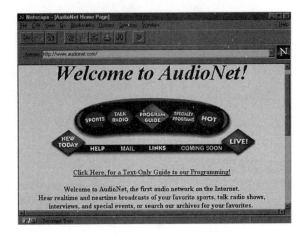

For those of you lucky enough to be connected to the Internet by a high-speed connection, another multimedia resource is beginning to gain a place on the World Wide Web: video. Until very recently it was simply not practical or possible for all but the most powerful computer systems to play moving images and sounds. But with the increased availability of fast Pentium and PowerPC computers, such capabilities are moving into the realm of reality.

There are, however, still a number of logistical difficulties that need to be resolved before the general public can start viewing the latest feature movies on the Internet. Of these, the most pressing is the need for very high-speed connections to the Internet. For example, a low-quality 30-second movie will probably require at least 2MB of storage space. If you tried to download this movie using a 28,800bps modem, the transfer would take anywhere from 10 to 20 minutes, a speed which could hardly be referred to as realtime.

While these sorts of transfer speeds may not be suitable for movies on demand, there are already a number of Web sites that allow you to download small video clips like the 30-second one mentioned in the last paragraph. One of the most popular of these is the MovieWEB site shown in Figure 1.6. To visit this site, point your Web browser to `http://movieweb.com/movie/movie.html`.

Note: You point your Web browser to a Web page by telling your Web browser to open the Web page indicated by the URL in question. (See Chapter 2 for an in-depth discussion of the Netscape Navigator 2.0 Web browser and its use.)

Figure 1.6.

You can download trailers and teasers for all the latest feature movies via MovieWEB.

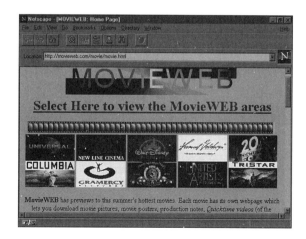

What Is Interactive Access?

Unlike most other Internet-based services, the World Wide Web is a highly interactive environment. When you click on a hyperlink, the World Wide Web responds by giving you new information to view. Such a level of interaction would on its own not be considered that exciting. After all, when you select a file for downloading using FTP, it, too, responds by sending you new information.

What makes the World Wide Web different is its ability to accept information from users and perform various actions based on these responses. To do this the World Wide Web uses what are called *forms*. (See Figure 1.7.)

Figure 1.7.

Forms enable people to interact with the World Wide Web.

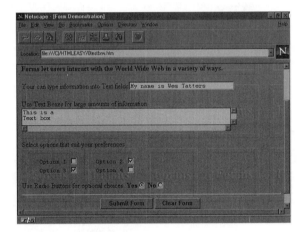

A form is a special Web page that includes text fields, check boxes, radio buttons, menus, and popup lists that give the user the ability to interact with the World Wide Web. Forms are used all over the World Wide Web in a wide variety of applications. For example, if you want to order a book while online, the simplest way to do so is by filling out an online order form. Other sites use forms to conduct surveys, obtain feedback, provide input for search tools, and tailor their sites to best suit a user's needs.

What Is Dynamic Updating?

Many people have likened the World Wide Web to a global encyclopedia. Like an encyclopedia, the World Wide Web contains a wealth of information on almost every imaginable topic, yet it differs from an encyclopedia by constantly changing and evolving.

When you purchase an encyclopedia you obtain a set of books that contain accurate and up-to-date information. But within weeks, parts of the encyclopedia will be out of date. This has been especially evident in recent years with the political changes in Eastern Europe that have seen entire countries disappear. As a result, trying to keep an encyclopedia up-to-date has become a nearly impossible task.

The World Wide Web, on the other hand, is always as up-to-date as its latest entry, and what's more important, the end user does not even need to know when changes are being made. The dynamic nature of the World Wide Web means that all a person needs to do to obtain the latest information is select the appropriate hyperlink.

> **Caution:** Although the World Wide Web has the potential to be the best source of up-to-date information, information still needs to be placed on the World Wide Web by someone. This leads to a question of reliability. In some cases the latest information on the World Wide Web may not be very up-to-date simply because no one has bothered to update it!

What Is Cross-Platform Support?

In the world of computers, the most harrowing question you can ask a computer programmer is Will that program you wrote from my Apple Macintosh run on the IBM PC I have at home? Unfortunately, the answer is no!

From the moment the first computer scientists realized they could make their computers better than the rest by doing things differently, the issue of compatibility has plagued the computing world. Today you have UNIX computers that won't run software written for Microsoft Windows, Macintosh programs that won't run under MS-DOS, and more recently Windows 95 software that won't run under Windows 3.11.

What makes the World Wide Web so radically different from most other aspects of computing life is the fact that it can be run on just about any type of computer system ever developed, and in most cases it looks and feels the same regardless of what computer you are using. In fact, all that is needed to take advantage of the World Wide Web is a Web browser designed for the type of computer you use.

Who Owns the World Wide Web?

The simple answer to this question is no one! Yet at the same time it can be argued that everyone owns the World Wide Web. Like much of the Internet, the World Wide Web is more of a collaborative effort between all the people who publish Web pages. Certainly it can be said that people who create Web pages own their contents, in terms of copyright and other legal issues, but when it comes to the World Wide Web itself, it is not possible to assign ownership to a single group.

Although no one owns the Web, there is an organization that attempts to coordinate the development and future direction of the World Wide Web: the W3 Consortium.

The W3 Consortium

The W3 Consortium was formed by the Massachusetts Institute of Technology (MIT) and the French National Institute for Research in Computing and Automation (INRIA) in collaboration with CERN, to take responsibility for the long-term coordination of the World Wide Web and the various standards such a global system demands.

The purposes of the consortium are

- To support the advancement of information technology in the field of networking, graphics, and user interfaces by developing the World Wide Web into a comprehensive information infrastructure
- To encourage the industry to adopt a common set of World Wide Web protocols

To achieve this, the consortium plans to design a common World Wide Web protocol suite, develop publicly available reference code, promote the common protocol suite throughout the world, and encourage industry to create products that comply with the common protocol suite.

If you are interested in finding out more information about the consortium's activities and its members, you can go to a World Wide Web site that has been set up to provide detailed information about many of the projects currently under development, along with a wide variety of resource documents dealing with all aspects of the World Wide Web. The contents page for this site, as shown in Figure 1.8, can be found by pointing your Web browser to `http://www.w3.org/`.

Figure 1.8.
The W3 Consortium home page.

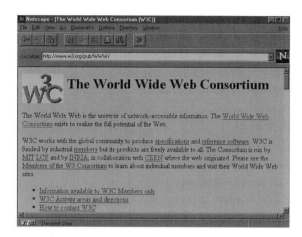

Web Browsers

To access the World Wide Web and explore the many services it offers, you first need some way to communicate with it. The best way to communicate with the World Wide Web is to use a Web browser such as the Netscape Navigator, which is discussed in Chapter 2 and throughout this book.

When Tim Berners-Lee designed the first Web browser, he set out to create a program that would replace all the various Internet tools that people had previously used to communicate with the Internet. However, as the project developed, his original Web browser became more than just a replacement for all the old tools. Instead, it evolved into a new method of communicating with the Internet that also encompassed all the previous methods.

How Does a Web Browser Work?

At its most basic level, a Web browser is a program that can retrieve any sort of information from just about any computer connected to the Internet and display it in a recognizable format. All the Web browser needs to know is the location of the required information.

Uniform Resource Locators

To tell the Web browser where a file or any other resource is located, a special kind of address called a uniform resource locator (URL) is used. In fact, you have already encountered a number of URLs while reading this chapter. When I told you to point your Web browser to `http://movieweb.com/movie/movie.html`, what I was really saying was that `http://movieweb.com/movie/movie.html` is the URL of the Web document for the MovieWEB site.

A URL is designed in such a way that it contains all the information needed by the Web browser to obtain the file you require. The first part of the URL (the *protocol*) tells the Web browser what type of file or service it needs to communicate with. This might be `ftp:`, `gopher:`, `news:`, or a Web page (`http:`). Following the protocol definition comes the *domain name* of the computer where the information is held. In the case of MovieWEB this is `movieweb.com`. After the domain name are the directory and name of the actual file: `/movie/movie.html`.

As you learn more about the World Wide Web, you will find that URLs are the lifeblood of the Internet. You can use a URL to jump straight to a Web page by entering it directly into your Web browser, and you will also find that all the hyperlinks buried in Web pages are, in fact, URLs that point to the location of the required information.

Note: For more information about the different types of URLs and protocols supported by the World Wide Web, turn to Chapter 9, "Working with Links and URLs."

HTML—The Language of the World Wide Web

Although a Web browser can communicate with a variety of different Internet services, most of the time you will find yourself using your Web browser to display Web pages.

To easily define the contents of a WWW page, a simple method was needed that could encompass the large amounts of text many pages include and incorporate all the graphical elements and combinations of hypertext links that may be included on any given page. Also, a system was needed that could allow the same information to be displayed on a wide variety of both text and graphical WWW browsers.

As a result, it was decided that instead of defining WWW pages in a rigid typographic sense, a language would be developed to describe the information and the way its creator expected it to appear. The WWW browser could then take this information and display it in the best way possible, given its particular operating environment.

To do this, the *hypertext markup language* (*HTML*) was developed. HTML uses text files that include a limited set of instructions to define special items such as hyperlinks, images, and a limited number of typographic elements. (See Figure 1.9.) This allows WWW pages to be created by anyone with a simple text editor or word processor.

Figure 1.9.
HTML lets anyone with a text editor create pages that can be displayed by a World Wide Web browser.

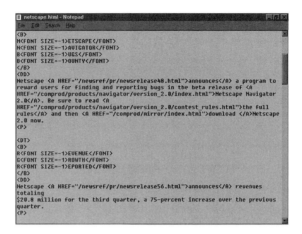

Once a page of HTML has been created and stored on a WWW server, anyone can add a link to the new document from his or her own HTML page, assuming of course that they know the URL of the Web page in question. By doing this, the new page effectively becomes part of the World Wide Web and can then be called up by anyone with a WWW browser and Internet access. For example, the page of HTML shown in Figure 1.9 is actually a part of the main Web page for the Netscape Communications shown in Figure 1.4.

If you look closely, you might be able to see how the various references made in the HTML document become pictures and hyperlinks in a WWW browser. However, don't be too concerned, at this early stage, if everything looks a bit like a Russian food recipe. After all, if you could already read HTML fluently, you probably wouldn't be reading this chapter.

Web Servers

As mentioned previously, you use a Web browser to display Web pages. But how do these pages get onto the World Wide Web in the first place?

The best way to publish Web pages on the World Wide Web is to use what is called a *Web server*. A Web server is a special type of program that sits on a computer connected to the Internet and waits for requests from Web browsers. When you click on a hyperlink using your Web browser, the browser works out which Web server looks after the information you are interested in. It then sends a request to that Web server, asking for a copy of the selected file, and the server then organizes the transmission of the file back to your Web browser.

Note: It is technically possible to publish Web pages without using a Web server. You could use either an FTP client or a Gopher server, but doing so greatly reduces the level of interaction your pages can provide, as you will learn in Chapter 13, "Installing Your Web Pages on a Web Server."

Web servers are also responsible for handling any interactive activities that might be demanded of a Web page that includes forms. For example, when you fill out an online order form, it is the Web server that organizes the information you have entered into a format that will result in the products you have ordered being delivered to your doorstep.

Note: On Day 5, Chapter 13 and Chapter 16, "Interacting with the Web Server by Using CGI," explain the principles behind working with a Web server.

Home Pages

If you spend even a short amount of time exploring the World Wide Web you will come across the term *home page.* Although this term is in widespread use, there are currently a few different opinions about exactly what a home page is.

The Web Browser Home Page

Every Web browser has a default home page, which is configured when the browser is first installed. This is the Web page that your browser displays when you first start running it. For the Netscape Navigator the Web page shown in Figure 1.4 is the default home page.

Once you become familiar with your Web browser, you will be able to alter the default home page and set it to any Web page you like. After you do this, the new page, rather than the original default home page, will be loaded every time you start your Web browser. (See Chapter 2 for information about changing Netscape's default home page.)

Tip: I have set my Web browser home page so that it points to the powerful World Wide Web search tool called Lycos: `http://www.lycos.com/`. Doing this gives me direct access to an index that now encompasses over 90% of the World Wide Web.

The Web Server Home Page

The second way the term home page is used is to refer to the main page of a Web server.

One of the most difficult concepts to come to grips with when dealing with the World Wide Web is the fact that it has no top or bottom. There is effectively no front door to the World Wide Web or, for that matter, back door. For this reason, most Web sites create a special page—a bit like a table of contents—which acts as the home page for that Web site.

There are many definitions of what actually constitutes a home page. Regardless of what the technical definitions are, most people consider a Web server home page to be any location on the World Wide Web that acts like a front door to a collection of Web pages that are stored on a single Web server.

Personal Home Pages

The third and final "popular" usage of the term home page relates to Web pages that act as a front door to a specific collection of pages.

For example, I have a collection of Web pages stored on a Web server whose server home page is `http://www.webcom.com/`. If you used this URL, a contents page describing all the information stored at Web Communications is displayed. On the other hand, if you used the URL of my personal home page—at `http://www.webcom.com/taketwo/`—you would see my private contents page, instead of the server home page.

Sites such as `http://www.webcom.com/` can contain literally thousands of personal home pages, on every topic imaginable.

Summary

In this chapter you have learned about the basics of the World Wide Web, including what it is and how it operates. You should now have a general understanding of what the terms HTML and URL mean and how they relate to the World Wide Web. In addition, you should now know the difference between a Web browser and a Web server, and understand what is meant by the term home page.

With these basics under your belt, you are ready to move on the next chapter, where you will learn about the Netscape Web browser and explore many of the features it offers.

Workshop

Welcome to the Workshop. Throughout this book, at the end of each chapter you will find a section similar to this one, which provides you with some homework, so to speak.

The first section of the Workshop lists some of the common questions people ask about the World Wide Web along with a brief answer to each. Next is a quiz about the chapter you have just read. If you have problems answering any of the questions in the quiz, you can turn to Appendix E, "Answers to Quiz Questions."

Finally, the best way to learn about Web publishing is to actually create Web pages. To get you started, each chapter lists a number of exercises that you might like to try.

Q&A

Q How large is the World Wide Web?

A One recent estimate reported that there are more than 10 million pages of information on the World Wide Web, and another reported that the number of pages is doubling every 6 months. The problem, however, is that no one is really sure. Because of the distributed nature of the World Wide Web, it is very difficult to account for every Web server.

Q If the World Wide Web is so large, how can anyone ever find what they are looking for?

A One of the best ways to locate information on the World Wide Web is to use a service called Lycos. To use Lycos point your Web browser to `http://www.lycos.com/`.

Basically, Lycos is an enormous database that contains links to more than 10 million WWW pages. When you enter a word or group of words into the search field located on the Lycos home page, Lycos uses its database to create a list of WWW pages that contain matches for any or all of the words. By default, Lycos lists the first 10 sites that match your request, with the WWW pages that contain the most matches being listed first. Alternatively, if you want Lycos to display more matches or change the way the search is conducted, select the Search Options link on the Lycos home page. If you select this option, you will be presented with a search page that gives you greater control of how Lycos operates.

As an added bonus, Lycos includes what its developers claim is the most up-to-date "top sites" listing on the Internet. Lycos generated this list by cross-referencing the millions of WWW links located by special programs it calls "spiders," as they roam the World Wide Web looking for new sites. The result is a list of the 250 WWW pages that contain the most links from other sites.

Q I have a friend who set up a shop on the Internet to sell greeting cards, but since she installed the service no one has placed a single order. Is the World Wide Web all hype?

A There is a great danger in thinking that the World Wide Web is somehow going to magically make you money. Certainly there are many companies that claim considerable success selling products on the World Wide Web, and yes, there is no doubt that many have met with little success.

The World Wide Web is not all hype, but at the same time, it is also not the "Great White Hope." Like any new venture, it will take some time before your Web site becomes known. You can help this situation by promoting the existence of your site on not only the Internet, but also on your business cards, letterhead, flyers, and maybe even bumper stickers.

Just remember the saying "If you build it, they will come!"

Quiz

1. Where was the World Wide Web created?
2. What do the letters HTML stand for?
3. Name four attributes of the World Wide Web.
4. What do the letters URL stand for?
5. Who is the father of the World Wide Web?
6. What is a hyperlink?
7. How many roads must a man walk down?
8. Who owns the World Wide Web?

Exercise

Before you embark on the development of your own Web pages, you need to spend some time examining as many different Web pages as you possibly can. More importantly, however, you need to develop a feeling for what constitutes a good Web page and what does not.

Choose 5 Web pages and create a list of pros and cons. For each page, you should attempt to list at least 10 comments discussing what you like about the site or what you don't like. Then, once you have created the list, compare your comments for each site and attempt to come up with 5 general ideas about what you feel constitutes a good Web page.

2

Getting to Know the Netscape Navigator

Now that you have an understanding of what the World Wide Web is all about, it's time to take a look at Netscape Navigator 2.0, the Web browser this book revolves around.

In this chapter you will learn about the following topics:

- ☐ The early years of Netscape
- ☐ Installing Netscape 2.0
- ☐ Working with Netscape 2.0
- ☐ Configuring Netscape 2.0
- ☐ Advanced capabilities

Netscape—The Early Years

Unlike most other Internet tools, whose histories can be traced back to the formative days of the Internet, the World Wide Web is a relative youngster.

As mentioned briefly in the last chapter, it was not until late in 1990 that the first World Wide Web browser, designed by Tim Berners-Lee, appeared at CERN. Over the next 12 months, this browser and a less-capable, text-based version were brought online at CERN and were gradually enhanced to include all the capabilities requested by the project staff. These features included the ability to read newsgroups, access anonymous FTP sites, and make use of both WAIS and gopher servers without the need to access any other client programs.

Although these browsers were available only in-house at CERN, it was not long before people outside of CERN began to hear rumors about this exciting new tool. They began looking for ways to make it available to the mainstream Internet world. To address these rumors, in 1992 CERN started to actively promote the existence of the World Wide Web tool it had developed.

Following this announcement, a number of World Wide Web browsers began to appear on most computer platforms, including Windows, Apple Macintosh, UNIX, and even smaller platforms such as the Commodore Amiga. Since then, the World Wide Web has erupted onto the Internet and single-handedly replaced many of the previously popular client applications. The Web has given people of different user levels simple and efficient access to all aspects of the emerging information superhighway.

NCSA Mosaic

Without a doubt, the best known of all World Wide Web browsers is the Mosaic browser developed by the National Center for Supercomputing Applications (NCSA) at the University of Illinois at Urbana-Champaign. Since the first NCSA Mosaic browser appeared in early 1993, it has become the de facto standard for World Wide Web browsers. (See Figure 2.1.)

Note: Although Mosaic is regarded as the de facto standard for World Wide Web browsers, there is also an official standard that specifies the visual functionality a Web browser should include. This standard is known commonly as the *HTML specification.* It describes the instructions that can be included in an HTML document and how they should appear when displayed by a Web browser.

Figure 2.1.
NCSA Mosaic.

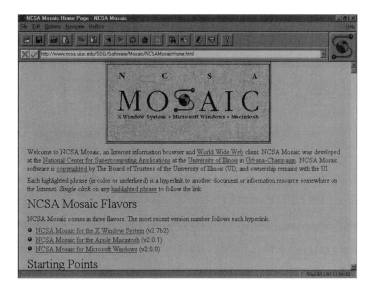

When the NCSA developed Mosaic, its aim was to create a World Wide Web browser that could be freely available to all members of the Internet community. At the same time, the ongoing development of Mosaic ensures that the World Wide Web continues to gain new functionality and evolve to meet the demands of an increasingly computer-literate community.

There are currently versions of Mosaic available for Windows (2.0.0), Apple Macintosh (2.0.1), and a variety of X11-based UNIX machines (Version 2.7b2). In addition, the full source code is available to those interested in exploring the internal workings of the program or in developing their own specialized versions.

To this end, many other World Wide Web browsers now available demonstrate their obvious heritage, which lies in the NCSA source code.

Note: NCSA Mosaic is available free of charge from `http://www.ncsa.uiuc.edu/SDG/Software/Mosaic/NCSAMosaicHome.html`, provided that you intend to use it for non profit or private use. On the other hand, if you wish to use it for commercial reasons, the Mosaic license requires the payment of a licensing fee.

Netscape Navigator

If you are not using a copy of Mosaic or one of the browsers based on its code, and since you are reading this book, chances are that you are using Netscape Navigator. (See Figure 2.2.) For many people, Navigator is the *only* World Wide Web browser. In fact, recent surveys have indicated that Navigator is now used by more than 75 percent of the Web community.

Figure 2.2.

The Netscape Navigator Web browser.

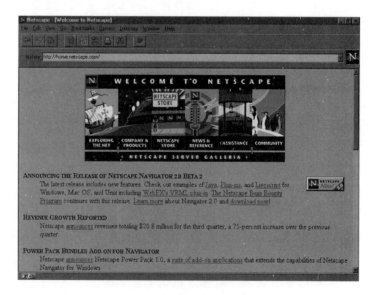

On the surface, the look and feel of Navigator is more than a little similar to NSCA Mosaic, possibly because many of the original NCSA personnel who developed Mosaic are now working for Netscape Communications, the company responsible for Netscape Navigator.

There are, however, a number of features offered by Navigator that Mosaic does not support. One of the most noteworthy is the ability to run Netscape Navigator on any Windows-based machine without the need for special 32-bit Microsoft libraries and support files. With the recent release of Navigator 2.0, the differences between Navigator and Mosaic have become more pronounced.

With Netscape enhancing its Web browser's capabilities and releasing updates on an almost monthly basis, Navigator is now regarded by many people as the most powerful and full-featured Web browser available. At the same time, its dominance of the marketplace means that many users will soon expect Web sites to take advantage of all these new features in the very near future.

Note: See the "The Netscape Debate" topic in Chapter 4, "Before You Start," for more information about the ramifications of the new features included in Navigator 2.0.

For the remainder of this book, you will be exploring the steps required to create Web pages that take advantage of the new features included in Navigator 2.0. Before that, it is important to take a look at how Netscape Navigator operates and learn about some of the features.

System Requirements for Netscape 2.0

For those of you who are not currently using Navigator 2.0, the following section describes how you can obtain a copy.

Note: Unlike previous versions of Netscape Navigator, which could be used for personal purposes without the payment of a licensing fee, Navigator 2.0 is a commercial product. When you download a copy, you are granted permission to use the program up to 90 days for evaluation purposes. If you continue to use Navigator 2.0 after this time, you are expected to purchase a software license from Netscape Communications.

Before you install a copy of Navigator 2.0 on your computer system, you should note that there are a few requirements you need to keep in mind. These requirements tend to vary for each of the computer platforms that Netscape Communications supports, so the following sections present each in turn.

Windows 3.x

Although the World Wide Web started as a tool designed mainly for UNIX-based computer systems that support the X Window (X11) standard, in recent years many of the new World Wide Web developments have revolved around the Microsoft Windows platform.

Navigator 2.0 will run quite comfortably on a Windows 3.1–based computer system. However, there are a few technical issues that need to be resolved first.

16-Bit Operation

With the introduction of Windows NT, and more recently Windows 95, a definition has been coined to describe programs that work on the various Microsoft Windows platforms.

Programs designed specifically for Windows NT and Windows 95 are *32-bit programs*, a designation that relates to the way they utilize memory and to other technical aspects of operation. On the other hand, Windows 3.1 and 3.11 applications are *16-bit programs*. If you want to run Navigator 2.0 under Windows 3.1 or 3.11, you need to download the 16-bit version.

Winsock

To explore the World Wide Web using Navigator 2.0 and Microsoft Windows, you will need a TCP/IP-based connection to the Internet. These connections come in a variety of forms, including SLIP, PPP, and ISDN connections. To link a TCP/IP connection with Netscape Navigator, you also need a special program called Winsock. This program looks after all the TCP/IP communications between your computer and the Internet.

Note: TCP/IP is the network protocol used by computer systems to communicate with each other via the Internet, and SLIP, PPP, and ISDN represent common methods of connecting computers using the telephone system.

A number of different Winsock programs are available, some commercially and others as shareware or public domain software. Of these, by far the most well known is Peter Tattam's Trumpet Winsock.

Note: Since a full discussion of the use and installation of Winsock is outside the scope of this book, you may want to check out one of the books in Sams.net's *Navigating the Internet* series that relates to your particular computer platform. These include *Navigating the Internet, Navigating the Internet with Windows 95, Navigating the Internet with your Macintosh, Navigating the Internet with America Online,* and *Navigating the Internet with CompuServe.*

Memory Requirements

To run Navigator 2.0 on a Windows 3.*x*–based system, you need to have at least 4MB of RAM installed. Though running Navigator 2.0 is possible with only 4MB, for all practical purposes you need 8MB of RAM to see the browser running at its full potential.

In addition to hardware-based memory, you also need to configure Windows virtual memory properly. Make sure that you have allocated at least 10MB of permanent virtual memory if your disk has enough space available to handle it. (Refer to your Windows User's Guide for more information.)

Note: At the time of this writing, the Windows 3.*x* version of Navigator 2.0 does not support the use of Java—the new, portable Internet-based language—and there are some indications that such support may never be included in this version.

Windows 95

Unless you live on the far side of the moon, you no doubt have heard some mention of Windows 95 in the last six months. For Internet users, Windows 95 opens up a new level of support and functionality that greatly simplifies connecting to the Internet and significantly improves the performance of many Internet applications.

Currently two versions of Navigator 2.0 will work under Windows 95. The first is the 16-bit application mentioned previously, and the second is a 32-bit application that uses Windows 95–specific capabilities. Naturally, there are a few special requirements for the use of this version.

Note: Although some 32-bit programs will work on a computer running Windows 3.11—provided that a utility called WIN32s is installed—this is not the case for the Windows 95 version of Navigator 2.0. It can be run only on a machine using Windows 95.

TCP/IP and Winsock

As with the 16-bit version of Navigator 2.0, you need a Winsock application to complete the connection with the Internet. But unlike the 16-bit version, which can use a variety of different Winsock programs, the Windows 95–specific version of Navigator 2.0 requires the Winsock program provided with Windows 95. For more information on installing the Windows 95 version of Winsock and the underlying TCP/IP communications software it contains, point your Web browser to `http://www.windows95.com/connect/index.html`. Once you get there follow the TCP/IP installation link.

Note: Under Windows 95, you can still use the 16-bit version of Navigator 2.0 with other Winsock programs, but you will lose access to many of the performance benefits that come with the 32-bit version.

Memory Requirements

The issue of memory and Windows 95 is a delicate subject at the best of times. According to its technical specifications, Windows 95 will work with as little as 4MB of memory. Most tests indicate, however, that 8MB is the minimum you should use.

When you add applications to the mix, the amount of memory required increases again. Netscape recommends that you have at least 8MB of memory when running Navigator 2.0, but you will find that having 16MB greatly improves overall performance.

Apple Macintosh

Netscape Navigator 2.0 is also well supported on the Apple Macintosh using both MacOS and the newer PowerPC operating systems. The minimum requirements for using Navigator 2.0 on a Macintosh computer are as follows:

- ☐ Macintosh System 7
- ☐ MacTCP
- ☐ Memory requirements

Macintosh System 7

Although many Macintosh users may still be opting to stay with Version 6 of the Macintosh operating system, only those people with System 7 or greater can use Navigator 2.0 on their computers.

MacTCP

As with Microsoft Windows, you need a program that acts as the glue between your computer and the Internet. The most popular and most readily available program is a system tool called MacTCP. If you have version 7.5 of the Macintosh operating system, MacTCP is included as a part of the package. Others should contact their nearest Apple support center to obtain a copy of MacTCP.

Memory Requirements

To run Navigator 2.0 on a Macintosh computer system, you need at least 4MB of RAM with 8MB being the preferred amount. You should also be careful using programs such as RAMDoubler, which increase the amount of memory available to your programs by using compression techniques. Some older versions of this program have caused problems with MacTCP.

UNIX

Because Netscape Navigator 2.0 is a graphical Web browser, not all versions of UNIX currently support it. To use Navigator 2.0 under UNIX, your system must be configured to support the X Window specification known commonly as X11.

Supported Platforms

If they support X11, the following computers systems can run Navigator 2.0:

- ☐ Digital Equipment Corporation Alpha computers (OSF/1 2.0)
- ☐ Hewlett-Packard 700 series computers (HP-UX 9.03)
- ☐ IBM RS/600 computers (AIX 3.2)
- ☐ Silicon Graphics IRIX 5.2 systems

☐ Sun SPARC computer systems (Solaris 2.4 and SunOS 4.1.3)

☐ 386/486/Pentium-based computers running BSDI

☐ Some Linux-based systems

Memory Requirements

To run Navigator 2.0 on any UNIX-based system, as a rule you will need at least 16MB of memory.

Obtaining a Copy of Netscape Navigator

There are three ways you can obtain a copy of Netscape Navigator 2.0 that is suitable for your computer system:

☐ Download a copy using a Web browser

☐ Download a copy using FTP

☐ Purchase a copy from a retail outlet

Downloading Navigator 2.0 by Using a Web Browser

If you already have an older version of Netscape Navigator or some other Web browser, the simplest way to obtain a copy of the latest version of Navigator 2.0 is to point your existing browser to `http://home.netscape.com/comprod/mirror/index.html`. (See Figure 2.3.)

Downloading 2.0 by Using FTP

If you don't have a Web browser yet, but you have access to an FTP client, you can download a copy of Netscape Navigator 2.0 using anonymous FTP. (See Figure 2.4.)

Netscape Communications operates an anonymous FTP server that can be reached at `ftp.netscape.com`. However, due to the number of people who visit this site every day, you may find that the main site is very busy. If this is the case, you should try `ftp2.netscape.com` or `ftp3.netscape.com`, and on up to `ftp8.netscape.com`. These sites are mirror images of the main FTP site.

Figure 2.3.
Select the computer platform you are using and follow the steps displayed on the screen.

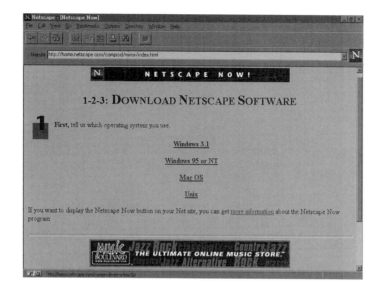

Figure 2.4.
With a program such as WS_FTP, you can download a copy of Navigator 2.0 using anonymous FTP.

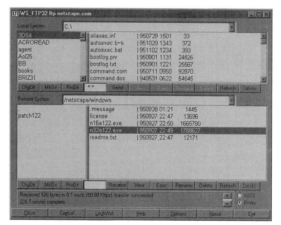

Purchasing a Copy from a Retail Outlet

With the rapid growth of popularity in the Internet and, more specifically, the World Wide Web, many computer suppliers and software houses now carry copies of Netscape Navigator as a regular part of their inventory. You can also purchase a copy directly from Netscape Communications by calling (415) 528-2555.

Note: You can, of course, purchase only the latest commercially released version from retail outlets. If you want to gain access to pre-release and beta versions of Navigator, you will need to do so online.

Installing Netscape Navigator on Your Computer

After you have obtained a copy of Navigator 2.0, you need to install it on your computer before you can use it. The file that you obtained, either online or on disk, will not start the Navigator program for you.

Windows and Windows 95

If you downloaded Navigator 2.0 from Netscape, you will first need to extract the contents of the file you received into a temporary directory. To do this, first create a temporary directory called something like \temp and then copy the file you downloaded into it. Finally, switch to the \temp directory and run the file. Within a few seconds the contents of the file will be unpacked into the temporary directory.

You then need to locate a special program called SETUP.EXE. This program contains all the instructions needed to properly install Navigator 2.0 on your computer. SETUP.EXE will be located somewhere in the \temp directory, as it is one of the programs that was created during the unpacking process.

To complete the installation process, run the SETUP.EXE program. You will then be guided through a series of simple steps that install Navigator 2.0 on your computer.

Note: If your copy of Navigator 2.0 came on a floppy disk, follow the installation instructions included with it.

Apple Macintosh

Installing Navigator 2.0 on a Macintosh is even easier than installing it on a Windows-based computer. All you need to do is double-click the Netscape Installer icon, located in the folder

where you put Navigator 2.0 when you downloaded it, or on the floppy disk, depending on how you obtained your copy.

Except for a few questions about which folder you want Navigator 2.0 to be stored in, the entire installation process is fully automated.

UNIX Versions

Unfortunately, installing programs on UNIX-based computer systems is often a little more complicated than doing so on Macintosh- or Windows-based machines.

As a result, each version of the UNIX Navigator contains a small readme file that explains the steps needed for that particular machine. To view the readme file, copy the Navigator 2.0 for UNIX file you obtained previously into a new directory and then type the following on the command line:

```
zcat filename.tarZ ¦ tar xvf -
```

You will need to replace `filename.tarZ` with the name of the file you downloaded. After the contents of the file have been unpacked, the readme file can be found in the same directory in which you saved the original file.

Working with Navigator 2.0

After Netscape has been installed on your computer and you have connected the computer to the Internet, using Netscape Navigator is a relatively simple process. In the following sections many of the major features of Navigator 2.0 will be examined. Because this book is about Web publishing, however, you should refer to any of the very good books devoted specifically to Netscape 2.0, such as *Netscape Unleashed*, for a more in-depth discussion of Navigator-specific usage.

Note: All the figures in this book refer to the Windows 95 version of Navigator 2.0. If you are using other versions, you may find that some of the figures vary slightly from what you see on your own computer. Regardless of which version you are using, the options and functions that are available should remain the same.

Starting the Browser

To start Navigator 2.0, all you need to do is locate the folder or directory in which it was saved during the installation process. After you locate Navigator 2.0, double-click its icon to activate the browser. This assumes, of course, that you have already obtained access to the Internet through an Internet service provider, school or college, your employer, or some other method.

Caution: Navigator 2.0 does not connect your computer to the Internet. This step is looked after by the TCP/IP software installed on your computer. When Navigator 2.0 starts, it expects to find an Internet connection. If it does not find one, you may encounter an error message. (Note that on some systems the TCP/IP software will attempt to create a connection when Navigator 2.0 starts. In this case, if the connection is successful Navigator 2.0 will start normally; otherwise you will again receive some sort of error message.)

The Document Area

The most important part of any Web browser is the *document area.* This is the area onscreen where Web pages are displayed. With Navigator 2.0, as with most Web browsers, the middle section of the screen is devoted to displaying Web pages as they are retrieved from the Internet. Regardless of which Web browser you use—whether it's the Macintosh, Windows, or UNIX versions—the document area will be basically the same.

In fact, the similar appearance of the document area, regardless of what system is displaying the document, is one of the most important features of the World Wide Web. When the concept of the Web was first proposed, one of the guiding principles of the project was the idea that any Web page developed on any computer platform must be viewable on any other computer platform, including the most basic text-based computer terminal. Naturally, you could not expect a text-based terminal to display computer graphics such as inline images, but the text and hypertext links for those images needed to be viewable.

Note: An inline image is an image that is displayed as a part of a Web page.

Occasionally you will notice some aesthetic differences between Web browsers in the areas of layout and physical display, but ultimately a hyperlink is still a hyperlink, and clicking one causes a new page to be loaded.

Tip: On occasions, you may find that the information contained on a Web page is larger than the space provided by the Web browser. To view this information, use the scrollbars at the top and sides of the document area.

Hyperlinks

The first thing you need to know when working with any Web browser is how to recognize a hyperlink. In Navigator 2.0 by default all hyperlinks are highlighted in blue text and are further enhanced by an underline. In addition, any graphics that have hyperlinks associated with them are normally highlighted by a blue border.

Tip: Web browsers such as Navigator 2.0 support an optional function that allows the default colors of hyperlinks to be altered by both the user and the Web developer. For this reason, most people now use underlines as the preferred method of displaying text-based hyperlinks.

When you click any of these hyperlinks, Navigator 2.0 opens a copy of the document that the link points to and displays it onscreen in place of the current page. For example, if you clicked on the link indicated by the pointer in Figure 2.5, the home page of Discovery Channel Online would eventually be displayed.

Figure 2.5.
Click on any of the underlined text to jump to a new Web page.

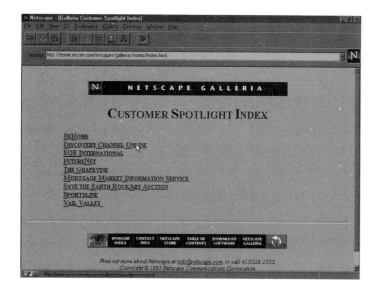

Note: When you select a hyperlink to explore a new page, Navigator 2.0 "remembers" the original page for the duration of your current session. If you return to the original page again, any of the hyperlinks that you have visited during the current session will now be displayed as purple text instead of blue text, or in the case of graphical hyperlinks, will be surrounded by a purple box.

The Control Console

The area at the top of the Navigator 2.0 main window above the document area is often referred to as the *control console*. You can easily navigate the World Wide Web by using the tools provided in this area.

The Menu Bar

Like all Windows-based programs, Navigator 2.0 has a menu bar across the top of the main window. To access the options provided by this menu bar, click the various menu options listed. When you do this, a pull-down menu appears displaying the options available:

File	The File menu contains functions to open new documents located on either your hard drive or any Web server connected to the Internet. You can also print copies of the page you are currently viewing and create messages to be sent via e-mail. And finally, you can even open additional browser windows.
Edit	There are commands on the Edit menu to copy the contents of a Web page onto the Windows Clipboard and copy URLs to and from the document line.
	There is also a search option built into Navigator 2.0 that can quickly locate specific text in the current Web page.
View	Most of the options on the View menu refresh the contents of different parts of the document window.
	This menu also provides two options that let you display the HTML source (information used to describe the content of a Web page) and other information relating to the current document.
Go	This menu duplicates the basic navigational options provided by the toolbar, and also displays a list of Web pages you have visited during your current session.
Bookmarks	With the bookmarks feature of Navigator 2.0, you can keep a list of sites that you visit on a regular basis. After a site is added to the

	bookmarks list, it is automatically displayed on the Bookmarks menu so you can easily return to the site whenever you want. When you select a page listed on this menu, Navigator 2.0 opens it as if you had selected the link by clicking on a hyperlink in a Web page.
Options	From this menu you can select any of the options that tailor the way Navigator 2.0 looks and operates. (See "Configuring Navigator 2.0" later in this chapter for more information.)
Directory	This menu contains a list of handy links maintained by Netscape Communications that give you immediate access to Netscape's home page, What's New pages, What's Cool pages, Web search tools, the Yahoo Internet directory, and Netscape's own "Galleria" commerce directory.
Window	With the options on this menu, you can open the Mail and News windows, the address book, bookmarks, and history windows. You can also switch between any other Navigator 2.0–specific windows that are currently open.
Help	This menu provides access to the Netscape online help system and also has an option for sending feedback to the developers at Netscape Communications.

The Toolbar

The toolbar displayed below the menu bar gives you access to many of the functions you will use regularly while exploring the World Wide Web.

By default, the toolbar contains both a graphical and textual description of its purpose. (See Figure 2.6.) As you become more familiar with the use of Navigator, you will probably want to adjust the settings so that only the graphical elements are displayed. (See Figure 2.7.) This can be achieved by altering the settings in the General Preferences dialog on the Options menu. By doing this, you increase the amount of space available in the document area for displaying Web pages.

Figure 2.6.
The Netscape Navigator toolbar.

Figure 2.7.
With the text turned off, the toolbar is considerably smaller.

The options provided by the toolbar are the following:

Back	As you begin to move around the World Wide Web, Navigator 2.0 keeps track of where you have been. If you click this button, the last page you accessed before the current one is recalled.
Forward	Click this button to return to the most recently visited page.
Home	When Navigator 2.0 is first installed, clicking this button opens the Netscape Communications home page; however, you can alter this default setting at any time to point to any page you choose.
Reload	Clicking this button forces Navigator 2.0 to reload the current page. If you stopped the retrieval of a large page, for example, you can use this button to retrieve the missing information.
Images	If you have configured Navigator 2.0 so that it does not load the images associated with a page, you can click this button to load the images associated with the current page. (See the "Auto Load Images" topic later in this chapter for more details about loading images.)
Open	This icon opens the small dialog box shown in Figure 2.8. If you enter the URL of a Web page in the field provided, and then click the Open button, Navigator will retrieve a copy of the page and display it onscreen.

Figure 2.8.
Enter the URL of a Web page and click the Open button.

Print	When you click this button, Navigator will send a copy of the current page to your printer.
Find	When you open a large Web page, it is sometimes handy to be able to search quickly through the contents of the page. The Find button allows you to open a small dialog box where you can enter the text to search for on the current page. (See Figure 2.9.)
Stop	If you need to halt the loading of a document, click this icon.

Figure 2.9.
You can search rapidly through large Web pages by using the Find dialog box.

Document Title

Immediately above the menu bar is an area that displays the title of the current Web page. Today most Web pages have a title associated with them, but for those that don't, the URL for the page is listed instead.

Document Location

The URL of the Web page currently displayed in the document area is—by default—shown in the document URL field, which is located just below the toolbar. It is the field with the `Location:` label in front of it. (In some older versions of Netscape Navigator the document URL field may also be labeled as `Netsite:`.)

You can also use this field to directly enter a URL for a Web page. When you do this, the Web browser will attempt to retrieve the page as though you had selected it via a hyperlink. (Note that when you start to enter a new URL, the `Location:` label in front of the document URL field is changed to `Go to:`.)

> **Note:** By clicking the drop-down arrow to the right of this field, you can call up a history list similar to the one provided by the Go menu. This time, however, you see a list of URLs instead of document titles.

Logo Animation

Apart from giving you something to look at, the animated logo to the right of the document URL field indicates when Navigator 2.0 is retrieving a Web page. If the animation is running, Navigator 2.0 is busy. If it is static, no pages are currently being retrieved.

Status Bar

The last area of the Navigator 2.0 screen is the status bar. It is located below the main document display area. The status bar displays a variety of information depending on what the browser is doing. When you place your mouse pointer over a hyperlink, the URL of the page or server that it points to is displayed on the left side of the status bar. Alternatively, when a new page is being loaded, a counter is displayed in this area to indicate the page size and the number of bytes already retrieved. At the same time, on the right side of the status bar, a bar graph is displayed to represent the percentage of the page that has been loaded.

Configuring Navigator 2.0

The Options menu shown in Figure 2.10 provides a list of menu commands that allow you to tailor the way Navigator 2.0 looks and operates. In the following sections, these menu items are discussed briefly.

Figure 2.10.

The Options menu gives you access to all the configurable parameters that control how Navigator 2.0 looks and operates.

General Preferences...

Selecting the **G**eneral Preferences item opens a dialog box where you can adjust settings that control how the Web browser component of Navigator 2.0 operates. The options available via this dialog box are separated into the following categories:

> **Note:** Besides being a Web browser, Navigator 2.0 can also send and receive e-mail, and read or post articles to Usenet newsgroups. In previous versions of Navigator these features were included as a part of the Web browser window, but as of Version 2.0, they have been split into separate components that use different windows.

Appearance	This area controls whether images or text are displayed on the toolbar, stores the location of the Web browser home page, and indicates whether hyperlinks are indicated using an underline.
Fonts	This area is used to configure the default fonts for displaying text on Web pages.
Colors	The default colors for links, text, and the background of Web pages can be altered in this area.

Images	The setting in this area controls whether images are displayed as they load or after they have finished loading. You can also control how Navigator 2.0 displays images on screens that can handle only a limited number of colors by setting the Choose color options.
Apps	This area is used to select the external programs that are used when you click on a hyperlink that points to a Telnet or TN3270 connection. In addition, you can set the default program for viewing the current Web page's HTML source code and define the directory to be used for temporary storage.
Helpers	This area contains a list of programs that work in concert with Navigator 2.0. These programs include an audio player, image browsers, file compression utilities, and video players.
Language	Netscape is currently starting to enhance Navigator 2.0's support for foreign languages. In this area, you can control which languages you want to see when viewing multilingual Web pages.

Mail and News Preferences...

Two of the major changes for Netscape Navigator with the release of Version 2.0 are greatly improved support for newsgroups and e-mail. As a reflection of this greatly enhanced support, a separate **M**ail and News Preferences dialog box has been added to the **O**ptions menu.

The options that this dialog box manage include the following:

Appearance	Use this area to configure the font and text styles used by Navigator 2.0 when it displays e-mail messages and newsgroup articles.
Composition	When you compose a new e-mail message or newsgroup article, Navigator 2.0 needs to be told how to handle the message. The composition area is where you do this.
Server	Use this area to tell Navigator 2.0 the location of your personal Internet mailbox and the domain name of the Usenet news server you are using.
Identity	The Identity area is where you store personal information about yourself, including your e-mail address, a default signature file for outgoing messages, and the name of your business or organization.

Organization	The settings in this area control the order in which new e-mail messages and newsgroup articles are displayed. The order can be sorted by date, subject, or sender.

Network Preferences...

Unlike standalone applications such as word processors, which need to communicate only with you and occasionally a printer, programs such as Navigator 2.0 need to communicate with thousands of different computer systems all around the world. While many of these activities occur automatically, Navigator 2.0 provides a number of preferences and other settings that allow you to tailor its performance across the Internet.

Network Preferences include the following:

Cache	Navigator 2.0 stores a copy of each page that you visit on your computer's hard drive, in what is called a *local cache*. This allows the pages to be reloaded without having to query the remote server again to download the pages. The Cache area controls the amount of memory and disk space used for cache purposes. The more memory and disk space you allocate, the more pages can be held in the local cache.
Connections	When Navigator 2.0 encounters a Web page that includes images, it starts downloading several images at the same time. Doing this allows the rest of the Web page to be displayed even though inline images are only partially downloaded. The Connections area is where you tell Navigator how many separate images and files it should attempt to download at the same time. (Note that raising the number of connections can slow down the time it takes to display a Web page, depending on the speed of your connection and computer. As a result, you really need to test this setting for yourself to determine an optimum value.)
Proxies	A number of businesses and other organizations connect their computer systems to the Internet through what are known as *firewalls*. Firewalls protect computer systems at the site from invasions by unwanted guests.
	If you are connected to the Internet via a firewall, you will usually need a proxy server to communicate with the World Wide Web and other Internet services. The Proxies area lets you configure Navigator 2.0 for use with a proxy server.

Security Preferences...

As more businesses move onto the World Wide Web, the issue of security has become a dominant factor in many Internet discussions. To cater to this growing area of concern, Netscape Communications has developed new security features that allow business transactions to be conducted on the Web with a high level of protection.

The Security **P**references settings, listed below, allow you to tailor the level of security provided by Navigator 2.0 to your specific needs:

General

These settings control the amount of information Navigator 2.0 provides about its security. In addition, there is an option that enables or disables support for Java applications.

Site Certificates

This area contains a list of site certificates for computer systems and people you want to communicate with in a secure manner. Site certificates are a bit like an electronic fingerprint, which can be used to sign and encrypt messages so that only certain people can view their contents.

But unlike traditional encryption systems, which simply scramble the information so it is unreadable by prying eyes, a site certificate can also be used as proof of identity, which guarantees that the sites or people you are sending information to are actually who they say they are.

Note: The implementation of security certificates is still in a state of constant flux. As a result, the options provided by this dialog box may very well change by the time you read this book. However, the basic principles involved will still remain the same. Refer to the release notes and online documentation provided by Netscape Communications at http://www.netscape.com/ for more details. In addition, the VeriSign site at http://www.verisign.com/ contains information about obtaining your own security certificate.

Show Toolbar

Selecting this menu item controls whether the toolbar is displayed below the menu area. The Show **T**oolbar item is on a toggle switch: Select it once to display the toolbar and select it again to hide it. (Note that when the option is active—the default—a small check mark or tick is displayed beside the menu item.)

Show Location

This menu item controls whether the document URL field is displayed below the toolbar. Like the Show Toolbar item, the Show Location item is also a toggle switch. Select it once to display the document URL field and again to hide it. (Note that when the option is active—the default—a small check mark or tick is displayed beside the menu item.)

Show Directory Buttons

Selecting this menu item adds an extra toolbar below the document URL field, as shown in Figure 2.11. This toolbar duplicates the links provided by the **D**irectory menu. When you click any of the buttons on this toolbar, Navigator 2.0 immediately retrieves the selected Web page. (Note that when the option is active—the default—a small check mark or tick is displayed beside the menu item.)

Figure 2.11.
The Directory toolbar gives you direct access to Web pages such as the online documentation for Netscape Navigator.

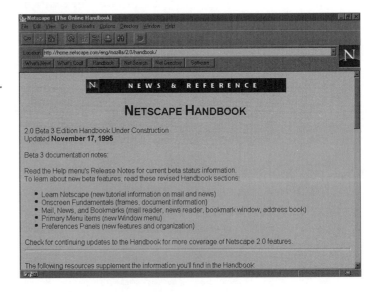

Show Java Console

This option is provided as a tool for people developing Java applications for use on the World Wide Web. If you activate this option, a window will be displayed that reports on the progress of running Java applets. (Note that when the option is active—deactivated is the default—a small check mark or tick is displayed beside the menu item.)

Note: For information about Java, refer to Chapter 21, "Java."

Auto Load Images

If you deselect the **A**uto Load Images item, Navigator 2.0 will load only the text of the document and insert placeholders where all the inline images are meant to go, as demonstrated in Figure 2.12. (Note that when the option is active—the default—a small check mark or tick is displayed beside the menu item.)

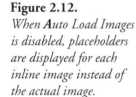

Figure 2.12.
*When **A**uto Load Images is disabled, placeholders are displayed for each inline image instead of the actual image.*

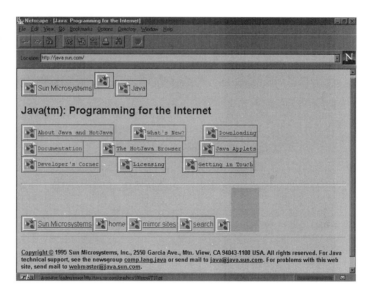

The main advantage of doing this is saving time. Using a 14,400bps modem, it will take 3 to 4 minutes to load the document shown in Figure 2.12 with all its images included. (See Figure 2.13.) Loading it with placeholders takes only seconds. When you consider that some pages may take up to 10 minutes to load using slower modems, deselecting the Auto Load Images option makes a lot of sense.

Note: The only disadvantage of not loading images is that you will not be able to use image maps. You can get around this, however, by using the Load Images button on the toolbar to retrieve images on pages where they are used.

Figure 2.13.
*Loading a Web page with **Auto Load Images** enabled greatly extends the amount of time taken to download the page.*

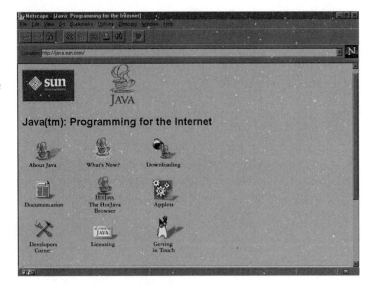

Document Encoding

With the development of support for languages such as Japanese and Chinese, there is a need for new methods of encoding and representing Web documents.

With Document Encoding item on the Options menu, you can tell Navigator 2.0 what encoding method it should use.

Save Options

Select this option to save any changes that have been made to the preference settings listed on the Options menu. If you do not save your changes, the next time you start Navigator 2.0 the changes will have been lost, and the preferences will have reverted to their previous settings.

Advanced Capabilities

Now that you have an understanding of the basic options provided by Navigator 2.0, let's take a look at some of the special features it offers to Web explorers.

In this section the following topics will be examined:

☐ Forms

☐ E-mail

☐ Newsgroups

☐ FTP

☐ Plug-ins

☐ Java and JavaScript

Forms

One feature of the World Wide Web that sets it apart from other Internet services is the ability to interact with users via what are known as *forms*.

On some Web pages, you will encounter fields like those shown in Figure 2.14. These fields allow you to submit information to a Web server by filling in the spaces provided. Depending on the Web page, this information might relate to a membership application, a search form, delivery details for an online purchase, or even your responses to online messages on a service such as WebChat.

The form shown in Figure 2.14 is a data entry form for the Lycos Internet catalog. By entering a word or words in the field provided and selecting from the parameters available, you can easily tell Lycos to search the World Wide Web and locate relevant Web pages.

In addition to data entry fields, many forms also contain radio buttons. With these buttons you can choose a single option from the list provided. Other forms also include check boxes. With check boxes you can select any or all of the options they correspond to.

Figure 2.14.

Lycos lets you search the World Wide Web using simple data entry forms.

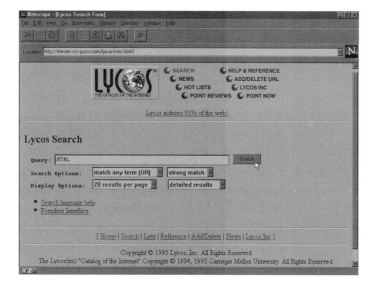

When you have provided the information requested by the form, you must then submit it to the Web server. On most forms you do this by clicking a submit button located somewhere on the form. In Figure 2.14, however, you need to click the search button indicated by the mouse pointer, while other pages use buttons labeled Verify, Send, Enter, Update, and many others.

> **Note:** If you mess up a form, you can often start it afresh by clicking the Reset Form button. Doing this removes all the information you have entered on the form. Not all forms include such a button, but those that do will in most cases display it beside the submit button.

E-mail

As you begin to explore the World Wide Web, you will occasionally come across a special type of hyperlink that looks something like this: mailto:wtatters@world.net.

If you select a hyperlink of this kind, Navigator 2.0 opens a dialog box similar to the one in Figure 2.15. Using this dialog box, you can send an e-mail message—usually to the creator of the Web page or to some other e-mail address he or she has chosen.

Figure 2.15.
The message dialog box lets you send e-mail messages using Navigator 2.0.

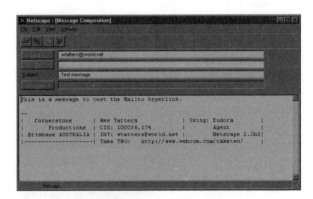

The field listed at the top of the dialog box contains the destination address of the e-mail message. The contents of the remaining fields are up to you. Obviously, a subject line is important, along with a message in the main text area of the dialog box. In the CC field, you can select people who should receive a copy of the message. (Note that Navigator 2.0 has also automatically included my standard signature lines at the end of the message.)

When you are happy with the message you have entered, click the Send button located in the toolbar on the dialog box. The send button is the first icon on the left.

Note: If you type `mailto:` on its own in the Document URL field, Navigator 2.0 will open the mail dialog box so that you can use Navigator 2.0 to send e-mail messages.

In addition to sending e-mail messages, Navigator 2.0 can also receive e-mail messages. To access this option, select the Netscape Mail option from the Window menu. When you do this, a window similar to the one in Figure 2.16 will be displayed onscreen. Then, provided that you have configured all the e-mail settings in Navigator 2.0 correctly, Navigator 2.0 will automatically retrieve any new messages from your Internet mailbox and display them.

Figure 2.16.
You can now send and receive e-mail messages using Navigator 2.0.

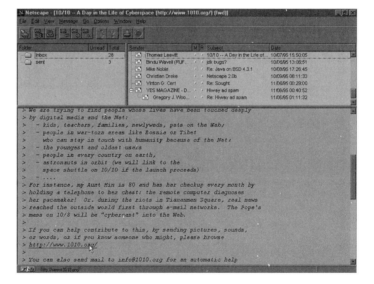

Newsgroups

Although the original specification for the World Wide Web required the ability to read newsgroups, few people regularly used this option as their primary method of reading newsgroup articles because the user interface was simply too unwieldy.

In an attempt to rectify the situation, Netscape Communications has completely revamped the newsreader included with Navigator 2.0. (See Figure 2.17.) Where previous versions of

Navigator used the document area to display articles, as of Version 2.0, the newsreader is contained in its own window. By doing this, Netscape has given the user far greater control over the way articles can be read.

Figure 2.17.
Navigator 2.0 also features a greatly enhanced Usenet newsreader.

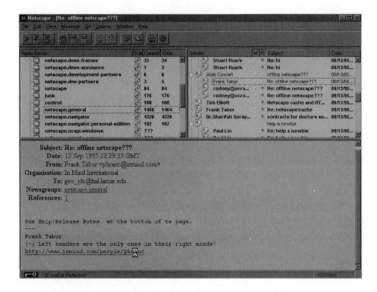

FTP

It is also possible to use Navigator 2.0 as an FTP client. To do this, simply enter the domain name of the FTP site you want to visit in the document URL field. To tell Navigator 2.0 that you want to open an FTP session, first enter `ftp://` followed by the domain name.

For example, if you wanted to visit the FTP site operated by Netscape Communications at `ftp.webcom.com`, enter `ftp://www.webcom.com/` in the document URL field and press the Enter key.

After a few seconds, you should see a page like the one shown in Figure 2.18. Along the left side of the main document, all the files and subdirectories in the root directory of the WebCom server are displayed, each represented as an underlined hotlink. All you need to do to select a directory or retrieve a file is to click on it.

Figure 2.18
The root directory of the WebCom FTP server

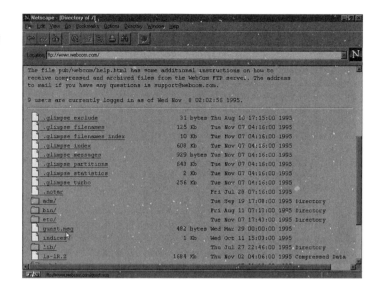

Note: Web Communications is one of the many companies that specialize in the rental of Web space. To find out more information about the services they offer, point your Web browser to http://www.webcom.com/. Alternatively, refer to http://union.ncsa.uiuc.edu/HyperNews/get/www/leasing.html for a list of other popular services.

Plug-Ins

In the past, if people wanted to view QuickTime movies, read Adobe Acrobat documents, explore experimental 3-D worlds, or listen to live audio on the Internet, they needed to install helper applications. Then, if their Web browser encountered a hyperlink that required the helper application, a separate program window was opened and the helper handled the special information.

With the release of Navigator 2.0, an entirely new type of helper applications—called plug-ins—is starting to appear. These applications, instead of using their own windows, can display information as part of a standard Web page. Already, a company called Paper Software has released a plug-in 3-D world viewer using the Virtual Reality Modeling Language (VRML), that gives people virtual worlds to explore via the World Wide Web. (See Figure 2.19.)

Figure 2.19.
*VRML brings the world
of virtual reality to the
World Wide Web.*

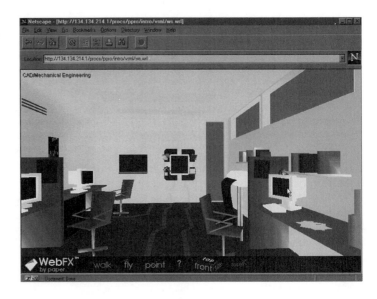

Note: See Chapter 11, "Using External Media and Plug-ins," for more information about plug-ins and Navigator 2.0.

In addition, Adobe is currently developing a plug-in for Acrobat documents, and Macromedia is doing the same for the popular Director multimedia system. What this means for the Web user is the availability of higher-quality applications and information via the World Wide Web, including online magazines that challenge the quality of printed material, access to real-time audio, and live video integrated into Web pages.

Note: To keep up-to-date with all the latest plug-in developments, watch the Netscape Communications home page at http://www.netscape.com/.

Java

Possibly the most significant development of Navigator 2.0 is support for the Java programming language developed by Sun Microsystems. Using Java, Web page developers can create custom-made programs called applets that enhance and extend the World Wide Web environment.

In fact, the possibilities offered by Java are almost endless. Using Java, options such as animated web pages with waving multicolor text are finally a reality. For people wanting greater control over data entry, real-time feedback, interactive online tutorials, or even Web-based games, Java is the answer. (See Figure 2.20.)

Figure 2.20.
Missile Commando via the World Wide Web, complements of Java.

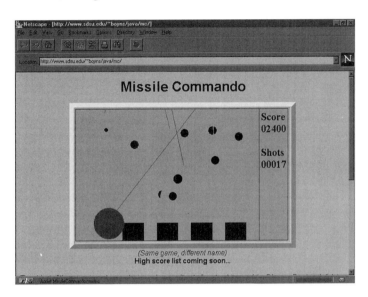

What makes Java even more versatile is the fact that Web users do not need to know it exists. Provided that their Web browsers are Java-aware, the new capabilities provided by Java applets will simply be downloaded to their computers as they are needed. If you load a Web page that includes a Java applet, any required information, including pictures, sounds, and program code, will be downloaded automatically. You don't even need to run the program once it has been downloaded since your Web browser will handle that as well.

JavaScript

In addition to Java support, Navigator 2.0 also introduces a scaled-down version of Java called JavaScript. JavaScript is ideal for creating small programs that control aspects of a Web page.

But unlike Java, which demands a good understanding of programming principles, JavaScript has been specifically design for ease of use, allowing Web publishers with little or no programming experience to create useful JavaScript programs and tools for their Web pages. For more information about JavaScript, refer to Chapter 19, "JavaScript," and Chapter 20, "Working with JavaScript."

Note: Occasionally you may encounter mention of a language called LiveScript. When Navigator 2.0 was first developed, JavaScript was in fact called LiveScript. But soon after the launch of LiveScript, Sun Microsystems decided to add its support to the concept of the scripting language that Netscape Communications proposed. As a result of this added support, LiveScript was renamed JavaScript.

Summary

In this chapter you have learned about the features and services provided by Navigator 2.0. You have found out how to obtain a copy of the latest version and install it, and you have also examined the configuration options available to you. In addition, you have been introduced to some of the advanced capabilities included in Navigator 2.0.

Workshop

The first section of the Workshop lists some of the common questions people ask about the World Wide Web along with a brief answer to each. Next is a quiz about the chapter you have just read. If you have problems answering any of the questions in the quiz, you can turn to Appendix E, "Answers to Quiz Questions."

Q&A

Q Why do I need to use Netscape Navigator 2.0 as my Web browser?

A If you plan to develop Web pages that take advantage of the features available in Navigator 2.0, you will need a way to test whether the pages work correctly. At this stage plug-ins, Java and JavaScript, and some of the features you will learn about later in this book are supported only by Navigator 2.0. As a result, it is the only Web browser you can use to fully test your Web pages.

Q This begs another question. If all these new features are only supported by Navigator 2.0, won't I be disfranchising part of the Web community if I use Netscape-specific options?

A As a rule, the way that the World Wide Web was designed means that this will not be the case. For the most part, if a feature is not supported by a particular Web browser, that option is ignored. The Web page will still be displayed by the Web browser but may not look exactly like its developer intended.

At the same time, Netscape Communications is actively involved in the development of Web standards such as HTML 3.0. As a result, it is hoped that many if not all of the features provided by Navigator 2.0 will one day be supported by other Web browsers. (For more information of the ramifications of developing Netscape-specific Web pages, see "The Netscape Debate" in Chapter 4.)

Q I've been trying for three days to download the latest version of Netscape Navigator, but all I ever seem to get is a message telling me that the FTP server is busy or is being access by too many users. What's the problem?

A When Netscape releases a new version of their products, within hours their Web site is flooded with thousands of people trying to download it. The simple fact is that there is only room for so many people on their computer system. You have one of two options: Keep trying or check to see if there are any sites that maintain a copy in your local area. Netscape lists all of the sites—called mirrors—that maintain copies of the latest versions of programs like Netscape Navigator at `http://www.netscape.com/comprod/mirror/index.html`.

Quiz

1. What computer platforms are currently supported by Navigator 2.0?

2. Where would you find a switch to stop images from automatically being displayed when a new Web page is loaded?

3. Can Navigator 2.0 receive e-mail messages?

4. What setting do you need to adjust if you are connected to the Internet via a firewall?

5. Can I run the 32-bit version of Navigator 2.0 under Windows 3.11?

Exercises

1. If you have not already done so, now would be a good time to download a copy of the latest version of Netscape Navigator.

2. Whenever Netscape Communications releases a new version of their programs, they update all of their online documentation at the same time. The problem is that few people ever bother to read through this information. At the very least, you should check the Release Notes regularly for news about bugs, patches, and updates. Your second exercise for this chapter is to locate the release notes for Netscape Navigator and read them.

3

HTML Assistants: Editors and Converters

HTML Assistants: Editors and Converters

In the following chapters you will learn about the various elements that create a Web page. During these discussions, you will be taught how a simple text file—created by a text editor— is magically transformed into a singing, dancing, multimedia Web site. What you won't be told about, however, are the many tools now available that reduce the amount of work involved in designing a Web site—and there is a very good reason for this.

At its heart, HTML—the language used to describe Web pages—is basically a simple text-based language. As a result, to be fully conversant in this language, you need to understand, in detail, how all the elements fit together. The best way to do this is by getting your hands dirty and hard coding some Web pages manually. This is the way you will do it throughout this book.

Having said that, writing HTML documents by hand in a text editor is probably the most cumbersome way to write HTML. You must type all the tags, remember what the elements are called, remember to close your two-sided tags, remember to include closing quotation marks on attributes, and remember a host of other details. And, of course, you must know something about which tags can go where. With all that to keep in mind as you produce an HTML page, it sometimes becomes difficult to remember what you're actually writing.

Note: Scared yet? Don't be! All the terms used in this discussion, and many others you encounter in this chapter, will be explained in the days to come. For now, just accept the fact that there is more to a Web page than meets the eye, and enjoy reading the rest of the chapter.

Also, as you begin to learn more about HTML and Web publishing, you will soon see where programs like the ones discussed here can be used to their best advantage.

To reduce the amount of work required to create a Web page, a number of HTML editors, utilities, and assistants have begun to appear on the market. These programs look after many of the more mundane tasks usually associated with creating Web pages, and in some cases they also give you a visual approximation of what your final Web page will look like.

However, if you go looking for a full-featured HTML editor that enables you to see the results of your work quickly, insert links, anchors, and inline graphics quickly and easily, build a form using element widgets you can drag from a toolbox, or manage multiple sets of documents and the structure among them, you'll be looking for a very long time.

Note: By the time you see this book on the shelves, such a program should have been delivered by Netscape Communications. As this book goes to press, Netscape GOLD is in beta testing, which means that it should be commercially available sometime in early 1996. Netscape has indicated that this program will be the ultimate HTML editor, and judging by Netscape's past record, it probably will be.

All this is not to say that good tools for writing HTML files don't exist; on the contrary, there are lots of them, and there are even more converters and filters available that enable you to work in a program you know well and then output HTML. But none of these tools really creates a good HTML development environment. A truly excellent HTML development environment has yet to be produced. I recommend trying several editors and converters to see what works for you. You might end up finding an editor that makes writing HTML documents fast and easy—or you might find that none of them works as well as a "dumb" text editor and a list of tags.

In this chapter I'll describe some of the more common tools that claim to make writing HTML easier. They fall into a few categories:

☐ Tag editors—text editors that help you create HTML files by inserting tags or managing links

☐ Near-WYSIWYG editors

☐ Converters—programs that enable you to convert files created by popular word processing programs or other formats to HTML

I'll also discuss the advantages and disadvantages of using a converter versus working directly in HTML.

This chapter is by no means a complete catalog of the available editors and converters for HTML, but only a sample of some of the more popular tools. Also, this is a rapidly growing field, and by the time you read this book, it is likely that newer, better, and more powerful tools will be available for HTML development. For this reason, Appendix D, "Sources of Additional Information," provides some pointers to lists of editors and filters. These lists are being constantly updated and are the best source for finding tools that might not be described in this chapter.

Note: As an added bonus, copies of a number of the tools and utilities mentioned in this chapter have been included on the CD-ROM that accompanies this book. Watch out for the CD icon!

Tag Editors

Tag editor is a term I use to describe a simple standalone text editor or an extension to another editor. Tag editors help you write HTML documents by inserting the tags for you. They make no claim to being WYSIWYG—all they do is save you some typing. Tag editors generally provide shortcuts for creating HTML files. With tag editors, you don't have to remember whether selections in forms are specified by the <SELECT> tag or the <SELECTION> tag, and you won't have to worry about typing both the opening and the closing parts of a long tag by hand—tag editors usually provide windows or buttons with meaningful names that insert the tag into the text for you at the appropriate spot. You're still working with text, and you're still working directly in HTML, but tag editors take away a lot of the drudgery involved in creating HTML documents.

Most tag editors work best if you already have a document prepared in regular text with none of the tags. Using tag editors as you type a document is slightly more difficult; it's best to type the text and then apply the style after you're done.

For Microsoft Windows

If you use Windows to develop HTML files, you have no shortage of tag editors. There are seemingly hundreds of them. Four of the most popular are HTML Assistant, HotDog, HTML Easy!, and WebEdit.

HTML Assistant

HTML Assistant (see Figure 3.1) is one of the older, but still one of the most popular, tag editors for Windows. HTML Assistant enables you to insert tags by clicking buttons in a toolbar and to preview your work with your favorite browser. The interface is simple and intuitive, with all the important tags available on a toolbar. With a basic understanding of HTML, you can get started right away with HTML Assistant.

Figure 3.1.
HTML Assistant.

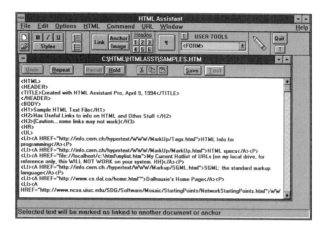

One of this tag editor's best features is the capability to collect URLs from hotlists or bookmark files generated by Mosaic and Cello and to enable you to create links to those URLs. With this feature, you might never have to type a URL into your HTML documents.

HTML Assistant comes in a freeware version with enough features for most HTML files, and a commercial Pro version that includes more features (HTML tags, filtering, searching, and so on). The free version of HTML Assistant supports HTML 2.0, including forms, whereas the Pro version supports more of the recent tags. You can also add new tags through a User Tools menu.

The FAQ (Frequently Asked Questions) for HTML Assistant is at `ftp://ftp.cs.dal.ca/htmlasst/htmlafaq.html`. (You can get to the actual program from that URL as well.)

HotDog

HotDog, from Sausage Software, is a full-featured HTML tag editor with support for just about every HTML feature, either existing or proposed, including HTML 2.0, tables, forms, many of the new Netscape extensions, and even some of the proposed HTML 3.0 tags. (See Figure 3.2.)

Using HotDog is reasonably intuitive; you insert tags by using a toolbar or menu items. One very handy feature is that when you start a new document, all the HTML structuring tags—`<HTML>`, `<HEAD>`, and `<BODY>`—are inserted for you. Because I include these tags in all my HTML files, having them automatically inserted saves some time over inserting them by hand. HotDog's linking feature is also quite nice, enabling you to build a URL from parts and showing you the result as you build it.

Figure 3.2.
HotDog.

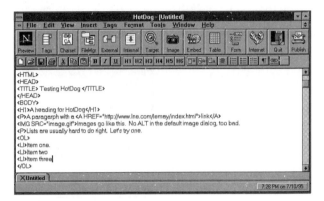

HotDog's biggest drawback is that it tries to support everything. If you're actually working with the proposed HTML 3.0, you might need all these tags, but if you just want to create something simple, all the extra tags and features can be overwhelming. (I was confused, and I've worked with HTML 3.0!) Given that most browsers don't even support most of HTML 3.0 right now and that the standard is changing, it is a bit premature to include support for all of HTML 3.0. It complicates the use of an otherwise terrific editor.

You can get more information about the shareware HotDog and its forthcoming commercial equivalent from Sausage Software's Web site at `http://www.sausage.com/`.

HTML Easy!

HTML Easy!, although not as striking to look at (see Figure 3.3) as HotDog, lives up to its name in that is it far easier to use. It supports HTML 2.0 and most Netscape extensions, including forms and tables.

Figure 3.3.
HTML Easy!

There are some oddities in HTML Easy!'s use. For example, although it supports the HTML tags for <HEAD> and <BODY> (more on these tomorrow), it does not support the <HTML> tag itself—you must include it by hand. Also, when it inserts tags for you, it then selects both tags, requiring you to click the mouse in between them so that you can type the content of the tag (other editors will set the insertion point for you after inserting the tags).

You can find out more about HTML Easy! from `http://www.seed.net.tw/~milkylin/`.

WebEdit

Like HotDog, the shareware WebEdit, shown in Figure 3.4, aims to support the full suite of HTML 2.0, 3.0, and Netscape tags. Also like HotDog, this means dozens of tags and options and alternatives to choose from, without any distinction of which tags are actually useful for real-life Web presentations. And all these choices needlessly complicate the use of the editor for creating simple pages.

Figure 3.4.
WebEdit.

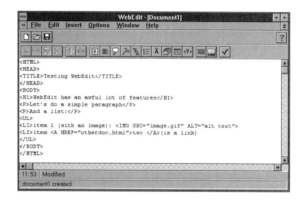

WebEdit's interface for inserting elements (you choose an element and then select features of that element) is quite elegant and easy to use—if you have a reason to use all the features of that element. For most common uses, however, all the extra features get in the way.

Find out more about WebEdit from `http://www.nesbitt.com/`.

For Macintosh

For those who are developing HTML files on the Macintosh, HTML.edit provides a HyperCard-like environment for inserting HTML tags into text files and managing related documents. If you're used to working on a more full-featured text editor, such as Alpha or BBedit, note that there are also HTML extensions for both of these packages.

HTML.edit

HTML.edit is a HyperCard-based HTML tag editor (see Figure 3.5), but it does not require HyperCard to run. It provides menus and buttons for inserting HTML tags into text files, as well as features for automatic indexing (for creating those hyperlinked table-of-contents lists) and automatic conversion of text files to HTML.

Figure 3.5.
HTML.edit.

HTML.edit's most interesting feature, however, is its Index page, which enables you to collect a set of related HTML documents, sort of like a project in THINK C or a book file in FrameMaker. After a file is listed on the Index page, that file appears in a list of files you can link, so you can create navigation links between related files quickly and easily.

I found the interface to HTML.edit somewhat confusing, but a quick read through the online help answered most of my questions. HTML.edit supports all of HTML 2.0, including forms as well as tables. It does not support the Netscape extensions.

You can get information about HTML.edit from `http://ogopogo.nttc.edu/tools/HTMLedit/HTMLedit.html`.

HTML Extensions for Alpha and BBedit

Alpha and BBedit are two of the more popular shareware text editors available for the Macintosh. Both provide mechanisms to add extensions for working in particular languages and writing text that conforms to a particular style. Extensions exist for both Alpha and BBedit to help with writing HTML tags.

There are significant advantages to using a standard text editor with extensions as opposed to using a dedicated HTML tag editor. For one thing, general text editors tend to provide more features for writing than a simple HTML text editor, including search-and-replace and spell checking. Also, if you're used to working in one of these editors, being able to continue to use it for your HTML development means that you don't have to take the time to learn a new program to do your work.

Versions after 5.92b of the Alpha editor include the HTML extensions in the main distribution. You can get Alpha and its HTML extensions from `ftp://cs.rice.edu/public/Alpha/`.

There are actually two extension packages for HTML development in BBedit. The first, called HTML Extensions for BBedit, was written by Charles Bellver. You can get information about this package from `http://www.uji.es/bbedit-html-extensions.html`. The second package, HTML BBedit Tools, which is based on Charles Bellver's extensions, includes some additional features. You can get more information about it at `http://www.york.ac.uk/~ld11/BBEditTools.html`.

For UNIX

tkHTML is a nice graphical HTML tag editor (see Figure 3.6) for the X11 Window system that uses the tcl language and the tk toolkit. It enables you to insert tags into text files, easily convert existing text to HTML, and automatically preview your HTML files using a WWW browser called WWwish. You can get more information about tkHTML from `http://alfred1.u.washington.edu:8080/~roland/tkHTML/tkHTML.html`, or download the source directly from `ftp://ftp.u.washington.edu:/public/roland/tkHTML`.

Figure 3.6.
tkHTML.

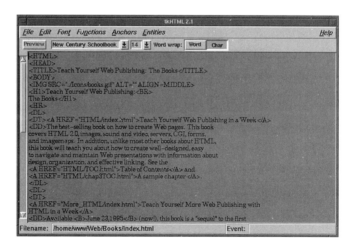

If you prefer to work in Emacs, the popular text editor-slash-kitchen sink, you have three HTML-mode packages to choose from:

- ☐ html-mode, the original, available at `ftp://ftp.luth.se/pub/infosystems/www/ncsa/html/elisp/html-mode.el`.

- ☐ html-helper-mode, an enhanced version of the preceding package. You can get information about it at `http://www.santafe.edu/~nelson/tools/`.

☐ hm--html-menus, which is also based on html-mode but provides additional features for Lucid Emacs (now called Xemacs) and GNU Emacs 19. Information is available at `http://www.tnt.uni-hannover.de/data/info/www/tnt/soft/info/www/html-editors/hm--html-menus/overview.html`.

If you use Emacs extensively, you might also want to look at William Perry's Emacs w3-mode, which turns Emacs into a full-featured Web browser with support for most advanced features of HTML. It includes support for much of HTML 3.0, many of the Netscape extensions, and just about anything else you can imagine. Get more information about w3-mode from `http://www.cs.indiana.edu/elisp/w3/docs.html`.

WYSIWYG Editors

The concept of a true WYSIWYG editor for HTML files is a bit of a fallacy, because each Web browser formats HTML documents in slightly different ways, and most enable readers to configure their browsers to use their favorite fonts, colors, and in some cases, backgrounds and sounds. The closest an editor could come to WYSIWYG would be if it enabled you to select the browser that would be viewing your document—and you could look at your document under Lynx, then under Mosaic for X, then under Cello.

Because HTML's design relies on the fact that it is not truly WYSIWYG, be suspicious of any editor that claims to be fully WYSIWYG or that claims you need absolutely no knowledge of HTML to use it. Many of these editors generate very poor HTML code, and these claims might betray a lack of understanding of HTML by their authors.

Some editors purport to be near-WYSIWYG; that is, they provide some WYSIWYG capabilities while still reminding you of the existence of the HTML underneath. This section describes a few of those editors.

For Microsoft Windows

For near-WYSIWYG HTML editing under Windows, you have essentially three choices: any of a number of template packages for Microsoft Word 2.0 or 6.0, SoftQuad HoTMetaL, or LiveMarkup.

Template Packages for MS Word

If you like Microsoft Word Version 2.0 or Version 6.0, you can choose from several template packages, assigning styles as you would in any Word document and selecting HTML features (such as links and inline images) from a toolbar. All also enable you to export your files to HTML format. Note, however, that if you make changes to the HTML document you've exported, you cannot import it back into Word.

There are three well-known template packages:

- [ ] CU_HTML (from Chinese University of Hong Kong, hence the CU). Information is available at `http://www.cuhk.hk/csc/cu_html/cu_html.htm`.

- [ ] GT_HTML (from Georgia Tech Research Institute). See the information at `http://www.gatech.edu/word_html/release.htm`.

- [ ] ANT_HTML (by Jill Smith; according to an information file that comes with the package, "the acronym is a secret"). You can retrieve the entire package from `ftp://ftp.einet.net/einet/pc/ANT_HTML.ZIP`.

Microsoft's Internet Assistant

Microsoft is in the HTML editor market with a tool called Internet Assistant. Internet Assistant is a plug-in for Word for Windows 6.0 and Word for Windows 95 that enables you to create your HTML files in Word and then save them as HTML. If you stick to the style sheet included with Internet Assistant and understand HTML's limitations, creating HTML documents can be almost easy.

Internet Assistant also doubles as a Web browser, enabling you to visit sites on the Web from within Word. The browser support is quite slow, however, in comparison with dedicated browsers such as Netscape or Mosaic.

You can get Internet Assistant from Microsoft's Web site (information is at `http://www.microsoft.com/msoffice/freestuf/msword/download/ia/default.htm`) or by calling Microsoft's support lines.

WordPerfect Internet Publisher

Similar to Microsoft's Word plug-in is WordPerfect's Internet Publisher for WordPerfect for Windows 6.1. Internet Publisher includes a template for editing files for the Web and a converter program that enables you to add links and convert the document to HTML.

You can get more information about WordPerfect Internet Publisher from the WordPerfect (Novell) Web site at `http://wp.novell.com/elecpub/intpub.htm`. You can also download it from that page or by calling the WordPerfect support lines.

SoftQuad's HoTMetaL

SoftQuad's HoTMetaL, shown in Figure 3.7, is an excellent standalone editor that has very near-WYSIWYG capabilities without trying to hide the fact that you're still working in HTML. You still work with tags in HoTMetaL, and you can insert tags only where they are legal. (You can't, for example, put regular paragraphs into a `<HEAD>` section.) This is a good thing; it means that if you use HoTMetaL, you cannot write an HTML document that does

not conform to correct HTML style. HoTMetaL supports all of HTML 2.0 as well as the Netscape extensions and HTML 3.0.

Figure 3.7.
HoTMetaL.

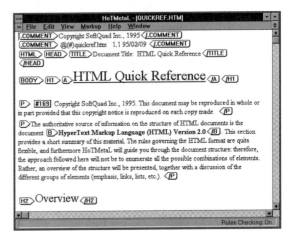

HoTMetaL comes in several configurations: a free version, a Pro version that offers more features, and a 2.0 Pro version with still more advanced features and an improved interface. Information about HoTMetaL and SoftQuad's other SGML-based tools is available at `http://www.sq.com/`.

Live Markup

One of the latest, and by far the most WYSIWYG-capable, HTML editors has been developed by Mediatec at `http://www.mediatec.com/`. Their Live Markup and Live Markup Pro editors (see Figure 3.8) let you edit HTML documents in an environment that looks as close to a real Web page as possible.

Forms, tables, and images can be laid out visually in Live Markup, giving a very close approximation of how the Web page will appear when displayed by your Web browser. Apart from the soon to be released Netscape GOLD HTML editor, which actually incorporates Navigator 2.0, Live Markup is just about the next best thing to being there.

Figure 3.8.
Live Markup.

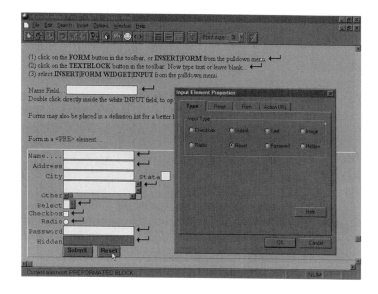

For Macintosh

Several near-WYSIWYG HTML editors exist for the Macintosh. Only two, however, stand out as being easy to use and having enough features to make them worthwhile for day-to-day use: HTML Editor and HTML Web Weaver.

The commercial version of SoftQuad's HoTMetaL is also available for the Macintosh, although the free tryout version had not been released as I was writing this book. Given HoTMetaL's respect in the Windows and UNIX worlds, I recommend trying it when the free version becomes available.

HTML Editor

HTML Editor is a wonderful application that enables you to insert tags into your file and see the result in a WYSIWYG fashion—at the same time. (See Figure 3.9.) The tags are shown in a lighter color than the surrounding text, and the text looks like it would look in Mosaic, although you can change the appearance of any style and apply it across the document. There are options to hide the tags in your document to get the full effect, and you can also preview the document using your favorite browser.

Figure 3.9.
HTML Editor.

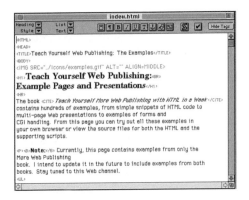

HTML Editor's current version is 1.1.1. It supports only the basic HTML 2.0 tags, not including forms. It does not include any of the Netscape extensions or HTML 3.0 tags. It has a feature for including custom tags, however, so you can customize the application to include these new tags.

The documentation for HTML Editor is available at http://dragon.acadiau.ca/~giles/ HTML_Editor/Documentation.html. You can get the actual package from ftp://cs.dal.ca/ giles/HTML_Editor_1.1.1.sit.hqx.

HTML Web Weaver

HTML Web Weaver (formerly called HTML Super Text) is like HTML Editor in that it shows the text of a document in a semi-WYSIWYG form, with the tags in a smaller font and a different color. HTML Web Weaver's interface is quite elegant (see Figure 3.10), making it easy to create lists and links. Because it splits the URL over several text fields, however, creating a link the first time can be confusing.

Figure 3.10.
HTML Web Weaver.

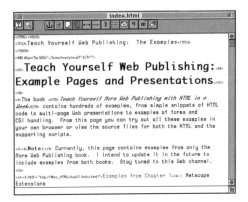

One very odd part of HTML Web Weaver is that it doubles as a regular editor. You can create documents and apply different fonts, sizes, and styles to the text, and never end up with HTML as the final result. This can be very confusing to a beginner who might assume that all he has to do is Save As to end up with HTML. The only way to create an HTML document in HTML Web Weaver is to use the HTML tags.

HTML Web Weaver supports HTML 2.0, minus forms, and includes the Netscape extensions. You can also create custom tags.

You can get more information about HTML Web Weaver and the latest version from `http://www.northnet.org/best/`.

For UNIX

Two WYSIWYG tools are available for UNIX systems running X: SoftQuad HoTMetaL and tkWWW.

SoftQuad HoTMetaL

SoftQuad's HoTMetaL HTML editor, described in the section on Windows editors, is also available for many UNIX workstations running X11 (Motif). See `http://www.sq.com/` for more information.

tkWWW

tkWWW is a World Wide Web browser and editor that runs using the tcl language and tk toolkit under X. Because it is both an editor and a browser, it can rightfully claim WYSIWYG-ness if you use tkWWW as your only browser. In tkWWW, you choose items and styles from menus, and correct HTML is produced when you save the document. This is nice if you can't stand looking at HTML tags—using tkWWW, you never have to see one.

tkWWW requires tcl and tk. An overview of its features is available at `http://uu-gna.mit.edu:8001/tk-www/help/overview.html`; you can retrieve the package itself from `ftp://ftp.aud.alcatel.com/tcl/extensions`.

Converters

What if you'd prefer not to work in HTML at all—you have your own tool or language that you're familiar with, and you'd prefer to work in that? Many programs exist that convert different formats into HTML. This section describes many of those converters.

If you use a commercial word processor and you don't see a converter for it listed here or in Appendix D, try calling the vendor of that word processor. Conversion to HTML has been a hot topic for most word processing and desktop publishing companies, and that vendor might have a converter available.

For Windows

Converters for Windows are available for two of the most popular word processing systems: Microsoft Word and WordPerfect.

Microsoft Word

The CU_HTML, ANT_HTML, and GT_HTML packages, as well as Microsoft's Internet Assistant, can be used to convert Word documents to HTML. For information, see the discussions about these packages earlier in this chapter.

Microsoft Word can also export files in RTF (rich text format), which can then be converted to HTML using the RTFTOHTM filter for Windows. You can get more information about this filter from `http://www.w3.org/hypertext/WWW/Tools/RTFTOHTM.html`.

WordPerfect

In addition to the Internet Publisher program I mentioned previously in this chapter, other converters exist. WPTOHTML is a set of WordPerfect macros that converts WordPerfect 5.1 and 6.0 for DOS files to HTML. WordPerfect can also export RTF files, enabling you to use the RTF converter mentioned in the preceding section on Microsoft Word.

For more information about the WPTOHTML macros, take a look at `http://www.lib.ox.ac.uk/~hunter/`.

For Macintosh

Converters for Macintosh files lag behind other platforms, but good ones do exist, including rtftohtml, an excellent RTF-to-HTML converter. Because many popular word processing and desktop publishing programs can export RTF (including Microsoft Word, PageMaker, QuarkXpress, and FrameMaker), this might be the only converter you need. You can get information about rtftohtml at `ftp://ftp.cray.com/src/WWWstuff/RTF/rtftohtml_overview.html`.

If you use ClarisWorks, you definitely should check out `http://ai.eecs.umich.edu/highc/software/translator/XTND_HTML_Translator.html`, which contains information about a Claris XTND translator for HTML files.

If you use QuarkXPress, you can either use the RTF converter mentioned previously, or export your Quark files to "tagged text" and then use the converter mentioned later, in the section on QuarkXPress.

For UNIX

UNIX, of course, has all the good converters. Many of these are written in the Perl language, which means that if you have a Perl port for your system, these converters might work there as well.

Here's a quick rundown of the more popular converters for UNIX.

Plain Text

If you have files in plain text format that you want to convert to HTML quickly and easily, two simple filters will do it for you, both called txt2html. See `http://www.seas.upenn.edu/~mengwong/txt2html.html` for more information.

RTF (Rich Text Format)

Although RTF is a more popular format for desktop word processors, the filter mentioned under Macintosh converters also exists for UNIX systems. That URL, again, is `ftp://ftp.cray.com/src/WWWstuff/RTF/rtftohtml_overview.html`.

LaTeX

For converting LaTeX files to HTML, you can use latex2html. One capability it includes is conversion of equations into GIF files for inclusion in the HTML document. You can get latex2html at `http://cbl.leeds.ac.uk/nikos/tex2html/doc/latex2html/latex2html.html`.

FrameMaker

Several filters to convert FrameMaker files exist for UNIX, including the following:

☐ Frame2HTML from Norwegian Telecom does an excellent job of converting whole books to HTML, including preserving interdocument hypertext links as HTML tags and also converting internal graphics into GIF files with the GhostScript and PBM filter packages installed. See `http://www.w3.org/hypertext/WWW/Tools/fm2html.html` for more information.

☐ WebMaker is a similar package for converting FrameMaker documents to HTML. It is available in binary form for several popular platforms, including SunOS, Solaris, HPUX, and IRIX. You can get more information from `http://www.cern.ch/WebMaker/wmum/AboutWebMaker.html` or `http://www.harlequin.com/webmaker/2.0/buy.html`.

FrameMaker has advertised its support for exporting files to HTML in its newest version (5.0), which is available for many different platforms, including Macintosh and Windows. This filter promises to be interesting. FrameMaker files can contain images, tables, and hypertext links within pages in the file and elsewhere on the Web.

QuarkXpress

QuarkXpress files themselves cannot yet be converted to HTML, but Quark can output tagged text that can then be converted to HTML. More information is available at `http://the-tech.mit.edu/~jeremy/qt2www.html`.

PostScript

Information about a general-purpose PostScript-to-HTML converter can be found at `http://stasi.bradley.edu/ftp/pub/ps2html/ps2html-v2.html`. You will need GhostScript to use this converter.

Working Directly in HTML Versus Using a Converter

With all these converters from word processors to HTML, you can often do most of your HTML development in those programs and deal with converting the files to HTML at the last minute. For many projects, this might be the way to go.

Consider the advantages of using a converter:

☐ Authors do not have to keep track of tags. Having to memorize and know the rules of how tags work is a major issue if all one wants to do is write.

☐ Fewer errors end up in HTML documents (misspelling words, forgetting to close tags, using overlapping tags). Because the HTML is automatically generated, there's less chance of "operator error" in the final output.

☐ Authors can use a tool they're familiar with. If they know MS Word and live and die by MS Word, they can work in MS Word.

On the other hand, working in a converter is not a panacea. There are pitfalls, including these:

☐ No tools can provide all the features of HTML, particularly with links to external documents. Some handworking of the final HTML files will generally be required after you convert.

☐ You must deal with the split-source issue. After you convert your files from their original form to HTML, you'll have two sources you will have to monitor. To make changes after you do the conversion, you'll have to either change the original and regenerate the HTML (wiping out any hand-massaging you did to those files), or make sure you make the change to *both* the original source and the HTML documents. For large projects, splitting the source at any time except the last minute can create enormous headaches for everyone involved.

Working directly in HTML, for all its hideous text-only markup what-you-see-is-nothing-like-what-you-get glory, does have advantages, including these:

☐ All your work is done in one file; no extra step to generate the final version is needed.

☐ HTML files are text only, making it possible for them to be filtered through programs that can easily do automatic tasks such as generating tables of contents of major headings (and hyperlinking them back to those headings) or testing for the validity of the links in those files. The files also can easily be put under source-code control.

☐ You have the full flexibility of the HTML language, including the capability to code new features as they appear rather than having to wait for the next revision of the converter.

Summary

In this chapter you have learned about some of the many HTML editors, utilities, and converters that can be used to assist you in the creation of Web pages. You won't find any mention of these tools throughout the remainder of this book, however, since you are going to be learning HTML from the ground up.

Having said that, once you have a good understanding of the workings of HTML and Web creation techniques, using such tools can be a valuable aid to your Web publishing efforts. Certainly feel free to explore the capabilites offered by any of the tools listed in this chapter, but remember that sound knowledge can never be fully replaced by the use of add-on tools and utilities.

Workshop

There is no Workshop for this chapter, so because it is the end of the day, put your feet up, kick back, and relax.

On the other hand, some of you might be so keen to get on with the business of Web publishing that you are tempted to jump straight into Day 2, "Creating Simple Web Documents." Go on, I dare you to! <Grin>

DAY 2

Creating Simple Web Documents

4

Before You Start

On Day 1, "Introducing the World Wide Web, Hypertext, and Netscape," you learned how the World Wide Web operates and explored some of the tools that help you work with Web pages. But what about creating your own pages? After all, that is what this book is all about.

In today's lessons you will explore the basics of Web publishing and create your first Web page. To get you started, this chapter looks at the following topics:

- ☐ Deciding what you want to do
- ☐ The Netscape debate
- ☐ Planning your Web site

Deciding What You Want to Do

You might think I am stating the obvious by telling you that the first thing you need to do when developing a Web site is decide what you want to do with the World Wide Web. Yet it is ironic that many Web sites are developed without anyone ever establishing a clear definition of what the site will achieve.

For private home pages and the like, the feet-first, get-one-page-running-and-then-do-the-rest style of development might be acceptable. But with more and more commercial enterprises moving onto the World Wide Web, there is an ever-increasing movement toward high-quality, professional Web sites that demonstrate a high level of preproduction planning. After all, businesses need to ensure that they show their best face to the viewing public from day one.

As a bonus, by defining up front what you want to achieve, planning the site in detail before you start production, and allowing for future expansion, in most cases the ongoing maintenance requirements for a site are considerably reduced.

So how do you go about deciding what to do on the World Wide Web? The best place to start is by taking a look at what you can do with the World Wide Web.

What Can You Do on the World Wide Web?

Due to the nature of the World Wide Web, the correct answer to this question is Just about anything. A quick trip to a popular Web directory such as Yahoo—http://www.yahoo.com/—reveals the extent of the possibilities offered by the World Wide Web. (See Figure 4.1.)

Figure 4.1.
Yahoo—one of the most popular Web directories currently available.

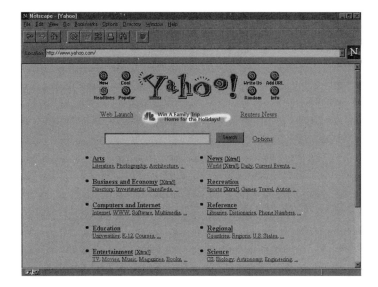

Although the possibilities are limitless, most Web sites fall into one or more of the following categories:

Advertising

Until the advent of the World Wide Web, commercial activities were very much frowned on by the Internet community. But now it seems that just about everyone is using the World Wide Web for advertising and promotion.

There is a danger, however, in mistakenly thinking that the World Wide Web is the ideal advertising tool. It certainly can be a very good tool for advertising products and services, but don't fire the company ad agency just yet.

Customer support

Many computer companies now offer online support for their products via the Internet and the World Wide Web. This can include access to program fixes and patches, new product information, discussion groups, and feedback forms.

Although the area of online customer support is still mainly the domain of the computer industry, there is nothing stopping non-computer-related organizations from offering customer support via the World Wide Web as well.

Education	With the Internet's background historically so closely associated with educational institutions, the amount of education-related information on the World Wide Web is very great. Universities, colleges, grade schools, and private educators all over the world operate Web sites that contain information about their campus facilities, classes, research projects, faculty, students, and almost anything else you can imagine.
Electronic shopping	Many businesses are attracted to the World Wide Web by the prospect of selling their products and services online.
	The World Wide Web offers a new level of interactivity that provides even the smallest company with the means of publishing catalogs online and also provides the mechanisms that enable customers to place orders for listed products.
	In addition, with the inclusion of secure transaction processing systems in Web browsers such as Netscape, customers can now provide information such as credit card details over the World Wide Web, safe in the knowledge that it will be seen only by the company or person it was sent to.
Entertainment	In the past, tools such as Internet relay chat (IRC) and multiuser dungeons (MUDs) offered limited forms of entertainment to Internet users. But now, with the availability of multimedia-capable Web browsers, the World Wide Web is bringing new meaning to the term *online entertainment*.
	Using the World Wide Web, you can listen to radio programs, play games, watch film clips of the latest Hollywood blockbusters, read books and magazines, explore virtual worlds, and in the not-too-distant future, maybe even view feature movies while online.
Information gathering	With tools such as forms, a Web site can be used to gather information. This can take the form of surveys, questionnaires, application forms, suggestion boxes, feedback pages, or any other type of information.

Information providers | When the World Wide Web was first proposed, one of the principal reasons for its development was to provide easy access to information, whether online documentation, news and press releases, company profiles, scientific papers, articles, commentaries, or the like.

Now, although the World Wide Web provides the mechanism for accessing all of these types of information, someone still needs to publish the information online before anyone can read it. In reality, most Web sites are information providers of some sort.

Personal information | Have you ever wanted to tell the world how incredibly wonderful you are, announce what you want for breakfast, or express your feelings about the meaning of life? With the World Wide Web, you can. But whether anyone is really interested is an entirely different subject.

What Can You Put on a Web Page?

When you are deciding what to do on the World Wide Web, you need to have an understanding of the various types of information that can be included as a part of a Web page. These elements are covered in the following sections.

Text

By far the most common use of Web pages is for the presentation of textual information. Basically, anything that has ever been entered into a computer can be displayed by the World Wide Web.

There are, however, a few limitations on the way your text is displayed by Web browsers. For example, you cannot take a formatted word processing document and expect it to look the same on the World Wide Web. You can take the text of the document and publish it, but the way the document appears on the World Wide Web is largely determined by the capabilities of the Web browser displaying the information.

This is not to say that all your Web pages will have the appearance of an old text-based computer terminal. You do have control of several formatting elements, including boldface, italics, text sizes, text alignment, and tables (on some Web browsers).

Links Within a Web Page

When creating large Web pages, you probably should include an index at the top of the page that enables people to move quickly through the document to the information they are looking for.

When you create a Web page, you can define any number of links to other places within the current documents. When you select one of these links, the Web browser automatically scrolls up or down the page to the appropriate location.

 Tip: Adding cross-reference links and links that take people back to the top or bottom of a page, is also considered to be good practice.

Links to Other Web Pages

Creating very large Web pages brings up a problem. For people with 14,400bps or 28,800bps modem connections, loading a 100+KB Web page takes some time. In a world that demands instant access, waiting around for a Web page to load is often deemed unacceptable.

To get around this problem, most Web publishers split large Web pages into smaller Web pages. All the smaller pages are then linked together using hyperlinks. For example, the first page might contain a table of contents that lists all the topics. (See Figure 4.2.) When you select a topic by clicking its hyperlink, the appropriate Web page is loaded. On this new page you usually find a hyperlink that returns you to the contents page, and possibly to the next and previous subjects.

Links to Other Web Sites

By far, the most powerful feature of the World Wide Web is the capability to include links on a Web page that point to documents stored at other Web sites. All you need to do is include the URL of the remote page as a hyperlink on your Web page, and the Web browser takes care of locating and displaying the information for you.

In fact, many Web sites—such as Yahoo—do little more than display lists of links to other Web sites. Because the World Wide Web has no formal table of contents, some people have taken it upon themselves to create directory lists of the most popular sites. What makes the World Wide Web so unique, however, is that each of these directories is itself simply another collection of Web pages, which can in turn also be pointed to by other people.

Figure 4.2.
Linking small pages together with hyperlinks reduces the need for large Web pages.

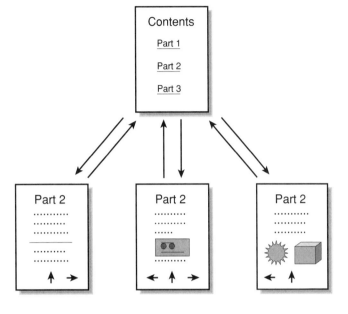

Using hyperlinks also gets around another potential problem: copyright. If you were to copy the contents of someone else's Web page and publish it yourself, you would technically be in breach of the laws dealing with copyright. If, however, you instead add a hyperlink to a person's site, there is no breach, because you have not republished anything—you have only told people where to find the information.

Note: For more information about how copyright and intellectual property issues affect the Internet, the best place to start is the Electronic Frontier Foundation's "Intellectual Property Online: Patent, Trademark, Copyright" archive. This archive is located at `http://www.eff.org/pub/Intellectual_property/`.

Links to Other Services

In addition to links with other Web pages, you can include links to other Internet services as a part of a Web page. These services include FTP, Gopher, Usenet, e-mail, and telnet.

When a Web browser encounters a link that points to any of these services, it automatically adjusts its operation to communicate with the service indicated by the hyperlink. Most Web browsers, however, do not support direct access to telnet sites. Instead, when a person selects a telnet-based hyperlink, a separate program is launched by the browser to handle the telnet session.

Including links to other services as a part of a Web page might at first glance seem like a strange idea, but using such capabilities can greatly enhance the usability of a Web page. For example, if you want to give people the ability to download files from your site, including a direct link to the file offers a simple one-click approach to FTP. You could just list the location of the file as a part of your Web page and let the user start his or her own FTP client and download the file. The better approach is to add an FTP hyperlink to the Web document that performs the download automatically.

Forms

In addition to providing information, a Web page can be used to gather responses from visitors to your Web site. By using forms, you can request information and then respond accordingly.

For example, a feedback form might be used to collect comments from people about the way a Web site looks. (See Figure 4.3.) When a user fills out the feedback form, the Web server that houses the form can be programmed to automatically send a thank-you message, forward the comments to the Web site's owner for evaluation, and even automatically display a new Web page.

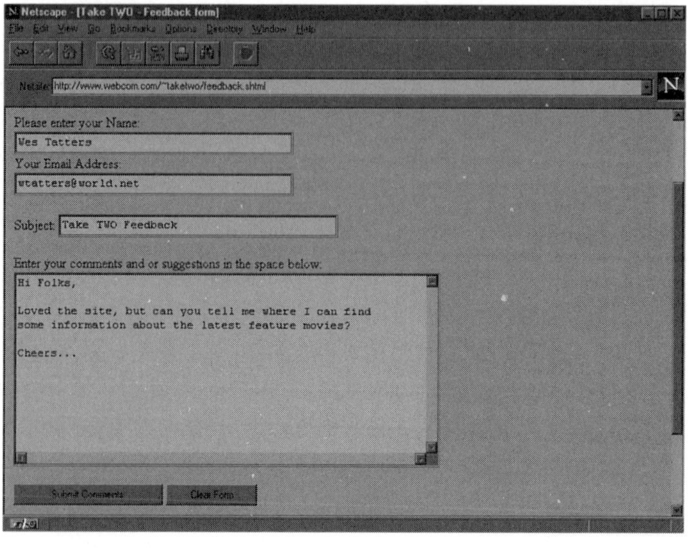

Figure 4.3.

Forms let people interact with your Web site.

Inline Graphics

Inline images are graphics that can be displayed as an integral part of a Web page. Inline images can be used to liven up a Web page by displaying

- ☐ Corporate logos
- ☐ Fancy borders and bullets
- ☐ Product images
- ☐ Graphics hyperlinks
- ☐ Photographs of your family cat

There is no limit to the images that can be displayed as a part of a Web page. You should, however, keep some practical considerations in mind. First, try to keep your images as small as possible. Your Web page might look great when displayed on your local screen, but only the very patient will wait 15 minutes for it to download using a 14,400bps modem.

Second, there are four image formats currently supported by Web browser for the presentation of inline images:

GIF	The Graphical Interchange Format (GIF) is the de facto standard for inline images. There are, however, two versions of the GIF standard: GIF87 and GIF89 (commonly known as Transparent GIF). All the popular graphics Web browsers can display inline images based on either format, but only newer browsers, such as Netscape Navigator, can take advantage of the transparency feature provided by GIF89.
Interlaced GIF	An Interlaced GIF image is a special type of GIF file that allows for the partial display of images as a Web page is being downloaded. If you have ever visited a Web site where the inline images start off looking chunky and then gradually increase to full quality, you have seen Interlaced GIF images at work.
JPEG	The Joint Picture Experts Group developed the JPEG or JPG image format to solve some of the limitations imposed by formats like GIF. GIF images contain only 256 colors, and even a small image can take up a large amount of storage space. JPEG images, on the other hand, can contain up to 16 million colors and are considerably smaller than their GIF counterparts.

Progressive JPEG

Progressive JPEG images are similar to Interlaced GIF images in that they allow a JPEG image to be built up layer by layer. Of all the image formats currently available, progressive JPEG images are the fastest-displaying images.

Note: Although progressive JPEG images look like the obvious format of choice for inline images, there are some limitations on their use. First, they are currently supported only by Navigator 2.0, second, they cannot be used with image maps, and finally, they do not support transparency.

Multimedia Presentations

It was not so long ago that multimedia on the Internet, and even the World Wide Web, meant the provision of a hyperlink to an occasional audio file as a novelty. But now, the availability of realtime audio, video playback, and 3D virtual reality, as well as access to multimedia presentation systems such as Adobe Acrobat and Macromedia Director, heralds the dawn of a new level of multimedia interaction via the World Wide Web.

External Multimedia

Currently, the most common way to integrate multimedia capabilities with the World Wide Web is by using helper applications. These applications are programs that can be called by a Web browser when it encounters information it cannot process internally.

For example, the Web site shown in Figure 4.4 contains a hyperlink to a new type of online video file called VDOLive. When you click on such a hyperlink, a helper application called the VDOLive Player—the window shown on the right side of Figure 4.4—is started. After a few seconds, live video begins to appear in the small display.

Note: Unlike other video helper applications that require you to download an entire file to your local computer before it can be displayed, VDOLive displays the file as it is being transferred. To learn more about VDOLive, point your Web browser to http://www.vdolive.com/.

Figure 4.4.
View moving images in realtime with VDOLive.

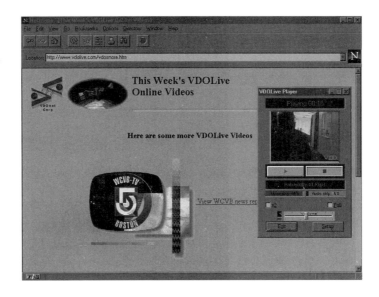

The main advantage of using helper applications is that your Web browser does not need to understand how the information is displayed or played. As a result, just about any Web browser can use helper applications, because it is the helper application, not the Web browser, that does all the work.

Inline Multimedia

With the release of Navigator 2.0, a new type of helper application called a plug-in (or live object) has become available. Whereas traditional helper applications are separate programs that operate independently of the Web browser, plug-ins provide a way for multimedia elements to be included directly on a Web page.

In Figure 4.5, the two graphics boxes on the left side of the Web page are, in fact, plug-in elements that represent objects constructed using the Virtual Reality Modeling Language (VRML). If you place your cursor over one of these boxes, you can move around the image and zoom in and out, because the box is really a window into a 3-D virtual world.

Figure 4.5.
Plug-ins enable Web publishers to include multimedia information directly on a Web page.

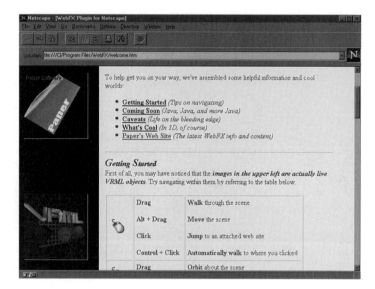

Taking the Plunge

Still having trouble deciding what to do on the World Wide Web?

If not, great—go to the head of the class. Well, not exactly. Instead, feel free to skip forward to the section titled "The Netscape Debate." There you'll learn about some important considerations you need to take into account when creating a Web site.

Be Creative

One of the most amazing things about the World Wide Web is that you can never tell what will and won't work. Some of the most ridiculous or downright unusual Web sites are in fact the most popular. Take, for example, the Useless Pages "America's Funniest Home Hypermedia" site at `http://www.primus.com/staff/paulp/useless.html`.

This site contains an up-to-date directory of the most useless Web pages ever created. Thrilling stuff, huh? Yet more than a million people have visited the site since it was created.

So even if you have an idea for a Web site that you think is way out, maybe you already have a winner. In fact, sometimes taking your brain out and just letting the ideas wash in is a good way to come up with new concepts.

Practical Ideas

Apart from the weird and wonderful, there are many opportunities for Web sites opening up each week on the World Wide Web. Do you belong to a club or an association, for example? If so, maybe you should consider creating a Web page devoted to it. You might be surprised to find out how many other people have interests similar to your own.

Creating a Web page devoted to your local community can be an enjoyable and possibly profitable activity. Have you ever tried searching the World Wide Web for information about the town or city you live in? In fact, this is the first thing many people do when starting out on the World Wide Web, yet so few towns and cities are represented. Imagine the surprise, then, when people in your community discover the Web page you have created.

Hobbies are another valuable source of ideas for interesting Web sites. As an exercise, pick a hobby you enjoy, and use the Lycos search tool at `http://www.lycos.com/` to see whether any Web sites are devoted to it. If you can't find such a site, maybe you should consider starting one.

Are you beginning to get the picture? There really is no limit to what you can do on the World Wide Web. In most cases, all it takes is a bit of lateral thinking.

The Netscape Debate

The introduction of plug-ins and a few other features as a part of Navigator 2.0 raises a few difficult questions for Web publishers.

In the past, as long as Web publishers developed Web pages according to the standards defined by the HTML 2.0 specification, they could be reasonably confident that anyone with a Web browser would be able to view their pages via the World Wide Web. Publishers still had to put up with the fact that their pages might look slightly different on each Web browser, but in general, most elements would remain the same.

Note: The HTML 2.0 specification is the internationally recognized guideline for the creation of HTML documents. It describes all the elements of a Web page and their use.

HTML 3.0

Things started to become more complex when people began talking about the HTML 3.0 specification. This specification includes layout and formatting features that affect the visual appearance of a Web page. By taking advantage of these new features, a Web publisher has far greater control over the way a Web page appears. But the problem is that only those Web browsers that recognize and support the HTML 3.0 elements can display the page as it was intended. The page shown in Figure 4.6 uses many of the new HTML 3.0 features, including Justification, Centering, Tables, and Background Images.

Figure 4.6.

The HTML 3.0 specification gives Web publishers greater control over the layout of their Web pages.

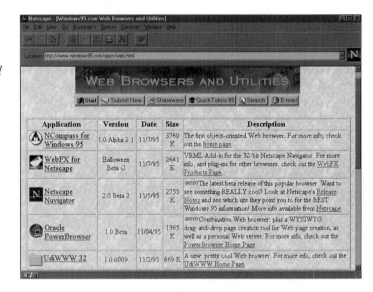

Web browsers that don't support HTML 3.0 can still display the text and inline images contained on the Web page, but all the HTML 3.0 formatting controls are lost. Figure 4.7 shows the Web page displayed in Figure 4.6 when viewed by an old version of the Cello Web browser that does not recognize HTML 3.0 formatting.

As you can see in Figure 4.7, when an HTML 3.0–formatted page is viewed on a Web browser that does not support the new standard, the results are often less than perfect. Certainly, all the information is still there, but visually things could be a lot better. This situation led to a new problem. Because many Web sites are now virtual storefronts for commercial operations, having a Web site that looks bad, on any Web browser, is regarded as bad business. Most companies want to look their best regardless of the situation.

Figure 4.7.
Web browsers that don't support HTML 3.0 still display the contents of the Web page, but not in the proper layout.

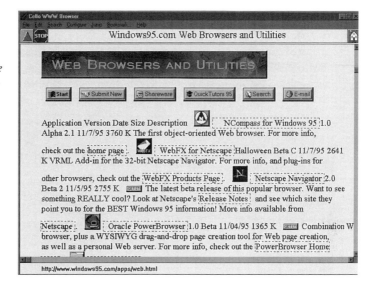

Obviously, you can't make a Web browser do things it was not designed for. Instead, some Web publishers create two separate sets of Web pages for their sites, one set suited to HTML 2.0–based browsers and text-based browsers, and one suited to HTML 3.0–based browsers. In this way, users who have a browser that supports HTML 3.0 receive the benefits of better layout and design, while other users can still access the site and view the Web pages in a visually suitable way.

This solution is, however, fraught with its own problems, not the least of which is the added workload involved in maintaining two separate sites. In addition, if you do not have your own Web server and are instead renting space from a Web service provider, the additional storage space required to maintain two separate sets of Web pages often makes doing so an expensive proposition.

As a result, many Web publishers who create Web sites that take advantage of the features provided by HTML 3.0 have adopted the attitude that if you don't have a suitable browser, it's time you upgraded. To this end, you will often encounter messages such as "This site is best viewed using Netscape 1.2" displayed on home pages, accompanied by a hyperlink to the appropriate Web site, so that users can download a copy for themselves.

Netscape Navigator 2.0 and NHTML

Since the release of Navigator 2.0, the problems associated with supporting different versions of HTML have again become the subject of many sometimes heated discussions.

The debate revolves around some new features that currently are available only in Navigator 2.0. Netscape Communications has submitted proposals recommending the inclusion of many of these features in the final HTML 3.0 specification, but the very existence of what is currently Netscape-specific HTML, or NHTML, means that Web publishers must again make decisions about what they will and will not use on their Web pages.

Note: The term NHTML has become the de facto means of describing HTML elements included in the Navigator 2.0, which currently have no equal in the HTML 3.0 or earlier specifications. It is not an official format or specification, but instead is a common term used by many participants in the various debates about Netscape versus the rest.

Frames

Support for separate windows on a Web page is one of the most long-awaited features in the history of HTML development. Whereas a traditional Web page consists of a single page of information, by using frames—Netscape's answer to separate windows—you can display multiple Web pages on a single screen. (See Figure 4.8.)

Figure 4.8.
Hyperlinks in one window can be used to control the contents of another window.

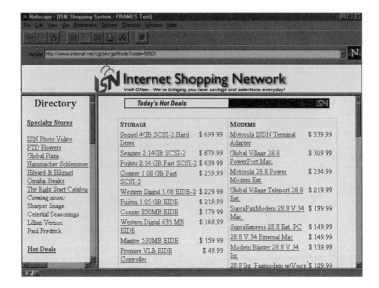

More important, you can change the contents of one window without affecting the contents of all the other windows. Or you can open new pages in one window by clicking hyperlinks located in another. For example, Figure 4.8 shows a frames-based version of the Internet Shopping Network's (ISN's) online catalog. In the left window is a Web page showing the directory for the ISN catalog. When you click any of the hyperlinks listed in this directory, the window on the right side is updated to display the section of the catalog pointed to by the link. In addition, the directory window is unaffected by this change and remains on-screen so that you can select other sections of the catalog.

 Note: To learn more about frames take a look at Chapter 12, "Linked Windows and Frames."

There is a big problem, however, with frames and Web browsers that don't support their use. Due to the way pages associated with frames operate, there is currently no way to represent such pages on a Web browser that does not have frames support. Unlike most other HTML 3.0–specific features that are simply ignored by older Web browsers. Attempting to display the page shown in Figure 4.8 on the Cello browser previously mentioned produces the results shown in Figure 4.9. As a result, Web publishers who plan to use frames need to create separate pages for browsers that don't support frames.

Figure 4.9.
A Web publisher needs to create separate pages for browsers that don't support frames.

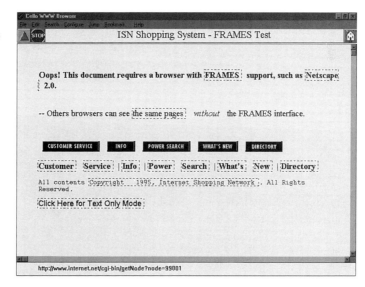

Java and JavaScript

Because Navigator 2.0 is currently the only Web browser that supports Java applications—apart from HotJava, the experimental Web browser written in the Java language—using Java applets with your Web pages effectively demands that people use Navigator 2.0 to explore your site.

The same is true for the JavaScript scripting language, which is also currently supported only by Navigator 2.0. However, the recent indications of support for JavaScript and Java, both by Sun Microsystems, and a host of major industry players does bode well for future support in other Web browsers.

The Verdict

Because you are reading this book, it would be reasonably safe to assume that you plan to include many of the new Navigator 2.0–specific features in your future Web sites. As a result, you need to decide fairly early on in your Web development projects exactly how having a Navigator 2.0–only site will affect your site's prospects.

On the plus side, access to features such as frames, Java, JavaScript, and plug-ins can greatly improve the way your Web sites look and how they operate. But on the downside, by using such features, you effectively prevent people without Navigator 2.0 from using your site to its best advantage.

So which way should you go? Ultimately, the choice is up to you. With an estimated 75 percent of all Web users currently using Netscape Navigator, it is clear that having a Navigator 2.0–only site will not relegate it to the Internet wastelands. But at the same time, if you want to reach every Web user, you might need to make some plans for alternative Web pages.

Note: If you do decide to create alternative Web pages, make sure you take into consideration the fact that in the future when you need to update any information, it will need to be done twice. As a result, while setting up alternative pages may at first seem like a reasonably simple task, if you are not careful, you can wind up with a maintenance nightmare down the track.

Planning Your Web Site

After you have decided what you want to do with your Web site, it is a good idea to spend a little time planning how your Web site will work.

I realize that you are probably itching to get your hands dirty creating your first Web page, and the last thing you want to do is sit down with a piece of paper and a pencil—but that is exactly what you should do. (OK, OK, you can use your computer if you prefer.)

Outlines and Strategic Plans

Whether you're writing a book, designing a house, starting a new business, or building an ocean liner, the first step in the process is always to create an outline of some sort. For a book, the outline is usually a preliminary table of contents; for a business, it's a strategic plan. When developing a Web site, you should do the same.

Establish Your Goals

The first part of your plan should define the goals you hope to achieve. To put this in business terms, you need to define the mission or objective for your Web site.

When creating a list of goals, you should attempt to include answers to the following questions:

- ☐ What do you hope to achieve by creating the Web site?
- ☐ What do you want people to be able to do with the Web site?
- ☐ What makes this Web site different from other sites?

Defining the Outline for Your Site

After you have established the goals for your Web site, you need to create a list that describes in detail what you want to include as a part of the Web site. You can adopt various approaches at this stage, but the one I find most useful is to treat each Web site like a book.

First, you need to organize the contents of your proposed site into a list of main topics or ideas. For example, I operate a Web site called TakeTwo—`http://www.webcom.com/taketwo/`—that contains a directory of film and television sites and a set of Web forms on which people can submit their own movie reviews. When I first created this site, I listed the following items in my initial outline:

- ☐ Table of Contents
- ☐ Television Information
    World Wide Web Sites
    Newsgroups
- ☐ Film Information
    World Wide Web Sites
    Newsgroups

☐ User Reviews

Movie Reviews

Television Reviews

☐ My Personal Information Page

☐ Search Tools

Defining the Contents of Each Web Page

After you have developed a basic outline, you should keep refining it until each item represents a single Web page. When you are happy with the outline, the next step is to create a list for each page that itemizes the information it will include.

This list should include the text, any inline images, sound and multimedia files, any hyperlinks located on the page, and finally, if the page is a form, what information it will collect and what will be done with the information.

Note: If you are creating a site that includes Web directories or information that will be entered by users, obviously you cannot define the exact content at this stage. You should, however, still attempt to create as detailed an outline and contents list as possible, because this information will be used to create your initial Web pages.

Evaluating Your Site's Performance

The one part of a good outline most people forget about is a description of how you will evaluate the success of your site after it is operational. Although nothing is stopping you from putting a site up on the World Wide Web and forgetting about it, most people will want to update their site on a regular basis and react to the comments of people who visit.

When establishing your performance-evaluation process, make sure that you include the following items:

☐ An explanation of how you plan to collect feedback, Web forms, and e-mail.

☐ An evaluation timetable that shows when you will review the site and update information.

☐ An explanation of how you plan to determine the popularity of your site.

Note: No one will come knocking on your door if you don't keep to the timetable you set; however, a page with outdated information and bad links will gain few followers. If you want people to visit your site, you need to keep the information it contains accurate and up-to-date.

Developing a Storyboard

The final step before you start creating your Web pages is the development of a storyboard. If you have worked through the steps discussed previously, creating the storyboard should be a fairly straightforward task.

In the film and television industry, storyboards are used by production teams to depict the action that will take place in a film. Each separate shot in the film is drawn on a storyboard before it is ever recorded. In this way, the director and other staff can get a general impression of how the final product will look. By using a storyboard, the production team can quickly locate areas of potential problems and examine the flow of the film.

When you are developing a Web site, a storyboard comes in very handy for the same reasons. A storyboard enables you to look at the layout of your Web site as a whole and helps you understand where each page fits in the overall structure of the site. You have, in fact, already seen a rudimentary storyboard earlier in this chapter. Figure 4.2 contains a storyboard that represents the flow and layout of a simple four-page Web site.

To create a storyboard for your site, take each list you created when defining the contents of each page, and determine how these pages will be linked together. You should then use this information to draw a picture that indicates the links between each page and the relationships of the different pages.

At this stage, you should also determine how you plan to let people navigate around your site. Will there be a link on every page that returns you to the home page or the table of contents? Will you include elements such as a signature or logo on each Web page? Also, do you plan to include any alternative pages for different Web browsers, and how will they be linked with all the other pages?

Tip: As you work through the creation of your storyboard, be sure to keep referring to the outline you established previously, and keep checking that your site is consistent with your chosen goals. Doing this helps ensure that your Web site remains focused on its objectives.

Publish Away

By now, you should have a stack of lists, outlines, and storyboards that describe the contents of your new Web site. With these items in hand, you are ready to create your first Web page.

> **Note:** Actually, nothing can stop you from creating your Web pages without doing any planning at all. If you want, you can simply start with a home page and build your site as you go. You will often find, however, that creating a site in this way takes considerably longer, due to the inevitable rebuilds and restructurings as you discover new elements that should have been included at the start.

Summary

In this chapter you have learned some of the reasons people create Web pages and examined the basic elements that can be included on a Web page. You have also been introduced to the issues surrounding the development of Netscape-only Web sites, and you have developed an outline and a storyboard for a Web site.

In the next chapter, you will learn about the basics of HTML and create your first Web page.

Workshop

The first section of the Workshop lists some of the common questions people ask about the World Wide Web along with a brief answer to each. Next is a quiz about the chapter you have just read. If you have problems answering any of the questions in the quiz, you can turn to Appendix E, "Answers to Quiz Questions."

Q&A

Q I really do want to publish pictures of my cat on the World Wide Web. Do I still need to bother with outlines and storyboards?

A It's up to you. Techniques such as storyboards and outlines exist to help you define what you want to do on the World Wide Web. If you are confident you know what you want, feel free to jump right in and start Web publishing. If, however, you plan to embark on a major Web project, spending a little time planning the site often saves many hundreds of hours later.

Q I like this idea of being able to link to other people's sites, but how do I know that they won't move the information?

A You don't. Unfortunately, the World Wide Web is in a state of constant flux. People regularly change information, redesign their sites, and even relocate entirely. That is why I suggested that you create a timetable defining when you will evaluate and update your site. Part of the evaluation process should include a check of the entire site to make sure that all your hyperlinks are still valid.

Quiz

1. What graphics formats can be used when displaying inline images?
2. What Web browsers support the use of frames?
3. What is the difference between inline and external multimedia support?
4. How large does a business need to be before it can use the World Wide Web for electronic shopping?
5. What feature of the World Wide Web can be used to collect responses from people who visit a Web site?

Exercise

Today's exercise is a simple one. Create a list of five ideas for new Web sites and conduct a search of the World Wide Web to see whether any similar sites already exist. If a similar site exists, remove the idea from your list and think of a new one. Keep going like this until you have a list of five ideas for new Web sites.

5

Basic HTML and the World Wide Web

With all the planning and preparation out of the way, finally you are ready to create your first Web page. In this chapter you will learn about HTML and explore some of the basic Web page formatting techniques.

You will do this by examining these topics:

☐ What is HTML?

☐ The structure of an HTML document

☐ Basic document tags

What Is HTML?

Before you create your first Web page, you need to understand what HTML is and why you need to use it. Unless you have been skipping chapters, you have already encountered the term HTML earlier in this book. But for those who jumped straight to this chapter, and as a quick refresher for everyone else, here is the short version.

HTML is an abbreviation for Hypertext Markup Language. This is the language you use to describe the contents of your Web pages. For this reason, Web pages are often described as HTML documents. Although these two terms can be used interchangeably, throughout this book the term *HTML document* is used in reference to the contents and information that defines a Web page. The term *Web page* is used in reference to the resultant information that is displayed by a Web browser.

Note: HTML is based loosely on another language called the Standard Generalized Markup Language, or SGML for short. SGML is used primarily by the printing and publishing community when describing the contents and general appearance of printed documents.

HTML Describes Structure, Not Page Layout

Unlike other popular page-description languages such as PostScript or a word processor such as Microsoft Word, which are used to describe in great detail how pages of text and other information will look, HTML is used to describe only the contents and structure of a Web page. It is then up to the Web browser to take this information and determine the final page layout, based on the browser's capabilities.

This is an important concept to understand as you begin to develop Web pages. Although you can spend many hours formatting a Web page so that it looks perfect on your own Web browser, the moment the page is displayed on another brand of Web browser, there is no guarantee as to how the page will look. In fact, differences can become apparent even when the same Web browser is being used on two different computer systems.

For example, compare the Web page shown in Figure 5.1 with the one shown in Figure 5.2. Although the same HTML source was used in both screen shots, and even the same Web browser was used, the final appearance and layout of the pages are different.

Figure 5.1.

The Web browser determines the ultimate appearance of a Web page.

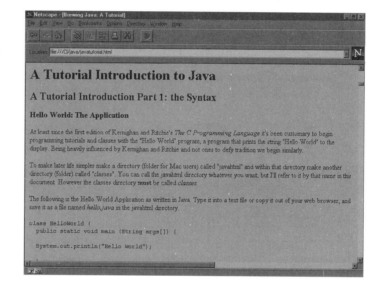

In Figure 5.1 the browser was configured—by its user—to display text using a Times Roman font, whereas in Figure 5.2 a different-sized Arial font was used. As a result, the size of the text displayed on each page, the amount of information displayed onscreen, and the physical placement of the text are different.

You, the Web page developer, have little or no control over what settings a user might define for his Web browser or how the browser will lay out your Web pages. Therefore, the information you code into an HTML document needs to be specific enough to provide the Web browser with general instructions, yet flexible enough to let many kinds of Web browsers display the resulting page.

Figure 5.2.

Even when the same Web browser is used, personal preferences and other optional settings can alter the appearance of a Web page.

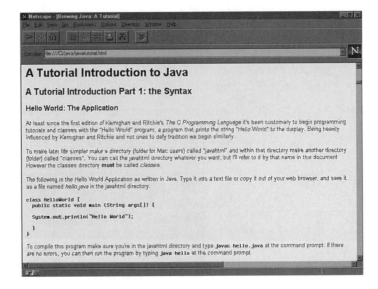

Style Sheets and HTML

To achieve this balance between the general and the specific, the HTML specification uses a technique similar to that adopted by many word processor and document formatting tools. If you have ever used a program such as Microsoft Word, PageMaker, or QuarkXPress, you probably have used their built-in style sheet tools.

Style sheets provide writers with the means of formatting the standard components they used in a document. These components usually include body text, headings, subheadings, notes, quotations, and other user-definable categories. Using style sheets when writing greatly reduces the chance of inconsistencies in a document, which often result from the accidental use of different formatting for one or more elements.

The page shown in Figure 5.3 demonstrates how a word processor uses styles to simplify the writing process. After you define a text style, you can reuse it throughout the document, and the word processor always ensures that the text defined for a given style is displayed and printed correctly. In addition, if you decided to alter the appearance or format of a style, all the text throughout the document which uses that style is automatically updated to reflect any changes.

Figure 5.3.
Using styles when writing helps you organize your text.

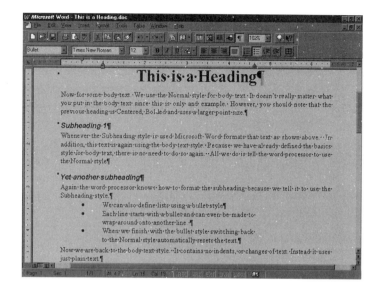

The HTML specification uses a similar concept for the creation of Web pages, although it does not give you the same level of control provided by a word processor. What HTML does give you is a set of predefined generic styles you use to indicate how text and other elements of your Web page should look. These generic styles include those for headings and paragraphs, some limited formatting tools, and a set of Web-specific elements.

You use these styles to tell the Web browser how each block, or paragraph, of text should be displayed. The Web browser then uses this information to format the page as best it can, depending on the browser's built-in capabilities.

Note: Web browsers such as Navigator 2.0 that take advantage of the HTML 3.0 specification provide much greater control over the physical layout of a document than do their predecessors. Yet at the same time, for the most part, they still adhere to the multiplatform principles outlined in the original HTML specification.

Tags and Text

Apart from the layout limitations inherent in HTML, the other main difference between an HTML document and a word processing document is the way information is stored in an HTML document.

HTML documents are created using plain ACSII text files like those created by a text editor. Unlike word processing documents and most other document-formatting utilities that bury complicated binary codes in their documents, making them unreadable without a dedicated program, you can read and write HTML documents using the simplest of text editors. To achieve this, HTML documents use what are called *tags* to define the various document styles (or elements), formatting options, hyperlinks, and even graphical images to be displayed by a Web browser.

The most basic style available in an HTML document is plain text. Plain text should be considered the default style because there is no physical need to define text. Basically, any text not included in a formatting tag is displayed by your Web browser using the browser's default text style, whereas any text surrounded by formatting tags is displayed according to the information included in the tags.

So what does an HTML tag look like? I'm glad you asked! Most HTML tags have a format similar to this:

`<TAGNAME>Some text</TAGNAME>`

In this syntax, `TAGNAME` is replaced by the HTML element you want to use. For example, the tag `<H1>` tells the Web browser that the text following the tag should be displayed using a Heading style. If you were to use this tag with the preceding example, you would write this:

`<H1>Some text</H1>`

This tells the Web browser that the words `Some text` should be displayed using a Heading style, in this case Heading1 style.

Note: See the section "Basic Document Tags," later in this chapter, for more information about heading tags.

The other important piece of information you should note from this example is the `</H1>` element following `Some text`. This tells the Web browser where the block of text affected by the `<H1>` tag ends. Most tags act like switches: When a Web browser encounters a tag in an HTML document, it tells the browser to "turn on" a style or formatting element. This style remains in force until it is "turned off" by a corresponding end tag. End tags have a / symbol added to the front of the tag name. So `</H1>` is the corresponding end tag for `<H1>`.

There are a few exceptions—tags that are said to be single sided—but as a rule, most tags consist of both a start and an end code.

> **Tip:** HTML tags are not case sensitive. In other words, `<H1>` could also be
> written as `<h1>`. It is, however, regarded as standard practice to use uppercase
> letters for tags. This convention makes tags easier to locate in an HTML
> document.

Tag Attributes

Throughout this book, many of the tags you encounter will also have what are called *tag
attributes* associated with them. Tag attributes supply the Web browser with additional
information about how a tag should be represented or treated.

When a tag has tag attributes associated with it, the tag takes the following format:

```
<TAGNAME ATTRIBUTE="ATTRIBUTEVALUE">Some text</TAGNAME>
```

All the attributes associated with a specific tag must be included before the > symbol. For
example, the `<H1>` tag, mentioned previously, can have an alignment attribute associated with
it. This attribute—`ALIGN`—tells the Web browser to center, left justify, or right justify the text
associated with the heading tag. To tell the Web browser to center the words `Some text` using
the Heading1 style, you would use the following HTML source:

```
<H1 ALIGN="CENTER">Some text</H1>
```

▼ Exercise: Learning by Example

Now it's your turn to do some work. One of the best ways to learn about the makeup of
HTML documents is to examine the contents of Web pages created by other people. Unlike
computer programming languages, which go to great lengths to hide the secrets of their
internal code, the source for HTML documents is publicly available to everyone. (To read,
but not copy!).

Like many Web browsers, Navigator 2.0 provides a built-in mechanism that enables you to
view the HTML source for any Web page you visit. To access this feature, load a Web page
you want to examine using any method you prefer, and then open the **V**iew menu and select
the Document **S**ource item, as shown in Figure 5.4. For this exercise, try using the W3
Consortiums home page at `http://www.w3.org/`. If you have not taken the opportunity to
visit this site yet, now would be a good time to do so.

Figure 5.4.

Select the Document Source item from the View menu.

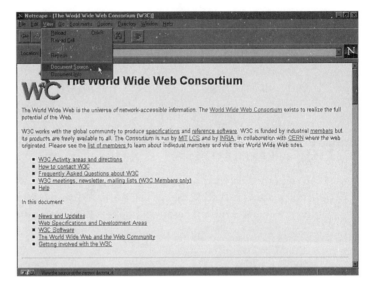

After you select the Document Source item, Navigator 2.0 opens a new window like the one shown in Figure 5.5. In this window Navigator 2.0 displays the HTML source for the currently displayed document and adds some highlighting features to help you differentiate tags, attributes, attribute values, and basic text.

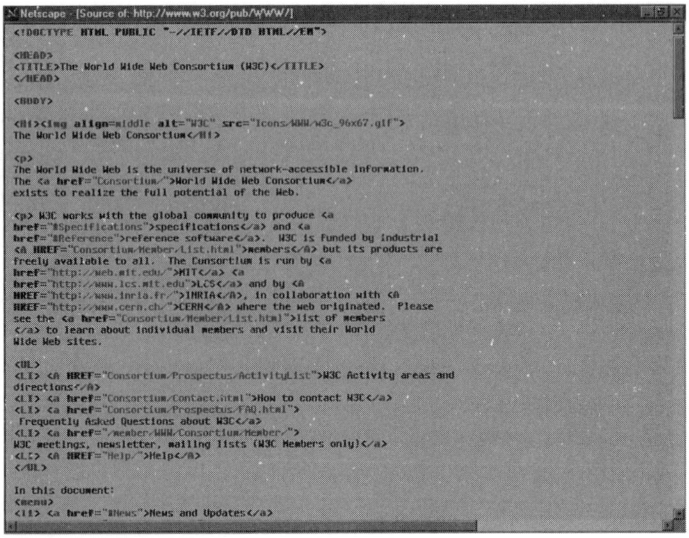

Figure 5.5.

Navigator 2.0 highlights HTML commands, tags, attributes, and attribute values in different colors to make the HTML source easy to read.

After spending some time looking at the HTML source for the W3 Consortium home page, feel free to visit any other sites you like and examine its HTML source as well.

When looking at the HTML source for a page, flip back and forth between it and the Web page, and try to locate the different tags that control the elements you are looking at. Don't, however, be too disappointed at this stage if the HTML source looks to you like Egyptian hieroglyphics. After all, this is only Chapter 5, and you still have a way to go. By the time you finish this book, you will be able to look at a page of HTML source code and know what it all means.

The Structure of an HTML Document

Although most HTML tags are used to control the way blocks of text in a Web page look, a few tags don't affect the appearance of the page. Instead, these tags give some additional structure to the HTML documents you create by separating the major components into individual blocks of information. These are the tags:

- [ ] `<HTML>`
- [ ] `<HEAD>`
- [ ] `<BODY>`

Note: Although most Web browsers will display Web pages properly if these tags are missing, good HTML writing style demands their inclusion. As a result, they will be included throughout this book and you should include them in all your own HTML documents.

5

<HTML>...</HTML>

Every HTML document you create should start with `<HTML>` and end with `</HTML>`. Doing this informs the Web browser that everything within these two tags should be treated as HTML source code.

Note: Currently, if you don't include an <HTML> tag at the start of an HTML document, most Web browsers simply assume that there is one by default and display the document correctly. There are, however, moves to extend the HTML specification to include other markup information, either before or after the HTML section. If such a change does occur, pages that don't include an HTML block defined by the <HTML> tag might break future Web browsers.

<HEAD>...</HEAD>

The <HEAD> tag should always be placed immediately after the <HTML> tag. In the block of text bracketed by the <HEAD> and </HEAD> tags you place any information that is used to describe the contents of your Web page. This block of text takes the following form:

```
<HTML>
<HEAD>
<TITLE> My first HTML Document </TITLE>
    Other document information goes here.
</HEAD>

    The rest of your HTML source goes here.
</HTML>
```

For most users, the only information you need to include in this section is a document title. The <TITLE> tag is a special tag that tells the Web browser not to display the text between it and the </TITLE> tag as part of the physical Web page. (See the following section for more information regarding the <TITLE> tag titles.)

Note: The <HEAD> block of your HTML document should not contain any displayable information. Although most Web browsers will attempt to display such text as part of the Web page, it is regarded as bad practice to do so.

<BODY>...</BODY>

The area where you type the information you want displayed as part of your Web page is bounded by the <BODY> and </BODY> tags. In this block of text you include the text of your Web page, any hyperlinks and graphics, and all the formatting elements.

The <BODY> tag is usually placed immediately after </HEAD>, and the </BODY> tag immediately before the </HTML> tag. Doing this gives a standard HTML document the following structure:

```
<HTML>
  <HEAD>
      Basic document information is placed here.
  </HEAD>
  <BODY>
      The contents of your Web page are placed here.
  </BODY>
</HTML>
```

Exercise: Creating Your First HTML Document

Now that you understand what the <HTML>, <HEAD>, and <BODY> tags do, you are ready to create your first HTML document.

Open your text editor of choice, and enter the following text:

```
<HTML>
<HEAD>
<TITLE>My first HTML Document</TITLE>
</HEAD>
<BODY>
<H1 ALIGN="CENTER">This is my first HTML Document</H1>
Here is my very first Web page, brought to you by Netscape Navigator 2.0.
</BODY>
</HTML>
```

By now, you should recognize all the tags shown here. Start your HTML document with an <HTML> tag, followed by a <HEAD>...</HEAD> block that includes a <TITLE> block. Add a small <BODY> block that includes an <H1> block and some straight text. And finally, close the document using a </HTML> tag.

After you have entered this text into your text editor, save it to your hard disk with an .html extension. Give the file a name like myfirst.html, and save it in an appropriate directory or folder.

5

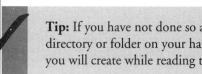

Tip: If you have not done so already, now would be a good time to create a new directory or folder on your hard drive where you can store all the HTML files you will create while reading this book.

Note: If the computer you are using is running MS-DOS, you cannot save HTML documents with an .html extension. Instead, you must settle for an .htm extension. If you are going to create many HTML documents, this limitation in MS-DOS provides a good argument for upgrading your system to Windows 95, which supports longer file extensions and, incidentally, longer filenames.

Whenever you create a new HTML document, the first thing you need to do is test it using your Web browser. To do this, start Navigator 2.0 and open the File menu. Select Open File and use the dialog box to locate the HTML document you just saved. When you open this file, you should see a Web page like the one shown in Figure 5.6. If your Navigator 2.0 screen does not look similar to this one, check your HTML document to make sure that all your tags are spelled correctly and that you have not missed any < or > symbols.

Figure 5.6.
Use Navigator 2.0 to test your HTML documents.

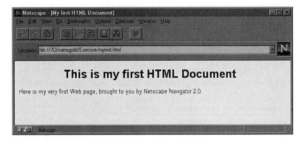

Basic Document Tags

In the final section of this chapter, you will learn about many of the basic formatting tags you will encounter in most of the Web sites you visit, and you will learn about the tags you will use in nearly all the HTML documents you create in the future.

Document Titles

The *title tag* <TITLE> is a special element that can appear only between the <HEAD> and </HEAD> tags at the start of your HTML document. It takes the following form:

```
<TITLE>My first HTML Document</TITLE>
```

The <TITLE> tag is also one of the special groups of tags that don't affect the physical appearance of your Web page. Instead, the text surrounded by the <TITLE> and </TITLE> tags is displayed by Navigator 2.0 in the title area, located at the top of the browser window, as shown in Figure 5.7.

Figure 5.7.
Navigator 2.0 displays the document title in the top section of the Web browser screen.

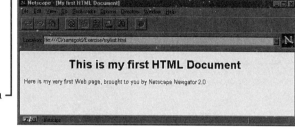

The title area ⎤

You should attempt to make your page titles as descriptive as possible so that people understand immediately what your Web page is about. Although you might understand exactly what is meant by titles such as "My home page," "Order Form," or "Chapter 1," they would be of little use to anyone visiting your pages via the World Wide Web. On the other hand, "The Wes Tatters Home Page," "Games World Order Form," and "The Great American Novel - Chapter 1" all provide people visiting your site with useful information about what the Web page is and does.

Note: Technically, the inclusion of a document title on each of your Web pages is not a requirement of the HTML specification. If you don't include a title, Navigator 2.0 displays the URL of the current page in the title area. However, not including a title is regarded as bad form by most of the Web community.

Headings

Six *heading tags*, which take the following form, are provided by the HTML specification:

```
<H1>Heading 1 is the largest heading style</H1>
<H2>This is an example of Heading 2</H2>
<H3>This is an example of Heading 3</H3>
<H4>This is an example of Heading 4</H4>
<H5>Heading 5 and heading 6 produce text that is smaller than plain
text on most browsers</H5>
<H6>Heading 6 is the smallest heading style</H6>
```

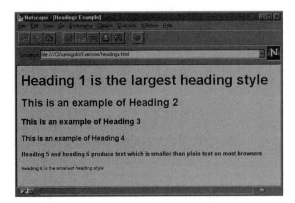

Output

Figure 5.8.
*Six heading styles are
provided by the
HTML specification.*

When you display this HTML source on a Web browser, it produces the results shown in Figure 5.8. Using the tags that represent Heading 1 through Heading 4 on a Web page produces bold text that is larger than the standard text displayed by your Web browser. Heading 5 and Heading 6, on the other hand, produce text that is smaller than standard text. In addition, regardless of which heading style you use, the Web browser always leaves a blank line following a heading, equal in height to that of the heading.

How you actually use the heading tags in your Web pages is basically up to you. You should, however, try to adhere to a few guidelines:

☐ There should be only one <H1> tag on any given page, and it should contain the same text you included in your <TITLE> tag.

☐ Don't use headings when you want to make text stand out. There are far better ways of doing this, which you will learn about soon.

☐ The headings in this book are organized in a hierarchical structure with the major topics displayed using the largest heading and subtopics displayed using smaller headings. When creating Web pages, you should adopt a similar principle for your headings. Try using <H2> for your main topic headings and <H3> for subtopics.

☐ Although text within a heading tag automatically wraps around onto a new line if it can't fit on a single line, you should try to keep headings as short as possible.

Heading Attributes

As mentioned previously, heading tags can take the optional *alignment attribute* `ALIGN` as part of their definition. When you include the `ALIGN` attribute as part of a heading tag, you tell the browser where you want the heading placed. Three values are currently supported by the `ALIGN` attribute regarding heading tags: `ALIGN="LEFT"`, `ALIGN="CENTER"`, and `ALIGN="RIGHT"`.

Figure 5.9 demonstrates how the use of the `ALIGN` attribute affects the display of the following HTML source:

```
<H2 ALIGN="LEFT">This heading is left justified</H2>
<H2 ALIGN="CENTER">This heading is centered</H2>
<H2 ALIGN="RIGHT">This heading is right justified</H2>
```

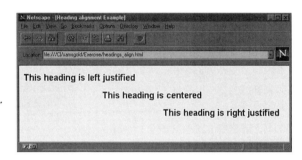

Figure 5.9.
With the `ALIGN` *attribute, you can left justify, center, or right justify headings.*

Paragraph Formatting

If you have spent any time playing with the HTML source from the preceding exercise, "Creating Your First HTML Document," you might have noticed a very important feature of HTML. When you display your HTML documents using Navigator 2.0, it takes no notice of where you put carriage returns, tabs, or white space.

Take, for example, the HTML fragment shown next. When Navigator 2.0 displays this HTML source, it looks like the Web page shown in Figure 5.10. The spaces between the words "Navigator" and "2.0" have been removed along with those between "you" and "put." In addition, all the text has been brought back onto a single line.

```
<BODY>
Navigator          2.0 ignores
any carriage returns
or white space you        put in your HTML
documents.
</BODY>
```

Figure 5.10.
Web browsers ignore any carriage returns, tabs, or white space in an HTML document.

As a result, because all Web browsers ignore any carriage returns you place in your HTML documents, when you really do want to start your text on a new line, you need to use paragraph formatting tags.

The *
* Tag

The *line break tag*
 is one of the few tags in the HTML specification that don't have a corresponding end tag. Tags like this are called single-sided tags.

Wherever you place a <BR> tag in an HTML document, the text immediately following it is moved to the start of a new line. For example, if you want to space out the text from the preceding example so that it appears on separate lines (see Figure 5.11), use the following HTML source:

```
<BODY>
Navigator          2.0 ignores<BR>
any carriage returns<BR>
or white space you       put in your HTML<BR>
documents.<BR>
</BODY>
```

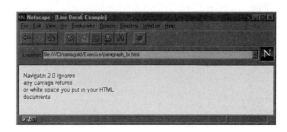

Figure 5.11.
Web browsers ignore any carriage returns, tabs, or white space in an HTML document.

It is important that you understand that the <BR> tag is what tells the Web browser when to start a new line. Because the <BR> tag has this function, you can achieve the same result using the following HTML source:

```
<BODY>
Navigator 2.0 ignores<BR>any carriage returns<BR>or white space you put in
 your HTML<BR>documents.<BR>
</BODY>
```

The <P> Tag

In the original HTML 1.0 specification, the *paragraph tag* <P> was a single-sided tag like the <BR> tag. Under this specification, you placed a <P> tag in an HTML document to indicate the end of a paragraph of text.

When the Web browser encountered a <P> tag, the text following the paragraph tag was moved to the start of a new line and separated from the preceding text by an additional blank line. Visually, using the <P> in a document had the same result as putting two <BR> tags side by side, giving the effect of separating blocks of text into paragraphs, as shown in Figure 5.12:

```
<BODY>
The only problem with demonstrating the effect<BR>
of the paragraph tag on a document<BR>
is that you need to type a few of lines of text<BR>
to see it happening.<P>
The only problem with demonstrating the effect<BR>
of the paragraph tag on a document<BR>
is that you need to type a number of lines of text<BR>
to see it happening.<P>
</BODY>
```

Figure 5.12.
The <P> tag can be used to separate blocks of text into paragraphs.

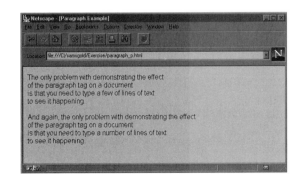

The *<P>...</P>* Tag

With the advent of HTML 3.0, the paragraph tag has become a double-sided tag, although just about all Web browsers still support the single-sided version as well.

Surrounding a block of text with a <P> and a </P> tag extends the concept of text styles down to the level of standard text. In the past, straight text within an HTML document was not bounded by any formatting tags. But now, with the inclusion of the new double-sided paragraph tag, all the text within a document can be bounded by its own style tags, as shown in the following example, which duplicates the Web page shown in Figure 5.12. This time, however, instead of single-sided paragraph tags indicating where the paragraph breaks go, double-sided paragraph tags indicate the text to be included in each paragraph:

```
<BODY>
<P>The only problem with demonstrating the effect<BR>
of the paragraph tag on a document,<BR>
is that you need to type a few of lines of text<BR>
to see it happening.</P>
<P>The only problem with demonstrating the effect<BR>
of the paragraph tag on a document,<BR>
is that you need to type a number of lines of text<BR>
to see it happening.</P>
</BODY>
```

You can use either paragraph style in your HTML documents, but it is important that you remain consistent in your usage. If you mix single- and double-sided paragraph tags on the same page, you can wind up with paragraph breaks appearing in strange places on your Web pages.

Note: Although the single-sided paragraph tag is still in use at many Web sites, for the remainder of this book, the double-sided paragraph style is used to indicate all standard text blocks.

Paragraph Attributes

The introduction of double-sided paragraph tags adds an important new feature to the presentation of straight text within a Web page. As with the heading tags, you can now include the ALIGN attribute as part of a double-sided paragraph tag. To use the ALIGN attribute with a paragraph tag, you must use the following format:

```
<P ALIGN="LEFT">Left justify the text in this paragraph</P>
<P ALIGN="CENTER">Center the text in this paragraph</P>
<P ALIGN="RIGHT">Right justify the text in this paragraph</P>
```

> **Note:** Because the `ALIGN="LEFT"` attribute represents the default text format, currently you need not include it in your documents. However, this situation might change in the future when additional paragraph attributes, such as full justification and paragraph style sheets, become a reality. For this reason, to maintain a level of consistency, some Web developers are now including the `ALIGN="LEFT"` attribute in all their paragraph tags.

Character Formatting

All the tags you have looked at so far format or control the general appearance of blocks of text within your Web page. Now it is time to look at some of the formatting tags used to format individual words and characters within a paragraph or even a heading.

Two main types of character style tags are defined in the HTML specification: *physical style tags* and *logical style tags*. Physical style tags tell the Web browser how your text should be formatted, whereas logical style tags tell your Web browser what your text is used for and lets the browser itself determine the text's physical appearance.

In the following sections, the steps involved in using all the character style tags shown in Figure 5.13 are discussed by examining the physical style tags and then the logical style tags.

Figure 5.13.
Physical and logical style tags help you control the appearance of text within your HTML documents.

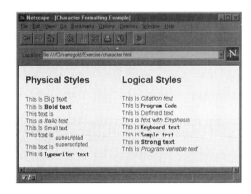

Physical Style Tags

The eight physical style tags shown in Table 5.1 can be used anywhere in an HTML document to alter the appearance of the text they surround. With these tags, you can display text using attributes such as bold, italics, subscripts, or even a monospaced typewriter font, provided of course that your hardware and Web browser can handle the different formats. (If a format or style is not available on a particular system, most Web browsers attempt to substitute a similar one.)

Table 5.1. Physical style tags.

Tag Code	Name	Description
`<BIG>`	Big text	Text uses larger font than standard text
`<B>`	Bold	Text is bold
`<BLINK>`	Blinking	Text blinks
`<I>`	Italic	Text is italic
`<SMALL>`	Small text	Text uses smaller font than standard text
`<SUB>`	Subscript	Text is subscripted
`<SUP>`	Superscript	Text is superscripted
`<TT>`	Typewriter	Text uses monospaced typewriter font

Tip: The `<BLINK>` style was added to Netscape Navigator almost as a joke and was never intended to be part of the HTML specification, but because so many people now use `<BLINK>` on their pages, it remains in Navigator 2.0. You should, however, refrain from using `<BLINK>` in your HTML documents for two reasons: It might not be included in future versions of the Netscape Navigator, and blinking text annoys the living daylights out of most people.

To format text using any of the physical style tags, surround the text you want highlighted using the appropriate tag, remembering that you must include both a start and an end tag, as shown here:

```
This text uses <B>Bold</B> to highlight a word.
```

In addition, you can create text that uses more than one physical style by simply surrounding the text with more tags. For example, to display text using bold, italic, typewriter text, follow this example:

```
This text combines the <B><I><TT>bold, italic and typewriter</TT></B></I>
➥physical style tags.
```

Tip: When using more than one style tag at the same time, be sure to turn off each style in the reverse order in which you turned them on—for example, `bold on <B> italic on <I> some text </I> italic off </B> bold off`. Doing this helps you account for each tag and not leave any style changes hanging without a corresponding off tag.

Note: Occasionally, you might encounter a <U> style tag when examining the contents of other people's Web sites. This tag was used in earlier versions of Netscape Navigator to indicate underlined text, but because most people expect underlined text to indicate hyperlinks, its use is being phased out.

Logical Style Tags

The logical style tags shown in Table 5.2 are used in the same way as physical tags. However, whereas physical style tags tell the Web browser exactly how you want your text to be displayed, logical style tags tell the Web browser what type of information is being displayed. It is then up to the Web browser to decide how to format this text for display.

Table 5.2. Logical style tags.

Tag Code	Style Name	Use
<CITE>	Citation	For quotes and references
<CODE>	Program code	For computer-program source code
<DFN>	Defined	For word definitions
<EM>	Emphasis	When italic emphasis is required
<KBD>	Keyboard	When showing text people need to type
<SAMP>	Sample	For examples
<STRONG>	Strong	When bold text is required
<VAR>	Variable	For names of program variables

Many people argue that logical character styles should be used in place of physical styles wherever possible, because they let different Web browsers format the text in a way that is best suited to the browser's capabilities. Physical styles, on the other hand, effectively demand that a Web browser support all the documented styles before they can represent text according to the wishes of you, the Web publisher.

If, however, you are developing Web pages aimed at the Navigator 2.0 world, you can be reasonably confident that all the physical styles will be displayed correctly.

Logical styles are very useful, though, when you want to keep the presentation of special elements such as program code listings consistent throughout your Web pages. By using the available logical styles, you no longer need to remember that you are displaying program listings using small, bold, monospaced typewriter text. Instead, using the built-in program code tag <CODE> makes a lot of sense. You do have to accept the text styles chosen by the <CODE> and other logical tags, but in most cases, they are ideally suited to the tasks they describe.

Comments and Notes

The final tag for this chapter is one that has no effect whatsoever on your Web page. Instead, the comment tag gives you a way to include notes and other comments as a part of your HTML documents.

All comments begin with <!-- and end with -->, and they take the following form:

```
<!-- This is a comment -->
<!-- This text will not be displayed by your web browser -->
<!-- You can also
split comments over
a number of lines -->
<!-- and any <B>tags</B> will also be ignored <P> including the paragraph -->
```

Many people use the comment tags to indicate who wrote the document source, when the document was created and last revised, and the document's name. For example, you might want to include the following information at the top of all your HTML documents:

```
<HTML>
<!-- Document Name:        test_comments.html -->
<!-- Document created by:  Wes Tatters (wtatters@world.net) -->
<!-- Creation Date:        12 November 1995 -->
<!-- Late Revision Date:   15 November 1995 -->
<HEAD>
<TITLE>
    the rest of your HTML document goes here
</HTML>
```

 Tip: Because comments can span more than one line, you can use them to hide information in an HTML document quickly by simply putting a comment around the information.

Summary

In this chapter you have learned what HTML is and why you need to use it when designing Web pages. In addition, you have learned about the structure of a basic HTML document and discovered the purpose for the tags listed in Table 5.3.

Table 5.3. New tags discussed in this chapter.

Tag	Description
`<HTML>…</HTML>`	HTML document tag
`<HEAD>…</HEAD>`	The document heading area
`<BODY>…</BODY>`	The main document content area
`<TITLE>…</TITLE>`	The document title
`<H1>…</H1>`	Heading 1—the largest heading style
`ALIGN`	The `ALIGN` attribute for all heading tags can be set to `LEFT`, `CENTER`, or `RIGHT`
`<H2>…</H2>`	Heading 2
`<H3>…</H3>`	Heading 3
`<H4>…</H4>`	Heading 4
`<H5>…</H5>`	Heading 5—smaller than normal text
`<H6>…</H6>`	Heading 6—the smallest heading style
` `	Line break tag
`<P>`	Paragraph break tag
`ALIGN`	The `ALIGN` attribute of the `<P>` tag can be set to `LEFT`, `CENTER`, or `RIGHT`
`<P>…</P>`	Paragraph text block
`<BIG>…</BIG>`	Big text
`<B>…</B>`	Bold text
`<BLINK>…</BLINK>`	Blinking text
`<I>…</I>`	Italic text
`<SMALL>…</SMALL>`	Small text
`<SUB>…</SUB>`	Subscript text
`<SUP>…</SUP>`	Superscript text
`<TT>…</TT>`	Typewriter text
`<CITE>…</CITE>`	Citation text
`<CODE>…</CODE>`	Program code text
`<DFN>…</DFN>`	Defined text
`<EM>…</EM>`	Emphasized text—italic
`<KBD>…</KBD>`	Keyboard text

5

continues

Table 5.3. continued

Tag	Description
<SAMP>...</SAMP>	Sample text
<STRONG>...</STRONG>	Strong text—bold
<VAR>...</VAR>	Variable text
<!-- ... -->	Comment tag

Workshop

The first section of the workshop lists some of the common questions people ask about the World Wide Web along with a brief answer to each. Next is a quiz about the chapter you have just read. If you have problems answering any of the questions in the quiz, you can turn to Appendix E, "Answers to Quiz Questions."

Q&A

Q Some of the Web sites I visit don't include document tags such as <HTML> and <HEAD>, yet their Web pages display perfectly on my Web browser. So why do I need to use document tags in my HTML documents?

A It all comes down to good HTML publishing style and planning for the future. If you want, you can leave out document tags in your pages as well, but there is no guarantee that they will work properly on future Web browsers.

Q All this information about document formatting and character styles is great, but what I really want to know is how to include hyperlinks in HTML documents. When will we start to learn about this?

A Good question and easy answer. In the next chapter!

Q You mentioned that the <BLINK> tag is supported only by Netscape Navigator. What happens when a different browser encounters the <BLINK> tag?

A Other browsers simply ignore the <BLINK> tag and display the text it surrounds using whatever style the rest of the text in the document is using.

Quiz

1. What tag would you use to define the smallest possible heading available on a Web page?
2. What attribute values can be used with the ALIGN attribute in a paragraph <P> tag?
3. Can you center text displayed using a heading tag such as <H1>?
4. Which logical style tag would be appropriate to format the text of a quotation?
5. Can a comment tag extend over more than one line in your HTML documents?

Exercises

1. This exercise is the first in an ongoing series, designed to help you create a set of personal HTML reference notes like the Web page shown in Figure 5.14. At the end of each chapter, you will be asked to create an HTML document that demonstrates all the new tags discussed in that chapter. Doing this helps you get a better understanding of the way each tag operates, while providing you with a handy quick-reference guide for future use.

Figure 5.14.
Exercise 1.

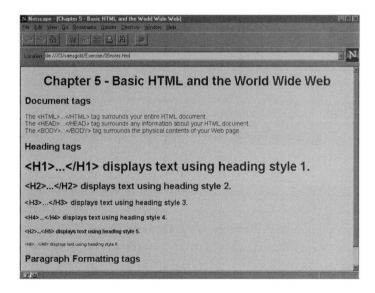

First, create a new directory or folder on your hard drive where these HTML documents will be stored. Then open your text editor and create a new file with a name like 05notes.html. It does not really matter what you call the file, but keep in mind that you will create other HTML documents in later chapters that should use a name similar to this one.

The next step—writing the HTML document—is up to you. But to help you get started, here are the first few lines of HTML code from the Web page shown in Figure 5.14:

```
<HTML>
<HEAD>
<TITLE>Chapter 5 - Basic HTML and the World Wide Web</TITLE>
</HEAD>
<BODY>
<H1 ALIGN=CENTER>Chapter 5 - Basic HTML and the World Wide Web</H1>
<H2>Document tags</H2>
<P>
The &ltHTML&gt...&lt/HTML&gt tag surrounds your entire HTML document.<BR>
```

You need to pay attention to two special codes in the last line of this text. Because the < and > symbols are used to indicate the start and end of an HTML tag, you cannot enter them individually into an HTML document. For this reason, if you do want to display a < on your Web page, you must type the code &lt. Likewise, if you want to display a > symbol on a Web page, you must type the code &gt into your HTML document.

2. In preparation for the next chapter, list your 20 favorite Web pages. In this list, you should include the name of each page, a short description of the Web page's contents, and the URL that describes its location.

6

TWO

Linking Web Pages Together

In Chapter 5, "Basic HTML and the World Wide Web," you learned how to create a simple HTML document with different text styles and some paragraph formatting, but you can do that sort of thing on any old word processor. Where the World Wide Web comes into its own, however, is through its capability to link your HTML documents together using hyperlinks.

In this chapter you will learn how to include hyperlinks in your HTML documents by examining the following subjects:

- ☐ <A>: the link tag
- ☐ Linking local Web pages
- ☐ Creating links to other documents on the World Wide Web
- ☐ Making links work for you, not against you

<A>: The Link Tag

No doubt you're keen to get started linking your HTML documents together, so let's get straight into it!

To create a hyperlink, you use the <A> tag. This tag enables you to do two things. First, you use it to define the text that will be highlighted or underlined by your Web browser to indicate the *hotspot text* for the hyperlink. And second, you use it to describe the location of the file pointed to by the hyperlink.

When people first see the link tag <A>, they often wonder why the letter *A* was used rather than the seemingly more logical letter *L*. The reason for the use of an *A* is that the link tag is sometimes referred to by an alternative name. If you ever read any early papers and documents dealing with hyperlinks, you will often find the link tag referred to as a *Reference Anchor*—hence the use of the <A> in the link tag. These days, however, the term *anchor* is normally used only when discussing a special use of the <A> tag called a *Named Anchor*. (Chapter 9, "Working with Links and URLs," discusses the use of anchors.)

Note: The <A> tag is also used for hyperlinks represented by images rather than text. Chapter 10, "Adding Images to Your Web Documents," explains how the <A> tag is used when images are involved.

The Hotspot

Until now, this book has referred to a hyperlink as a single component, but now, to help clarify which part of the hyperlink is being referred to, a couple new terms are needed.

The first of these terms is *hotspot text*. The hotspot text is the visible part of the hyperlink, the text Navigator 2.0 and most other Web browsers display—by default—as underlined blue text. In other words, it is the text that users will click to select the hyperlink.

You define the hotspot text for a hyperlink in much the same way that character styles were applied in Chapter 5. To do so, you place an <A> tag at the start of the hotspot text and a matching </A> at its end, as shown here:

```
This is <A>the hotspot text</A> for a hyperlink.
```

The *HREF* Attribute

On its own, the preceding example does very little. In fact, if you had tried to test it using your Web browser, you would have found that no hyperlink was displayed.

Before your Web browser can represent the hotspot text as a hyperlink, it needs to be told the location of the file that the link points to. You do this by including a special attribute in the <A> tag called the HREF attribute. When included as part of a hyperlink, the HREF attribute takes the following form:

```
This is <A HREF="file/location.html">the hotspot text</A> for a
hyperlink.
```

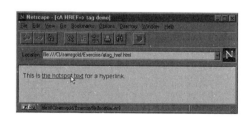

Figure 6.1.
The HREF attribute indicates the location of the file pointed to by a hyperlink.

As you can see in Figure 6.1, after adding the HREF attribute, the Web browser can properly format the text surrounded by the <A> tag as a hyperlink. The only problem now is knowing what to include inside the quotation marks on the right side on the HREF attribute.

Basically, any valid URL can be referenced by the HREF attribute, but for the time being, this chapter restricts itself to linking HTML documents together. (Chapter 9 looks at the other types of files and services that can be pointed to by a hyperlink.)

Note: Other attributes can be associated with the <A> tag, including TARGET and NAME. These attributes are discussed in later chapters.

Linking Local Web Pages

For a hyperlink to be of any use, there must be some sort of file or service associated with it. In the preceding section, you learned that the HREF attribute is used to tell the hyperlink what it is pointing at. And now, in the following sections, you will learn about some of the ways this information can be described.

Absolute Addressing

To define the location of a file in a hyperlink, you need to tell the Web browser three pieces of information: the service type, its location, and its name.

You do this using a URL that takes the following form:

```
protocol://domain.name/directory_name/filename.html
```

The first part of a URL is called the *protocol section*. This section tells the Web browser what type of information (service type) the hyperlink points to. Because this section is discussing Web pages stored on your local hard drive, you need to use the file: protocol. This protocol tells the Web browser that the file will be loaded from your local hard drive. (Later in this chapter, you will learn about the http: protocol, which loads files from Web servers.)

Immediately after the protocol definition, most URLs require the inclusion of two backslashes (//) as a separator. However, as you will learn later, there are a couple exceptions to this rule.

The next section of the URL—/directory_name/—describes the location of the file you want the hyperlink to load. This includes the location of the hard drive where the file is stored and the list of directories and subdirectories you must follow to locate the file, starting at the root or top directory of your computer system and working your way down.

Note: MS-DOS users might have noticed that forward slashes (/) were used in the URL shown previously, rather than the backslashes (\) they are no doubt familiar with. This is due to the fact that all Web browsers use the UNIX method of describing file paths. On UNIX systems, forward slashes are used to separate directories.

Depending on the type of computer system you are using, the exact contents of the file location section will take different forms. Table 6.1 lists the different formats used by MS-DOS, Windows 95, Macintosh, and UNIX computer systems.

Table 6.1. Absolute pathname formats by computer system.

Platform	Pathname	Comments
MS-DOS	`file:///C¦/path/file.htm`	The hard drive on an MS-DOS system is represented using its drive letter followed by a vertical bar (¦). Also, because MS-DOS systems limit file extensions to three letters, `.html` is shortened to `.htm`.
Windows 95	`file:///C¦/path/file.html`	Windows 95 permits the use of long extensions.
Macintosh	`file:///Drive/path/file.html`	On Macintosh systems, the name of the hard drive is included before the file path.
UNIX	`file:///path/file.html`	On UNIX systems, you simply list the directory path to the file you are interested in.

The last part of the URL is simply the name of the file you want to load.

When these three pieces of information are combined together as a URL describing the destination of a hyperlink, the result is called an absolute address, because this URL describes *absolutely* the location of the file you are looking for.

6

Relative Addressing

As you might well imagine, entering an entire absolute URL address for every hyperlink you want to include in an HTML document does become very time-consuming. So to reduce the amount of information you must type, a special form of URL called a *relative address* was developed. Using relative addressing, you include only enough information about the new file to describe its location *relative* to the currently displayed Web page—hence the name relative addressing.

In its simplest form, the HREF attribute defines the name of the file that a hyperlink points to. For example, typing HREF="myfile.html" inside an <A> tag tells your Web browser to open a file called myfile.html.

Your Web browser knows how to locate this file by using relative addressing. In the preceding example, myfile.html must be located in the same directory or folder as the HTML document that called it. When you click on the hyperlink to myfile.html, your Web browser uses the location of the current HTML document as the base location for myfile.html.

For example, assume that <A HREF="myfile.html"> is part of a hyperlink in an HTML document called first_file.html, and this file is located on your computer's drive C: in a directory called htmlfiles. Using an absolute path, the URL of this file would be described as file:///C¦/htmlfiles/first_file.html. When you click the myfile.html hyperlink, your Web browser uses this URL as the base location for the relative address of myfile.html. Basically, it takes the location information from the current file and fills in the missing pieces of the relative address, thus creating an absolute address for the new file: file:///C¦/htmlfiles/myfile.html.

You can also include additional path information in a relative address to describe the location of files that are not stored in the same directory as the current HTML document. Table 6.2 lists some of the possible variations you can use with relative addressing.

Table 6.2. Relative pathname formats.

Path and Filename	Comments
file.html	This file is located in the /chapter6 directory.
extra/file.html	This file is located in a subdirectory of /chapter6 called /extra.
../file.html	The ../ symbol is used to refer to the directory above the current one. Therefore in this example, file.html would be located in the /htmlfiles directory.
../www/file.html	This file is located in a subdirectory of the /htmlfiles directory called /www.

Path and Filename	Comments
`../../file.html`	This file is located in the root directory of drive C:.
`../../Other/file.html`	This file is located in a subdirectory of the root directory called `/Other`.

All the examples listed in this table use a hard drive with the directory structure shown in Figure 6.2, and they are hyperlinks in an HTML document that has the following absolute address:

```
file:///C¦/htmlfiles/chapter6/relative.html
```

Figure 6.2.
The directory structure for Table 6.2.

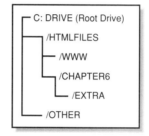

Absolute or Relative— Which Should I Use?

To answer this question, you really need to look at what you are using hyperlinks for.

When linking your own Web pages together, using relative addressing makes your HTML documents more portable. You can easily move all your HTML documents to a new set of directories or even to a different hard drive and be reasonably confident that all your links will remain intact. If you did the same thing to a set of pages with absolute references, you would need to re-edit each HTML document and update all the URLs before any of the hyperlinks would work.

Relative links become even more useful when you start moving your Web pages onto a Web server for publication. As you will discover in the next section, when you create a link that references a document stored on a Web server, you normally use the `http:` protocol rather than the `file:` protocol discussed previously. If you were using absolute references for all your HTML documents, you would need to re-edit each one before loading it onto the Web server and change any local `file:` protocol references to online `http:` references. If you use relative references (ones without `file:` at the start) for all your local links, the Web browser automatically looks after the process of deciding which protocol to use.

On the other hand, when you are creating links to other people's Web pages, you have little choice but to use absolute addressing, unless of course they happen to be stored on the same Web server as your own pages. In addition, should those files be moved from the Web server that you share, the relative addresses will no longer work.

Exercise: Building a Table of Contents

It's time for you to do some work again. As you begin to create more HTML documents for your HTML reference notes, as discussed in Exercise 1 in Chapter 5, you will no doubt get to a stage where you are tired of having to use the Web browser's pull-down File menu each time you want to load any of the documents in your HTML reference library.

So why not create a Table of Contents page that links all these pages—05notes.html, 06notes.html, and those from future chapters—together using hyperlinks? After all, that is what the World Wide Web was designed for.

To create the Table of Contents page, open your text editor in the same directory where you saved the 05notes.html document created in Exercise 1 in Chapter 5. This makes it easy to use relative addressing when linking the 05note.html document to your table of contents.

In a new file called html_contents.html, type the following text:

```
<HTML>
<HEAD>
<TITLE>HTML Reference - Table of Contents</TITLE>
</HEAD>
<BODY>
<H1 ALIGN="CENTER">HTML Reference - Table of Contents</H1>
<A HREF="05notes.html"><H2>Chapter 5</H2></A>
<P>This chapter discusses document tags, headings, character styles
and the comment tag. </P>
<A HREF="06notes.html"><H2>Chapter 6</H2></A>
<P>This chapter discusses the link tag &lt;A&gt;.</P>
</BODY>
</HTML>
```

Figure 6.3.
The HTML Reference - Table of Contents page.

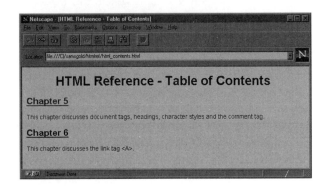

After you have entered the text, save the file and then test it using your Web browser. If you entered everything correctly, you should see a Web page similar to the one shown in Figure 6.3.

When you click the `Chapter 5` hyperlink, your Web browser automatically calls up and displays the contents of `05notes.html`. But if you click the `Chapter 6` hyperlink, your should receive an error informing you that the file could not be found—unless of course you have already created `06notes.html`.

This exercise also demonstrates an important feature of the link tag. Both of the links used on this exercise have an `<H2>` tag buried inside the `<A>` and `</A>`. This way, the hotspot text is both underlined and displayed using heading style 2. And besides the heading styles, you can include character formatting as part of the hotspot for a hyperlink.

Note: As an added exercise, re-edit the `05notes.html` document, and add a hyperlink that sends you back to the contents page using `<A HREF="html_contents.html">Contents</A>`.

Creating Links to Other Documents on the World Wide Web

Although linking all of your own HTML pages together is very useful, the main reason most people add hyperlinks to their documents is not to link their own pages together, but instead to add hyperlinks to Web pages published by other people.

Note: Throughout this book, hyperlinks that point to HTML documents on your own personal computer system are referred to as local links and those that point to documents stored on a Web server as remote links.

The only difference between a local link and a remote link is the URL associated with the `HREF` attribute. To create a hyperlink that points to a Web page located anywhere on the World Wide Web—including your personal Web server—you use a URL that takes the following form:

```
protocol://domain.name:port/directory_path/filename.html
```

The Communications Protocol

The most common protocol used when referring to HTML documents is http, which is the protocol used by Web browsers when communicating with a Web server. Because most Web pages are housed on a Web server, this is the protocol you will use the most. Occasionally, however, you might encounter HTML documents stored on FTP or Gopher servers, in which case you will need to use the ftp: and gopher: protocols, respectively.

The Domain Name

Immediately after the protocol: section and the // separator comes the address of the computer system that operates the server that maintains the Web page you want to link to. The most common method of addressing a computer on the Internet is by using its domain name. Alternatively, you can use a computer's IP address, but doing so can lead to problems if the IP address associated with a domain name changes. By using a domain name, if a site's IP address does change, your hyperlinks will still be able to find the correct computer system.

Note: An IP address consists of four numbers separated by dots. These numbers represent the unique electronic address of every computer system on the Internet. For example, the IP address of my Internet service provider is 192.190.215.9. The problem with numbers, however, is that they are often difficult to remember. For this reason, a second addressing system called a *domain name address* was developed. Basically each IP address has a corresponding domain name address associated with it. The domain name of my Internet service provider is world.net.

Most of the computer systems you want to connect to use a standard socket on their computer system called *port 80* for all http:-based communications. Occasionally, however, you will encounter a Web site that uses a different port. If you want to access an HTML document stored on such a site, you need to append its port number to the end of its domain name. For example, when addressing a normal Web site, you would use a URL like this:

```
http://www.world.net/
```

This indicates that the Web site you want to connect to is called www.world.net and uses the standard communications port. If, however, this site used port 8000 rather than 80, you would need to address it as shown here:

```
http://www.world.net:8000/
```

The Directory Path

The next section of the URL—the directory path—describes the physical location of the file you want the hyperlink to point to. This includes the list of directories and subdirectories you must follow to locate the file, starting at the root or top directory of the Web site indicated by the URL's domain name and working down to the subdirectory where the file is stored.

Note: If the file you want to load is stored in the top directory of a Web site, you need to include only the / that represents the root directory. For a file stored in the root directory of `www.world.net`, you would write `http://www.world.net/`.

The Document Name

The last part of the URL is simply the name of the document you want to load. On most systems, the file ends with an `.html` extension, but on MS-DOS systems, it ends with `.htm`.

When all the pieces of the URL are combined together, they define the absolute location of the HTML document you want to load. You can also use relative addressing when referring to HTML documents stored on a Web server, but as a rule, you would do this only for files stored on your own server.

You should also be aware of a special version of the document name—or its lack thereof. To access the home page of many Web sites, you do not include a document name in the URL at all. For example, to access the home page at Netscape Communications, you use `http://www.netscape.com/`. When the site's Web server receives a request for this page, it automatically works out which HTML document should be sent back to the Web browser. There is a physical home page HTML document stored at the Web site, but you need not enter it in your URL.

Note: For more information about default home pages, refer to Chapter 13, "Installing Your Web Pages on a Web Server."

6

Exercise: Building a Favorite Web Sites Page

The best way to learn about using hyperlinks that point to documents on the World Wide Web is by example.

In Exercise 2 at the end of Chapter 5, you were asked to list your favorite Web pages. To complete this exercise, you need to dig out that list, because it will form the basis of one of the most common types of Web page you will find anywhere on the World Wide Web.

Just about every Web site you visit contains a list of hyperlinks that point to the Web page developer's favorite Web pages. And after you finish this exercise, you too will have a list of favorite sites like the one shown next. How you lay out your HTML document is up to you—Figure 6.4 shows one possible layout, but there are many others. But to help you get started, here is the HTML source that created Figure 6.4:

```
<HTML>
<HEAD>
<TITLE>Wes Tatters' favorite Web sites</TITLE>
</HEAD>
<BODY>
<H1 ALIGN="CENTER">Wes Tatters' favorite Web sites</H1>
<H3>Web Development Sites</H3>
<A HREF="http://www.netscape.com/">Netscape Communications</A>
➥<BR>
<A HREF="http://java.sun.com/">HotJava Home Page</A> <BR>
<A HREF="http://www.macromedia.com/">Macromedia! Home Page</A>
➥<BR>
<A HREF="http://www.pointcom.com/">Point Communications Corporation
➥</A> <BR>
<A HREF="http://www.webcom.com/">Webcom Home Page</A> <BR>
<H3>Leading edge technology</H3>
<A HREF="http://www.paperinc.com/">P a p e r S o f t w a r e</A>
➥<BR>
<A HREF="http://www.vdolive.com/partner.htm">VDOLive Beta Program</A>
<A HREF="http://www.dspg.com/cool.htm">DSP Group, Inc.</A> <BR>
<A HREF="http://www.itelco.com/">Internet Telephone Company -
➥WebPhone(tm)</A>
<BR>
<A HREF="http://www.worlds.net/">Worlds Inc.</A> <BR>
<H3>Fun Sites</H3>
<A HREF="http://www.webcom.com/taketwo/">Take TWO Home Page</A>
➥<BR>
<A HREF="http://tvnet.com/TVnet.html">TV Net®</A> <BR>
<A HREF="http://www.rutgers.edu/x-files.html">The X-Files</A> <BR>
<A HREF="http://www.mcp.com/">Macmillan USA Information SuperLibrary
➥(tm)</A>
<BR>
<A HREF="http://tvp.com/>The Virtual Press</A> <BR>
<A HREF="http://espnet.sportszone.com/">ESPNET SportsZone</A> <BR>
<A HREF="http://www.cyberpet.com/cgibin/var/cyberpet/
➥index1.htm">Cyber-Pet</A>
<BR>
<P>
Don't forget to visit my
<A HREF="../htmlref/html_contents.html">HTML reference library</A>
➥while you're here.
```

```
</P>
</BODY>
</HTML>
```

Output

Figure 6.4.
Wes Tatters'
favorite Web sites.

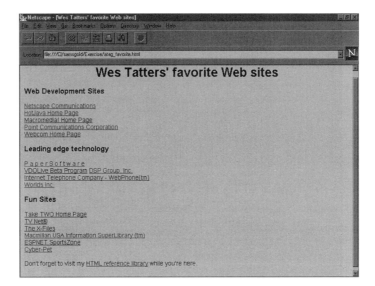

Try to include as many of the HTML elements you have already learned about as possible in this new page. You should use at least two different heading styles, the `<BR>` and `<P>` tags, and of course the `<A>` tag. In addition, include a link to the `html_contents.html` file created in the preceding exercise by using relative addressing.

Making Links Work for You, Not Against You

Although hyperlinks are a very powerful tool, they are relatively simple to use. Unfortunately, as a result, they are often badly used. To help you avoid some potential pitfalls and hiccups so often associated with hyperlinks, the last section of this chapter looks at some of the ways you can enhance your Web pages when using links without detracting from the page's overall objective.

Inline Links

The most common form of hyperlink found on Web pages is the inline link. An inline link is any hyperlink that appears as part of the text of a Web page, as opposed to being listed separately, on a line of its own.

Basically, no limitations are placed on the contents or makeup of the inline links you place in your HTML documents. Inline links can contain as many words as you want, they can also be images (as you will discover in a later chapter), and they can be displayed using any of the character-formatting styles currently available.

You should, however, keep a couple guidelines in mind when adding inline links to your HTML documents:

- ☐ Keep your hotspot text short and self-explanatory
- ☐ Limit the use of character formatting
- ☐ Avoid the "here" syndrome
- ☐ Use transparent links where possible

Keep Your Hotspot Text Short

The concept behind all inline hyperlinks is accessibility without intrusion. When you add a hyperlink to a Web page, it should blend into the page and not overwhelm it. By keeping the length of your hotspot text to a minimum, you greatly reduce the possibility of your hyperlinks taking over the Web page.

You should always attempt to select only enough words for your hyperlink that people understand what the link is pointing to. For example, in Figure 6.5, using just the words Netscape Communications as a hyperlink is just as effective as highlighting all the words shown highlighted in the second paragraph. And at the same time, it clutters the page less, giving a cleaner visual appearance.

Figure 6.5.
Keep the length of your hotspot text to a minimum.

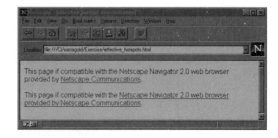

Limit Character Formatting

Although you can alter the formatting of a hyperlink using character formatting, as a rule you should avoid doing so, because the Web browser will have already highlighted the link using a different color and most probably an underline. All you achieve by adding additional formatting is making the hyperlink stand out even more when you really want it to blend in with the surrounding text. After all, this is the purpose of inline links. As a result, if you think that a link is important enough to highlight using other attributes, maybe you should consider placing it on a line of its own rather than inline.

Avoid the "Here" Syndrome

By far, the most common trap people fall into when creating inline hyperlinks is something called the "here" syndrome. If you find yourself creating hotspot text that includes the word "here," chances are that you too have become a victim.

The first paragraph of Figure 6.6 demonstrates some text that is suffering from both the "here" syndrome and its friend, "this link," which sometimes gets abbreviated to just "this." The second paragraph shows the same information rewritten so that it no longer uses either "here" or "this link." The result is a paragraph of text that is easier to read and that uses links that, themselves, describe what they are pointing to.

Figure 6.6.
Avoid the "here" syndrome in your Web pages.

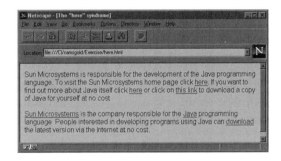

Use Transparent Links Where Possible

In keeping with the concept of accessibility without intrusion, you should always attempt to make your hotspot text grammatically transparent.

The first paragraph of Figure 6.7 practically shouts that it is a hyperlink. Writing "this is the link" serves no logical purpose in the sentence; people can already see where the link is because it is underlined and displayed in blue text. The second paragraph provides the user with the same basic information, but this time the hotspot text is an integral part of the sentence, not something that has been tacked onto the end almost as an afterthought.

Figure 6.7.
Links should be grammatically transparent.

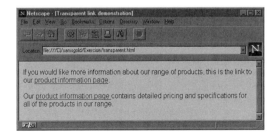

Lists of Links

Apart from inline links, the other common method of presenting hyperlinks on a page is as part of a list or a *link menu* like the one demonstrated in the earlier exercise "Building a Table of Contents." Link menus are ideal for any type of list, catalog, or index that demands the presentation of a collection of hyperlinks in a format that is easily accessible.

There is very little you can do wrong when creating link menus if you keep these three concepts in mind:

- ☐ Make link-menu text descriptive
- ☐ Use character formatting where appropriate
- ☐ Mix paragraphs of descriptive text with link menus

Make Link-Menu Text Descriptive

When creating link menus, you are not writing entire sentences for each link. Instead, you want to describe the link using just a few words. You need to ensure, however, that the user has been given enough information to work out what the hyperlink points at, without having to select it. And if adding a few words of descriptive text to a menu item enhances its meaning—as is the case in Figure 6.8, on the line that says The FAQ for the English Premier League—then do so!

Figure 6.8.

Use character formatting and bullets where appropriate when creating link menus.

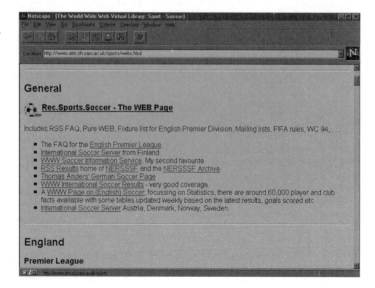

Use Character Formatting Where Appropriate

Unlike inline text, for which additional formatting is normally not recommended, when dealing with link menus, people often use heading styles and bold to highlight separate categories in a list or as a quick and simple method of creating hierarchical menus. In addition, there is a special formatting attribute, which you will learn about tomorrow, that allows you to add bullets to the front of menu lists as shown in Figure 6.8.

Mix Paragraphs of Descriptive Text with Link Menus

Figure 6.9 demonstrates a hybrid link menu that incorporates a separate paragraph of descriptive text for each link. Basically, there is no limit to what you can do with link menus; however, you should always try to maintain a consistent approach. Try not to mix different styles of menu on a single Web page, because doing so gives your pages a jumbled, disorganized appearance.

Figure 6.9.

Mixing paragraphs of descriptive text with link menus.

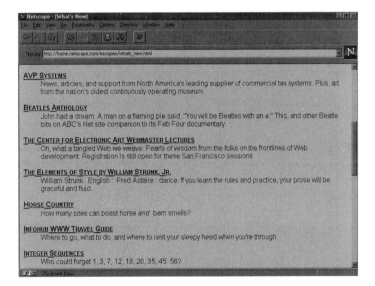

Summary

As you come to the end of another day's study, you should now be able to create an HTML document, format its contents using headings and character styles, and insert hyperlinks that point to other documents on your local hard drive and on Web servers all over the World Wide Web.

With all this knowledge under your belt, you are ready to advance to the next level of HTML development. On Day 3, "Building on the Basics," you will learn about advanced formatting techniques, as well as how to use tables and how to create hyperlinks that point to other Internet services, such as anonymous FTP sites.

Workshop

The first section of the Workshop lists some of the common questions people ask about the World Wide Web along with a brief answer to each. Next is a quiz about the chapter you have just read. If you have problems answering any of the questions in the quiz, you can turn to Appendix E, "Answers to Quiz Questions."

Q&A

Q Why can't I use the `http:` protocol to load files from my local hard drive? Isn't `http:` the protocol for the World Wide Web?

A `http:` is the protocol used by a Web browser when communicating with a Web server. In this sense, yes, it is the protocol for the World Wide Web. But when you are loading files from your local hard drive, your Web browser is not actually communicating with the World Wide Web. Instead, it is communicating with your hard drive. In this case, you must use the `file:` protocol.

Q To me, blue text is boring. Why can't I make my hyperlinks red so that they really stand out?

A You actually can change the color of your hyperlink text, as you will learn tomorrow in Chapter 7, "Advanced Formatting Options." However, using some colors, such as red, in Web pages can cause problems for people using monochrome displays. It is very hard to detect the difference between red and black on such screens, so for these people your hyperlinks would not stand out at all.

Q I've visited some Web sites where none of the absolute URLs seems to include a protocol section. How does this work?

A Most Web browsers automatically default in the protocol used by the currently displayed Web page when they encounter a missing protocol. This is effectively a type of relative addressing solely for the protocol information. About the only benefit to be gained from leaving out the protocol section is the time saved in the creation of the HTML document (five keystrokes per URL). On the negative side, leaving out the protocol section can occasionally cause strange and unpredictable side effects, so you are better off including it.

Q **In the last section, I noticed that you referred to a link that people could select to download a file, yet I don't recall being told how this is done. Did I skip a page somewhere?**

A No, you didn't! This subject is covered tomorrow in Chapter 9.

Quiz

1. What attribute is used by the <A> tag to describe the location of the file pointed to by a hyperlink?

2. For what reasons would you choose absolute addressing over relative addressing?

3. What is the ../ symbol used for in a relative address?

4. Why would you need to include a port number in a URL?

5. Can you display the hotspot text of a hyperlink in bold or italics?

Exercises

1. Your first task is to create the 06notes.html document for your HTML reference collection. Be sure to include a description, and demonstration, of the differences between an absolute and a relative link, and also include an example of a link to a remote document and a link to the favorite-Web-sites document you created earlier in the exercise "Building a Favorite Web Sites Page."

   Also, if you have not already done so, skip back to the 05notes.html document and add a hyperlink that points to the html_contents.html document you created earlier in this chapter. And don't forget to include a link to this document in 06note.html.

2. The second exercise involves creating a new version of the favorite-Web-sites document you created earlier in the exercise "Building a Favorite Web Sites Page." This time, instead of using a link menu to display your list of favorite sites, use inline links.

   To do this, write a short paragraph that describes each of your favorite sites using an inline link to show the location of the site. Remember to avoid using words such as "here" and "this" as your hotspot text.

DAY 3

Building on the Basics

7

Advanced
Formatting
Options

Over the course of the past two days, you have covered a lot of ground learning about how the World Wide Web operates, discovering what HTML is, and writing your first HTML documents. And now, as you begin Day 3, "Building on the Basics," it is time to build on this basic knowledge and delve further into the mysteries of Web publishing.

Today you will learn how to add tables to your Web pages and examine the different types of files and services you can call using hyperlinks. But first, in this chapter you will learn about some of the more advanced formatting options by exploring the following topics:

☐ Adding lists to your documents

☐ Advanced paragraph formatting

☐ Advanced text formatting

☐ Displaying special characters

Adding Lists to Your Documents

In the preceding chapter, you created a table of contents and a list of your favorite Web sites. Although these two lists were functional and performed the tasks required of them, from a visual perspective they were somewhat lacking.

To help improve the appearance of menus and many other types of lists, the HTML specification includes a set of tags that enable you to include bullets and numbers in front of lists of information. Figure 7.1 demonstrates the use of both *unordered lists* and *ordered lists* in the Table of Contents for the HTML 3.0 specification. If you want to examine this page for yourself, point your Web browser to `http://www.w3.org/pub/WWW/MarkUp/html3/Contents.html`.

Figure 7.1.

The HTML 3.0 specification Table of Contents demonstrates the use of both ordered and unordered lists.

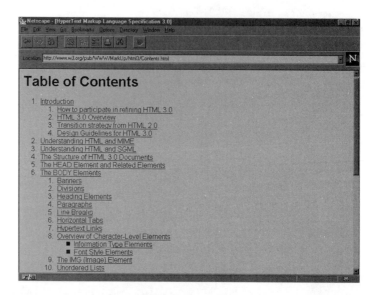

In addition to unordered and ordered lists, the HTML specification includes a third type of list, called a *definition list* or *glossary list*, shown in Figure 7.2. Glossary lists are ideal for lists that itemize the meanings of words, but they can be used for many other purposes, as well.

Figure 7.2.
Glossary lists are often used when describing the meanings or definitions of words.

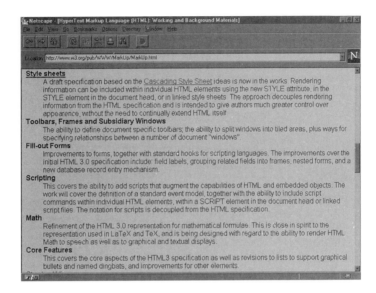

Unordered Lists

As their name indicates, unordered lists are used when the items in the list are not organized in any particular order. To indicate that there is no particular order, a *bullet* is placed in front of each element.

The *<UL>* Tag

You create an unordered list by using the <UL>...</UL> tag. This tag tells your Web browser that everything between the start tag and the end tag is to be included as part of an unordered list.

In addition, you can include a TYPE attribute as part of the <UL> tag to indicate which of the three possible bullet types should be used. Currently, Navigator 2.0 supports the use of TYPE="DISC", TYPE="CIRCLE", and TYPE="SQUARE".

The *<LI>* Tag

Within the <UL> tags, you place an <LI> tag where you want each item of the list to start. The <LI> tag indicates to the Web browser where the bullets should be placed, as shown in Figure 7.3:

```
<UL>
<LI><A HREF="http://www.netscape.com/">Netscape Communications</A>
<LI><A HREF="http://java.sun.com/">HotJava Home Page</A>
<LI><A HREF="http://www.verisign.com/">VeriSign Home Page</A>
<LI><A HREF="http://www.pointcom.com/">Point Communications Corporation</
A>
<LI><A HREF="http://www.macromedia.com/">Macromedia! Home Page</A>
<LI><A HREF="http://www.webcom.com/taketwo/">Take TWO Home Page</A>
<LI><A HREF="http://www.webcom.com/">Webcom Home Page</A>
</UL>
```

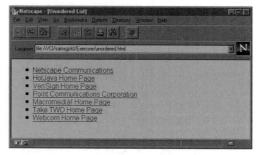

Figure 7.3.
An unordered list with bullets.

> **Note:** You do not need to include <BR> tags to separate the individual lines of your list, because the <LI> tag automatically causes each bullet to be placed on a new line.

As with the <UL> tag, you can also include a TYPE attribute as part of the <LI> tag to indicate which of the three possible bullet types should be used. This enables you to change the appearance of bullets item-by-item. Whenever you use the TYPE attribute, in either the <UL> or the <LI> tag, all the bullets following it will be affected as well. Figure 7.4 demonstrates the appearance of the three bullet types by using the following code:

```
<UL>
<LI TYPE="DISC">This is a TYPE="DISC" bullet
<LI TYPE="CIRCLE">This is a TYPE="CIRCLE" bullet
<LI TYPE="SQUARE">This is a TYPE="SQUARE" bullet
</UL>
```

Figure 7.4.
Navigator 2.0 currently supports three types of bullets: DISC, CIRCLE, and SQUARE.

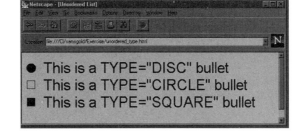

Note: The appearance of each bullet type tends to vary depending on the computer platform and the font used by the Web browser. Using DISC, CIRCLE, and SQUARE will result in the display of three different bullets, but they might not always look exactly like a disc, circle, and square.

Ordered Lists

Ordered lists differ from unordered lists in one main way. Instead of a bullet being placed in front of each item, each item has a number, letter, or roman numeral in front of it. The most basic of all ordered lists is a numbered list, in which the first item in the list is preceded by a 1; the second item, a 2; the third, a 3; and so on.

The *<OL>* Tag

You create an ordered list by using the <OL>...</OL> tag. This tag tells your Web browser that everything between the start tag and the end tag is to be included as part of the ordered list.

In addition, you can also include a TYPE attribute as part of the <OL> tag to indicate which of the five ordered types should be used. Currently, Navigator 2.0 supports the use of TYPE="A", TYPE="a", TYPE="I", TYPE="i", and TYPE="1".

The *<LI>* Tag

The <OL> tag uses the <LI> tag in much the same way as the <UL> tag does. With the <OL> tag, you place an <LI> tag where you want each new item of the list to start. Figure 7.5 demonstrates how similar the coding of an ordered and unordered list are by displaying the list shown in Figure 7.5 as an ordered list. The only change required was the alteration of the <UL> and </UL> tags to their corresponding <OL> and </OL> tags:

```
<OL>
<LI><A HREF="http://www.netscape.com/">Netscape Communications</A>
<LI><A HREF="http://java.sun.com/">HotJava Home Page</A>
<LI><A HREF="http://www.verisign.com/">VeriSign Home Page</A>
<LI><A HREF="http://www.pointcom.com/">Point Communications Corporation</A>
<LI><A HREF="http://www.macromedia.com/">Macromedia! Home Page</A>
<LI><A HREF="http://www.webcom.com/taketwo/">Take TWO Home Page</A>
<LI><A HREF="http://www.webcom.com/">Webcom Home Page</A>
</OL>
```

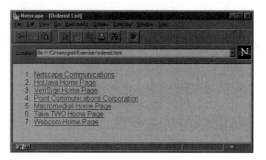

Figure 7.5.
An ordered list with numbers.

You can also include a TYPE attribute as part of the <LI> tag to indicate which of the five ordered list types should be used for each item. This enables you to change the appearance of the ordered list item by item. As was the case for the unordered lists, whenever you use the TYPE attribute with either the <OL> tag or the <LI> tag, all the items following it will be affected as well. Figure 7.6 demonstrates how each of the five ordered lists looks when used in the following code:

```
<OL TYPE="1">
<LI>Item 1 using TYPE=1
<LI>Item 2 using TYPE=1
<LI>Item 3 using TYPE=1
</OL>
<OL TYPE="A">
<LI>Item 1 using TYPE=A
<LI>Item 2 using TYPE=A
<LI>Item 3 using TYPE=A
</OL>
<OL TYPE="a">
<LI>Item 1 using TYPE=a
<LI>Item 2 using TYPE=a
<LI>Item 3 using TYPE=a
</OL>
```

```
<OL TYPE="I">
<LI>Item 1 using TYPE=I
<LI>Item 2 using TYPE=I
<LI>Item 3 using TYPE=I
</OL>
<OL TYPE="i">
<LI>Item 1 using TYPE=i
<LI>Item 2 using TYPE=i
<LI>Item 3 using TYPE=i
</OL>
```

Figure 7.6.
*Navigator 2.0 supports
five types of ordered list.*

The *START* and *VALUE* Attributes

The <OL> tag supports an additional attribute—START—that enables you to alter the starting
value of a list. For example, to start an ordered list at 5 rather than the default of 1, you type
<OL START="5">.

To complement the START attribute, when the <LI> tag is used in an ordered list, you can alter
the value of any given item using the VALUE attribute. The following HTML source demonstrates the use of both the VALUE and the START attributes in the creation of the Web page
shown in Figure 7.7:

```
<OL TYPE="1" START="10">
<LI>Item 1 using TYPE=1 starting at 10
<LI>Item 2 using TYPE=1
<LI>Item 3 using TYPE=1
</OL>
<OL TYPE="1">
```

```
<LI>Item 1 using TYPE=1 starting at item 1
<LI VALUE="5">Item 2 using TYPE=1 then changing to item 5
<LI>Item 3 using TYPE=1
</OL>
<OL TYPE="A" START="10">
<LI>Item 1 using TYPE=A starting at item 10 which is 'J'
<LI>Item 2 using TYPE=A
<LI>Item 3 using TYPE=A
</OL>
<OL TYPE="A">
<LI>Item 1 using TYPE=A starting at item 1
<LI VALUE="5">Item 2 using TYPE=A then changing to item 5 which is 'E'
<LI>Item 3 using TYPE=A
</OL>
```

Figure 7.7.
*An ordered list with
numbering changed by
the START and VALUE
attributes.*

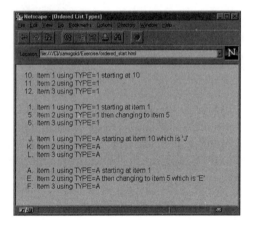

Nesting Lists

As you might have already gathered from Figure 7.1, shown at the beginning of this chapter, or from Figure 7.8, you can nest ordered and unordered lists in various ways.

Figure 7.8 shows three possible nesting combinations, but there are many others. In the first example, unordered lists have been nested to demonstrate how Navigator 2.0 automatically selects a different bullet type for each new level, up to a maximum of three levels. After you nest past the third level, the bullet type remains the same.

To nest lists, begin each subsequent level after the list items of the level above it. The end tags for each level follow all the list items. This is important since you need to make sure that each start tag has a corresponding end tag as shown in the HTML source for the first example:

```
<UL>
<LI>This is level one.
<UL>
<LI>This is level two.
<UL>
```

```
<LI>This is level three.
</UL>
</UL>
</UL>
```

Figure 7.8.
*Ordered and unordered
lists can be combined and
nested.*

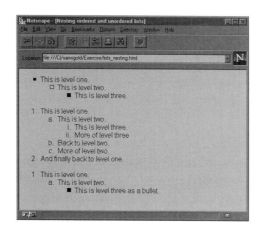

In the second example three ordered lists have been nested. But unlike nesting unordered lists, nesting ordered lists does not automatically alter the list type. As a result, to create the output shown in Figure 7.8, in which a numbered list is used for level one, an alphabetic list is used for level two, and roman numerals are used for level three, each <OL> tag that indicates a new level must have a TYPE attribute associated with it. The HTML source for the second example looks like this:

```
<OL>
<LI>This is level one.
<OL TYPE="a">
<LI>This is level two.
<OL TYPE="i">
<LI>This is level three.
<LI>More of level three.
</OL>
<LI>Back to level two.
<LI>More of level two.
</OL>
<LI>And finally back to level one.
</OL>
```

The final example demonstrates how ordered and unordered lists can be nested together. When you're nesting different types of lists together, it is very important that you don't get your end tags out of sequence. Remember to close each menu level in the reverse order in which they were opened, as shown here:

```
<OL>
<LI>This is level one.
<OL TYPE="a">
```

```
<LI>This is level two.
<UL>
<LI>This is level three as a bullet.
</UL>
</OL>
</OL>
```

Definition Lists

Definition lists are ideal for any Web pages that list the meanings of words or that demand the use of indented blocks of text that are directly associated with a line of non-indented text.

The *<DL>* Tag

To declare a definition list, you use the <DL>...</DL> tag combination. Any text included inside these two tags is considered to be part of the definition list.

Whereas the <UL> and <OL> tags use the <LI> tag to indicate the start of each line item, a slightly different approach is required when you are creating definition lists. This is because each single item is actually composed of two separate parts: a term and its definition.

The *<DT>* Tag

To indicate the start of a new term, the <DT> tag is used. Whenever the Web browser encounters a <DT>, it starts a new line. The <DT> tag takes the following form:

```
<DL>
<DT>Term
  The rest of the definition list.
```

The *<DD>* Tag

Each <DT> tag definition must be followed by a complementary <DD>. The <DD> tag indicates the start of the term's definition. Like the <DT> tag, the <DD> tag will as a rule cause the Web browser to start a new line. The text of the definition, however, does not start at the edge of the screen, but instead is indented as shown in Figure 7.9. To create a definition list like the one in Figure 7.9, you make the following entry:

```
<DL>
<DT>HTML
<DD>Hypertext Markup Language
<DT>HTTP
<DD>Hypertext Transport Protocol
<DT>hypertext
<DD>puts the hyperlink into the World Wide Web.
<DT>SGML
<DD>Standard Generalised Markup Language
</DL>
```

Figure 7.9.
A definition list, as created by the <DT> and <DD> tags.

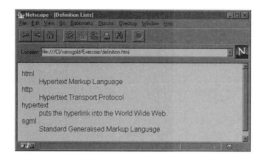

> **Tip:** To make the term section of a definition stand out, many people add some form of character style to it, with bold or emphasis being the most popular. Terms can also be hotspot text for hyperlinks, and inline hyperlinks can also be embedded in the definition section, as can any character formatting.

The *COMPACT* Attribute

The <DL> tag includes support for a special attribute that, under certain circumstances, can reduce the amount of space taken up by a definition list. This attribute, the COMPACT attribute, takes the following form:

```
<DL COMPACT>
```

If the COMPACT attribute is included in the source of the preceding example, the Web page shown in Figure 7.10 is the result. Where the length of the term section is sufficiently small, the Web browser brings the definition section onto the same line.

Figure 7.10.
Using the COMPACT attribute can reduce the amount of space taken up by a definition list.

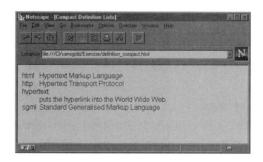

> **Note:** Because there is no way to know exactly how small a term will need to be before most Web browsers will compact it, the COMPACT attribute is not considered a viable tool by most people.

Directory and Menu Lists

In your travels, you might occasionally encounter tags for two other types of lists, namely the <DIR> and <MENU> tags. These two types of lists are no longer in common use. They are both part of the HTML 1.0 and HTML 2.0 specifications but are not considered to be part of the proposed HTML 3.0 specification.

If you really do want more information about the use of these two tags, check out the HTML 2.0 specification at the W3 Consortium home page at http://www.w3.org/. It is likely, however, that future Web browsers will no longer support the use of these tags. In addition, because similar layouts can be created using the unordered list and definition list tags, the use of the <DIR> or <MENU> tags is even less relevant to current Web publishing needs.

Advanced Paragraph Formatting

Back in Chapter 5, "Basic HTML and the World Wide Web," you learned about basic page layout using the paragraph <P> and line break <BR> tags. Although these two tags are suitable for most layout needs, in some circumstances the use of dedicated tags can greatly enhance the appearance of a Web page.

In this section, you will learn about some new tags that enable you to easily control the following design elements:

- ☐ Preformatted text
- ☐ Addresses
- ☐ Quotations
- ☐ Divisions
- ☐ Horizontal rules
- ☐ Line break extensions

Preformatted Text

To date, much has been made of the fact that the formatting and final layout of a Web page are the responsibility of the Web browser and not the Web designer. The Web browser removes such elements as white space, carriage returns, and line feeds, and it even looks after text wrapping.

At times, however, what is really required is complete control over the layout of a block of text. For example, if you wanted to display an online price list for your customers, ideally you would want to create a table that included product codes, a description, and a price. But if you attempted to create such a table using the elements discussed so far, the result would be

less than satisfactory, because it would be nearly impossible to get the columns of your price list to line up.

To create such a list on a Web page, you need to use a special tag called the preformatted text tag—<PRE>...</PRE>. Surrounding a block of text with the <PRE> tag basically disables all the Web browser layout controls that strip out such things as white space and carriage returns. Any text inside the <PRE> block will be displayed exactly as you enter it.

Using the <PRE> tag, the previously mentioned price list would look something like the one shown in Figure 7.11:

```
<PRE>
Bob's Widgets                                    Customer Price List
===================================================================
Product Code    Description                Size        Price
-------------------------------------------------------------------
AA1010          All purpose Widget         10x10         1.50
AA1015          All purpose Widget         10x15         1.75
BX1000          Bob's private collection   Box          10.50
CA1010          Colorful Widget            10x10         2.00
CA1015          Colorful Widget            10x15         2.25
OA0510          Old Widget                 05x10         0.75
OA1020          Old Widget                 10x20         1.35
RA1010          Red Widget                 10x10         1.75
RA1015          Red Widget                 10x15         1.95
XX1000          Widget Gift Set            Box          18.95
-------------------------------------------------------------------
</PRE>
```

Figure 7.11.
The <PRE> tag displays text exactly as it is entered.

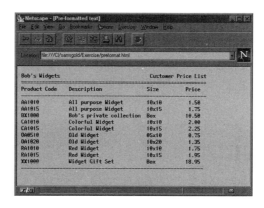

Note: Since the introduction of HTML 3.0, there has in fact been a far better way to create tables. You will learn about the <TABLE> tag and its use in Chapter 8, "Adding Tables to Web Pages."

Addresses

The <ADDRESS>...</ADDRESS> tag is designed to contain information about the Web page's author, including e-mail addresses, postal or business addresses, phone numbers, or other contact information. The best way to think of the <ADDRESS> tag is to think of it as a signature for your Web page.

In use, the <ADDRESS> tag is much like a dedicated version of the paragraph tag that appears only once on a page, usually at the bottom. All the text inside the address tag will be displayed using emphasis or italics. (See Figure 7.12.)

The <ADDRESS> tag takes the following format:

```
<ADDRESS>
<B>Wes Tatters<B><BR>
wtatters@world.net<BR>
wtatters@msn.com<BR>
100036.174@compuserve.com
</ADDRESS>
```

Figure 7.12.
*The <ADDRESS> tag
displays the text it
surrounds using italics.*

**Note:** Text within the <ADDRESS> tag can be further formatted using character styles if you want to enhance the author's name (see Figure 7.12) or some other information. In addition, hyperlinks can also be embedded in the address area if required.

Quotations

On those occasions when you choose to enter a quotation onto a Web page, instead of simply adding a hyperlink to the relevant text, you can either format the layout of the quotation manually—possibly using the <CITE> tag— or use the <BLOCKQUOTE> tag.

Text surrounded by the `<BLOCKQUOTE>` tag will be indented from the left side of the screen to separate it from any other text. (See Figure 7.13.) It is important to note that you still need to surround the text with a paragraph block, in addition to the `<BLOCKQUOTE>` tag, as shown in the following example:

```
<BLOCKQUOTE>
<P>We hold these truths to be self-evident, that all men are created
equal, that they are endowed by their Creator with certain unalienable
Rights, that among these are Life, Liberty and the pursuit of
Happiness.<BR>
- Declaration of Independence</P>
</BLOCKQUOTE>
```

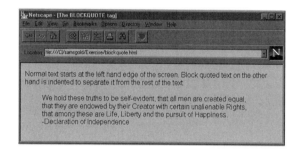

Figure 7.13.
Text formatted with the
BLOCKQUOTE tag.

Note: When quoting another person's work, be sure to attribute the quote correctly, giving recognition to those to whom it is due.

Divisions

As of Version 2.0 of Netscape Navigator, a new paragraph formatting tag—`<DIV>`—has been introduced. Currently, it is functionally similar to the `<P>` tag, except that the `<DIV>` tag does not introduce a blank line between each separate block of text. (See Figure 7.14.)

In addition, like the paragraph tag, the `<DIV>` tag supports the `ALIGN` attribute, as shown in the following HTML source:

```
<DIV ALIGN=LEFT>The only problem with demonstrating the effect<BR>
of the DIV tag on a document<BR>
is that you need to type a few of lines of text<BR>
to see it happening.</DIV>
<DIV ALIGN=CENTER>The only problem with demonstrating the effect<BR>
of the DIV tag on a document<BR>
is that you need to type a few of lines of text<BR>
to see it happening.</DIV>
<DIV ALIGN=RIGHT>The only problem with demonstrating the effect<BR>
```

167

```
of the DIV tag on a document<BR>
is that you need to type a number of lines of text<BR>
to see it happening.</DIV>
```

Figure 7.14.
The <DIV> *tag enables you to format text using the* ALIGN *attribute.*

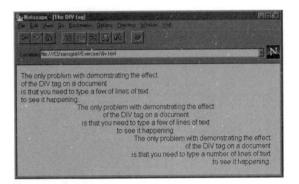

Note: Features of the <DIV> tag currently supported by Navigator 2.0 represent only a small part of the proposed new HTML 3.0 formatting capabilities. Other, as yet unsupported, options include full text justification, style sheets, user-defined styles and classes, and categorization of document sections by division.

Horizontal Rules

A horizontal rule is a line placed across a Web page, usually to separate different parts of document. To draw a horizontal rule on a Web page, all you need to do is use the <HR> tag.

You can also alter the appearance, width, size, and justification of the horizontal rule using four attributes. Table 7.1 lists the attributes and explains their use.

Table 7.1. Horizontal rule attributes.

Attribute	Description
SIZE="*pixels*"	Enter the size in pixels to set the thickness of the horizontal rule.
WIDTH="*pixels*"	Enter the size in pixels to set the width of the horizontal rule.
WIDTH="*percentage%*"	Enter the size as a percentage to set the width of the horizontal rule as a percentage of the width of the page.

Attribute	Description
ALIGN="LEFT"	Align the horizontal rule on the left side of the page.
ALIGN="CENTER"	Align the horizontal rule in the middle of the page. (This is the default.)
ALIGN="RIGHT"	Align the horizontal rule on the right side of the page.
NOSHADE	Turn off the shading and embossed appearance of the horizontal rule, leaving just a solid line.

You can mix any or all of the attributes supported by the <HR> to create an almost limitless number of horizontal rules. The following HTML source demonstrates some possible combinations, shown in Figure 7.15:

```
<HR>
<HR SIZE="10">
<HR WIDTH="50">
<HR WIDTH="50%">
<HR WIDTH="200" ALIGN="LEFT">
<HR WIDTH="200" ALIGN="CENTER">
<HR WIDTH="50%" ALIGN="RIGHT">
<HR NOSHADE>
```

Figure 7.15.
Horizontal rule types currently supported by Navigator 2.0.

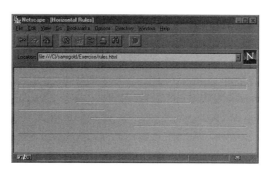

Line Break Extensions

Navigator 2.0 supports two unusual extensions to the basic line break tag: the no break tag—<NOBR>...</NOBR>—and the word break tag—<WBR>.

The no break tag is designed for those rare occasions when you don't want a line of text wrapped around onscreen. Instead, Navigator 2.0 continues to print the line out past the right edge of the screen. Any text you enter inside the <NOBR> tags is considered to be part of the line you don't want wrapped around. To view such a line, you must use the scrollbars at the bottom of the document area.

If finding a use for the <NOBR> tag is a rare event, then finding a use for the <WBR> tag is probably even rarer. You use the <WBR> tag to tell Navigator 2.0 where it would be OK to include a line break. If Navigator 2.0 decides that a line break is required, based on the size of the screen, the font, and other formatting considerations, it will use the location indicated by the <WBR> tag.

The following example demonstrates how the <NOBR> and <WBR> tags are used to create the Web page shown in Figure 7.16. In particular, pay special attention to the location of the <WBR> tag—it causes the text to wrap after the document rather than after the is, as was the case in the first paragraph:

```
<P>The only problem with demonstrating the effect
of the NOBR tag on a document
is that you need to type a few lines of text
to see it happening.</P>
<P><NOBR>The only problem with demonstrating the effect
of the NOBR tag on a document
is that you need to type a few lines of text
to see it happening.</NOBR></P>
<P><NOBR>The only problem with demonstrating the effect
of the NOBR and WBR tag on a document<WBR>
is that you need to<WBR> type a few lines of text
to see it happening.</NOBR></P>
```

Figure 7.16.
Using the NOBR and WBR
tags to format lines.

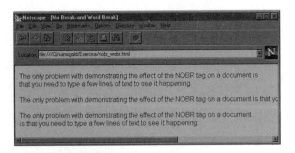

Advanced Text Formatting

One of the most popular additions to the HTML specification—especially for Navigator 2.0 uses—is the availability of a range of new character formatting elements that enable you to change the colors of fonts, hyperlinks, visited hyperlinks, and even the screen. When these new elements are coupled with the new font elements that enable you to alter the size of individual characters, the new possibilities for creativity are amazing.

Changing Text Colors

To accommodate the need for different-colored text on Web pages, a new group of attributes has been added to the <BODY> tag. These attributes enable you to define the color of text on

your Web page, the color of link text, the color of active links, and the color of visited links, along with the background color for the entire page.

These are the names of these new attributes:

- ☐ BGCOLOR—background color
- ☐ TEXT—text color
- ☐ LINK—link color
- ☐ ALINK—active link color
- ☐ VLINK—visited link color

When included as part of the <BODY> tag, each of these attributes takes the following format:

```
ATTRIBUTE="#rrggbb"
```

The color values of *r*, *g*, and *b* each represent a hexadecimal value between 0 and F. For each of the three color groups—rr (red), gg (green), and bb (blue)—00 repents the absence of a color, and FF represents the maximum possible value. By mixing different amounts of each color, all the colors of the spectrum can be obtained.

For example, to set the TEXT color to black, you write TEXT="#000000". You set it to all red with TEXT="#FF0000", to all green with TEXT="#00FF00", and to all blue with TEXT="#0000FF". In addition, a color such as yellow can be obtained by mixing equal amounts of red and green as in TEXT="#FFFF00" or a darker yellow by using a value such as TEXT="#7F7F00".

Or you can also use words to describe colors. For example, TEXT="RED", TEXT="GREEN", TExT="BLUE", and naturally the colors BLACK and WHITE are supported. (See Appendix C, "Colors by Name and Hex Value," for a complete list of colors supported by Navigator 2.0.)

Therefore, to create a Web page with a BLACK background, WHITE text, RED hyperlinks, YELLOW visited links, and links that turn GREEN as you click them, you would type the following:

```
<BODY BGCOLOR="BLACK" TEXT="WHITE" LINK="RED" VLINK="YELLOW" ALINK="GREEN">
```

Alternatively, you could type this:

```
<BODY BGCOLOR="#000000" TEXT="#FFFFFF" LINK="#FF0000" VLINK="#FFFF00"
ALINK="#00FF00">
```

> **Note:** Navigator 2.0 also supports a third method of color definition that takes the form ATTRIBUTE="rrggbb". In this format, there is no # symbol; however, good HTML style really demands the use of the ATTRIBUTE="#rrggbb" version.

The *<FONT>* Tag

Whereas the <BODY> tag, and heading tags such as <H1> act on blocks of text, the <FONT> tag provides Web publishers with a means of controlling the appearance of individual characters. Currently, two attributes are supported by the <FONT> tag: COLOR and SIZE.

The *COLOR* Attribute

The COLOR attribute takes the same values as those discussed previously for the color attributes of the <BODY> tag. For example, to define a single word in the color red, you would write this:

```
<FONT COLOR="RED">Red</FONT>
```

or this:

```
<FONT COLOR="#FF0000">Red</FONT>
```

Be sure to include the </FONT> tag so that any text following your red word will be displayed in the text color defined for the whole document.

With a little careful planning, you can even create rainbow-colored text by using the following source:

```
<H1>
<FONT COLOR="RED">R</FONT>
<FONT COLOR="ORANGE">A</FONT>
<FONT COLOR="YELLOW">I</FONT>
<FONT COLOR="GREEN">N</FONT>
<FONT COLOR="BLUE">B</FONT>
<FONT COLOR="VIOLET">O</FONT>
<FONT COLOR="RED">W</FONT>
</H1>
```

The *SIZE* Attribute

The second attribute provided by the <FONT> tag is the SIZE attribute. By using this attribute, you can change the size of words and characters within a Web page. Seven text sizes are available, with size 3 being equivalent to the size of standard text, or what is called the default base font size. The following HTML source demonstrates the seven available text sizes by creating the Web page shown in Figure 7.17:

```
<P>
Normal Text
<FONT SIZE="1" >R</FONT>
<FONT SIZE="2" >A</FONT>
<FONT SIZE="3" >I</FONT>
<FONT SIZE="4" >N</FONT>
<FONT SIZE="5" >B</FONT>
<FONT SIZE="6" >O</FONT>
<FONT SIZE="7" >W</FONT>
```

```
</P>
<P>
Normal Text
<FONT SIZE="1" >R</FONT><FONT SIZE="2" >A</FONT><FONT SIZE="3" >I</FONT>
➥<FONT SIZE="4" >N</FONT><FONT SIZE="5" >B</FONT><FONT SIZE="6" >O</FONT>
➥<FONT SIZE="7" >W</FONT>
</P>
```

Figure 7.17.
The SIZE attribute of the <FONT> tag enables you to adjust the size of words and characters on a Web page.

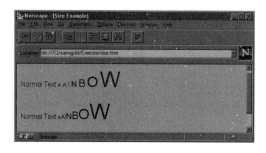

Caution: The second line of text in Figure 7.17 demonstrates what appears to be a fault in the current version of Navigator 2.0. The horizontal spacing for the two lines of text are different even though technically they should be identical. It appears that because the individual characters are on separate lines in the HTML source for the first row, some extra spacing is forced between each character. To avoid this problem, keep any font size changes on the same line of your HTML source.

Defining the Base Font

By using the <BASEFONT> tag, you can alter the base font size that governs the display of all standard text within a Web page. As mentioned in the preceding section, the default base font size is font size 3. Under most circumstances, it is best to leave the base font set to this size and use the <FONT> tag to display smaller and larger text sizes.

If, however, you want to adjust the physical base font size, you do so by writing <BASEFONT SIZE="*newsize*">, in which *newsize* is a value between 1 and 7.

Altering the base font size will affect the appearance of all the standard text within your HTML document that follows the <BASEFONT> tag. It does not, however, have any effect on the size of heading styles or the <FONT SIZE="?"> tag, unless you deliberately specify that the font size setting is relative to the current base font.

To specify a relative font size change, instead of writing <FONT SIZE="5">, you write <FONT SIZE="+2">, based on the fact that the default base font size is 3. When the relevant text is displayed, Navigator 2.0 takes the current base font size and adds the relative size—+2—to arrive at the correct size for the font, which in this case would be size 5.

As a result, if the base font size were changed to 4, then <FONT SIZE="+2"> would display text using font size 6, as shown in Figure 7.18. In addition, normal text and <FONT SIZE="4"> text will look identical.

Figure 7.18.
Changing font sizes with the <FONT> *and* <BASEFONT> *tags.*

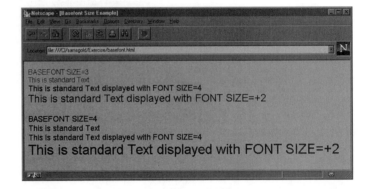

Displaying Special Characters

If you cast your mind back to Chapter 5, you will recall that to display the < symbol on a Web page, a special code is required. The code you used was <.

< and >, the two codes you used in the first exercise in Chapter 5, are part of a special set of elements called *character entities*. Character entities enable you to place characters and symbols on your Web page that are not normally associated with ASCII text files.

When you create a text file, the only characters that can be entered directly into the file are part of what is called the ASCII 7-bit character set. This character set is a collection of 127 letters, numbers, and symbols. All the upper- and lowercase letters in the English alphabet are included in this set, along with the numerals 0 through 9 and the symbols ~!#$%^&*()_+|`-=\,./;'[]<>?:"{}.

What are not included, however, are the characters associated with many foreign languages and some special symbols such as the copyright and registered trademark. This second group of characters is part of what is called the extended ASCII 8-bit character set. Unfortunately, due to the nature of the Internet, it is not possible to include these characters directly on a Web page.

Instead, you describe these characters using character entities. Three types of character entities are currently available:

- Special entities
- Named entities
- Numeric entities

> **Note:** An additional level of complexity is associated with representing characters in the extended ASCII set. Unfortunately, many different computer systems place characters in the upper (8-bit) section of the extended ASCII character set in different locations or order. As a result, there are varying standards for ASCII (8-bit) tables. To maintain a level of transportability, all Web browsers must use what is called the ISO-8859-1 (ISO-Latin-1) version.

Special Character Entities

All entities start with an ampersand (&) symbol and end with a semicolon (;).

The < and > entities are part of the small group of special character entities. These entities are used to represent characters that are in fact part of the ASCII 7-bit character set, but because they are used in the HTML syntax, they cannot be directly entered into an HTML document. Table 7.2 lists the four special character entities supported by Navigator 2.0.

Table 7.2. Special character entities.

Special Entity	Character Displayed on Web Page
&amp;	&
&gt;	>
&lt;	<
&quot;	"

Named and Numeric Entities

The remaining character entities all take one of two forms. They can be represented either as a named entity or as a numeric entity.

Named entities have a similar appearance to special entities. They all start with the & symbol and end with a semicolon. The name of the character (usually an abbreviation) is then placed between the & and the semicolon to describe the character to be displayed. For example, to display the registered trademark symbol (®) on a Web page, you use the named entity ®.

Unfortunately, however, very few Web browsers—including Navigator 2.0—recognize all the named entities set down in the original HTML specification. As a result, to display characters that don't have named entities, you need to use a numeric entity.

To represent a numeric entity, you still start with an & symbol and end with a semicolon, but instead of placing a name in the middle, you enter a # (pound sign) followed by a number that indicates the character's position in the ISO-8859-1 ASCII 8-bit character set. Therefore, if you wanted to display the British pound currency symbol (£) on a Web page, you would type £. This tells the Web browser to display the 163rd character in the ISO-8859-1 character set.

Note: Appendix B, "Character Entities," lists all the characters in the upper section of the ISO-8859-1 ASCII 8-bit character set, along with their corresponding named and numeric entities.

Summary

In this chapter you have learned about many of the advanced formatting options supported by Navigator 2.0. You have examined the three standard types of lists, discovered how to change the color and size of text on a page, and learned how to apply formatting to individual characters and words. In addition, you now know how to use tags to sign your Web pages and add quotations.

To recap what you have learned in this chapter, Table 7.3 lists all the new tags you have explored.

Table 7.3. New tags discussed in this chapter.

Tag	Description
BGCOLOR	The BGCOLOR attribute of the <BODY> tag sets the background color of the current Web page.
TEXT	The TEXT attribute of the <BODY> tag sets the text color for the current Web page.

Tag	Description
LINK	The LINK attribute of the <BODY> tag sets the link color for the current Web page.
ALINK	The ALINK attribute of the <BODY> tag sets the active link color for the current Web page.
VLINK	The VLINK attribute of the <BODY> tag sets the visited link color for the current Web page.
<UL>…</UL>	Signals an unordered list, more commonly known as a bulleted list.
<OL>…</OL>	Signals an ordered list, more commonly known as a numbered list.
START	The START attribute of the <OL> sets the starting number for an ordered list.
<LI>	Indicates the start of each line item in an unordered or ordered list.
TYPE	For unordered lists the TYPE attribute of the <LI> tag can be set to DISC, CIRCLE, or SQUARE. For ordered lists the TYPE attribute of the <LI> tag can be set to 1, A, a, I, or i.
VALUE	For ordered lists the TYPE attribute of the <LI> sets the number of a list item.
<DL>…</DL>	Declares a definition list or glossary list.
COMPACT	The COMPACT attribute of the <DL> tag causes the definition list to be compacted where possible.
<DT>	Indicates the start of each new term in a definition list.
<DD>	Indicates the start of the definition section. Each <DD> tag must be preceded by a corresponding <DT> tag.
<PRE>…</PRE>	Displays preformatted text exactly as it is typed into an HTML document.
<ADDRESS>…</ADDRESS>	Contains information you include as a signature for your Web page.
<BLOCKQUOTE>…</BLOCKQUOTE>	Displays quotations indented from the rest of the text on a Web page.
<DIV>…</DIV>	Acts like the <P> tag, but does not place a blank line between each block of text.

continues

Table 7.3. continued

Tag	Description
ALIGN	The ALIGN attribute of the <P> can be set to LEFT, CENTER, or RIGHT
<HR>	Draws horizontal lines across a Web page.
SIZE	The SIZE attribute of the <HR> tag sets the thickness of the horizontal rule.
WIDTH	The WIDTH attribute of the <HR> tag sets the width of the horizontal rule.
ALIGN	The ALIGN attribute of the <HR> tag sets the horizontal rule alignment to LEFT, CENTER, or RIGHT.
NOSHADE	The NOSHADE attribute of the <HR> tag lets you turn off the shading and embossed appearance of the horizontal rule.
<NOBR>…</NOBR>	Displays all the text inside this tag on a single line.
<WBR>…</WBR>	Indicates suitable locations for line breaks in long lines of text.
<FONT>…</FONT>	Alters the size and color of words and individual characters within a Web page.
SIZE	The SIZE attribute of the <FONT> tag is used to alter the size of text displayed inside the <FONT> tag block.
COLOR	The COLOR attribute of the <FONT> tag is used to alter the color of text displayed inside the <FONT> tag block.
<BASEFONT>	Defines the base size for all standard text.
SIZE	The SIZE attribute of the <BASEFONT> tag sets the base size of text displayed on the current Web page.

Workshop

The first section of the Workshop lists some of the common questions people ask about the World Wide Web along with a brief answer to each. Next is a quiz about the chapter you have just read. If you have problems answering any of the questions in the quiz, you can turn to Appendix E, "Answers to Quiz Questions."

Q&A

Q Using the `<PRE>` tag doesn't seem like the easiest way to create tables. Isn't there a better approach?

A There sure is. In the next chapter you will learn all about the `<TABLE>` tag. By using this tag, you can create tables with multiple columns, headers, text attributes, and much, much more.

Q At a couple sites I've visited, I've seen HTML documents that include `<DD>` tags without any corresponding `<DT>` tags. How is this possible?

A Most Web browsers are very forgiving and will let people get away with just about anything. As a result, some people have discovered that the `<DD>` tag can be used to create indented lists that don't have corresponding term sections. As with all the workarounds and tricks that people discover, however, there is no guarantee that they will be supported in future Web browsers or that they won't break existing ones. Therefore, the bottom line is that if you want to write reliable and consistent HTML documents, adhere to the guidelines set before you. That way, you won't get into trouble later.

Q I liked the rainbow text example you demonstrated earlier, but what I really would like is rainbow text that changes color. Is that possible?

A If that question had been asked even a few months ago, the answer would have been a resounding "not possible." With the introduction of the Java programming language, however, such feats are now well within the realm of possibility. To see an example of flashing rainbow text, along with a host of other exciting Java applets, take a look at `http://www.gamelan.com/Beta.html`.

Quiz

1. What two tags are used when creating an ordered list?
2. What purpose does a `<DD>` tag serve?
3. What are the four attributes used by the `<HR>` tag?
4. What tag is used to create a signature for your Web pages?
5. What color is represented by `"#00FF00"`?
6. What are the five color attributes used by the `<BODY>` tag?
7. How many font sizes can be used with the `<FONT SIZE="?">` tag attribute?
8. What is the character entity for the ampersand (&) symbol?

Exercises

1. With so many new tags to learn about in this chapter, you have had a bit of a free ride (no exercises to get in your way) with all the examples provided for you.

   The best way, however, to learn about HTML is still by creating your own Web pages. To this end, your first exercise for this chapter is to go back to the `html_contents.html` document you created previously and use the unordered list tags to turn the table of contents into a list. While you are editing this document, don't forget to add an <ADDRESS> tag to the bottom of the page as your signature. You might also want to add a couple of horizontal rules, one after the page heading and one before the <ADDRESS>, to break up the page.

   Also, update the `05notes.html` document to include <ADDRESS>, <HR>, and possibly list tags.

2. Your second task today is to create the `07note.html` document for your HTML reference collection. Be sure to include an example of each list type, using all the available attributes. Sign this document as well, by using the <ADDRESS> tag. Add a hyperlink to point back to the `html_contents.html` document, and one in the contents document to point to `07note.html`.

   Finally, include a hyperlink in `07note.html` to point to the following page maintained by Martin Ramsch: `http://www.uni-passau.de/~ramsch/iso8859-1.html`. This page contains a list of all the character entities relevant to the ISO-8859-1 character set.

8

Adding Tables
to Web Pages

Adding Tables to Web Pages

As you discovered in Chapter 7, "Advanced Formatting Options," the use of preformatted text is not the most ideal method of portraying tables of information on a Web page. In a pinch, it will get the job done, but the lack of control over individual elements in the table leaves a lot to be desired.

In this chapter you will learn about a far better method of displaying tables on a Web page—which was introduced as part of the HTML 3.0 specification—by exploring the following topics:

- ☐ Building a basic table
- ☐ The <TABLE> tag
- ☐ Defining rows and cells
- ☐ Advanced table formatting
- ☐ Table alignment options

Building a Basic Table

With the introduction of tables to the HTML specification, many previously impossible layout techniques are now available to Web page designers.

In their most simple form, tables give you far greater control over the appearance of tabular information. With a bit of planning, however, the table specification also introduces the possibility of side-by-side (newspaper style) text columns and Web pages whose appearance approaches that of popular magazine layouts.

What is even more significant, from the Web publisher's perspective, is the relative ease with which such layouts can be achieved, given the fact that only five tags control the entire table system. These are the tags:

- ☐ <TABLE>...</TABLE>
- ☐ <TR>...</TR>
- ☐ <TD>...</TD>
- ☐ <TH>...</TH>
- ☐ <CAPTION>...</CAPTION>

The <TABLE> Tag

To indicate the presence of a table within a document, a new <TABLE> tag has been introduced. Netscape Communications defines this tag as "the main wrapper for all other table tags."

In many ways the <TABLE> tag is a lot like the <HEAD> and <BODY> document tags. On its own, the <TABLE> tag has no effect on a Web page; instead, it is used to indicate the type of information it surrounds. But unlike the other document tags, which are optional, a <TABLE> tag must be included before the other table tags can have any effect. (Remember, while <HEAD> and <BODY> tags are both optional, good HTML style demands their inclusion.)

When used in an HTML document, the <TABLE> tag takes the following form:

```
<BODY>
  Any HTML source
<TABLE>
  Table definition goes here
</TABLE>
  Any other HTML source
</BODY>
</HTML>
```

Defining Rows and Cells

Tables within a Web document consist of data cells that are divided into rows. If you have any experience using spreadsheets, the concept of cells should be reasonably familiar to you, but if not, don't be too concerned because it is not a difficult concept to come to terms with. Figure 8.1 shows a simple table that demonstrates how rows and data cells in a table are organized.

Figure 8.1.
Tables consist of some data cells divided into rows.

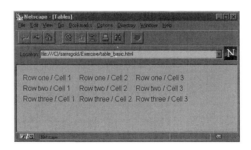

▼ Exercise: Creating Your First Table

To demonstrate how rows and data cells in a table are defined, in this exercise you will create the table shown in Figure 8.1.

First, to indicate the start of a table in an HTML document, you need a <TABLE> tag. As mentioned previously, without the <TABLE> tag, none of the other tags you are about to use will have any effect on your Web pages.

For each row in your table, you need to define a table row tag block—`<TR>`…`</TR>`. To define the three rows required for the table shown in Figure 8.1, you would write this:

```
<TABLE>
<TR> <!-- this is the start of row 1 -->
</TR>
<TR> <!-- this is the start of row 2 -->
</TR>
<TR> <!-- this is the start of row 3 -->
</TR>
</TABLE>
```

> **Tip:** To help you sort through all the tags in a table, use the `<!-- comment -->` tag to indicate the start of each row.

Finally, you need to define a data cell—`<TD>`…`</TD>`—for each block of text in the table. Working across your table from left to right, row by row, enter the contents of each data cell between a set of `<DT>` tags, inside the cell's corresponding row tag, as shown here:

```
<HTML>
<BODY>
<TABLE>
<TR> <!-- this is the start of row 1 -->
<TD>Row one / Cell 1 </TD>
<TD>Row one / Cell 2 </TD>
<TD>Row one / Cell 3 </TD>
</TR>
<TR><!-- this is the start of row 2 -->
<TD>Row two / Cell 1 </TD>
<TD>Row two / Cell 2 </TD>
<TD>Row two / Cell 3 </TD>
</TR>
<TR><!-- this is the start of row 3 -->
<TD>Row three / Cell 1 </TD>
<TD>Row three / Cell 2 </TD>
<TD>Row three / Cell 3 </TD>
</TR>
</TABLE>
</BODY>
</HTML<
```

After you have entered the preceding document into your text editor, save the file as `table.html`, and then load it into Navigator 2.0 to verify the results.

Note: You might have noticed that there is nothing in the preceding table definition to indicate the width of each cell. This is because the Web browser looks after this task for you, by calculating the widest cell in each column and then setting the width of all the other cells in the column to match it.

This is also the reason all the cells in the preceding exercise have a trailing space between the last character of the cell data and the </TD> tag. For calculation of the width of a cell, this trailing space is taken into account. To verify this, try table.html with and without the trailing space. You should find that the width of each column is slightly wider when the trailing space is included. Adding more than one trailing space, however, does not increase the width any further.

Table Borders

In your travels around the World Wide Web, you possibly have visited Web sites whose tables include a fancy border around each cell, yet the table shown in Figure 8.1 includes no such border. The reason for this is that by default, tables do not include borders. To turn on the display of borders for a table, you must include a BORDER attribute inside the <TABLE> tag, which takes the following form:

```
<TABLE BORDER>
```

Including the border attribute in the table created for the preceding exercise produces the results shown in the first table of Figure 8.2.

Figure 8.2.
Tables with different border values.

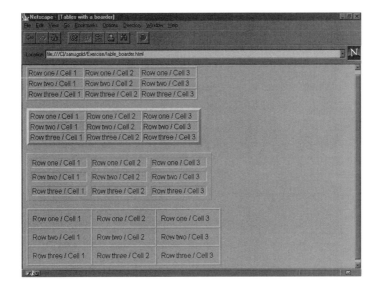

BORDER="value"

The BORDER attribute can also have a value associated with it that specifies the size—in pixels—of a bevel-edged border that is placed around the outside of the entire table. Using a setting of BORDER="5" produces the second table shown in Figure 8.2. (If no value is assigned to the BORDER attribute, a default value of zero is used.)

CELLSPACING

When you include the BORDER attribute in a <TABLE> tag, the size of the border that surrounds each cell is determined by an attribute called CELLSPACING. By default, the CELLSPACING for a table is set to 2. You can override this default setting by including the CELLSPACING attribute as part of the <TABLE> tag.

For example, to define a CELLSPACING of 10, as was the case for the third table in Figure 8.2, you would type this:

```
<TABLE BORDER CELLSPACING=10>
```

CELLPADDING

One additional table attribute affects the positioning of borders. The CELLPADDING attribute defines the amount of space left between the contents of each cell and its surrounding border. By default, the CELLPADDING value for a table is set to 1.

The bottom table in Figure 8.2 demonstrates a table that has been assigned a CELLPADDING value of 10 with the following code:

```
<TABLE BORDER CELLPADDING=10>
```

Note: The BORDER="value", CELLSPACING="value", and CELLPADDING="value" attributes can be used in combination to create various borders, each with a unique appearance.

Table Headings

A large percentage of the tables you create on Web pages will require some sort of column headings to describe the contents of the cells that appear below them.

To assist you in this area, a special type of data cell has been defined that replaces the normal <TD> tag with a <TH> tag. The <TH> tag is functionally identical to the <TD> tag, except that text inside a <TH> tag is displayed in bold and aligned with the middle of the cell instead of being left justified.

As a result, to add a set of column headings to the preceding example, all you need to do is define a new table row and include a <TH> tag block for each column heading. The HTML source required to include the column headings shown in Figure 8.3 looks like this:

```
<TABLE>
<TR> <!-- this is the start of the heading row -->
<TH>Column 1 </TH>
<TH>Column 2 </TH>
<TH>Column 3 </TH>
</TR>
<TR> <!-- this is the start of row 1 -->
<TD>Row one / Cell 1 </TD>
<TD>Row one / Cell 2 </TD>
<TD>Row one / Cell 3 </TD>
</TR>
  the rest of your table goes here.
</TABLE>
```

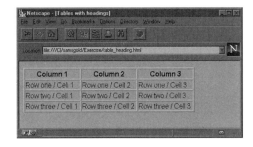

Figure 8.3.
A table with column headings.

Note: Technically, the <TH> tag can replace any <TD> cell in a table. Traditionally, however, headings should only appear either on the top row of a table or in the cells of the first column at the left side of the table.

Creating a Table Caption

The final table tag—<CAPTION>...</CAPTION>—does not actually affect the appearance of the table itself. Instead, it is used to define a title or caption to be displayed above or below the table. As a rule, you should place the <CAPTION> tag immediately after the <TABLE> tag and before any table cell or row tags.

If you want to display a title above a table, you use the <CAPTION> tag with its ALIGN="TOP" attribute set. Alternatively, if you want to display a caption below the table, you use <CAPTION ALIGN="BOTTOM">. For example, to define a title (see Figure 8.4) for the table shown in Figure 8.3 you would enter this:

```
<TABLE>
<CAPTION ALIGN="TOP">This is a table caption</CAPTION>
<TR> <!-- this is the start of the heading row -->
<TH>Column 1</TH>
     the rest of your table goes here.
</TABLE>
```

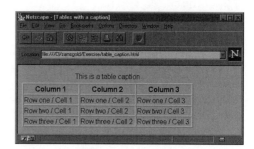

Figure 8.4.

Text inside the <CAPTION> tag is displayed above the table as a title.

Caution: You cannot include both a caption and a title in the same table. Doing so produces unpredictable results. Specifically, Navigator 2.0 will ignore any additional <CAPTION> tags and will probably place any text included within them after the table (but not as a caption.)

Advanced Table Formatting

To give you greater control over the appearance of your tables, a rich set of attributes is supported by the various table tags. These attributes enable you to override the default cell width and height, control the alignment of text within each cell, span cells across multiple rows and columns, and alter the border size or cell spacing.

Width and Height Controls

By using the HEIGHT and WIDTH attributes with either the <TABLE> tag or the <TH> and <TD> tags, you can control, with a reasonably high level of accuracy, the size of a table and the cells it contains.

When used with the <TABLE> tag, the HEIGHT and WIDTH attributes both take on one of two forms. You can define HEIGHT (or WIDTH) either as a percentage of the Web page or by using a physical number of screen pixels. For example, to define a table that has a width equivalent to 90% of the current page width and that is 300 pixels high, you would write this:

```
<TABLE BORDER WIDTH="90%" HEIGHT="300" >
```

Note: When you specify a set of specific sizes for a table, these size attributes attempt to override the normal cell height and width calculations. However, if, for example, you specified a width of 50 pixels for a table with five columns, the Web browser would override the width you specified so that all the columns would still fit inside the table.

Using the HEIGHT attribute with a <TH> or <TD> tag enables you to control the height of all the cells in a row. And likewise, using the WIDTH attribute with the <TH> or <TD> tag lets you control the width of all the cells in a column. For example, in Figure 8.5, the width of column 1 is set to 60% of the table width, and the height of all the cells in row 2 is set to 100 pixels. It is important to also note that it does not matter which data cell in a row or column you place the size attributes in, because all the cells in the affected row or column will be altered to the new setting.

To create the table shown in Figure 8.5, which also includes the <TABLE> width and height settings discussed previously, you would use the following HTML source:

```
<TABLE BORDER WIDTH="90%" HEIGHT="300">
<TR> <!-- this is the start of the heading row -->
<TH WIDTH="60%">Column 1</TH>
<TH>Column 2</TH>
<TH>Column 3</TH>
</TR>
<TR> <!-- this is the start of row 1 -->
<TD>Row one / Cell 1 </TD>
<TD>Row one / Cell 2 </TD>
<TD>Row one / Cell 3 </TD>
</TR>
<TR> <!-- this is the start of row 2 -->
<TD HEIGHT="100">Row two / Cell 1 </TD>
<TD>Row two / Cell 2 </TD>
<TD>Row two / Cell 3 </TD>
</TR>
<TR> <!-- this is the start of row 3 -->
<TD>Row three / Cell 2 </TD>
<TD>Row three / Cell 2 </TD>
<TD>Row three / Cell 3 </TD>
</TR>
</TABLE>
```

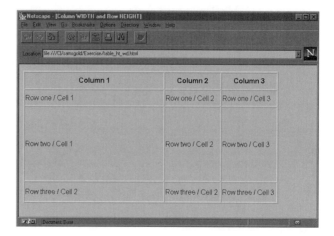

Figure 8.5.
A table with column width and row height specified.

Note: In the current version of Netscape Navigator, there is no support for percentage sizes when setting the height of a row of cells. As a result, if you want to specify a cell's height, you must use pixels.

Text Alignment

Like the paragraph <P> and division <DIV> tags, which allow you to alter the text alignment of blocks of text, you can also adjust the alignment of text within each individual cell in a table. Figure 8.6 demonstrates all the possible alignment attributes for the <TD>, <TH>, and <TR> tags.

Figure 8.6.
The effects of alignment attributes on table formatting.

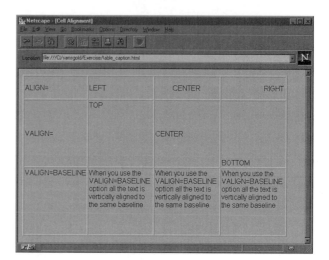

Horizontal Alignment

The ALIGN attribute controls the horizontal alignment of text within a data cell. It currently takes the values ALIGN="LEFT", ALIGN="CENTER", and ALIGN="RIGHT". If there is no ALIGN attribute, the default value for each cell is ALIGN="LEFT".

The HTML used to create the top row of the table in Figure 8.6 looks like the following HTML source. You should also note the use of the HEIGHT and WIDTH attributes in this example to set the size of all the cells in the table to an equal width and height:

```
<TR> <!-- this is the start of row one -->
<TD HEIGHT="50" WIDTH="25%">ALIGN=</TD>
<TD WIDTH="25%" ALIGN="LEFT">LEFT </TD>
<TD WIDTH="25%" ALIGN="CENTER">CENTER </TD>
<TD WIDTH="25%" ALIGN="RIGHT">RIGHT </TD>
</TR>
```

Note: When the ALIGN attribute is applied to a <TR> tag, all the cells in that row are affected, but when ALIGN is applied to either the <TD> tag or the <TH> tag, only the corresponding cell is affected.

Vertical Alignment

Where a data cell is larger than one line high, the VALIGN attribute can be used to control the vertical alignment of the text within a cell. Four values are currently supported by the VALIGN attribute: VALIGN="TOP", VALIGN="CENTER", VALIGN="BOTTOM", and VALIGN="BASELINE". If no alignment is specified for a data cell or its surrounding row tag, the alignment defaults to VALIGN="CENTER".

The second line of Figure 8.6 demonstrates the use of the first three VALIGN values using the following source:

```
<TR> <!-- this is the start of row two -->
<TD HEIGHT="150">VALIGN=</TD>
<TD VALIGN="TOP">TOP </TD>
<TD VALIGN="CENTER">CENTER </TD>
<TD VALIGN="BOTTOM">BOTTOM </TD>
</TR>
```

The third line of Figure 8.6 demonstrates the use of the VALIGN="BASELINE" value and also shows how placing an alignment attribute inside a row tag affects all the cells within the row. Currently, the VALIGN="BASELINE" value produces the same effect as the VALIGN="TOP" attribute. The partial HTML source for this line looks like this:

```
<TR VALIGN=BASELINE> <!-- this is the start of row three -->
<TD HEIGHT=150>VALIGN=BASELINE</TD>
```

```
<TD >When you use the VALIGN=BASELINE option all
the text is vertically aligned to the same baseline</TD>
<TD >When you use the VALIGN=BASELINE option all
the text is vertically aligned to the same baseline</TD>
<TD >When you use the VALIGN=BASELINE option all
the text is vertically aligned to the same baseline</TD>
</TR>
```

Note: When the VALIGN attribute is applied to the <TR> tag, all the cells in that row are affected, but when VALIGN is applied to a <TD> or <TH> tag, only the corresponding cell is affected.

Word Wrapping

When the Web browser encounters a data cell that contains more text than can be made to fit on a single line, the contents of the cell are automatically wrapped onto additional lines by increasing the height of the rows. However, because of the way the automatic table and cell sizing routines work, cells with only a small amount of text also have their contents word wrapped and, more significantly, their width reduced to make room for more text on each line of any cells with a lot of text. The first table in Figure 8.7 demonstrates the effect word wrapping has on the appearance of cells in the table.

In some circumstances, however, you will not want small lines of text to be automatically word wrapped. To prevent word wrapping, you include a NOWRAP attribute in the data cell's <TD> or <TH> tag. The effect of the NOWRAP attribute is demonstrated in the second cell of the bottom table in Figure 8.7.

Figure 8.7.

The NOWRAP attribute disables word wrapping for a data cell.

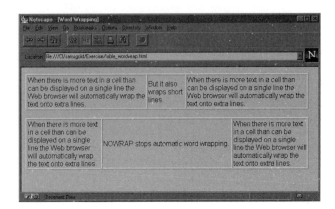

> **Note:** When the NOWRAP attribute is defined for a data cell, you can still use the <BR> tag and the <P> tag to force physical line and paragraph breaks within the cell.

Spanning Data Cells

8

All the table examples you have seen so far have had an equal number of cells in each row and, likewise, an equal number of cells in each column. But as you are about to learn, this does not always need to be the case.

The HTML 3.0 specification defines two attributes—COLSPAN and ROWSPAN—that enable you to span a single cell across a number of columns or down through a number of rows. By using these attributes, in combination with many of the features already discussed, you can create complex tables like the one shown in Figure 8.8.

Figure 8.8.

By using the ROWSPAN and COLSPAN attributes, you can create complex tables.

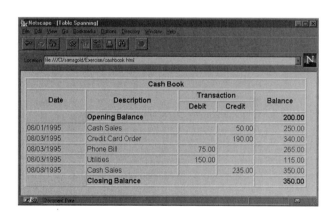

Exercise: Spanning Columns

The COLSPAN attribute is used when you want the contents of a data cell to span two or more columns of a table. To help you understand how the COLSPAN attribute works, in this exercise you will create the table shown Figure 8.9.

Figure 8.9.

With COLSPAN, you can make attribute cells span two or more columns of a table.

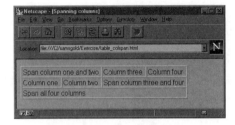

First, define the table and three row tags, as shown in the preceding exercise, "Creating Your First Table":

```
<TABLE BORDER>
<TR> <!-- this is the start of row one -->
</TR>
<TR> <!-- this is the start of row two -->
</TR>
<TR> <!-- this is the start of row three -->
</TR>
</TABLE>
```

Tip: To include a border around your tables, remember to include the BORDER attribute inside the <TABLE> tag.

The next step is to start adding the cells for each row. On the top row, the first cell needs to span both columns one and two. To do this, you need to include a COLSPAN attribute with a value of 2 inside the data cells <TD> tag as shown here:

```
<TD COLSPAN=2>Span column one and two</TD>
```

As before, you need to place each data cell inside its corresponding <TR> tag, working from left to right through the cells in the row. Note also that the cells to be placed in columns three and four span only a single column, so there is no need to include a COLSPAN attribute, as shown here in the completed definition for row one:

```
<TR> <!-- this is the start of row one -->
<TD COLSPAN="2">Span column one and two</TD>
<TD>Column three</TD>
<TD>Column Four</TD>
</TR>
```

In the middle row, the situation is reversed. The first two cells span only a single column, but the last cell spans two columns. To define this row, enter the appropriate data cells inside the second row's tag:

```
<TR> <!-- this is the start of row two -->
<TD>Column one </TD>
<TD>Column two </TD>
<TD COLSPAN="2">Span column three and four </TD>
</TR>
```

Finally, row three contains only a single data cell that spans all four columns of the table. To code this data cell, you use COLSPAN="4" as shown here:

```
<TR> <!-- this is the start of row three -->
<TD COLSPAN="4">Span all four columns </TD>
</TR>
```

After you have entered all the code, save it in a file called colspan.html, and then check out your handiwork using Navigator 2.0. If your table looks different from the one shown in Figure 8.9, backtrack through the HTML source, making sure that you have not missed any < or > elements around your tag, and make sure that each tag is also spelled correctly.

Exercise: Spanning Rows

Whereas the COLSPAN attribute enables you to span the contents of a data cell across columns within a table, ROWSPAN enables you to span a data cell across rows, as shown in Figure 8.10.

Figure 8.10.
The ROWSPAN attribute lets cells span across two or more rows of a table.

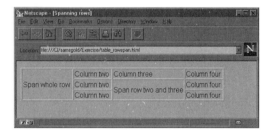

To duplicate the Web page shown in Figure 8.10, first define your table and three row tags:

```
<TABLE BORDER>
<TR> <!-- this is the start of row one -->
</TR>
<TR> <!-- this is the start of row two -->
</TR>
<TR> <!-- this is the start of row three -->
</TR>
</TABLE>
```

After this is done, you need to define the data cells for the first row, remembering to indicate that column one is to be spanned across three rows. You do this using ROWSPAN="3", as shown here:

```
<TR> <!-- this is the start of row one -->
<TD ROWSPAN="3">Span whole row </TD>
<TD>Column two </TD>
<TD>Column three </TD>
<TD>Column four </TD>
</TR>
```

Moving to row 2. The first column of row 2 is actually part of a cell spanned from row one, so there is no need to define a `<DT>` tag in row 2 for this cell. When creating complex tables, however, many people find it helpful to include a `<!-- comment -->` tag to indicate the existence of a spanned data cell in the row. Using this technique often goes a long way toward resolving any alignment problems you might encounter in a table. In the HTML source for this example, the inclusion of a `<!-- SPANNED ROW -->` comment indicates clearly that the row in fact contains four columns, even though only three data element tags have been defined.

The second row also includes the start of another spanned data cell, which this time needs to span two rows. You do this by using `ROWSPAN="2"`. The completed definition for row 2 of the table now looks like this:

```
<TR>  <!-- this is the start of row two -->
<!-- SPANNED ROW -->
<TD>Column two </TD>
<TD ROWSPAN="2">Span row two and three</TD>
<TD>Column four </TD>
</TR>
```

Finally, you need to define the third row of the table. In this row, there are only two new data cells because the two other cells are spanned from either the first or the second row. As before, be sure to include a comment tag to indicate where the spanned rows will appear in the current row, as shown here:

```
<TR> <!-- this is the start of row three -->
<!-- SPANNED ROW -->
<TD>Column two </TD>
<!-- SPANNED ROW -->
<TD>Column four </TD>
```

After you have typed the entire table, save it to your hard drive with a name like `rowspan.html`, and then test it by using Navigator 2.0.

Note: There is no physical requirement in the HTML specification for including placeholder comments. Including them, however, does tend to make your HTML source more understandable and greatly reduces the chance of alignment and layout mistakes. You might also want to consider using `<!-- SPANNED COLUMN -->` as a placeholder for spanned data cells.

Nesting Tables

To add even greater flexibility to your tables, you can embed entire tables inside any data cell, as shown in Figure 8.11. To do this, all you need to do is include a new <TABLE>...</TABLE> block within any <TD>...</TD> cell. In fact, you can even include tables, within tables, and within tables if you so desire.

To demonstrate how you embed one table within another, take a look at the HTML source used to create the Web page shown in Figure 8.11:

```
<TABLE BORDER WIDTH= "80%">
<TR> <!-- This is the start of row one of the main table -->
<TD>Column 1 </TD> <!-- This is column 1 of row one -->
<TD> <!-- this data cell has an entire table embedded inside it -->
    <TABLE BORDER=4 CELLSPACING=0 WIDTH= "100%">
    <TR> <!-- This is the start of row one of the embedded table -->
    <TD>Column 1 </TD>
    <TD>Column 2 </TD>
    </TR>
    <TR> <!-- This is the start of row two of the embedded table -->
    <TD>Column 1 </TD>
    <TD>Column 2 </TD>
    </TR>
    </TABLE>
</TD>   <!-- this data cell has an entire table embedded inside it -->
</TR>
<TR> <!-- This is the start of row two of the main table -->
<TD>Column 1 </TD>
<TD>Column 2 </TD>
</TR>
</TABLE>
```

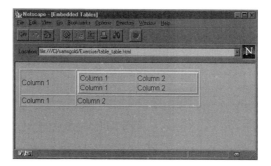

Figure 8.11.
Entire tables can be embedded inside any data cell.

In the HTML source code shown above, the second cell (column 2) of row one in the main table has a <TABLE>...</TABLE> block definition inside its <TD> tags. Using this technique allows you to define a new table which will be displayed inside a single cell of the main table.

Creating Blank and Empty Data Cells

Tables displayed by Navigator 2.0 can represent an empty data cell in one of two ways. If you write `<DT>…</DT>`, the Web browser displays what is called a blank cell. A blank cell is one that has no border.

Alternatively, if you include either a `<BR>` tag or a character entity called a nonbreaking space as the only text in a data cell, the Web browser displays the cell with a border. To use a nonbreaking space, you would write `<DT> </DT>`. Figure 8.12 demonstrates the appearance of both a blank and an empty data cell.

The cell shown below the "Blank Cell" heading has no border around the cell area, while the cell shown below the "Empty Cell" heading does have a border. To create the example shown in Figure 8.12 for yourself, use the following HTML source code:

```
<TABLE BORDER WIDTH="100%" >
<TR>
<TH>Blank Cell</TH>
<TH>Empty Cell</TH>
</TR>
<TR>
<TH> </TH>          <!-- this creates a blank cell -->
<TH> </TH>     <!-- this creates an empty cell -->
</TR>
</TABLE>
```

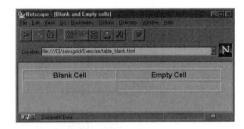

Figure 8.12.
Data cells can be either blank or empty.

Table Alignment Options

To complete this discussion of tables, one final group of options needs to be examined. Figure 8.13 demonstrates some of the possible table alignment options available. Unlink the alignment options discussed previously that control the alignment of cells within a table. This last set of options controls the alignment of tables within a Web page.

Figure 8.13.
Examples of table alignment.

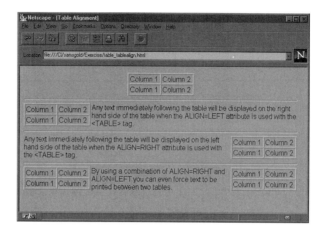

Table Justification

By placing a table within a `<DIV>` tag block, you can cause the alignment attributes normally associated with the `<DIV>` tag to be applied to a table. For example, to center a table as shown in Figure 8.13, you would enter this:

```
<DIV ALIGN="CENTER">
<TABLE BORDER>
<TR>
<TD>Column 1 </TD>
<TD>Column 2 </TD>
</TR>
<TR>
<TD>Column 1 </TD>
<TD>Column 2 </TD>
</TR>
</TABLE>.
</DIV>
```

You can also align a table with the right side of the Web page by using `<DIV ALIGN="RIGHT">`.

Note: Some HTML tutorials refer to the `<CENTER>` tag as another means of centering a table. The `<CENTER>` tag, however, is currently being phased out in favor of the `<DIV>` tag.

Text Wrapping

The other three examples shown in Figure 8.13 demonstrate the different ways that the ALIGN attribute can be used when associated with the <TABLE> tag. When used with the <TABLE> tag, the ALIGN attribute can take a value of LEFT or RIGHT. It takes the following form:

```
<TABLE ALIGN="LEFT">
```

What the ALIGN attribute actually does, in this case, is control the placement of a table in relation to the text immediately following it in an HTML document. When ALIGN="LEFT" is set, the table is aligned with the left side of the Web page, and any text that follows it is wrapped down the right side of the table. On the other hand, when ALIGN="RIGHT" is used, the table is aligned with the right side of the Web page, and any text that follows the table is wrapped down the table's left side.

Regardless of which value you use, the HTML source required to create this effect looks similar to this:

```
<TABLE BORDER ALIGN="LEFT">
<TR>
<TD>Column 1 </TD>
<TD>Column 2 </TD>
</TR>
<TR>
<TD>Column 1 </TD>
<TD>Column 2 </TD>
</TR>
</TABLE>
<DIV>Any text immediately following the table will be
displayed on the right-hand side of the table
when the ALIGN="LEFT" attribute is used with the &lt;TABLE&gt; tag.</DIV>
```

Note: The text following the table has been wrapped in a <DIV> tag rather than the more common <P>, because the text may not wrap correctly around the table when some versions of Netscape Navigator encounter a <P> tag. More specifically, a blank line is added to the start of the wrapped text.

The final example at the bottom of Figure 8.13 uses both the ALIGN="LEFT" attribute and the ALIGN="RIGHT" attribute in two separate tables to produce the "text bounded by two tables" effect. To create this effect, your HTML source should take the following format:

```
<TABLE BORDER ALIGN="LEFT">
<TR>
<TD>Column 1 </TD>
<TD>Column 2 </TD>
</TR>            .
<TR>
```

```
<TD>Column 1 </TD>
<TD>Column 2 </TD>
</TR>
</TABLE>
<TABLE BORDER ALIGN="RIGHT">
<TR>
<TD>Column 1 </TD>
<TD>Column 2 </TD>
</TR>
<TR>
<TD>Column 1 </TD>
<TD>Column 2 </TD>
</TR>
</TABLE>
<DIV>The text to be placed between the two tables goes here,
 and once again it is surrounded by a &ltDIV&gt tag</DIV>
```

Summary

Now that you have completed this chapter, you should be able to create many kinds of tables that include spanned columns and rows, row and column headings, and table captions. In addition, this chapter has taught you how to align text within a data cell and how to align tables within a Web page.

To recap what you have learned, Table 8.1 lists all the new tags you have explored in this chapter.

Table 8.1. New tags discussed in this chapter.

Tag	Description
<TABLE>…</TABLE>	The wrapper tag that surrounds a table.
BORDER	Indicates whether the table should be drawn with or without a border. BORDER can also have a value indicating the width of the border.
CELLSPACING	The amount of space between the cells in the table.
CELLPADDING	The amount of space between the edges of the cell and its contents.
WIDTH	The width of the table on the page, in either exact pixel values or as a percentage of page width.
ALIGN	Determines the alignment of a table.
<TR>…</TR>	The table row tag.
ALIGN	The horizontal alignment of the contents of the cells within this row. Possible values are LEFT, RIGHT, and CENTER.

continues

201

Table 8.1. continued

Tag	Description
VALIGN	The vertical alignment of the contents of the cells within this row. Possible values are TOP, MIDDLE, BOTTOM, and BASELINE.
<TD>...</TD>	The data cell tag.
ALIGN	The horizontal alignment of the contents of the cell. Possible values are LEFT, RIGHT, and CENTER.
VALIGN	The vertical alignment of the contents of the cell. Possible values are TOP, MIDDLE, BOTTOM, and BASELINE.
ROWSPAN	The number of rows this cell will span.
COLSPAN	The number of columns this cell will span.
NOWRAP	Do not automatically wrap the contents of this cell.
WIDTH	The width of this column of cells, in exact pixel values or as a percentage of the table width.
<TH>...</TH>	The data cell header tag. (Recognizes the same attributes and the <TD> tag.)
<CAPTION>...</CAPTION>	The tag that displays titles above the table or captions below the table.
ALIGN	The position of the caption. Possible values are TOP and BOTTOM.

Workshop

The first section of the Workshop lists some of the common questions people ask about the World Wide Web along with a brief answer to each. Next is a quiz about the chapter you have just read. If you have problems answering any of the questions in the quiz, you can turn to Appendix E, "Answers to Quiz Questions."

Q&A

Q I see no mention of images with relation to tables. Is it possible to include an image in a data cell?

A Yes, you can. Because you have not yet learned about inline images, however, the discussion of this subject has been left to Chapter 10, "Adding Images to your Web Documents."

In fact, you can include any HTML elements, including hyperlinks, images, headings, other tables, and even special features such as embedded plug-ins and Java applets, inside a data cell.

Q A friend of mine mentioned that the table specification includes the capability to change the background color of individual cells. Is this possible?

A Currently, you cannot change the background color of cells in Navigator 2.0, but you can change the color of the text by using the <FONT> tag. This feature might, however, be introduced in a future release of Netscape Navigator.

Quiz

1. What tag is used to indicate a heading cell?

2. What are the four possible values associated with the VALIGN attribute?

3. What attribute do you need to include in the <CAPTION> tag to define a caption that is printed below a table?

4. How do you alter the size of the border around a table?

5. What attribute is used to define data cells that span two or more rows of a table?

Exercises

1. As usual, your first task is to create the 08note.html document for your HTML reference collection. Be sure to include an example of all the table tags, using all the available attributes. Also, don't forget to sign the document using the <ADDRESS> tag, and add a hyperlink to point back to the html_contents.html document and one in the contents document to point to 08note.html.

2. Your second task is to attempt to re-create the Web page shown in Figure 8.14. To create this table, you need to use many of the main table tags and attributes presented in this chapter.

Figure 8.14.

Your mission for Exercise 2 (should you accept it) is to re-create this complex table.

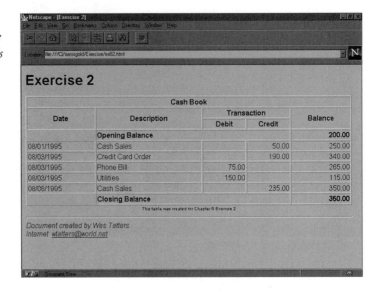

If you are have difficulties getting the table to work, the actual source code used to created this example is listed next. You should, however, first attempt to create the table yourself. Here is the code:

```
<HTML>
<HEAD>
<TITLE>Exercise 2</TITLE>
</HEAD>
<BODY>
<H1>Exercise 2</H1>
<TABLE BORDER WIDTH="100%" >
<CAPTION ALIGN="BOTTOM"><FONT SIZE="1">
This table was created for Chapter 8 Exercise 2
</FONT></CAPTION>
<TR> <!-- This is the start of row one -->
<TH COLSPAN="5">Cash Book</TH>
<!-- SPANNED COLUMN -->
<!-- SPANNED COLUMN -->
<!-- SPANNED COLUMN -->
<!-- SPANNED COLUMN -->
</TR>
<TR> <!-- This is the start of row two -->
<TH ROWSPAN="2">Date</TH>
<TH ROWSPAN="2">Description</TH>
<TH COLSPAN="2">Transaction</TH>
<!-- SPANNED COLUMN -->
<TH ROWSPAN="2">Balance</TH>
</TR>
<TR> <!-- This is the start of row three -->
<!-- SPANNED ROW -->
<!-- SPANNED ROW -->
<TH>Debit</TH>
<TH>Credit</TH>
<!-- SPANNED ROW -->
```

```
</TR>
<TR> <!-- This is the start of row four -->
<TH></TH> <!-- this is an empty cell -->
<TH ALIGN="LEFT" COLSPAN="3">Opening Balance</TH>
<!-- SPANNED COLUMN -->
<!-- SPANNED COLUMN -->
<TH ALIGN="RIGHT">200.00</TH>
</TR>
<TR> <!-- This is the start of row five -->
<TD>08/01/1995</TD>
<TD>Cash Sales</TD>
<TD ALIGN="RIGHT"><BR></TD> <!-- use the <BR> tag to indicate a blank cell -->
<TD ALIGN="RIGHT">50.00</TD>
<TD ALIGN="RIGHT">250.00</TD>
</TR>
<TR> <!-- This is the start of row six -->
<TD>08/03/1995</TD>
<TD>Credit Card Order</TD>
<TD ALIGN="RIGHT"><BR></TD>
<TD ALIGN="RIGHT">190.00</TD>
<TD ALIGN="RIGHT">340.00</TD>
</TR>
<TR><!-- This is the start of row seven -->
<TD>08/03/1995</TD>
<TD>Phone Bill</TD>
<TD ALIGN="RIGHT">75.00</TD>
<TD ALIGB="RIGHT"><BR></TD>
<TD ALIGN="RIGHT">265.00</TD>
</TR>
<TR> <!-- This is the start of row eight -->
<TD>08/03/1995</TD>
<TD>Utilities</TD>
<TD ALIGN="RIGHT">150.00</TD>
<TD ALIGB="RIGHT"><BR></TD>
<TD ALIGN="RIGHT">115.00</TD>
</TR>
<TR> <!-- This is the start of row nine -->
<TD>08/08/1995</TD>
<TD>Cash Sales</TD>
<TD ALIGB="RIGHT"><BR></TD>
<TD ALIGN="RIGHT">235.00</TD>
<TD ALIGN="RIGHT">350.00</TD>
</TR>
<TR> <!-- This is the start of row ten -->
<TH></TH> <!-- this is an empty cell -->
<TH ALIGN="LEFT" COLSPAN="3">Closing Balance</TH>
<!-- SPANNED COLUMN -->
<!-- SPANNED COLUMN -->
<TH ALIGN="RIGHT">350.00</TH>
</TR>
</TABLE>
<HR>
<ADDRESS>Document created by Wes Tatters<BR>
Internet: <A HREF="mailto:wtatters@world.net">wtatters@world.net</A>
</ADDRESS>
</BODY>
</HTML>
```

9

Working with Links and URLs

Back in Chapter 6, "Linking Web Pages Together," you learned how the <A> tag is used to link HTML documents together. At that time, you were told that the <A> can also be used to indicate links to other Internet services and files.

In this chapter you will learn how to use the <A> tag to point to these Internet services, and you will discover the purpose for the special <A> tag called a Reference Anchor. You will learn about these HTML techniques by exploring the following topics:

- ☐ Links and anchors within a document
- ☐ URLs explained
- ☐ Types of URLs

Linking to Anchors Within a Document

All the hyperlinks discussed in Chapter 6 were designed specifically to create links between HTML documents, either on your local hard drive or on a remote Web site. But what about creating hyperlinks that point to different parts of the same Web page? Or for that matter, hyperlinks that point to different sections of another Web page?

The Reference Anchor

To create a link that points to any part of a Web page other than its top, you first need to place an *anchor* in the target Web page to indicate the hyperlink's destination. An anchor is a bit like a section heading in a book; it is a point in the document that can easily be identified and can act as a target for a hyperlink.

When you create a basic hyperlink, there is no need for an anchor in the target Web page because your browser automatically displays any new page starting at the top. To point to any other part of a Web page, however, you need some sort of reference point.

To create this reference point, you use a special form of the <A> tag called a reference anchor. When used as a reference anchor, the <A> tag takes the following form:

```
<A NAME="anchorname">Displayed text</A>
```

Unlike previous <A> tag examples that used the HREF attribute, when creating a reference anchor, you need to use the NAME attribute. Exactly what value is assigned to the NAME attribute is up to you. All that is important is that the value assigned to each anchor in a single HTML document is unique. When possible, however, the name should be reasonably descriptive of the section of a Web page it anchors.

The other major difference between a reference anchor and the reference links discussed in Chapter 6 is that the `Displayed text` included between the `<A>` and `</A>` tags is not highlighted or emphasized in any way. Apart from the fact that the text is surrounded by an `<A>` tag, it is no different from standard text.

That having been said, you can alter the appearance of this text using character formatting or any of the heading styles. If, however, you want to use anchor text that is displayed with a heading style, you must place the reference anchor tag inside the heading tag, and not the other way around. In other words, this form is correct:

```
<H1><A NAME="contents">Page Contents</A></H1>
```

And this form is incorrect:

```
<A NAME="contents"><H1>Page Contents</H1></A>
```

The Reference Link

After you have defined an anchor in your target page, you can create a hyperlink, either in the same HTML document or in a separate one that points to that anchor.

To create a hyperlink that points to a reference anchor, you use the `<A>` tag in one of the following forms:

```
<A HREF="directory/name.html#anchorname">hotspot text</A>
```

```
<A HREF="http://domain.name/directory/name.html#anchorname">hotspot text</A>
```

If you examine these two examples closely, you will see that the difference between these hyperlinks and those discussed in Chapter 6 is the inclusion of the # symbol followed by an *anchorname* at the end of the document URL.

When you click the hotspot text of either of these links, your Web browser first loads the appropriate Web page in the same way as was done in previous hyperlink examples. However, after the HTML source of the new Web page has been loaded, if there is a # symbol followed by an *anchorname* in the URL, the browser searches the new HTML document for an anchor reference that corresponds to the *anchorname*. If such an anchor reference tag is found, the Web page is scrolled down until the anchor reference is at the top of the Web browser's document window.

Note: When you're creating hyperlinks to reference anchor points within the current document, by taking full advantage of relative addressing, all you need to include in the HREF value is the anchor name. For example, `<A HREF="#bottom">` would point to a reference anchor named `bottom` located on the current page (probably at the bottom of the document).

▼ Exercise: Working with Anchors

To help you understand how reference anchors work, using your text editor, open the file called 05notes.html that you created in Chapter 5, "Basic HTML and the World Wide Web." When displayed in your Web browser, this document should look something like the Web page shown in Figure 9.1.

Figure 9.1.

05notes.html.

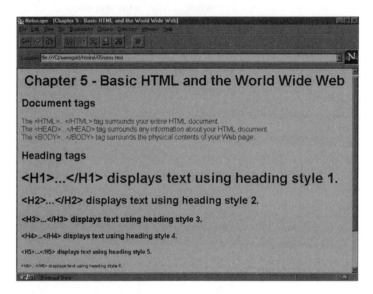

To enhance the table of contents for your HTML reference, in this exercise you need to add a reference anchor to each topic heading in 05notes.html and later to the other chapter references as well.

First, locate the line that creates the Document tags heading, and add a reference anchor with the name Document_tags, as shown here:

```
<H2><A NAME="document_tags">Document tags</A></H2>
```

Then do the same for Heading tags:

```
<H2><A NAME="heading_tags">Heading tags</A></H2>
```

And finally, do the same for the Paragraph Formatting tags heading as well:

```
<H2><A NAME="paragraph_tags">Paragraph Formatting tags</A></H2>
```

After you save the new 05notes.html document, open the html_content.html document. In this document, you will add hyperlinks that point to each of the new anchors in 05notes.html.

Below the Chapter 5 hyperlink and the descriptive paragraph that follows it, include a separate hyperlink for all three anchors, using an unordered list to place each hyperlink onto a separate line. For each hyperlink, the HREF value consists of the document name, 05notes.html, followed by a #, and then the appropriate anchor name, as shown here:

```
<DT>
<A HREF="05notes.html"><H2>Chapter 5</H2></A>
<DD>
<P>This chapter discusses document tags, headings, character styles
and the comment tag. </P>
<UL>
<LI><A HREF="05notes.html#document_tags">Document Tags</A>
<LI><A HREF="05notes.html#heading_tags">Heading Tags</A>
<LI><A HREF="05notes.html#paragraph_tags">Paragraph Formatting tags</A>
</UL>
```

After you save the updated html_contents.html document and load it into Navigator 2.0, you should see a Web page that looks similar to the one shown in Figure 9.2. If you click any of the new hyperlinks, the appropriate section of 05notes.html is displayed onscreen.

Figure 9.2.
Reference anchor tags in a document.

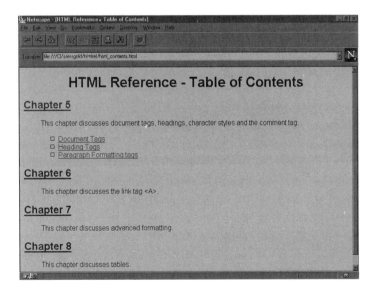

Note: This exercise demonstrates the embedding of an unordered list within the definition section of a definition list. (In Chapter 7, "Advanced Formatting Options," the first exercise turned the table of contents into a definition list.) In much the same way as an ordered list can be embedded in an unordered list, or vice versa, you can also embed ordered and unordered lists within a definition list; however, you should embed them only within the definition section.

URLs Explained

In Chapter 6 you learned how the `http:` and `file:` URLs are used with the `<A>` tag to indicate the location of HTML documents both on local hard drives and across the Internet. These are, however, only two of the forms a URL can take when referencing a location, file, or service on the World Wide Web and more generally on the Internet as well.

The remainder of this chapter discusses the various other forms of URLs that can be associated with a hyperlink. But first, as a quick refresher, take another look at exactly what a URL is.

What Is a URL?

A URL, or uniform resource locator, is part of a small group of standards designed for the Internet and more specifically the World Wide Web. URLs exist solely to provide a simple and effective method of identifying any file, service, or resource located anywhere on the Internet, using a simple and consistent addressing method.

And, more significantly, a URL not only indicates the location of the file or service, but also indicates the type of server or service the URL points to. This is very important when you're dealing with a system like the World Wide Web, which can access many different Internet services.

Parts of a URL

As mentioned in Chapter 6, there are normally four main parts to a URL:

☐ The communications protocol
☐ The domain name and port address
☐ The directory path
☐ The filename

When combined into a URL, these four parts look like this:

`protocol://domain.name:port/directory_path/filename.extension`

It is important, however, to point out right now that not all URLs demand the presence of all four parts, as you will learn later in this chapter.

The Communications Protocol

Every URL you create must include a communications protocol definition. The communications protocol is used by your Web browser to control the method used to access the file

or resource specified in the remainder of the URL. Table 9.1 lists all the protocols currently supported by most Web browsers. For more information on the specifics of each of these protocols, refer to the appropriate topic in the later section titled "Types of URLs."

Table 9.1. URL communications protocols.

Protocol	Service
`file:`	In addition to referencing information located on the Internet, most WWW browsers can also access files stored on your local hard drive. If `file:` is followed by a `///C¦`, the URL points to a file on your local drive C:.
`ftp:`	If the URL link points to a file stored on an anonymous FTP server, or private FTP server, it must begin with this definition.
`http:`	All HTML documents are usually stored on a WWW server. HTTP (hypertext transfer protocol) refers to the communications protocol used by these servers.
`https:`	This protocol indicates the use of a special type of WWW server that supports secure transactions. When the `https:` protocol is used, information sent between the Web browser and Web server is encoded.
`gopher:`	All WWW browsers can also navigate their way around a Gopher server by using this protocol definition.
`mailto:`	This is a special type of URL that enables you to send an e-mail message.
`news:`	Links that point to Usenet newsgroups must be declared using this protocol.
`snews:`	As with the secure `http` protocol, there is also a secure Usenet news protocol supported by Navigator 2.0.
`telnet:`	To indicate that a link needs to open a telnet session, the URL begins with `telnet:`. Most WWW browsers can't open a telnet session themselves. Instead, they usually launch a separate telnet client when such links are selected.
`wais:`	In theory, all WWW browsers can access WAIS (Wide Area Information System) servers. Use of the WAIS protocol, however, is slowly being phased out in place of WAIS gateways such as WAISgate, which is located at `http://www.wais.com/`.

The Domain Name and Port Address

Following the protocol definition, the next item of information to be defined by a URL is the location of the server housing the file or resource pointed to by the hyperlink.

As with all other Internet services, this can be done by using either the domain name of the server or its corresponding IP address. The use of IP addresses, however, is frowned on by most of the WWW community because it does not describe the name of the site that the URL refers to in an easily understandable form.

Note: An IP address is a unique number assigned to each individual computer connected to the Internet. It is represented by four separate 8-bit numbers that take the form 192.190.215.5. Due to its appearance, the IP address is often referred to as a dotted quad.

When the protocol definition and the domain name are combined using the // symbol, the result is a URL definition that accurately indicates the location and type of server the URL points to.

There is one additional piece of information that might sometimes be required to provide a complete definition of a server's location. By default, WWW browsers use the protocol definition to determine the port number they should use to access a specific server. On certain occasions, however, when a server uses a port different from the default, a separate port number might need to be appended to the domain name. To do this, simply append the port number to the domain name, separated by a colon, as in http://www.netscape.com:80/.

The Directory Path and Filename

Depending on the type of URL, you might need to include a directory path and possibly a filename at the end of the URL to complete the definition. The directory path should start at the top directory associated with a Web server and continue down to the directory where the specified file is located.

Note: When including a directory, as mentioned previously, people from the MS-DOS world need to remember to use a forward slash (/) rather than the backslash (\) associated with pathnames on their computer system.

> **Tip:** Where there is only a directory path in a URL, and no filename, be sure to add a trailing / to the pathname. If you don't, some older Web browsers might attempt to treat the last directory in the path as a file, which can lead to unpredictable results. But most often you will receive "file not found" errors.

The File Extension

The file extension is the one part of a URL that has not yet been examined in any detail, but it is important because it serves to demonstrate a popular misconception many people have regarding the `http:` protocol.

The `http:` protocol does not indicate the presence of a Web page. Instead, it indicates only the communications protocol. When a Web browser looks at a URL, it uses the file extension to determine the type of file associated with the URL. Based on the file extension, the Web browser then decides how the file should be displayed.

To demonstrate this situation, choose any of the HTML documents you have created so far, and resave the document with a `.txt` extension rather than an `.html` extension. Now load the new file into Navigator 2.0. When you do so, instead of seeing a properly formatted Web page, you will see the contents of the file as it appeared in your text editor, tags and all.

As a result, it is vitally important that all of your HTML documents have an `.html` or `.htm` extension.

Spaces and Other Special Characters

As with HTML documents, the characters that can be directly included as part of a URL are limited to those in the 7-bit ASCII character set. More specifically, this means the letters a through z and A through Z, the numbers 0 through 9, and the symbols minus (-), plus (+), underscore (_), dot (.), and dollar sign ($). In addition, you cannot include a space inside a URL.

Nevertheless, at times you will need to include either a space or characters from the extended ISO-8859-1 character set as part of a URL. To do this, you must use an approach similar to that adopted for character entities. This time, however, instead of using the ampersand (&) symbol, the percentage (%) sign is used. Also, instead of using a number to represent the character, you must use the hexadecimal number that corresponds to the position of the character in the ASCII table.

For example, when indicating files maintained on Gopher sites, you need to include the name of the menu item associated with the file. On Gopher servers, menu items can contain a space.

To represent the spaces in a menu item when it is included as part of a URL, you type %20 rather than each space, as shown here:

```
gopher://gopher.tc.umn.edu:70/11/Information%20About%20Gopher
```

For the time being, don't be concerned about what the rest of the URL means, because this is discussed in the following section.

Note: A full list of the hexadecimal numbers that correspond to each character in the ASCII table is included as part of the character entities table in Appendix B, "Character Entities."

Types of URLs

The rest of this chapter examines the appearance of each protocol outlined in Table 9.1.

HTTP

The Hypertext Transfer Protocol (http) is the communications protocol used by a Web browser when communicating with a Web server. Just about every Web page you will ever visit when exploring the World Wide Web is, in fact, transferred to your computer by using the http: protocol.

What makes the World Wide Web so powerful is that people using it don't need to worry about how the Web pages they select are transferred to their computers, because the Web browser performs all the required communications tasks without any user intervention.

To make this system work, it is up to you as a Web publisher to provide the Web browser with all the information it needs, to first work out which communications protocol to use, then to locate the correct computer system and finally access the appropriate file or resource. You do this by providing the Web browser with hyperlinks that contain properly formed URLs.

As you have already discovered in Chapter 6, a URL that uses the http: protocol takes the following form:

```
protocol://domain.name/directory_name/filename.html
```

Where protocol: is replaced by http:, giving this:

```
http://domain.name/directory_name/filename.html
```

Note: When creating hyperlinks to join the different pages of your own Web sites together, it is common practice to create URLs that omit the `http://` specification and the domain name. Doing this enables you to take advantage of relative addressing, something that makes relocating your Web pages relatively easy.

As mentioned in Table 9.1, one version of the `http:` protocol is designed specifically for use with secure Web servers such as the Netscape Communications Commerce server. To indicate that a page should be transmitted using a secure, encoded protocol, you must use a URL that looks like this:

```
https://domain.name/directory_name/filename.html
```

It is important to note, however, that there will be little or no cause for you to use the `https:` protocol with a URL associated with a hyperlink. As a rule, this protocol is restricted to script-based actions that deal with Web forms and interactive pages. (See Chapter 17, "Forms and CGI," for more information about forms and scripts.)

Since the subject of secure transactions and the specifics of the `https:` protocol are outside the scope of this book, if you want to learn more about Internet and World Wide Web security, you should take a look at the following:

```
http://home.netscape.com/newsref/ref/index.html
http://home.netscape.com/newsref/ref/internet-security.html
http://home.netscape.com/newsref/ref/netscape-security.html
```

Files

The `file:` protocol is technically not a true Internet communications protocol. Instead, it represents the internal computer procedures used to access files from your local hard drive. When you select the **O**pen File item from the **F**ile menu in Navigator 2.0, it is basically the `file:` protocol that is used to load the file from the hard drive.

A URL using the `file:` protocol takes the following format:

```
file:///drive/directory_name/filename.html
```

As you learned in Chapter 6, the drive specification for the file protocol can take various forms, depending on the type of computer system you are using. To refresh your memory, refer to Table 6.1 in Chapter 6 for a list of the possible combinations.

Note: By taking advantage of relative addressing, you can develop and test an entire Web site on your local computer and then move it onto a remote Web site when you are satisfied that everything is working properly. If you specify only a relative path and filename for each Web page used by your Web site, your Web browser inserts the appropriate `http:` or `file:` protocol automatically, depending on whether you are online or offline.

It does this by defaulting in the protocol used by the currently displayed page. If you load your first Web page locally, all the relative hyperlinks that follow will also be made locally. Alternatively, if you load your first Web page from your Web site, all the relative hyperlinks will also be loaded from the Web site.

Gopher

Just about every Web browser currently available can be used to access files and menus maintained on Gopher servers. To include a Gopher site as the destination for a hyperlink, you use a URL that takes the following form:

```
gopher://domain.name:port/11/path
```

In place of `domain.name`, insert the domain name of the Gopher site you want to connect to. The `port` field usually contains `70`, which indicates the standard port for a Gopher server. And following the `/11/`, you need to enter the path and name of the Gopher menu or action you want to use.

For example, to access the "Information About Gopher" menu on the University of Minnesota Gopher server (see Figure 9.3), you would use this URL:

```
gopher://gopher.tc.umn.edu:70/11/Information%20About%20Gopher
```

If you look closely at this URL, you will notice that the spaces between `Information`, `About`, and `Gopher` have been replaced with `%20` as discussed previously. You need to do this because a URL cannot contain spaces. The `%20` symbol represents a space, which the WWW server will translate into the correct form at its end.

There is also a special form of the Gopher URL reserved for the top menu of each server. This menu is a bit like the home page of a Web site. To open this menu, you need not include a path or the full `/11/` section. As a result, to access the top menu of the Minnesota Gopher server (see Figure 9.4) you use this URL:

```
gopher://gopher2.tc.umn.edu:70/1
```

Figure 9.3.
Use %20 *to replace any spaces in the Gopher menu path or name.*

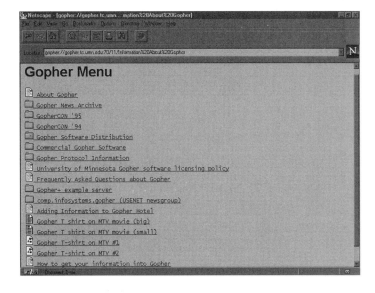

Figure 9.4.
You do not need to include a path when accessing the top menu of a Gopher server.

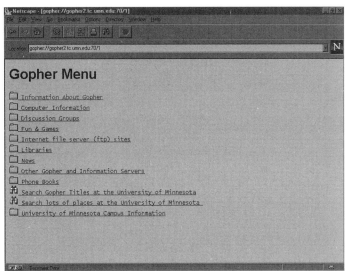

After you open a Gopher server using Navigator 2.0, you can navigate your way around it using the familiar hotlinks provided by the WWW browser. You can access all the menus and features offered by the Gopher server and even request files via FTP.

Newsgroups

To include a hyperlink that points to a Usenet newsgroup on your Web pages, you need to use a URL that takes the following form:

```
news:newsgroup.name
```

The first thing you should notice about this type of URL is the absence of the // characters. When defining a Usenet URL, you simply start with the news: protocol and follow it immediately with the newsgroup name. When this form is used, a Web browser attempts to open the indicated newsgroup using the Usenet news server configured by the user.

There is also a second form of the Usenet URL, which is currently supported only by Web browsers such as Navigator 2.0. When a newsgroup is located on a specific news server, you can specify the domain name of that server as part of the Usenet URL, as shown here:

```
news://domain.name/newsgroup.name
```

The most common use for this type of URL is for accessing a secure news server, like the one operated by Netscape Communications. Unlike most Usenet servers, the contents of which are visible to the entire Internet, the contents of the secure news server at Netscape Communications can be viewed only by people using Netscape Navigator. In addition, whenever you post an article to a secure server, the contents of the article are encoded before being transmitted across the Internet.

To access a newsgroup on a secure news server, you use a URL that takes the following form:

```
snews://domain.name/newsgroup.name
```

For example, to create a hyperlink that points to the netscape.testdrive newsgroup shown in Figure 9.5, which is located on the secure news server at secnews.netscape.com, you would write this:

```
<A HREF="snews://secnews.netscape.com/netscape.testdrive">
```

Anonymous FTP

To create a hyperlink that points to a file located on an anonymous FTP server, you use a URL that looks like this:

```
ftp://domain.name/directory_path/filename.extension
```

When you click a hyperlink that contains a URL with an ftp: protocol, your Web browser attempts to establish an anonymous FTP session with the selected FTP server. After the session has been established, the file indicated in the URL is downloaded to your local computer.

Figure 9.5.
When you click a hyperlink that points to a newsgroup, Navigator 2.0 automatically starts its built-in newsgroup reader.

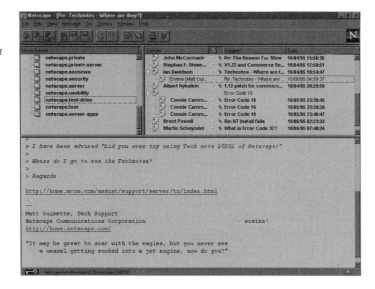

There is also a second form for URLs that uses the `ftp:` protocol. If you don't want to point to a specific file, but instead to a directory on an FTP server, you can do so by using a URL that takes this format:

```
ftp://domain.name/directory_path/
```

Note: As mentioned previously, always be sure to include a trailing slash (/) following the directory path. Most Web browsers can determine whether you are referring to a file or a directory, but to be on the safe side, including the / makes your intentions clear.

Private FTP

Not all FTP servers allow access via anonymous FTP. For those that don't, you must have a user ID and password before you can retrieve any files.

Although it is very rare that you would actually use this facility, there are provisions in the URL specification for a URL that can supply both the user ID and the password. To create such a hyperlink, you need to use a URL that takes this format:

```
ftp://userid:password@domain.name/directory_path/filename.extension
```

The *userid* is replaced by the username or login name for the FTP server and the password…well, you get the idea.

> **Caution:** If you choose to include this type of URL in a Web page, you run the risk of allowing everyone who visits the page to learn your user ID and password, because they will both be clearly visible to anyone who bothers to look.

telnet:

The `telnet:` protocol is about the only protocol supported by your Web browser that does not use the Web browser for its communications. Instead, when anyone clicks a hyperlink that has a `telnet:` URL associated with it, the Web browser attempts to start a separate telnet program.

Telnet URLs can take one of two formats:

`telnet:domain.name`

`telnet:loginname@domain.name.`

In the first format, the `domain.name` must be the name of a valid telnet server. When you click a hyperlink associated with such a URL, the Web browser passes the `domain.name` to the separate telnet application.

In the second format, the `loginname` field is used to indicate the login name that the user needs to use to log onto the telnet server. As a rule, however, this information is not passed directly to the telnet program by the Web browser. Instead, a small message box is displayed by the browser that contains a message telling the user to `"Login using loginname"`.

wais:

Over the past year or so, the `wais:` protocol has fallen very much into disuse. This has happened for a number of reasons, but the main reason is that the development of WAIS gateways has provided greatly improved methods of access to WAIS databases.

Of all the gateways currently available, the most notable one is operated by Wais Inc. (an America Online company). To learn more about WAISgate, the gateway provided by Wais Inc., point your Web browser to `http://www.wais.com/`.

mailto:

The final type of URL currently available to Web publishers uses the `mailto:` protocol. When you place a `mailto:` URL inside a hyperlink, clicking the hyperlink causes the Web browser to open an e-mail window where the Web user can compose a message and then send it to the person nominated in the URL.

A `mailto:` URL takes the following format:

`mailto:email@address`

By far the most common use of `mailto:` URLs is as part of your signature, inside an `<ADDRESS>` tag. For example, to spice up the `<ADDRESS>` example shown in Figure 7.12 in Chapter 7, you could write this:

```
<ADDRESS>
<B>Wes Tatters</B>
Internet: <A HREF="mailto:wtatters@world.net">wtatters@world.net</A>
Microsoft:<A HREF="mailto:wtatters@msn.com">wtatters@msn.com</A>
CompuServe:<A HREF="mailto:100036.174@compuserve.com">
100036.174@compuserve.com </A>
</ADDRESS>
```

In this example, each of my e-mail addresses has been associated with a hyperlink that includes a `mailto:` URL. Now, when anyone clicks either of these links, an e-mail message window is displayed where people can send me messages.

Summary

In this chapter you have learned how to create anchors on your Web page and how to create hyperlinks that point to them. In addition, you have learned about the types of protocols that can be included in a URL.

With three days of study now behind you, you are well on your way to becoming an accomplished Web publisher. In fact, with what you have learned so far, there is really nothing stopping you from starting to create your own Web pages. Most Web pages, however, contain more than just text and hyperlinks. They also contain images, movies, and sound files. Tomorrow, on Day 4, "Enhancing Your Web Page's Visual Appearance," you will learn all about adding images and other multimedia files to your Web page.

Workshop

The first section of the Workshop lists some of the common questions people ask about the World Wide Web along with a brief answer to each. Next is a quiz about the chapter you have just read. If you have problems answering any of the questions in the quiz, you can turn to Appendix E, "Answers to Quiz Questions."

Q&A

Q **I've tried to set up anchors and links, but they never seem to work properly. What am I doing wrong?**

A There are two main reasons people encounter problems with anchors. First, unlike most other aspects of HTML publishing, the names you assign to anchors are case sensitive. This means that if you type "TOP" as an anchor, using "#top" in the hyperlink won't work.

Second, a link might in fact be working properly although it does not appear to operate as advertised. If you click a link that points to an anchor which is already visible, the Web browser does not scroll the anchor to the top of the screen.

Q **I created a Web page that includes hyperlinks that point to all the files I've found useful. These files are located on anonymous FTP servers all over the Internet. The problem is that when I click some of the links, I am told to try again later. What's going on?**

A When setting up an FTP server, an organization needs to set some sort of limit on the number of people who can retrieve files simultaneously. What is happening when you click your hyperlinks is that your Web browser is being told by the FTP server that it has reached its connection limit. At this stage, there is nothing you can do but try again later.

Quiz

1. What does a reference anchor look like?
2. What symbol is used in a URL to indicate the location of a reference anchor?
3. What type of URL would you use to download a file located on any anonymous FTP server?
4. Which protocol would you use for a URL that points to a secure news server?
5. Why would you use the https: protocol?

Exercises

1. As usual, your first task is to create the 09note.html document for your HTML reference collection. Be sure to include an example of a reference anchor and its corresponding hyperlink. You should also include an example of each URL discussed in the chapter. Don't forget to sign the document using the <ADDRESS> tag, this time using a mailto: URL to add a hyperlink to your e-mail address. As before, add a hyperlink to point back to the html_contents.html document and one in the contents document to point to 09note.html as well.

2. While you're working on the html_contents.html document, your second task is to work back through all the pages you have already created and add reference anchors for the different sections in each document, as you did for 05note.html in the earlier exercise "Working with Anchors." After you have added the appropriate anchors, place hyperlinks to each anchor in html_contents.html. Also, while you're at it, update the <ADDRESS> tag in each document to include a hyperlink for your e-mail address.

DAY 4

Enhancing Your Web Page's Visual Appearance

10

Adding Images to Your Web Documents

Without a doubt, the one aspect of the World Wide Web that sets it apart from other Internet services is the capability to integrate images and text as part of a single Web page. It is this aspect of the World Wide Web that makes it the ideal tool for online publishing.

In this chapter you will learn how to integrate images with your Web pages by examining the following topics:

- ☐ Image formats
- ☐ Inline images
- ☐ Images with transparent backgrounds
- ☐ Images as hotlinks
- ☐ Adding document backgrounds
- ☐ Improving image performance

Image Formats

As with so many aspects of computing life, there are currently various methods, or formats, for storing images on a computer system. And as is the case for computer platforms, no two image formats are compatible.

To make matters worse, when you're dealing with the World Wide Web, only a few image formats are internally supported by most Web browsers. This means that if you want an image to be displayed directly on a Web page—as an inline image—you must first ensure that the image in question is stored in an appropriate format.

GIF

The Graphics Interchange Format (GIF) was originally developed by CompuServe Incorporated as a method for managing and displaying raster (or bitmap) images via CompuServe's own online service. Since its introduction, however, the GIF image format has become the de facto standard for image storage on just about all online computer systems.

To this end, the GIF image format has also been adopted by the World Wide Web community as the de facto standard format for inline images. According to documentation published by the W3 Consortium, as of December 1994, all graphical Web browsers now support the display of GIF images. In addition, as you will learn later, GIF is currently the only format that allows transparent images and image maps to be displayed on a Web page.

GIF does, however, have some limitations. First, any single image can contain no more than 256 separate colors. Second, due to the way images are stored, the size of GIF files often exceeds 100KB, making their use with slower modem-based Internet connections prohibitive.

Note: CompuServe recently announced the development of a new 24-bit GIF format that lets images include more than 16 million colors. This format, however, is not yet supported by any Web browsers.

JPEG Format

Due mainly to the excessive size of some GIF images, some Web browsers—including Navigator 2.0—now support the use of inline JPEG images.

The JPEG image format was developed by the Joint Photographic Experts Groups as a standard for the storage and presentation of full-color photographs. Included in its design is the capability to store images that contain more than 16 million colors, while at the same time using the smallest possible amount of storage space.

To achieve the extremely small files sizes possible using JPEG, however, there is often a slight degradation in image quality. It should be pointed out, though, that the visual effect is far less damaging than the losses involved in converting a 16-million-color photograph to GIF, in which case the number of colors would be reduced to 256.

On the plus side, JPEG images are often up to a tenth of the size of their corresponding GIF counterparts. As a result, it takes far less time to transfer JPEG images from a Web server to a Web page.

When examined in this light, JPEG format images appear to be the logical choice for all inline images. However, due to the limited number of Web browsers that currently support inline JPEG images, and the lack of support for transparent backgrounds, JPEG images are not yet in common use.

XBM Format

People who are familiar with the UNIX-based X Window or X11 environment will no doubt have encountered files stored in the X Bitmap format, or XBM for short. XBM is a raster image format designed specifically for the X Window environment, and as such it has little penetration onto other computer platforms.

Most Web browsers, however, can display inline XBM images, but as a rule, you should convert any such images to GIF format before using them with the World Wide Web.

10

Other Formats

When you encounter images stored in any other format, you have basically two options. First, you can convert the file to either GIF or JPEG format using any of the popular graphics manipulation and formatting programs currently available. To help you get started, these three programs all offer a good selection of image conversion and manipulation features:

☐ Microsoft Windows—Paint Shop Pro

```
ftp://ftp.jasc.com/pub/psp32bit.zip (Windows 95 & NT)
ftp://ftp.jasc.com/pub/psp311.zip (Windows 3.11)
http://www.jasc.com/psp.html (Additional Information)
```

☐ Macintosh—GraphicConverter

```
ftp://ftp.the.net/mirrors/ftp.utexas.edu/graphics/graphicconverter-222-
fat.hqx
```

☐ UNIX—ImageMagick

```
http://www.wizards.dupont.com/cristy/ImageMagick.html
```

Alternatively, if you don't want to convert the image from its original format, you can treat it as an external image. External images are not displayed as part of your Web page. Instead, you give the user access to them via a hyperlink. For example, to include the file `picture.tiff` as an external image, you would write something like this:

```
<A HREF="directory/picture.tiff">Hotspot text</A>
```

It is then up to the user to obtain a separate program or helper application that is capable of displaying the image in its native format. Netscape Communications lists various helper applications for different computer platforms at `http://home.netscape.com/assist/helper_apps/index.html`.

Inline Images

Having just read about the use of external images, you need to realize that the main thrust of image support on Web pages is oriented toward the use of inline images. Too many variables are involved in the use of external images to make their continued use practical for all but the most dedicated user. After all, users don't want to mess around with external viewers and helper programs just to view images at one or two sites. Instead, they want to look at documents in which the graphics and text are seamlessly integrated into a single Web page.

As a result, all the graphics, logos, images, and pictures you plan to use on your Web pages should be converted to GIF format or, when photorealistic quality is required, possibly JPEG format.

Obtaining Images to Use with Web Pages

This brings up an important point. How do you create the images that will be displayed on your Web pages? Or more to the point, if your artistic abilities aren't quite up to snuff, where can you find ready-made graphics and images?

In answer to the first question, many kinds of graphics and drawing programs are currently available, most of which can save images in GIF format. And if not, they will certainly be able to save the images in a format that one of the programs mentioned previously can read and then convert to GIF format. If you are looking for a good drawing program, paying a visit to `http://www2.ncsu.edu/bae/people/faculty/walker/hotlist/graphics.html` is not a bad idea. This site contains a directory of just about all the graphics and image-processing systems currently available anywhere on the Internet.

Regarding the second question, if you aren't an artist, you have several options. The first is to give it a go anyway! Get hold of a simple drawing program—for example, the Paint program that comes with Microsoft Windows—and experiment. If all you are doing is creating a few simple buttons, with a bit of effort, you will probably be able to produce quite usable results on your own.

On the other hand, if you are not happy with your own results, the World Wide Web itself is a valuable source of graphics and images. Various sites on the Internet contain collections of clip art, logos, buttons, rulers, and other pictures you can include in your own Web pages. The best way to locate such archives is by using a search program such as Lycos—`http://www.lycos.com/`. Trying using the word GIF in the search field. But for those of you who can't wait, try `http://aeiveos.wa.com/gif/gifs.html`. This is just one of the hundreds and possibly thousands of image archives currently available online.

If you can't find what you are looking for in any of the public archives, your next stop should be to check one of the commercial image libraries. These libraries contain tens of thousands of professionally digitized images and photographs that are copyright and royalty free. Some, such as PhotoDisc—`http://www.photodisc.com/`—even operate their own Web sites, where you can browse through an online catalog and arrange for the purchase of images you are interested in using.

The final option, if you are really serious about Web publishing, is to contract a graphic artist to produce your images. This option, however, can cost you a considerable amount of money. But on the plus side, a good graphic artist will also be able to help you design the complete visual layout for your Web pages.

10

The *<IMG>* Tag

After you have your GIF images ready to go, the next step in the process is to add them to your Web pages.

To indicate the location of an inline image on a Web page, you need to use the `<IMG>` tag. When used in an HTML document, the `<IMG>` tag takes the following form:

```
<IMG SRC="image.gif">
```

In its most basic form, the `<IMG>` tag takes only one attribute, and like the `<BR>` and `<HR>` tags discussed in previous chapters, it does not have a corresponding end tag. In the following sections you will learn about the other attributes that can be associated with the `<IMG>` tag, but for now, let's just deal with the `SRC` attribute.

The value you assign to the `SRC` attribute should be a URL that describes the location of the image to be displayed. It can be either an absolute or a relative address and can use the `http:`, `file:`, `ftp:`, or `gopher:` protocols, depending on the location of the server that holds the file. In addition, as mentioned previously, the image itself can be either a GIF or a JPEG format file; however, not all browsers can view inline JPEG images, so for the time being it is best to stick to GIF where at all practical.

As the name suggests, when your Web browser encounters an image tag, it places the image (inline) immediately after any preceding text. For example, the under-construction logo shown in Figure 10.1 is placed after the word "an" by typing the following HTML source:

```
<BODY>
<P>To include an <IMG SRC="images/undercon.gif">inline
image in a document all you need to do is
use the &lt;IMG&gt; tag.</P>
</BODY>
```

Figure 10.1.
The <IMG> tag is used to display inline images on a Web page.

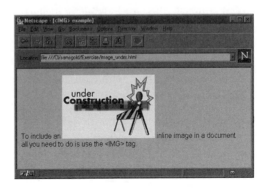

Tip: To keep your images and HTML documents separate, create a subdirectory called /images/ below the directory where you keep your HTML documents, and place any inline image files in it. You can then use relative addressing to locate the image files as shown in the preceding example.

Note: The under-construction logo shown in Figure 10.1 can be found at http://aeiveos.wa.com/gif/gifs.html and many other image archives.

Image Alignment

By default, inline images are aligned so that the bottom of the image sits flush with the current line of text. This, however, is not always the ideal place for an image to sit. To alter the position of an inline image, you must use the ALIGN attribute.

Three types of alignment can be associated with the ALIGN attribute:

- ☐ Alignment to text
- ☐ Floating text alignment
- ☐ Image spacing

Alignment to Text

Alignment to text enables you to position the inline image relative to the current line of text. Figure 10.2 demonstrates how ALIGN="TOP", ALIGN="MIDDLE", and ALIGN="BOTTOM" affect the position of an inline image. In addition, it demonstrates how text on the line following the inline image commences below the bottom of the image and does not wrap around the image. The HTML source used to create this example is shown here:

```
<P>The top of <IMG SRC="images/under2.gif" ALIGN="TOP" > the
image<BR>
is aligned with the text.</P>
<P>The middle of <IMG SRC="images/under2.gif" ALIGN="MIDDLE" > the
image<BR>
is aligned with the text.<BR></P>
<P>The bottom of <IMG SRC="images/under2.gif" ALIGN="BOTTOM" > the
image<BR>
is aligned with the text.<BR></P>
```

Figure 10.2.
Different ALIGN *values with inline images.*

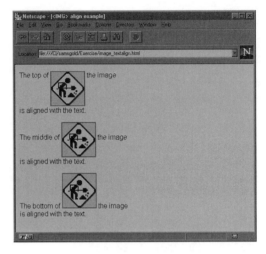

In addition to TOP, MIDDLE, and BOTTOM, Navigator 2.0 supports other alignment values. Table 10.1 discusses each of the possible text alignment values and their uses.

Table 10.1. Navigator 2.0 text alignment options.

ALIGN="*value*"	Description
TOP	Aligns the top of the image with the top of the tallest item on the current line.
TEXTTOP	Aligns the top of the image with the top of the tallest text on the current line.
MIDDLE	Aligns the middle of the image with the baseline of the current line.
ABSMIDDLE	Aligns the middle of the image with the absolute middle of the current line.
BASELINE	Aligns the bottom of the image with the baseline of the current line. (The baseline is the imaginary line on which a line of text sits.)
BOTTOM	Also aligns the bottom of the image with the baseline of the current line.
ABSBOTTOM	Aligns the bottom of the image with the absolute bottom of the current line. (The absolute bottom of a line of text is an imaginary line aligned with the bottom of the *descenders* of letters such as y, p, q, and g.)

Floating Text Alignment

The `<IMG>` tag also supports two text alignment values that allow text to be wrapped down either the left or the right side of an image, in much the same way as the `<TABLE ALIGN="value">` tag did in Chapter 9, "Working with Links and URLs."

Figure 10.3 shows three of the possible combinations that can be achieved by using `ALIGN="LEFT"` and `ALIGN="RIGHT"` text in the following HTML source. In the next section you will learn about the `<BR CLEAR="ALL">` tag used in this example. For now, just include the tags as shown:

```
<IMG SRC="images/under2.gif" ALIGN="LEFT" ><P> The top of the image
<BR>
is aligned with the top of the text,<BR>
and any additional text is wrapped down<BR>
the right hand side of the image.<BR CLEAR="ALL"></P>

<IMG SRC="images/under2.gif" ALIGN="RIGHT" ><P>The top of the image
<BR>
is aligned with the top of the text, <BR>
and any additional text is wrapped down<BR>
the left hand side of the page.<BR CLEAR="ALL"></P>

<IMG SRC="images/under2.gif" ALIGN="LEFT" >
<IMG SRC="images/under2.gif" ALIGN="RIGHT" ><P ALIGN="CENTER">
The top of each image<BR CLEAR="ALL">
is aligned with the top of the text, <BR>
and any additional text is wrapped down<BR>
between the two images.<BR CLEAR="ALL"></P>
```

Figure 10.3.

ALIGN="LEFT" and ALIGN="RIGHT" enable you to wrap text around an inline image.

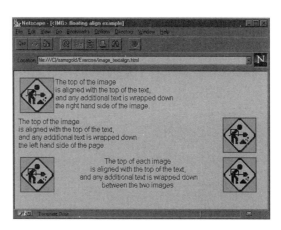

Note: In Figure 10.3 `<P ALIGN="CENTER">` is used to center justify the text between the two inline images. If this hadn't been done, the text would have wrapped hard against the right side of the left inline image.

The *CLEAR* Attribute

On some occasions, you might not want all the text following an inline image to wrap beside it. To stop text wrapping when the ALIGN="LEFT" or ALIGN="RIGHT" attributes are used with an inline image, you must use a special version of the <BR> that includes the CLEAR="ALL" attribute. Any text following the <BR CLEAR="ALL"> tag is moved to the first available line following the bottom of the inline image, as shown in Figure 10.4, which was created using this HTML code:

```
<IMG SRC="images/under2.gif" ALIGN="LEFT" > <P> The top of the image
<BR>
is aligned with the top of the text,<BR CLEAR="ALL">
and any additional text is wrapped down<BR>
the right hand side of the image<BR>
until it encounters a &lt;BR CLEAR=ALL&gt; tag.<BR CLEAR="ALL"></P>

<IMG SRC="images/under2.gif" ALIGN="RIGHT" > <P>The top of the image
<BR>
is aligned with the top of the text, <BR>
and any additional text is wrapped down<BR CLEAR="ALL">
the left hand side of the page beside the image<BR>
until it encounters a &lt;BR CLEAR="ALL"&gt; tag.<BR CLEAR="ALL"></P>
```

Figure 10.4.
The <BR
CLEAR="ALL"> *tag is
used to stop text
wrapping around an
inline image.*

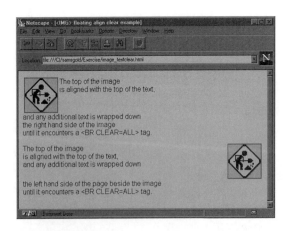

Tip: It is good practice to include a <BR CLEAR="ALL"> immediately after the last text that you want wrapped around an image. This way, you won't have pages that end up wrapping strangely on different computer platforms.

Image Spacing

When using the floating text alignment options, it is unlikely that you will want the text to be pushed up hard against the edge of the inline image. To prevent this from happening, the

VSPACE attribute can be used with the ALIGN attribute to control the vertical spacing above and below an image, and the HSPACE attribute can be used to control horizontal spacing to the left and right of an image.

For example, to place a 20-pixel gap between an inline image and its associated text, you would write this:

```
<IMG ALIGN="LEFT" HSPACE="20">
```

Likewise, to move the top of the image 10 pixels below the top of the first line of wrapped text, you would write this:

```
<IMG ALIGN="LEFT" VSPACE="10">
```

The *BORDER* Attribute

The BORDER attribute is another recent addition to the <IMG> tag. It enables you to control the size, in pixels, of the border that surrounds each inline image. By default, only images that represent hyperlinks are displayed with a border (more on these soon), but by using the BORDER attribute, you can assign any inline image a border.

When you assign a border to an inline image, the color of the border is taken from the current text color. Therefore, to display an inline image with a red 5-pixel border, you would write this:

```
<FONT COLOR="RED"><IMG SRC="images/under2.gif" BORDER="5"></FONT>
```

First, you set the FONT color to red. You then draw the image with a 5-pixel border and finally turn the red FONT color off again after displaying the image.

> **Caution:** You can assign a value of BORDER="0" to images that represent hyperlinks, but doing so will make it difficult for people to tell which images represent hyperlinks and which are simply inline images.

The *ALT* Attribute

The ALT attribute is a special addition to the <IMG> tag that has nothing to do with the appearance of the image. Instead, it has to do with the lack of an image.

Most graphical Web browsers provide their users with an option that disables the display of inline images, which is very useful when a slow modem-based Internet connection is being used. When this option is selected, the ALT attribute comes into play. Any text you assign to an ALT attribute is displayed where the inline image would go if its display were turned on.

For example, Figure 10.5 demonstrates the appearance of Figure 10.3 when inline images are turned off. In this case Netscape replaces each image with a placeholder graphic. In addition, as shown in the HTML source below, the top image and the two bottom images have ALT="Under Construction" included as part of their <IMG> tag, whereas the middle image has no ALT attribute:

```
<IMG SRC="images/under2.gif" ALIGN="LEFT" ALT="Under Construction" >
<P> The top of the image <BR>
is aligned with the top of the text,<BR>
and any additional text is wrapped down<BR>
the right hand side of the image.<BR CLEAR="ALL"></P>

<IMG SRC="images/under2.gif" ALIGN="RIGHT" >
<P>The top of the image <BR>
is aligned with the top of the text, <BR>
and any additional text is wrapped down<BR>
the left hand side of the page.<BR CLEAR="ALL"></P>

<IMG SRC="images/under2.gif" ALIGN="LEFT" ALT="Under Construction">
<IMG SRC="images/under2.gif" ALIGN="RIGHT" ALT="Under Construction">
<P ALIGN="CENTER">The top of each image <BR>
is aligned with the top of the text, <BR>
and any additional text is wrapped down<BR>
between the two images.<BR CLEAR="ALL"></P>
```

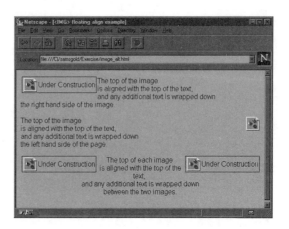

Figure 10.5.
Use the ALT attribute to describe the appearance of images when inline image display is turned off.

Tip: Good HTML design practices demand that an ALT attribute be assigned to every inline image, and especially to hyperlinks and image maps, as you will discover in Chapter 18, "Image Maps and Dynamic Documents."

Exercise: Including Images in Tables

Inline images can be included anywhere in an HTML document that standard text can be entered. Significantly, this includes inside a data cell as part of a table.

In this vein, to help you better understand some of the many possibilities offered by the <IMG> tag, in this exercise you will learn how to create the table shown in Figure 10.6.

Figure 10.6.
Inline images can be included in tables.

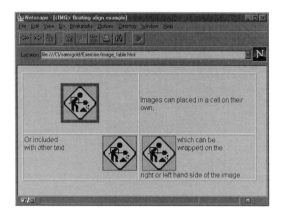

To commence this exercise, define a table with two rows and two columns, a border, and a width of 100%. If you are unsure about how to do this, refer to the exercise in Chapter 8, "Adding Tables to Web Pages," called "Creating Your First Table." But to help you get started, here are the first few lines:

```
<TABLE BORDER WIDTH="100%">
<TR> <!-- start of row one -->
<TD>
</TD>
    rest of table goes here.
</TABLE>
```

After you have your basic table defined, it is time to create the individual cells. The first cell includes a lone image that has been assigned a vertical spacing of 20 and a red border 5 pixels wide. In addition, the cell has a width of 50% and is center justified. To define this cell, write this:

```
<TD WIDTH="50%" ALIGN="CENTER">
<FONT COLOR="RED"><IMG SRC="images/under2.gif" VSPACE="20" BORDER="5"></FONT>
</TD>
```

The second cell on the top row is fairly straightforward because it includes only plain text. It looks like this:

```
<TD>
Images can placed in a cell on their own,
</TD>
```

10

The first cell of the second row should also be assigned a WIDTH of 50% to prevent Navigator 2.0 from overriding the width setting from the preceding row. This cell and the other one of row two also have a vertical alignment of TOP to ensure that the images and text line up properly. Finally, the image itself makes use of the ALIGN="RIGHT" attribute, as shown here:

```
<TR> <!-- start of row two -->
<TD WIDTH="50%" VALIGN="TOP" >
<IMG SRC="images/under2.gif" ALIGN="RIGHT"> Or included <BR> with other text
</TD>
```

All that is left now is the last cell. The image in this cell uses ALIGN="LEFT". In addition, there is a <BR CLEAR="ALL"> before the word "right" to force the bottom line of text to appear below the image. To create this cell, you need to write this:

```
<TD VALIGN="TOP">
<IMG SRC="images/under2.gif" ALIGN="LEFT"> which can be <BR>
wrapped on the<BR CLEAR="ALL">
right or left hand side of the image.
</TD>
```

To complete this exercise, as you have done in previous exercises, save the HTML source to a file, and then test it using Navigator 2.0.

Note: Don't worry if you don't have a copy of the correct inline images for this exercise. Just use a similar-sized image, remembering to change the value of the SRC to the appropriate location and filename. On the other hand, you can obtain a copy of the under-construction logo from the archives listed previously.

Images with Transparent Backgrounds

Currently, two GIF standards are supported by Navigator 2.0: GIF87a and GIF89a. Although there are technical differences between the two GIF versions, the most important difference between the two is the feature of GIF89a that gives it its common name.

Images saved using the GIF89a format can be assigned what is called a *transparent background*; as a result, this version of GIF is often referred to as the Transparent GIF format. To get a better understanding of what a transparent background is, look at the two images in Figure 10.7. The image on the left is stored in GIF87a format, and the one on the right is stored in GIF89a format with a transparent background enabled.

Figure 10.7.

Images with transparent backgrounds allow a Web page's background color or background image to show through.

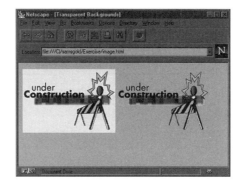

When a GIF89a image with a transparent background is used as an inline image, any parts of the image drawn in the image's background color become transparent, letting the Web page's background color or background image show through (you'll read more about background images soon).

Note: To ensure compatibility with older browsers, GIF89a images can still be displayed on browsers that don't support transparent backgrounds. On these browsers, the image looks exactly the same as its GIF87a counterpart.

Creating Transparent Images

The first step in creating a transparent image is to decide what parts of your image are to be transparent. Using a graphics program such as Adobe Photoshop on the Apple Macintosh, XV on X-11 UNIX systems, or Paint Shop Pro under Windows (see Figure 10.8), paint all the transparent areas of the image using a single color. It does not matter which color you use—just be sure that only transparent parts of the image are painted with it.

After you have painted all the transparent areas of your image using a single color, open the palette window of your graphics program and make a note of the index number that corresponds to the position of your chosen color in the image palette. In Figure 10.8 the color in index position 0 was used, but any position and color could have been chosen. With this information in hand, you are ready for the final step in the creation of your transparent inline image.

Depending on the type of computer and operating system you are using, various programs are available that can convert a standard GIF87a image into a GIF89a image with a transparent background.

Figure 10.8.
Using a single color, paint all the areas of your image that are to be transparent.

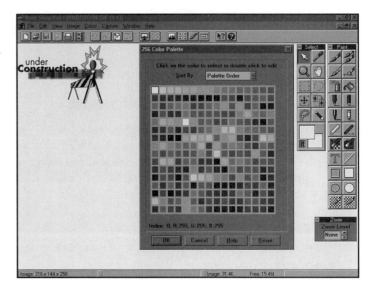

For people on UNIX systems, the best place to start is with a program called giftrans. To obtain a copy of the source code for giftrans—you will need to compile it yourself—try either `ftp://ftp.rz.uni-karlsruhe.de/pub/net/www/tools/giftrans.c` or `http://melmac.corp.harris.com/files/giftrans.c`. After the code is compiled, use a command like the following to covert your images:

```
giftrans -T index GIF87a.GIF > GIF89a.GIF
```

The `index` field is replaced with the index number for the color to be used as a background; it is a number from 1 to 256. `GIF87a.GIF` gets replaced by the name of the file you want to convert, and `GIF89a.GIF` is the name of the new file that will be created by giftrans. For example, to covert the file shown in Figure 10.8, you would enter this:

```
giftrans -T 1 undercon.gif > undercont.gif
```

In this example, the new file has a "t" appended to its name to indicate that it is a transparent image, but you can use any notation you desire for your own images. Also, note that an index position of 1 was used rather than 0, as indicated in Figure 10.8. Some programs list the index positions as a number between 1 and 256, whereas others use 0 to 255. All you need to do is ascertain which indexing method is being used by each program.

Both of the sites listed previously also contain an MS-DOS version of giftrans called `giftrans.exe`. For Windows users, however, a far better, and simpler, method of creating transparent GIFs involves the use of the Paint Shop Pro program discussed previously. This program enables you to select the background color using a graphical interface rather than the command-line process offered by giftrans.

Alternatively, you can also use another very good program called LView Pro 1.8, as shown in Figure 10.9. Copies of LView Pro can be obtained from the following:

```
ftp://ftp.std.com/ftp/vendors/mmedia/lview/lviewpro.zip (Windows 95)
ftp://ftp.std.com/ftp/vendors/mmedia/lview/lviewp1b.zip (Windows 3.11)
http://world.std.com/~mmedia/lviewp.html (Additional information)
```

Figure 10.9.

Programs such as LView Pro, Paint Shop Pro, and Transparency enable you to graphically select the transparent color.

Macintosh users need to get the program called Transparency. A copy of the latest version can usually be found at the Macintosh archive site operated by Gavin Bell at `http://www.qub.ac.uk/sigweb/mac-utils.html`. To obtain the current version as of this book's printing, try `ftp://src.doc.ic.ac.uk/packages/info-mac/gst/grf/transparency-10.hqx`.

Transparency, like Paint Shop Pro and LView Pro, provides a simple-to-use graphical interface that enables you to select the color you want to use as the background before saving the converted version to a separate file.

Images as Hotlinks

Because an `<IMG>` tag can be positioned anywhere that normal text can be placed, it is a simple process to turn an inline image into a hyperlink. In Chapter 6, "Linking Web Pages Together," you learned that the `<A>` tag is used to create hyperlinks using the following form:

```
<A HREF="URL">hotspot text</A>
```

By taking this knowledge and combining it with what you have just learned about inline images, you can see that you create a hyperlink image by using this:

```
<A HREF="URL"><IMG SRC="image" ALT="description"></A>
```

Instead of including `hotspot text` between the `<A>` and `</A>` tags, you include an inline image, defined by using the `<IMG>` tag. This example also emphasizes the importance of the `ALT` attribute, which is even more vital when an image represents a hyperlink. Without the `ALT` attribute, people with text-based Web browsers or who have inline image display turned off would have no idea what your hyperlink pointed to.

When used as a hyperlink, your images are displayed onscreen with a colored border, which by default is blue. If, however, the page includes any color definitions in the <BODY> tag, the color of the text surrounding the image is controlled by the LINK, VLINK, and ALINK attributes, in the same way as they control the color of the hotspot text.

Adding Document Backgrounds

If you have spent more than a few minutes exploring the World Wide Web with Navigator 2.0, you will no doubt have come across a few Web pages that contain images as backgrounds rather than the single-color backgrounds you have so far encountered in this book.

Creating Background Images

The background images that are now used by many Web pages are simply GIF or JPEG images that have been assigned to a Web page's backdrop rather than to an inline image tag. They are, however, treated slightly differently than a normal inline image.

When you use the <IMG> tag, this tells a Web browser to place a copy of the specified image on a Web page as a single inline image. But when you define a background image, you are actually telling the Web browser to tile the specified image across the back of your Web page. Figures 10.10 and 10.11 demonstrate how a small GIF image is tiled to fill the entire Web page when it is defined as the Web page's background image.

Figure 10.10.
A single GIF image.

Figure 10.11.
Images used as back-grounds are tiled so that they fill the entire Web page.

Online Sources of Background Images

Because background images are tiled, they can be designed in such a way that a small image gives the appearance of a single solid background, by carefully crafting the edges of the basic image. For example, when the small raindrop-textured image shown in Figure 10.12 is tiled onto a Web page, it gives the appearance of a single, much larger textured image (see Figure 10.13), which can be scaled to suit the size of the Web page.

Figure 10.12.
Images can be designed in such a way that each edge matches its corre-sponding edge.

Figure 10.13.
When tiled, textured images create the appearance of a single background texture or image.

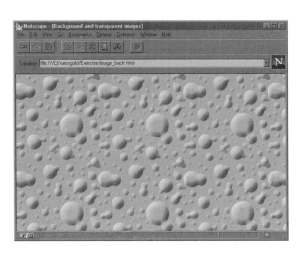

The only problem, however, is that designing such images can take a considerable amount of time and effort. But luckily for you (the Web developer), Netscape Communications realized this and, as a result, created a collection of predefined background images in various textures and different styles. You can use these images free of charge. To view all the images in this collection (see Figure 10.14), point your Web browser to `http://Home.netscape.com/assist/net_sites/bg/backgrounds.html`.

Figure 10.14.
Netscape Communications has designed a set of backgrounds that can be used on your Web pages.

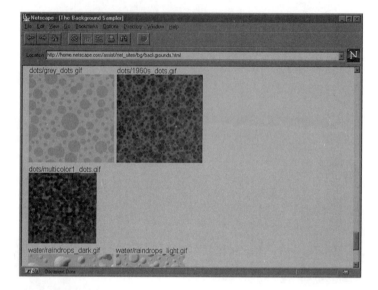

Note: The raindrops texture shown in Figure 10.13 can be found in the Netscape backgrounds collection as `http://home.netscape.com/assist/net_sites/bg/water/raindrops_dark.gif`.

The *BACKGROUND* Attribute

To include any of the images created by Netscape Communications or those of your own design as a background, you must use the BACKGROUND attribute.

The BACKGROUND attribute of the <BODY> tag is used to assign a background image to a Web page. To use this attribute to define the background image shown previously in Figure 10.14, you would write this:

```
<BODY BACKGROUND="http://home.netscape.com/assist/net_sites/bg/water/
raindrops_dark.gif">
```

In this example the background image has been addressed using the absolute address of its location at Netscape Communications. Netscape recommends that you use all the backgrounds it has created by absolute addressing; however, nothing is stopping you from downloading the file to your own hard drive as well. In this case, you could define the background image like this:

```
<BODY BACKGROUND="image/raindrops_dark.gif">
```

Note: Background images can be transparent GIF images. If you use a transparent GIF as a background image, the Web page's background color will show through between the tiles of the background image.

Tip: When adding background images to a page, it is common practice to alter the text and hyperlink colors to match the decor created by the background image. In doing so, however, many people fail to alter the background color to accommodate those people who have inline images turned off. Therefore, when defining a background image, also be sure to define a background color for the page that approximates the hue of the background image.

10

Improving Image Performance

Although inline images and background images can make your pages look very impressive, they can also cause considerable aggravation for people visiting your site.

The main reason for this is the amount of time it takes to download each of the images on a Web page. Obviously, if you have a 64KB ISDN connection to the Internet, a few hundred kilobytes of images will pose no problems. But a rapidly increasing portion of the Web community only has access to modems that at their best achieve rates in the region of 28,800bps. For these people, loading a 100KB image takes time.

To help reduce the amount of time, or at least the perceived amount of time, people must spend waiting for images to download, you have several performance options at your disposal.

Interlaced GIF Images

The first and by far the most used trick involves the use of what are called interlaced GIF images. *Interlaced GIF images* are normal GIF images that have been stored in a special format. When interlaced images are used, a chunky low-resolution version of the image is first downloaded to the Web page, followed by information that gradually builds the image up to full resolution, creating an effect similar to blinds being pulled down.

There is actually no true improvement in the amount of time it takes to display the full image, but because the user can see at least part of the image sooner, the perception of improved performance is achieved.

To create interlaced GIF images from standard GIF images, you again need to use a conversion program of some sort. Windows users need look no further than LView Pro or Paint Shop Pro, both of which can save GIF87a and GIF89a images in interlaced format.

 For the Macintosh, Netscape recommends GIFCONVERTER, which can be found at `http://wwwhost.ots.utexas.edu/mac/pub-mac-graphics.html#gifconverter-237`.

And finally, for people using UNIX-based systems, the ImageMagick program mentioned previously is a good place to start.

Progressive JPEG Images

The best way to improve the download and display of images on Navigator 2.0–specific sites is to use files stored in the JPEG image format when possible. Even JPEG images, however, can still take some time to download. For this reason, Navigator 2.0 now supports a new form of JPEG compression called progressive JPEG images.

When an image saved using the progressive JPEG format is downloaded to a Web site, it takes an appearance similar to that of an interlaced GIF image. First, a low-resolution version of the file is displayed, followed by enhancements that increase the image to full resolution. The visual effect of using progressive JPEG images on a Web page is that of a page that is ready for use almost instantly, even on slow modem-based connections.

The main problem with the progressive JPEG format at the moment, unfortunately, is the lack of image-processing tools capable of creating them. Currently, only a small number of Windows 95–specific programs, including LView Pro 1.C/32 and Polyview 2.18, fully support the creation and display of progressive JPEG images. (`http://www.windows95.com/` is a good place to look for Windows 95–specific files.)

Image Scaling

Netscape Navigator includes two special attributes for the <IMG> tag that can improve the apparent performance of a Web page. These attributes are HEIGHT and WIDTH.

In their most basic form, these two attributes are used to tell the Web browser the size of an image before it is downloaded. Doing this lets the browser lay out all the elements on a Web page before any inline images are loaded. If this size information is not included in your <IMG> tags, the Web browser can't start to display a Web page until the images are loaded and it knows how much space they take up. You include the HEIGHT and WIDTH attributes in an inline image like this:

```
<IMG SRC="images/under2.gif" HEIGHT="80" WIDTH="80">
```

In addition to defining the physical size of an image, the HEIGHT and WIDTH attributes can be used to scale the size of an inline image on the fly. Figure 10.15 demonstrates how altering the values of HEIGHT and WIDTH affects the appearance of an inline image when the following HTML source is used:

```
<IMG SRC="images/under2.gif" HEIGHT="80" WIDTH="80">
<IMG SRC="images/under2.gif" HEIGHT="40" WIDTH="40">
<IMG SRC="images/under2.gif" HEIGHT="160" WIDTH="160">
<IMG SRC="images/under2.gif" HEIGHT="160" WIDTH="40">
<IMG SRC="images/under2.gif" HEIGHT="40" WIDTH="160">
```

Figure 10.15.
The HEIGHT and WIDTH attributes can be used to scale inline images.

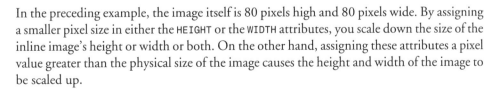

In the preceding example, the image itself is 80 pixels high and 80 pixels wide. By assigning a smaller pixel size in either the HEIGHT or the WIDTH attributes, you scale down the size of the inline image's height or width or both. On the other hand, assigning these attributes a pixel value greater than the physical size of the image causes the height and width of the image to be scaled up.

To give you even greater control over the displayed size of an inline image, you can replace the pixel values in the HEIGHT and WIDTH attributes with relative percentage values. For example, to set the height of an inline image to 40% of the total height of the Web page and 50% of the total width of page, you would write this:

```
<IMG SRC="images/under2.gif" HEIGHT="40%" WIDTH="50%">
```

As an exercise, create an HTML document with a few inline images, and experiment with the effects of percentage and absolute pixel values on their widths and heights.

Lo/High Image Loading

One final attribute of the <IMG> tag needs to be discussed in this section. Like the HEIGHT and WIDTH attributes, this attribute can be used to improve the perception of increased display speed.

The LOWSRC attribute gives you a method of associating two separate images with a single <IMG> tag. The reason for doing this is to allow the Web browser to quickly display a low-quality, low-resolution version of an image first, and then "fade in" the higher-resolution version after the entire Web page is displayed.

When included in an <IMG> tag, the LOWSRC attribute takes the following form:

```
<IMG SRC="highres.gif" LOWSRC="lowres.gif" HEIGHT="value" WIDTH="value">
```

Your main inline image should be assigned to the SRC attribute, and a version that uses a smaller file size—possibly progressive JPEG—should be assigned to the LOWSRC attribute. You also need to assign the HEIGHT and WIDTH attributes to equal the size of the SRC image. That way, if the image assigned to LOWSRC is physically smaller, it will automatically be scaled up to the same size as the main image.

Summary

The capability to integrate images and text on a single page is the main feature of the World Wide Web that sets it apart from other Internet services.

In this chapter you have learned how to add inline images to your Web pages and how to assign each page a background image. In addition, you have learned how to create interlaced and transparent GIF images and why progressive JPEG images display faster than those in any other formats. As a quick reminder, Table 10.1 lists all the new tags and attributes discussed in this chapter.

But images are not the only reason for the popularity of the World Wide Web. You can also integrate many other kinds of multimedia resources with a Web page, as you will learn in the following chapter.

Table 10.1. New tags discussed in this chapter.

Tag	Description
<IMG>	Insert an inline image into the document.
SRC	The URL of the image.
ALT	A text string that will be displayed in browsers that cannot support images.
ALIGN	Determines the alignment of the given image. If LEFT or RIGHT, the image is aligned to the left or right column, and all following text flows beside that image. All other values such as TOP, MIDDLE, or BOTTOM, or TEXTTOP, ABSMIDDLE, BASELINE, or ABSBOTTOM, determines the vertical alignment of this image with other items in the same line.
VSPACE	The space between the image and the text above or below it.
HSPACE	The space between the image and the text to its left or right.
WIDTH	The width, in pixels, of the image. If WIDTH is not the actual width, the image is scaled to fit.
HEIGHT	The width, in pixels, of the image. If HEIGHT is not the actual height, the image is scaled to fit.
BORDER	Set the size of the border in pixels to be drawn around the image.
LOWSRC	The path or URL of an image that will be loaded first, before the image specified in SRC.
<BR CLEAR="ALL">	Causes the text to stop flowing around an image.

Workshop

The first section of the Workshop lists some of the common questions people ask about the World Wide Web along with a brief answer to each. Next is a quiz about the chapter you have just read. If you have problems answering any of the questions in the quiz, you can turn to Appendix E, "Answers to Quiz Questions."

Q&A

Q **Many of the sites I visit contain images that can be clicked in different places. Depending on where you click, different Web pages are loaded. How do I create images like this?**

A The type of image you are referring to is called an image map. Creating image maps usually involves considerable interaction between a Web page and the Web server where the page is stored. For this reason, image maps are discussed in Chapter 18, after you have learned about Web servers and CGI scripts.

Q **Is there any limit on the number of inline images that can be included on a single page?**

A Technically, the answer is no. However, in keeping with past discussions about the time it takes to download and display a Web page, the more images you include on a page, the worse things become performance-wise.

Q **The text displayed by the ALT tag is very bland. Is there any way it can be jazzed up, maybe by making it bold or by using some other tag?**

A There is an undocumented way to do what you are asking about. If you place an image tag inside any of the character attribute tags—for example, `<B><IMG SRC="file.gif" ALT="text"></B>`—the text assigned to the ALT attribute is displayed using the specified attributes. As far as I know, however, this technique works only with Netscape Navigator and might not even be supported by it in future releases.

Quiz

1. Can JPEG images be used inline?
2. Why would I use the HEIGHT attribute in an `<IMG>` tag?
3. What are four of the text alignment values recognized by the ALIGN attribute when it is associated with the `<IMG>` tag?
4. How do you assign a background image to a Web page?
5. How do you create an image hyperlink?

Exercises

1. As usual, your first task today is to create the `10note.html` document for your HTML reference collection. Be sure to include an example of each image-alignment option and the various scaling parameters. At the same time, visit the background images collection maintained by Netscape Communications, and select a background texture for all the pages in your HTML reference. In this case, download a copy of the image to your local hard drive by following the online instructions.

   Also, don't forget to sign the document using the `<ADDRESS>` tag, including a `mailto:` URL as a hyperlink to your e-mail address. In addition, add a hyperlink to point back to the `html_contents.html` document and one in the contents document to point to `10note.html`.

2. One of the most common uses of image hyperlinks is for the creation of navigation buttons. In this exercise, you will create a set of common navigation buttons for use with your HTML reference documents.

   Using your graphics program of choice, create four images that say "Previous Chapter," "Contents," "Next Chapter," and "Favorite Places."

   After you have designed these images, place an image hyperlink using "Contents," "Next Chapter," and "Favorite Places" at the bottom of `05note.html`. "Contents" should link to `html_contents.html`, "Next Chapter" to `06note.html`, and "Favorite Places" to the document you created in the exercise in Chapter 6 called "Building a Favorite Web Sites Page." After you have completed work on `05note.html`, change to `06note.html` and repeat the process, this time including a "Previous Chapter" link to `05note.html` and a "Next Chapter" link to `07note.html`.

   Finally, do the same for `08note.html`, `09note.html`, and `10note.html`.

11

Using External Media and Plug-ins

As Chapter 10, "Adding Images to Your Web Documents," explains, inline images are images that can be displayed directly on the page along with text. The World Wide Web also supports other media, including images, sound, and video, that can be retrieved on demand and loaded in windows separate from the browser window. These forms of media on the Web are called external media because they are stored externally from your Web files.

In this chapter you learn about the following:

- ☐ What "external media" means
- ☐ How different browsers handle different forms of external media
- ☐ Specifying external media in your HTML file
- ☐ Using sound
- ☐ Using video
- ☐ Using plug-ins with Navigator 2.0

What's External Media?

External media, in its most general form, refers to any files that are not directly viewable by a Web browser on a Web page. External files can include just about any kind of file you can create: non-inline GIF files, MPEG video, PostScript files, zipped applications, and almost anything else. You can create a link in an HTML file to an external media file in exactly the same way that you link to another document: by using the <A> tag.

Whenever a server sends a file to your browser, it also includes information about what kind of file it is. It does this by sending a special message with the file. If the browser cannot internally display the type of file indicated by the special message, it then attempts to match the file type to a list of "helper" applications (sometimes called "viewers") configured in the browser. If the file type can be recognized and a helper application is available, the browser starts the helper application and hands it the file. The helper application in turn displays, runs, or plays the external media file that the browser could not read.

On the other hand, if the browser can't figure out what kind of file the server is trying to send, it usually asks the user what to do with it. At this stage, you can either save the file to disk or configure a helper application to view the file.

This process can often be confusing to newcomers. If you are still unsure about the steps involved in the process of loading and displaying external media, take a look at Figure 11.1. This figure presents the various steps taken by your Web browser in a diagrammatic form.

The browser can also execute helper applications for files it loads from the local disk, except it uses the extension of the file (`.gif`, `.jpeg`, and so on) to determine the type of the file and to execute the appropriate helper application. This is why the HTML and GIF files you've been working with locally must have the extensions `.html` and `.gif`—so that the browser can figure out what they are.

This system works especially well because it keeps the browser small (no need to include viewers or players for every strange media type out there). It's also configurable for new file types and new and better helper applications as they are written. Each browser has one list that maps file extensions to file types, and another list that maps file types to applications. You should be able to configure your browser to use the helper applications you want to use, as well as be able to add new file extensions to the list of file types.

Figure 11.1.
Browsers and other files.

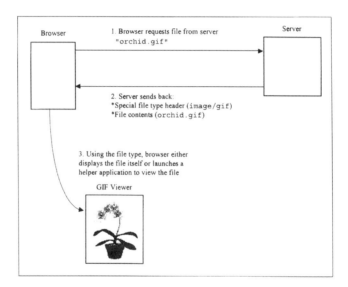

Note: The list of file types that browsers use in their helper application lists are drawn from a standard called MIME, which was originally intended for encoding media in electronic mail messages. You won't need to know this now, but it might be important when you start dealing with servers on Day 5, "Going Online."

Specifying External Media in HTML

To specify an external media file in HTML, you link to it just as you would any other document, by using the <A> tag and the HREF attribute. The path to the external file is a pathname or URL just as you would use if the file were another HTML document:

```
<A HREF="some_external_file">A media file.</A>
```

If you're going to make use of links to external media files, it is helpful if you include in the body of the link (or somewhere nearby) some information about the format of the media, such as the kind of file format and its file size.

Knowing the format of the file ahead of time is useful because this information indicates to your readers whether they can read the file. They're not going to want to retrieve a file if they can't do anything with it after it has been downloaded.

Telling the readers how big the file is enables them to decide before selecting the link whether they have the time (or the inclination) to sit and wait for the download to take place.

A few words as part of the link satisfy both of these suggestions:

```
<A HREF="bigsnail.jpeg">A 59K JPEG Image of a snail</A>
<A HREF="tacoma.mov">The Fall of the Tacoma Narrows Bridge </A>
 (a200K QuickTime File)
```

Using External Images

If you're using images inline on your Web page, the one format that all graphical browsers can read is GIF. Linking to external images, however, gives you slightly more flexibility in the image formats you can use.

Some popular image formats for external media include the following formats:

- ☐ GIF—Even though GIF files can be read inline, it often makes sense, particularly in the case of larger files, to link to external GIF files.
- ☐ JPEG—Although many browsers are supporting inline JPEG images, many more do not. So it makes sense to use JPEG as an external image. The combination of inline GIFs and external JPEGs is particularly useful.
- ☐ XBM—XBM files are X Window system bitmaps.
- ☐ PICT—PICT files are a common graphics format for the Macintosh.

□ TIFF—TIFF is a 24-bit format based on an international standard. Like JPEG, this format is used for full-color or True Color images. TIFF is very popular in the print and desktop publishing industry; however, the size of files used to store TIFF images can be very large (over 1MB in some cases).

□ BMP—BMP is the standard image format for Windows and Windows 95. It comes in two versions, BMP-8bit and BMP-24bit.

□ TARGA—TARGA is the de facto standard for high-resolution, high-quality images. It is based on a format designed by the Truevision company for the TARGA graphics cards.

Image processing programs such as Adobe Photoshop, Paint Shop Pro for Windows, XV for X11, the pbm conversion programs for UNIX, and deBabelizer for Macintosh and Windows should be able to convert among many of these formats.

After you have a converted file, you must name it with the appropriate extension so that your browser can recognize it. Extensions for graphics files are shown in Table 11.1.

Table 11.1. Image formats and extensions.

Format	Extension
GIF	.gif
JPEG	.jpg, .jpeg
XBM	.xbm
PICT	.PICT
TIFF	.tif, .tiff
BMP	.bmp
TARGA	.tga

▼ Exercise: Linking to External GIF and JPEG Files

A common practice in Web pages is to provide a very small GIF image (a "thumbnail") inline on the page itself. You then link that image to its larger counterpart. This technique has two major advantages over including the entire image inline:

□ It keeps the size of the Web page small, so the page can be downloaded quickly.

□ It gives your readers a "taste" of the image before they download the entire thing.

In this simple example, you'll set up a link between a small image and an external, larger version of that same image. The large image is a photograph of some penguins in GIF format, called `penguinsbig.gif` (shown in Figure 11.2).

First, create a thumbnail version of the penguins photograph in your favorite image editor. The thumbnail can be a scaled version of the original file, a clip of that file (say, one penguin out of the group), or anything else you want to use to indicate the larger image.

Here, I've created a picture of one penguin in the group to serve as the inline image. (I've called it `penguinslittle.gif`.) Unlike the large version of the file, which is 100KB, the small picture is only 3KB. By using the `<IMG>` tag, I'll put that image directly on a nearly content-free Web page:

```
<HTML>
<HEAD>
<TITLE>Penguins</TITLE>
</HEAD></BODY>
<H1>Penguins</H1>
<IMG SRC="penguinslittle.gif">
</BODY></HTML>
```

Figure 11.2.
Penguins.

Now, using a link tag, you can link the small icon to the bigger picture by enclosing the `<IMG>` tag inside an `<A>` tag:

```
<A HREF="penguinsbig.gif"><IMG SRC="penguinslittle.gif"></A>
```

The final result of the page is shown in Figure 11.3. Now if you click the small penguin image, the big image is downloaded and viewed by the helper application defined for GIF files for that browser.

Figure 11.3.
*The Penguins
home page with
link.*

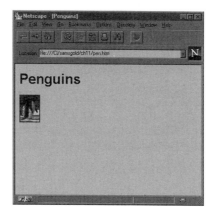

An alternative to linking the small image directly to the large image is to provide the external image in several formats and provide descriptive links for each, as mentioned previously. In this part of the example, I'll link to a JPEG version of that same penguins file.

To create the JPEG version of the penguin photograph, you need to use your image editor or converter again to convert the original photograph. Here, I've called it `penguinsbig.jpg`.

To provide both GIF and JPEG forms of the penguin photo, we'll convert the link on the image into a simple link menu (see Figure 11.4) that points to the GIF and JPEG files, remembering also to include some information about file size:

```
<IMG SRC="penguinslittle.gif">
<UL>
<LI>Penguins (<A HREF="penguinsbig.gif">100K GIF file</A>)
<LI>Penguins (<A HREF="penguinsbig.jpg">25K JPEG file</A>)
</UL>
```

Figure 11.4.
*The Penguins link
menu.*

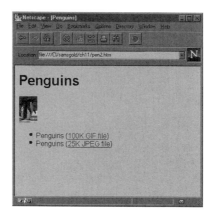

Using Sound

Including sound files on your Web page can provide optional annotations to existing text, welcome messages from you or someone important in your organization, or extra information that words and pictures cannot convey. If you're musically inclined, you can provide sound clips of your work on the Web or create archives of clips from your favorite bands— but be sure to get their permission first!

To include a link to an external sound on your Web page, you must have that sound sample in the right format, just as you would for an image. Various sound formats are beginning to appear on the World Wide Web, so here's a quick summary of the main contenders:

AU   Currently, the only fully cross-platform sound file format for the Web is Sun Microsystems's AU format. AU allows several kinds of sound sample encoding, but the most popular one is 8-bit μ-law. For this reason, AU files are often called simply μ-law files. AU files are of only barely acceptable quality, because the 8-bit sampling causes them to sound a bit like they are being transmitted over a telephone.

AIFF   For improved sound quality, the most popular Macintosh format is AIFF. This, however, is very much a Macintosh-specific file format, and as such, there are currently no compatible helper applications that support it on other platforms.

WAV   The WAV sound format is the de facto standard for Windows-based systems, and like AIFF, it can provide very high-quality (stereo CD) sound. But again, the limitation here is the availability of helper application support on other platforms.

TrueSpeech   This is a new sound format, developed by the DSP Group Inc. It uses a similar system to the WAV sound format. There are currently helper applications for Windows, Window 95, and Macintosh platforms. What makes this system different from the other formats mentioned is its capability to play continuous streams of sound in near realtime, as opposed to AU-type files where the entire file must be downloaded before the sounds can be played.

Using this system, a person can click a hyperlink when visiting your home page and listen to a selection of your favorite music while exploring the rest of the site. As an alternative, you could provide audio descriptions for information displayed on your pages. To learn more about TrueSpeech, point your Web browser to http://www.dspg.com/.

RealAudio   Like TrueSpeech, RealAudio is designed for the delivery of realtime or near-realtime audio streams. Its only limitation, unfortunately,

is the need for a dedicated RealAudio server on your host computer system before you can deliver realtime audio. The plus side of this system, on the other hand, is that it can broadcast live programming just like a radio station.

To learn more about RealAudio, point your Web browser to `http://www.realaudio.com/`. Also, while you are there, check out RealAudio 2.0—the new plug-in version for Netscape 2.0 (more on this later).

MPEG   Also, a recent addition to the already mind-boggling array of sound formats is MPEG audio. MPEG is generally better known as a video standard, but the audio portion of the standard allows for very high-quality sound, and players exist for many platforms.

QuickTime   Like MPEG, QuickTime is also better known as a video standard, but it too can also be used for sound files. (Note, however, that if you use either MPEG or QuickTime—or any other unusual formats—those sounds will probably not be playable cross-platform; therefore, you should be sure to indicate the format of the sound file in the link that points to it.)

So how do you get or create a sound file, and after you have it, how do you use it? Read on.

Getting Sound Files

Where can you get sound files? From various sources:

☐ Many systems enable you to record and digitize sounds or voice by using a microphone that comes with your system or inexpensive add-on equipment. (If you don't already know how to do this, dig out those manuals you threw aside when you opened the box your computer came in.)

☐ Some platforms with CD-ROM drives might enable you to record digital sounds directly off a standard audio CD; you'll need a CD-ROM drive that supports this feature, of course. Keep in mind if you go this route that most published audio material is copyrighted, and the owners might not appreciate your making their songs or sounds available free on the Internet.

☐ Many Internet archives have collections of small, digitized samples in the appropriate format for the platform they emphasize (for example, SND format files for Macintosh archives, WAV format for Windows, and AU for Sun's UNIX).

Note: Keep in mind that, like images, sounds you find on the Net might be owned by someone who won't like you using them. Exercise caution when using "found" sounds.

☐ Commercial "clip sound" products are available, again, in appropriate formats for your platform. These sounds have the advantage of usually being public domain or royalty free, meaning that you can use them anywhere without needing to get permission or pay a fee.

Converting Sound Files

After you have a sound file, it might not be in the right format—that is, the format you want it to be in. The programs introduced in this section can read and convert many popular sound formats:

UNIX	A program called SOX by Lance Norskog can convert many sound formats (AU, WAV, AIFF, Macintosh SND) and perform some rudimentary processing, including filtering, changing the sample rate, and reversing the sample.
MS-DOS	WAVany by Bill Neisius converts most common sound formats (including AU and Macintosh SND) to WAV format. In addition, a version of the SOX program is available for MS-DOS–based systems.
Windows	Waveform Hold and Modify (WHAM), for Windows, is an excellent sound player, editor, and converter that also works really well as a helper application for your browser. Also available at the RealAudio and TrueSpeech sites are special programs that you need to use when creating audio streams for these special formats.
Macintosh	The freeware SoundApp by Norman Franke reads and plays most sound formats, and converts to WAV, Macintosh SND, AIFF, and NeXT sound formats (but mysteriously, not Sun AU). The freeware program Ulaw converts Macintosh sounds (SND) to AU format.

FTP sources for each of these programs are listed in Appendix D, "Sources of Additional Information."

Including Sound Files on Web Pages

For a browser to recognize your sound file, it must have the appropriate extension for its file type. Common formats and their extensions are listed in Table 11.2.

Table 11.2. Sound formats and extensions.

Format	Extension
AU/μ-law	.au
AIFF/AIFC	.aiff, .aif

Format	Extension
WAV	.wav
RealAudio 1.0	.ra, .ram
RealAudio 2.0	.rp, .rpm
TrueSpeech	.dsp
MPEG Audio	.mp2

After you have a file in the right format and with the right extension, you can link to it from your Web page as with any other external file:

```
Laurence Olivier's "To Be or Not To Be" soliloquy from the film of the play
Hamlet (<A HREF="olivier_hamlet.au">AIFF format, 357K)</A>
```

Here are some additional hints for using sound files in your Web page:

☐ *Always* tell your readers that your link is to a sound file, and also be sure to note that sound file's format. This is especially important if you use a format other than AU; otherwise, your readers will have to download the file to find out whether they can handle it.

☐ Sound files tend to be quite large, so consider creating sound files of lesser quality for people on slower connections. In particular, mono sound files generally are smaller than stereo, and 8-bit files are smaller than 16-bit.

☐ If you use multiple sound files on your Web page, consider providing an explanatory note at the top of the page and then using a small inline GIF icon (such as the one shown in Figure 11.5) as the link to the sound files themselves. (Include the size of the file in the link as well.) Using a sound file icon provides an elegant way to show that a sound lurks on the other side of the link without needing to explain it in text all the time.

Figure 11.5.
A sound file icon.

Using Video

Video refers to any digitally encoded motion picture, which can include both animation and "real" video files.

For video files that can be read across platforms, the current standard on the Web is MPEG, but Apple's QuickTime format has been gaining ground as players have become more available for platforms other than the Macintosh. QuickTime also has the advantage of being able

to include an audio track with the video; although MPEG video files can have audio tracks, fewer existing players can play it. To complicate matters further, a third standard is also supported by Windows-based systems, called Video for Windows (.avi), and like QuickTime and MPEG, Video for Windows can also play live video with audio.

Which format should you use? This is a difficult question. QuickTime is developing a very large following, but Video for Windows is also growing in popularity. In the end, it really depends on the capabilities of the programs you use to create your video files. After all, each format seems to have as many strong supporters as detracters.

Getting and Converting Video Files

Just as with images and sound, you can get video clips by making them yourself, downloading them from the Net, or purchasing royalty-free clips you can read on your platform. Exactly how you go about digitizing your own video clips is greatly dependent on your computer system and the hardware you have available. In addition, achieving suitable results with even the most expensive equipment can be a difficult task. As a result, the best and easiest way to get video is to find it. Again, the best place to get short video clips is through royalty-free video libraries on CD-ROM or through sources over the Internet.

To convert video files between formats on the Macintosh, use the freeware program Sparkle. Sparkle can read and play both MPEG and QuickTime files and can convert between them. In addition, the program AVI->Quick can convert AVI (Video for Windows) files to QuickTime format.

On DOS/Windows systems, a commercial program called XingCD enables you to convert AVI files to MPEG. AVI-to-QuickTime converters are also available; one is a program called SmartCap from Intel, which can convert between AVI and QuickTime files that use the Indeo compression method. To use AVI files, you'll need the Video for Windows package, available from Microsoft or bundled with Windows 95. To use QuickTime movies, you'll need the QuickTime for Windows package, available from Apple. You'll need both to convert from one format to the other.

FTP locations and other information for these programs are in Appendix D.

Including Video Files on Web Pages

After you have a video file, you must do two things:

- [ ] Name the file appropriately. MPEG files should have an extension of .mpg or .mpeg; QuickTime movies have an .mov extension; Video for Windows movies use an .avi extension.
- [ ] Link to the file by using the <A> tag just as you did with external images and sounds.

In addition, if you want a QuickTime movie to be read on a platform other than the Macintosh, you will need to "flatten" that movie. On the Macintosh files contain resource and data forks for different bits of the file. Flattening a QuickTime file involves moving all the data in the QuickTime file into the data fork so that other platforms can read it.

A small freeware program called FastPlayer flattens QuickTime movies on the Mac; on Windows, try a program called Qflat. FTP locations are in Appendix D.

As with all external media files, you should be sure to tell your readers the type and size of file they are linking to. This information is especially important for video files, because the sizes are often frighteningly large. As I noted with sound files, linking to an icon on the Web page itself is often a nice design touch. (See Figure 11.6.)

Figure 11.6.
A video file icon.

Exercise: Creating a Media Archive

One of the uses of Web pages I have only vaguely mentioned up to this point is creating a media archive. A media archive is a Web page that serves only to provide quick access to image or other media files for viewing and downloading.

Previously on the Net, media was stored in FTP or Gopher archives. The text-only nature of these sorts of archives makes it difficult for people to find what they're looking for in images, sounds, or video. The filename is often the only description they have of the content of the file. Even reasonably descriptive filenames, such as `red-bird-in-green-tree.gif` or `verdi-aria.aiff`, aren't all that useful when you're talking about images or sounds. It's only by actually downloading the file that people can determine whether they want it.

Through the use of inline images and icons, and by splitting up sound and video files into small clips and larger files, you can create a media archive on the Web that is far more usable than any of the text-only archives.

11

Note: Keep in mind that this sort of archive, in its heavy use of inline graphics and large media files, is optimally useful in graphical browsers attached to fast networks. The Web does, however, provide advantages in this respect even for text-only browsers, simply because more room is available. Rather than having only the filename to describe the file, you can use as many words as you need. Here's an example:

A `<A HREF="organgefish.jpeg">34K JPEG file</A>` of an orange fish with a bright yellow eye, swimming in front of some very pink coral.

In this exercise, you'll create a simple example of a media archive with several GIF images, AU sounds, and MPEG video.

First, start with the framework for the archive. You'll include some introductory text; some inline images explaining the kinds of files; headings for each file type; and some of the special formatting options discussed in Chapter 10, including a background image, image alignment, and blue heading text. (Figure 11.7 shows how this code will look.)

```
<HTML>
<HEAD>
<TITLE>The Way Cool Media Archive</TITLE>
</HEAD>
<BODY BACKGROUND="waycool.gif">
<H1 ALIGN="CENTER"><FONT COLOR="BLUE">The Way Cool Media Archive</
➥FONT></H1>
<P>Select an image to download the appropriate file.</P>
<P><IMG SRC="penguinslittle.gif" ALIGN="MIDDLE"> Picture icons
➥indicate GIF images</P>
<P><IMG SRC="earicon.gif" ALIGN="MIDDLE"> This icon indicates an AU
➥Sound file</P>
<P><IMG SRC="film.gif" ALIGN="MIDDLE"> This icon indicates an MPEG
➥Video File</P>
<HR>
<H2>Images</H2>
<H2>Sound Files</H2>
<H2>Video Files</H2>
```

Figure 11.7.
The framework for the media archive.

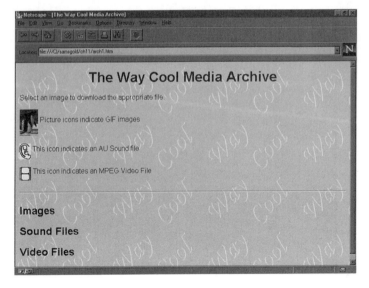

Tip: By putting a space immediately after each image tag, you create a small gap between the image and any text that follows it. For more precise control, you could use the HSPACE attribute, but for this exercise, the space will do the trick.

For the archive, we have four large GIF images:

- [ ] A drawing of a pink orchid
- [ ] A photograph of jelly beans
- [ ] The cougar from the Palo Alto Zoo home page
- [ ] A biohazard symbol

By using your favorite image editor, you can create thumbnails of each picture to serve as the inline icons, and you can insert <IMG> links in the appropriate spots in your archive file:

```
<H2>Images</H2>
<IMG SRC="orchidsmall.gif" ALT="a drawing of a pink orchid">
<IMG SRC="jellybeansmall.gif" ALT="a photograph of some jellybeans">
<IMG SRC="cougarsmall.gif" ALT="a photograph of a cougar">
<IMG SRC="biohazardsmall.gif" ALT="a biohazard symbol">
```

Note that I included values for the ALT attribute to the <IMG> tag, which will be substituted for the images in browsers that cannot view those images. Even though you might not intend for your Web page to be seen by nongraphical browsers, it's polite to at least offer a clue to people who stumble onto it. This way, everyone can access the media files you are offering on this page.

Now, link the thumbnails of the files to the actual images to form the output shown in Figure 11.8:

```
<A HREF="orchid.gif"><IMG SRC="orchidsmall.gif"
   ALT="a drawing of a pinkorchid"></A>
<A HREF="jellybean.gif"><IMG SRC="jellybeansmall.gif"
   ALT="a photograph of some jellybeans"> </A>
<A HREF="cougar.gif"><IMG SRC="cougarsmall.gif"
   ALT="a photograph of a cougar"> </A>
<A HREF="biohazard.gif"><IMG SRC="biohazardsmall.gif"
   ALT="a biohazard symbol"> </A>
```

Figure 11.8.
Image links to larger images.

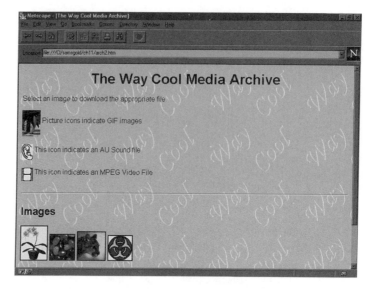

If I leave the archive like this, it looks nice, but I'm breaking one of my own rules: I haven't noted how large the files are. Here you have several choices for formatting. You could just put the size of the file inline with the image and let the images wrap on the page however they want, as illustrated in Figure 11.9:

```
<H2>Images</H2>
<A HREF="orchid.gif"><IMG SRC="orchidsmall.gif"
   ALT="a drawing of a pink orchid"></A>(67K)
<A HREF="jellybean.gif"><IMG SRC="jellybeansmall.gif"
   ALT="a photograph of some jellybeans"></A>(39K)
<A HREF="cougar.gif"><IMG SRC="cougarsmall.gif"
   ALT="a photograph of a cougar"></A>(122K)
<A HREF="biohazard.gif"><IMG SRC="biohazardsmall.gif"
   ALT="a biohazard symbol"></A>(35K)
```

Or you could put in line breaks after each image to ensure that they line up along the left edge of the page. I prefer the first method because it allows a more compact layout of images.

Figure 11.9.
Images with text.

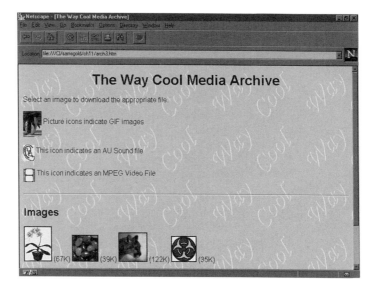

Now, moving on to the sound and video files. You have three sound files and two videos. Because these files can't be reduced to a simple thumbnail image, we'll describe them in the text in the archive (including the huge sizes of the files):

```
<H2>Sound Files</H2>
<P>A five-part a capella renaissance madrigal called "Flora Gave me Fairest
Flowers" (650K)</P>
<P>Some lovely wind-chime sounds (79K) </P>
<P>Chicken noises (112K)</P>
<H2>Video Files</H2>
<P>The famous Tacoma Narrows bridge accident (where the bridge twisted and
fell down in the wind)(13Meg)</P>
<P>A three-dimensional computer animation of a flying airplane over a
landscape (2.3Meg)</P>
```

Now add the icon images to each description—the ear icon to the sounds and the filmstrip icon to the videos. Here we'll also include a value for the ALT attribute to the <IMG> tag, this time providing a simple description that serves as placeholder for the link itself in text-only browsers.

And finally, just as you did in the image part of the example, link the icons to the external files. Here is the HTML code for the final list:

```
<H2>Sound and Video Files</H2>
<P><A HREF="flora.au"><IMG SRC="earicon.gif"
   ALT="[madrigal sound]"> A five-part a capella renaissance
 madrigal called "Flora Gave me Fairest Flowers" (650K)</A></P>
<P><A HREF="windchime.au"><IMG SRC="earicon.gif"
   ALT="[windchime sound]"> Some lovely wind-chime sounds (79K)</A></P>
<P><A HREF="bawkbawk.au"><IMG SRC="earicon.gif"
   ALT="[chicken sound]"> Chicken noises (112K)</A></P>
```

```
<P><A HREF="tacoma.mpeg"><IMG SRC="film.gif" ALT="[tacoma video]">
The famous Tacoma Narrows bridge accident (where the bridge twisted and fell
down in the wind) (13Meg)</A></P>
<P><A HREF="airplane.mpeg"><IMG SRC="film.gif"
 ALT="[3D airplane]">A three-dimensional computer animation of a
 flying airplane over a landscape (2.3Meg) </A></P>
```

And voila, you have your media archive, as shown in Figure 11.10. It's simple with the combination of inline and external images.

Figure 11.10.
Sound and video files.

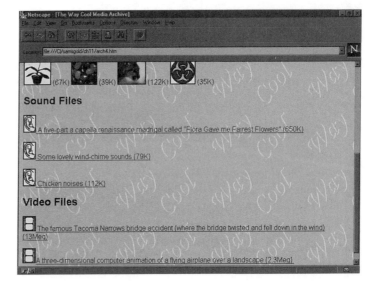

What Are Plug-Ins?

One of the main hassles associated with the use of helper applications is that as a Web publisher you have little or no control over the way these applications display the external media. In addition, users need to continually switch back and forth between the Web browser and the separate helper applications. On a system with a large monitor—17-inch or 21-inch—there is usually enough space on the screen for both programs to be displayed side-by-side, but when you come down to a 14-inch or smaller screen at resolutions around 640×480 pixels, there simply is not enough floor space to go around.

It is for both of these reasons that Netscape Communications has introduced the concept of plug-ins to Navigator 2.0. Basically, a plug-in is a special type of helper application that uses the Web browser's window for its own display purposes instead of creating a separate window and working environment.

Understanding the Differences Between Plug-Ins and Helper Applications

The best way to examine how plug-ins operate, and how they differ from normal external media or helper applications, is by examining a plug-in that was once a standalone helper application.

RealAudio as a Helper Application

When RealAudio released Version 1.0 of the realtime audio player, there was no such thing as a plug-in. Instead, the only way to integrate new features was to use a hyperlink to a file associated with a helper application—in the same way as you did earlier in this chapter for the exercise "Creating a Media Archive." For example, the QUICKNEWS icon shown in Figure 11.11 was linked to a RealAudio data file by the following code:

```
<A HREF=/rafiles/abc/thelatest.ram>
<IMG SRC="qwknews.gif" ALIGN="ABSMIDDLE" HSPACE="8" ALT="QUICKNEWS" BORDER="0">
</A>
```

When you click this icon, the separate helper application—in the small window at the lower right of Figure 11.11—is started by the Web browser so that the selected audio file can be played. When started, this application exists as an entirely separate entity from the Web browser. In fact, even shutting down the Web browser does not stop the RealAudio player.

Figure 11.11.
RealAudio 1.0 used hyperlinks to activate the RealAudio player.

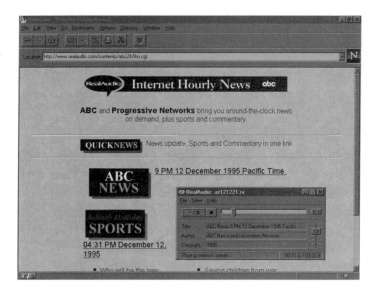

RealAudio as a Plug-In Application

RealAudio Version 2.0 has been upgraded considerably from its predecessor to include a new compression algorithm and higher-quality live audio over 28,800bps or faster links. To accompany this new release, a Navigator 2.0 plug-in version of RealAudio was also introduced. As a result, RealAudio providers can now directly integrate elements of the RealAudio player window as a physical part of a Web page, as shown in Figure 11.12.

Figure 11.12.
The plug-in version of RealAudio 2.0 enables you to integrate elements of the RealAudio player as a physical part of a Web page.

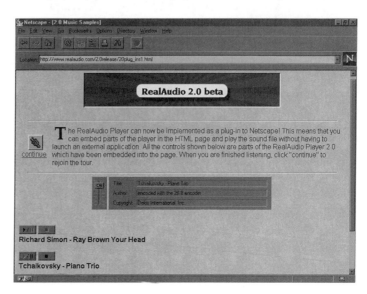

By clicking any of these elements, the user can directly control the RealAudio player without any need for interaction with a separate application, or the inevitable window switching such activities used to invoke.

This is the real power behind the new plug-in technology. The user—after installing the appropriate plug-in software—no longer needs to be concerned that a separate program even exists. In the user's eyes, she is simply viewing a Web page that has some fancy objects on it. The user can still use the Web browser in the usual way, and all the standard features of the browser are still available.

> **Note:** To learn more about how you can incorporate RealAudio technology into your Web page, take a look at the RealAudio home page located at `http://www.realaudio.com/`.

The *<EMBED>* Tag

To make all this new technology compatible with HTML, a new tag has been introduced by Netscape to declare plug-in elements for a Web page. This element, called the `<EMBED>` tag, is used rather than the `<A>` tag for adding plug-in–based information. As a general rule, the basic `<EMBED>` tag takes the following form:

```
<EMBED SRC="filename.extension" WIDTH="value" HEIGHT="value">
```

In this form, the `SRC` attribute indicates the information that is to be presented by the plug-in, and the file extension indicates which plug-in should be used. Basically, the `SRC` attribute takes a standard URL definition, be it a relative address or an absolute address. The `HEIGHT` and `WIDTH` values tell the Web browser how much space the plug-in uses, much as they did for the `<IMG>` tag. Also, all the `ALIGN` attributes supported by the `<IMG>` tag are also available to `<EMBED>` tags, including `ALIGN="TOP"`, `ALIGN="BASELINE"`, and `ALIGN="LEFT"`.

In addition to these tags, each plug-in module can define its own set of individual tags. Take, for example, the following two `<EMBED>` tags:

```
<EMBED SRC="/rafiles/20music/empty7.rpm"
       WIDTH="35"
       HEIGHT="75"
       CONTROLS="VolumeSlider"
       CONSOLE="_master">
<EMBED SRC="/rafiles/20music/empty5.rpm"
       WIDTH="50%"
       HEIGHT="75"
       CONTROLS="InfoPanel"
       CONSOLE="_master">
```

These two tags define the VolumeSlider and InfoPanel elements located in the middle of Figure 11.12. In each case, the `CONTROLS` and `CONSOLE` attributes are specific to the RealAudio plug-in. If they were included in an embedded tag for a different plug-in, they would have little or no effect on its operation.

The <NOEMBED> Tag

Because only Navigator 2.0 recognizes the <EMBED> tag, you need to include some information on your pages for people who don't have Navigator 2.0 or who have not installed the appropriate plug-in module.

To do this, you use the <NOEMBED> and </NOEMBED> tags, as shown here:

```
<EMBED SRC="cmx/canary.cmx" WIDTH="500" HEIGHT="200">
<NOEMBED>
<HR>
<H2>NOTE:</H2>
To view some elements on this page, you need to use
<A HREF="http://www.netscape.com/">Navigator 2.0</A>
and have the <A HREF="http://www.corel.com/corelcmx/">Corel CMX</A>
vector graphics Plug-in module installed.
<HR>
</NOEMBED>
```

When this page is viewed by Navigator 2.0—with the Corel CMX plug-in installed—a page like the one shown in Figure 11.13 is displayed. The canary image at the top of the screen is provided courtesy of the Corel CMX, which provides a mechanism for the presentation of vector graphics images on a Web page. When such a page is displayed by a Web browser that does not support plug-ins, however, you see the result shown in Figure 11.14. In this case, anything that was included inside the <NOEMBED> tags is displayed instead of the file associated with the embedded plug-in.

Figure 11.13.
The Corel CMX plug-in enables you to display inline vector graphics on a Web page.

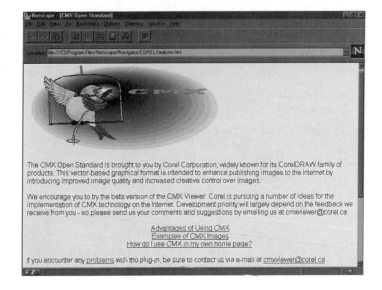

Figure 11.14.
A Web browser that doesn't support plug-ins displays any messages included between the `<NOEMBED>` *and* `</NOEMBED>` *tags.*

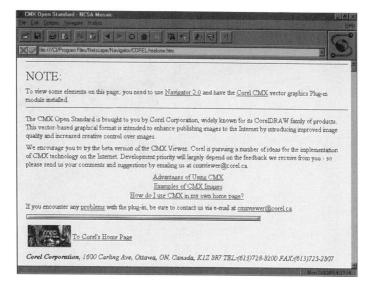

Note: To learn more about the Corel CMX plug-in and the CMX vector image format made popular by the CorelDRAW! suite of programs, point your Web browser to `http://www.corel.com/corelcmx/`.

Other Plug-In Modules

Apart from the RealAudio and CMX plug-ins already mentioned, a rapidly growing number of companies are introducing additional plug-ins, almost daily.

To give you some idea of the wide variety of possibilities offered by plug-ins, the following list examines some of the plug-ins that had been either announced or released before this book went to print:

11

 VDOLive

This plug-in plays live video streams over connections as slow as 14,400bps. Like RealAudio, VDOLive (see Figure 11.15) requires a dedicated VDO server to deliver live video streams, but after this is organized, the resulting video can be incorporated into any Web page. To learn more about the possibilities offered by VDOlive, take a look at the VDO home page located at `http://www.vdolive.com/`.

Figure 11.15.

VDOLive brings realtime video to the World Wide Web.

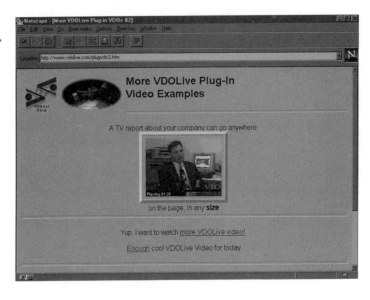

 Shockwave

Shockwave is a plug-in extension that brings MacroMedia Director presentations to the World Wide Web. For example, the Shockwave for Director logo, shown in Figure 11.16, is actually an animated spinning disc created by using the Director presentation system. When this page is viewed using Navigator 2.0, the logo rotates by itself. To see this and many other exciting possibilities offered by Shockwave, take a look at `http://www.macromedia.com/Tools/Shockwave/shock.html`.

Figure 11.16.

Shockwave brings the multimedia capabilities of MacroMedia Director to the World Wide Web.

 WebFX

Of all the plug-ins currently offered, WebFX has to be the most talked about. Using VRML—the virtual reality modeling language—WebFX enables you to explore interactive virtual worlds from the comfort of your Web browser. (See Figure 11.17.) Paper Inc., the company responsible for WebFX, can be found at `http://www.paperinc.com/`.

Figure 11.17.
Virtual reality worlds—all right, it's a house—on the World Wide Web, courtesy of WebFX.

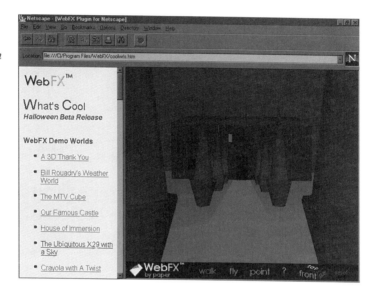

 Formula One/NET

This plug-in provides a mechanism for the inclusion of Excel worksheets and spreadsheets on a Web page and even allows them to be edited by the end user. (See Figure 11.18.) To find out more about Formula One/NET, check out `http://www.visualcomp.com/`.

QuickTime

Apple has announced that it plans to create a QuickTime plug-in that will allow QuickTime audio files and video files to be integrated directly into a Web page in much the same way as with VDOLive. It should be released by the time this book hits the streets.

 Adobe Acrobat

Adobe Acrobat PDF documents can now be displayed as a part of a Web page through the use of Adobe's new Amber plug-in. (See Figure 11.19.) To learn more about the Amber plug-in, point your Web browser to `http://www.adobe.com/Amber/Index.html`

Figure 11.18.
Formula One/NET enables you to include spreadsheets on your Web pages.

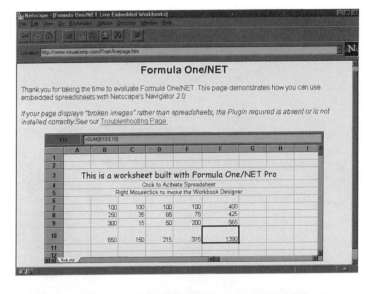

Figure 11.19.
The Amber plug-in from Adobe lets you integrate PDF files with a Web page.

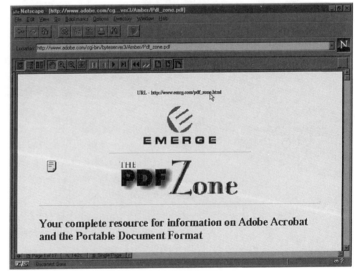

Summary

External media files are files that cannot be read directly by your Web browser. Instead, if you link to an external file, your browser starts up a "helper" application to view or play those files.

Non-inline images, sound, and video are the most popular external media files used on Web pages. In this chapter you've learned about the popular formats for each of these kinds of media and how to obtain samples of them. You've also learned about converting between formats and naming the files appropriately so that they can be recognized by Web browsers.

Unlike external media, plug-ins allow information not normally associated with a Web page to be included directly on it. In this chapter, you have learned about the <EMBED> tag, which provides the means for including plug-in objects on a page, and examined some of the recently released modules.

Workshop

The first section of the Workshop lists some of the common questions people ask about the World Wide Web along with a brief answer to each. Next is a quiz about the chapter you have just read. If you have problems answering any of the questions in the quiz, you can turn to Appendix E, "Answers to Quiz Questions."

Q&A

Q **My browser has a helper application for JPEG images listed in my helper applications list. But when I downloaded a JPEG file, the browser complained that it couldn't read the document. How can I fix this problem?**

A Just because an application is listed in the helper application list (or initialization file) doesn't mean that you have that application available on your system. Browsers are generally shipped with a default listing of helper applications that are most commonly used for the common external file formats available on the Web. You must locate and install each of those helper applications before your browser can use them.

Q **If JPEG files are so much smaller than GIF files, with some slight image degradation that is forgivable, why do browsers use only GIF files for inline images?**

A When image support was put into Mosaic (the first browser to use inline images), GIF was a much more popular format than JPEG, there were many more viewers across platforms for GIF than for JPEG, and the size issue was not as important. Now that JPEG has caught on more, some browsers (such as Navigator 2.0) are beginning to accept inline JPEG images in addition to GIFs.

Q I've been using AU files for my sound samples, but there's an awful hiss during the quiet parts. What can I do?

A Some sound editing programs can remove some of the hiss in AU files, but because of the nature of AU encoding, you'll usually have some amount of noise. If sound quality is that important to you, consider using AIFF or, if you have the converters, MPEG audio.

Q Why don't my MPEG files have sound?

A Maybe they do! The MPEG standard allows for both video and audio tracks, but few players can handle the audio track at this time. You have two choices if you must have sound for your MPEG movies: wait for better players (or bribe a programmer to write one) or convert your movies to QuickTime and show your readers how to install and use QuickTime players.

Quiz

1. What is the three-letter file extension for a JPEG file?
2. If I wanted to include a video clip as part of my Web page, what file formats could I use?
3. What is the name of the tag used to define a plug-in element on a Web page?
4. What is the file extension for a TrueSpeech file?
5. Which audio file format is currently supported by just about all Web browsers on every computer platform?

Exercises

1. If you have not already done so, take a look at all the new plug-ins available for Navigator 2.0. Using the plug-in pages at the Netscape Communications home site, download copies of all the plug-ins currently available for your operating system and spend some time testing each. At the same time, download any tutorials on the use of each, looking especially for descriptions of how you can use the plug-ins with your own Web pages.

2. Next up is your regular task. Create the `11notes.html` file for this chapter. Remember to include all the features discussed in previous chapters. In addition, try to include demonstrations of as many different examples of external images and plug-ins as you can.

   Finally, add a set of hyperlinks to the page that point to all the plug-in developers mentioned in this chapter or by Netscape Communications at the Web site.

12

FOUR

Linked Windows and Frames

Before you learn about the details of setting up your own Web site on Day 5, "Going Online," there is one final subject you need to cover. To round out Day 4, "Enhancing Your Web Page's Visual Appearance," this chapter explores the subject of frames by looking at the following topics:

☐ The Netscape debate revisited

☐ Working with linked windows

☐ Working with frames

☐ Creating complex framesets

The Netscape Debate Revisited

Most of the features and tags discussed in previous chapters will, as a rule, basically work on just about any Web browser. The appearance of the page might not be exactly what you had expected, but at the very least, people with older Web browsers can still view the text and links contained on the page.

In this chapter, however, you will learn about a new set of tags—used to create frames—that currently work only with Navigator 2.0. In addition, due to the nature of these tags, they will basically break any other Web browser, the result of which is Web pages that simply won't display using other browsers. The fact that frames can't be displayed on other Web browsers has made frames one of the most hotly debated topics of the "Netscape versus the rest" debate.

Note: Netscape Communications plans to submit the new frame tags for recognition as part of the HTML 3.0 standard, but it will probably be some time before you see the arrival of other browsers that include the features discussed in this chapter.

This said, for people who plan to develop Netscape 2.0–ready sites, the capabilities provided by the use of frames bring an entirely new level of layout control to Web publishing. Take, for example, the demonstration Web page created by Netscape Communications that is shown in Figure 12.1.

In this one screen Netscape has integrated information that would previously have taken many separate screen loads. In addition, because the information displayed on the page is separated into individual areas or frames, the contents of a single frame can be updated without the contents of any other frame being affected. For example, if you click any of the hotlinks associated with the photos in the left frame, the contents of the large frame on the

right are automatically updated to display the personal details of the selected staff member. When this occurs, the contents of the left frame and the bottom frame are not affected.

Figure 12.1.

A sample Web page with frames provided by Netscape Communications.

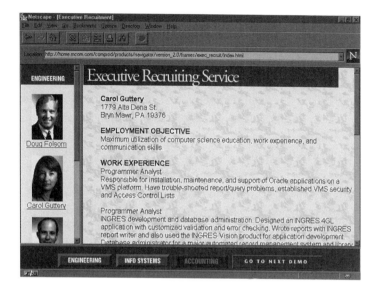

Apart from the demonstration pages provided by Netscape Communications, other sites are currently adding frame support to their Web pages. Of these, one site you might find handy is the color index page developed by InfiNet. (See Figure 12.2.) To visit this page, point your Web browser to `http://www.infi.net/wwwimages/colorindex.html`.

Figure 12.2.

The InfiNet color index provides a handy reference for many of the colors that can be displayed on a Web page.

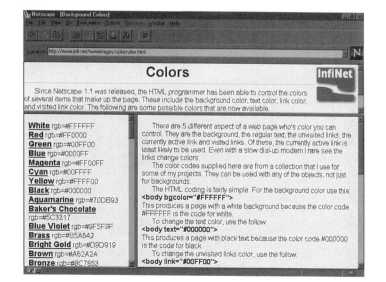

Working with Linked Windows

Before looking at how frames are added to a page, you first need to learn about a new attribute of the <A> tag. This new attribute takes the form TARGET="window_name".

Traditionally, when you click a hyperlink, the contents of the selected page replace the current contents. In a graphical environment, however, there is technically no reason the contents of the new page can't be displayed in a new window, leaving the contents of the calling page displayed onscreen in their own window.

The TARGET attribute enables you to do just that by telling the Web browser to display the information pointed to by a hyperlink in a window called *window_name*. You can call the new window anything you want, but you can't use names that start with an underscore (_). These names are reserved for a set of special TARGET values that you'll learn about later.

When you use the TARGET attribute in an <A> tag, Navigator 2.0 first checks whether a window with the name *window_name* exists. If it does, the document pointed to by the hyperlink replaces the current contents of *window_name*. On the other hand, if no window called *window_name* currently exists, a new browser window is opened and given the name *window_name*. The document pointed to by the hyperlink is loaded into the newly created window.

▼ Exercise: Working with Windows

In this exercise you will create four HTML documents that use hyperlinks, including the TARGET attribute. These hyperlinks will open two new windows called first_window and second_window, as shown in Figure 12.3. The top window is the original Web browser window; first_window is on the bottom left; and second_window the bottom right.

Figure 12.3.
Hyperlinks can be made to open new windows for each of the pages they

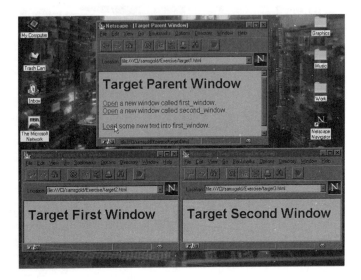

First, create the document to be displayed by the main Web browser window, shown in Figure 12.4, by opening your text editor of choice and entering the following lines of code:

```
<HEAD>
<TITLE>Target Parent Window</TITLE>
</HEAD>
<BODY>
<H1>Target Parent Window</H1>
<P>
<A HREF="target2.html" TARGET="first_window">Open</A>
 a new window called first_window.
<BR>
<A HREF="target3.html" TARGET="second_window">Open</A>
 a new window called second_window.
</P>
<P>
<A HREF="target4.html" TARGET="first_window">Load</A>
 some new text into first_window.
</P>
</BODY>
</HTML>
```

Figure 12.4.
The Target Parent window.

Save this HTML source as `target1.html`.

Next, create a document called `target2.html` that looks like the page shown in Figure 12.5, by entering the following code:

```
<HEAD>
<TITLE>Target First Window</TITLE>
</HEAD>
<BODY>
<H1>Target First Window</H1>
</BODY>
```

Figure 12.5.
target2.html
displayed in the
Web browser
window named
first_window.

After saving target2.html, create another document called target3.html that looks like the page shown in Figure 12.6. Do this by entering the following code:

```
<HEAD>
<TITLE>Target Second Window</TITLE>
</HEAD>
<BODY>
<H1>Target Second Window</H1>
</BODY>
```

Figure 12.6.
target3.html
displayed in the
Web browser
window named
second_window.

Finally, create a fourth document, called target4.html, that looks like the one shown in Figure 12.7:

```
<HEAD>
<TITLE>Target First Window</TITLE>
</HEAD>
<BODY>
<H1>Target First Window</H1>
<P>But this time with new text...</P>
</BODY>
</HTML>
```

To complete the exercise, load target1.html into your Web browser and click on the top two hyperlinks. This action opens two new windows; however, they probably won't be laid out like the ones shown in Figure 12.3. You still need to position each window manually to create the desired effect.

Finally, click the third hyperlink to replace the contents of first_window with the Web page defined by target4.html, as shown in Figure 12.7.

Figure 12.7.
target4.html
displayed in the Web
browser window
named first_window.

The *<BASE>* Tag

When using the TARGET attribute with links, you will sometimes encounter a situation in which all or most of the hyperlinks on a Web page point to the same window—especially when using frames, as you will discover in the following section.

In such cases, instead of including a TARGET attribute for each <A> tag, you can use another tag, called the <BASE> tag, to define a global target for all the links of a Web page. The <BASE> tag takes the following form:

```
<BASE TARGET="window_name">
```

If you include the <BASE> tag in the <HEAD>...</HEAD> block of a document, every <A> tag that does not have a corresponding TARGET attribute will display the document it points to in the window specified by <BASE TARGET="window_name">. For example, if the tag <BASE TARGET="first_window"> had been included in the HTML source for table1.html, the three hyperlinks could have been written this way:

```
<HEAD>
<TITLE>Target Parent Window</TITLE>
<BASE TARGET="first_window">        <!-- add <BASE TARGET="value" here -->
</HEAD>
<BODY>
<H1>Target Parent Window</H1>
<P>
<A HREF="target2.html">Open</A>      <!-- no need to include a TARGET -->
 a new window called first_window.
<BR>
<A HREF="target3.html" TARGET="second_window">Open</A>
 a new window called second_window.
</P>
<P>
<A HREF="target4.html">Load</A>      <!-- no need to include a TARGET -->
 some new text into first_window.
</P>
</BODY>
</HTML>
```

In this case, `target2.html` and `target4.html` are loaded into the default window assigned by the `<BASE>` tag; `target3.html` overrides the default by defining its own target window.

You can also override the window assigned by the `<BASE>` tag by using one of two special window names. If you use `TARGET="_blank"` in a hyperlink, a new browser window is opened that does not have a name associated with it. Alternatively, if you use `TARGET="_self"`, the current window is used rather than the one defined by the `<BASE>` tag.

Working with Frames

The opening introduction of frames in Netscape 2.0 heralds a new era for Web publishers. With the use of three simple tags, you can now create Web publications that duplicate all the common typographical elements found in print magazines. This includes features such as contents tables, banners, footnotes, and sidebars, just to name a few.

At the same time, frames also introduce a new concept to HTML development. Unlike all the previous examples, which have used a single HTML document to display a screen of information, when you create Web sites using frames, a single screen actually consists of a number of separate HTML documents that interact with each other. Figure 12.8 shows how a minimum of four separate documents is needed to create the screen shown in Figure 12.1.

Figure 12.8.
Separate HTML documents must be created for each frame.

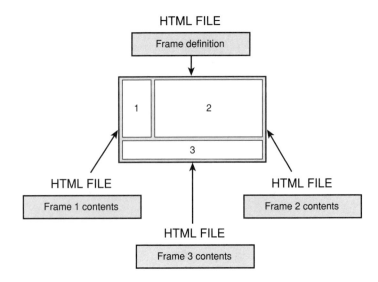

The first HTML document you need to create is called the frame definition document. In this document you enter the HTML code that describes the layout of each frame and indicates the name of the separate HTML document that contains the physical information to be displayed. The three remaining HTML documents contain normal HTML tags that define the physical contents of each separate frame area. These are the documents referenced by the frame definition document.

The *<FRAMESET>* Tag

To create a frame definition document, you use the `<FRAMESET>` tag. When used in an HTML document, the `<FRAMESET>` tag replaces the `<BODY>` tag, as shown here:

```
<HTML>
<HEAD>
<TITLE>Page Title</TITLE>
</HEAD>
<FRAMESET>
    your frame definition goes here.
</FRAMESET>
</HTML>
```

It is important that you understand up front how a frame definition document differs from a normal HTML document. If you include a `<FRAMESET>` tag in an HTML document, you cannot also include a `<BODY>` tag. The two tags are mutually exclusive. In addition, no other formatting tags, hyperlinks, or document text should be included in a frame definition document, except in one special case, which you will learn about later.

The *COLS* Attribute

When you define a `<FRAMESET>` tag, you must include one of two attributes as part of the tag definition. The first of these attributes is the COLS attribute, which takes the following form:

```
<FRAMESET COLS="column width, column width, …">
```

The COLS attribute tells Navigator 2.0 to split the screen into a number of vertical frames whose width is defined by *column width* values separated by commas. You define the width of each frame in one of three ways: explicitly in pixels, as a percentage of the total width of the `<FRAMESET>`, or with an asterisk (*) symbol. When you use the * symbol, Navigator 2.0 uses as much space as possible for the specified frame.

When included in a complete frame definition, the following `<FRAMESET>` tag creates a screen with three vertical frames. (See Figure 12.9.) The first frame is 100 pixels wide, the second is 50% the width of the screen, and the third uses all the remaining space:

```
<FRAMESET COLS="100,50%,*">
```

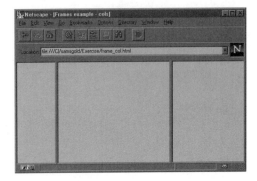

Figure 12.9.
The COLS attribute defines the number of vertical frames or columns in a frameset.

Note: Because you are designing Web pages that will be used on various screen sizes, you should restrict the use of absolute frame sizes to a minimum. In addition, whenever you do use an absolute size, ensure that one of the other frames is defined using an * to take up all the remaining screen space.

Tip: To define a frameset with three equal-width columns, use COLS="*, *, *". This way, you won't have to mess around with percentages, because Navigator 2.0 automatically gives an equal amount of space to each frame assigned an * width.

The *ROWS* Attribute

The ROWS attribute works the same as the COLS attribute except that it splits the screen into horizontal frames rather than vertical ones. For example, to split the screen into two equal-height frames, as shown in Figure 12.10, you would write this:

```
<FRAMESET ROWS="50%,50%">
```

Alternatively, you could use this:

```
<FRAMESET ROWS="*, *">
```

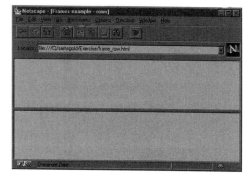

Figure 12.10.
*The ROWS attribute
defines the number of
horizontal frames or
rows in a frameset.*

Note: If you tried either of the preceding examples, you found that the
<FRAMESET> tag did not appear to work. The reason for this is that currently no
contents are defined for the rows or columns in the frameset. To define the
contents, you need to used the <FRAME> tag, which is discussed in the next
section.

The *<FRAME>* Tag

After you have your basic frameset laid out, the next step in the creation of the frame
definition document involves the association of an HTML document with each frame. To
do this, you use the <FRAME> tag, which takes the following form:

```
<FRAME SRC="document URL">
```

For each frame defined in the <FRAMESET> tag, you must include a corresponding <FRAME> tag,
as shown here:

```
<FRAMESET ROWS="*,*,*">
    <FRAME SRC="document1.html">
    <FRAME SRC="document2.html">
    <FRAME SRC="document3.html">
</FRAMESET>
```

In this example, a frameset with three equal-height horizontal frames has been defined. (See Figure 12.11.) The contents of `document1.html` are displayed in the first frame, the contents of `document2.html` in the second frame, and the contents of `document3.html` in the third frame.

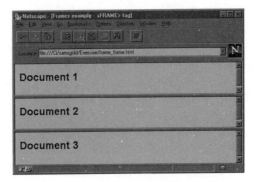

Figure 12.11.
The <FRAME> tag is used to define the contents of each frame.

> **Tip:** When creating frame definition documents, you might find it helpful to indent the <FRAME> tags so that they are separated from the <FRAMESET> tags in your HTML document. Doing so has no effect on the appearance of the resulting Web pages but does tend to make the HTML source easier to read.

Additional Attributes

A few extra attributes can be assigned to a <FRAME> tag to give you additional control over how the user interacts with your frames. To help you understand the purpose of these attributes, Table 12.1 describes the use of each one.

Table 12.1. Control attributes for the <FRAME> tag.

Attribute	Value	Description
SCROLLING	AUTO (default)	By default, if the contents of a frame take up more space than the area available to the frame, Navigator 2.0 automatically adds scrollbars to either the side or the bottom of the frame so that the user can scroll through the document.

Attribute	Value	Description
SCROLLING	NO	Setting the value of SCROLLING to NO disables the use of scrollbars for the current frame. (Note that if you set SCROLLING="NO" but there is more text in the document than can fit inside the frame, the user will not be able to scroll the additional text into view.)
SCROLLING	YES	If you set SCROLLING to YES, the scrollbars are included in the frame regardless of whether they are required.
NORESIZE		By default, the user can move the position of borders around each frame on the current screen by grabbing the border and moving it with his or her mouse. To lock the borders of a frame and prevent them from being moved, use the NORESIZE attribute.
MARGINHEIGHT	pixels	To adjust the margin that appears above and below a document within a frame, set MARGINHEIGHT.
MARGINWIDTH	pixels	The MARGINWIDTH attribute enables you to adjust the margin on the left and right sides of a frame.

The *<NOFRAME>* Tag

If you load a frame definition document into a Web browser that does not support frames, you get only a blank page. To get around this problem, Navigator 2.0 includes a special tag block called <NOFRAME> that enables you to include body text as part of the document. When used in an HTML document, the <NOFRAME> tag takes the following form:

```
<HTML>
<HEAD>
<TITLE>Page Title</TITLE>
</HEAD>
<FRAMESET>
 your frame definition goes here.
<NOFRAME>
  Include any text, hyperlinks, and tags you want to here.
</NOFRAME>
</FRAMESET>
</HTML>
```

12

None of the text you include inside the <NOFRAME> block will be displayed by Navigator 2.0, but when the page is loaded into a Web browser that does not support frames, it will be displayed. This technique provides you with a way to advise the user that the page requires a Web browser that supports the use of frames. You might also include a hyperlink to Netscape Communications along with a recommendation that the user download Navigator 2.0 to view your page.

On the other hand, if you have created a site that includes alternative pages for non-Netscape 2.0–specific browsers, you would naturally include hyperlinks that point to these pages.

Creating Complex Framesets

The framesets you have learned about so far represent the most basic types of frames that can be displayed by Navigator 2.0. But in day-to-day use, you will rarely use these basic frame designs. In all but the most simple sites, you will most likely want to use more complex framesets.

Therefore, to help you understand the possible combinations of frames, links, images, and documents that can be used by a Web site, this final section of the chapter explores the topic of complex framesets.

Exercise: Combining *ROWS* and *COLS*

The frame layout presented by Figure 12.1 at the beginning of the chapter provides a good basis for a simple example that explores the way framesets can be combined to create complex designs. To remind you of the basic layout, Figure 12.12 shows a screen that uses a similar design but without any contents.

> **Tip:** When you're designing complex frame layouts, storyboards are an invaluable tool. The storyboard helps you block out the structure of a frameset, and it can also be invaluable when you're adding hyperlinks, as you will see in the next exercise, "Using Named Frames and Hyperlinks."

In Figure 12.12 the top section of the screen is split into two vertical frames, and the third frame, at the bottom of the page, spans the entire width of the screen. To create a frame definition document that describes this layout, open your text editor and enter the following basic HTML structural details:

```
<HTML>
<HEAD>
<TITLE>Complex Frames Exercise</TITLE>
</HEAD>
<FRAMESET>
</FRAMESET>
</HTML>
```

Figure 12.12.
The "Combining ROWS and COLS" exercise.

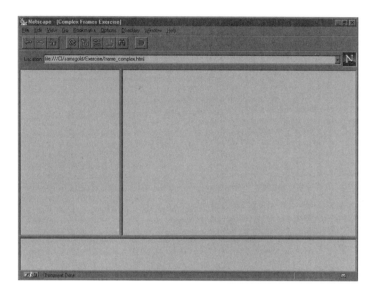

Next, you must decide whether you need to use a ROWS or COLS attribute in your base <FRAMESET>. To do this, take a look at your storyboard—in this case Figure 12.12—and work out whether any frame areas extend right across the screen or from the top to the bottom of the screen. If any frames extend from the top to the bottom, you need to start with a COLS frameset; otherwise, you need to start with a ROWS frameset. On the other hand, if no frames extend completely across the screen in either direction, you should start with a COLS frameset.

To put it more simply, here are some easily remembered rules:

- ☐ Left to right, use ROWS
- ☐ Top to bottom, use COLS
- ☐ Can't decide, use COLS

12

Note: The reasoning behind the use of the "left to right, use ROWS" rule relates to how Navigator 2.0 creates frames. Each separate <FRAMESET> definition can split the screen (or frame) either vertically or horizontally, but not both ways. For this reason, you need to define your framesets in a logical order to ensure that the desired layout is achieved.

In Figure 12.12 the bottom frame extends right across the screen from side to side. As a result, by using the rules mentioned previously you need to start with a ROWS frameset. To define the base frameset, write this:

```
<FRAMESET ROWS="*, 80">
   <FRAME SRC="dummy.html">  <!-- this is the frame for row 1 -->
   <FRAME SRC="dummy.html">  <!-- this is the frame for row 2 -->
</FRAMESET>
```

Doing this splits the screen into two sections: a small frame at the bottom of the screen that is 80 pixels high and a large frame at the top of the screen that uses the rest of the available space. Two <FRAME> tags have also been defined to represent the contents of each frame.

Tip: When laying out the basic structure of a frameset, you normally don't want to be bothered with such details as the actual contents of the frames. However, unless you define <FRAME> tags that include a valid document, your frameset will not be displayed properly when it is loaded into Navigator 2.0 for testing.

To get around this problem, create a small empty HTML document called dummy.html, and use it for all your frame testing. Alternatively, you can use a specific URL provided by Navigator 2.0 called about:blank which simply displays a blank Web page.

Nesting *<FRAMESET>* Tags

The next step in the process is to split the top frame area into two vertical frames. You achieve this effect by placing a second <FRAMESET> block inside the base <FRAMESET> block. When one <FRAMESET> block is nested inside another, the nested block must replace one of the <FRAME> tags in the outside frameset.

Therefore, to split the top frame into two frame areas, you replace the <FRAME> tag for the first frame with an embedded <FRAMESET> block. Doing this embeds the new frameset inside the area defined for the <FRAME> tag it replaces. Inside the <FRAMESET> tag for this new block, you then need to define a COLS attribute as shown here:

```
<FRAMESET ROWS="*, 80">
    <FRAMESET COLS="30%, *">        <!-- the frame for row 1   -->
        <FRAME SRC="dummy.html">    <!--  has been replaced     -->
        <FRAME SRC="dummy.html">    <!--    by an embedded      -->
    </FRAMESET>                     <!--     frameset block      -->
    <FRAME SRC="dummy.html">  <!-- this is the frame for row 2 -->
</FRAMESET>
```

The embedded COLS frameset defines two columns, the first being 30% the width of the embedded frame area and the second taking up all the remaining space in the embedded frame area. In addition, two <FRAME> tags are embedded inside the <FRAMESET> block to define the contents of each column.

> **Note:** When used inside an embedded frameset, any percentage sizes are based on a percentage of the total area of the embedded frame and not as a percentage of the total screen.

Finally, as you have done previously, save the finished HTML document to your hard drive and test it by using Navigator 2.0. Also, if you happen to have a copy of a different Web browser, try loading the document into it. (You should not see anything when you use the alternative browsers.)

Exercise: Using Named Frames and Hyperlinks

As mentioned earlier in this chapter, the frame definition document itself does not describe the contents of each frame. It is the documents indicated by the SRC attribute of the <FRAME> that actually contain the text, images, and tags displayed by the frameset.

As a result, to turn the frame definition document created in the preceding exercise into a fully working, frame-based Web page, you need to add some valid HTML documents to the definition. The frames are so powerful because any HTML document you have created previously can become the SRC for an individual frame. Therefore, it is easy to take the HTML reference documents you have been creating for each chapter and integrate them into a frameset. But first, so that you understand what you are about to create, Figure 12.13 shows the complete frameset you will create in this exercise.

12

Figure 12.13.
The HTML reference document as a frameset.

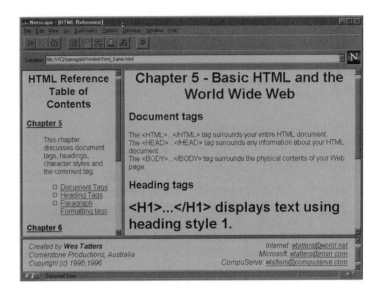

Adding Real Documents to Your Frameset

The first step in the process is simple. Take the frameset document you created in the exercise "Combining ROWS and COLS," and save a copy of it in the same directory as the HTML reference documents you created previously. Name the new file html_frame.html.

After you have created this new file, make the changes highlighted in bold as shown in the following text:

```
<FRAMESET ROWS="*, 80">
    <FRAMESET COLS="30%, *">
        <FRAME SRC="html_contents_frame.html">
        <FRAME SRC="05notes_frame.html">
    </FRAMESET>
    <FRAME SRC="html_footer.html">
</FRAMESET>
```

The first <FRAME> tag now points to a file called html_contents_frame.html. This file is a copy of the html_contents.html file you have been working with in previous chapters. However, because you will need to make some minor alterations to the document, it has been renamed so as not to alter the original. But for now, simply copy the html_contents.html file to html_contents_frame.html.

Tip: MS-DOS users must use an alternative naming scheme such as cont_f.htm and 05note_f.htm.

Do the same for `05notes.html` by copying it to `05notes_frame.html`, and then work through each of the other chapter documents and any other pages they reference.

You next need to make some alterations to `05notes_frame.html`. In previous exercises, you have added `<ADDRESS>` blocks and navigation buttons to each page. With frames, however, you don't need to include either of these elements, because in this exercise they will be handled in one way or another by other frames in the frameset. As result, you should remove the signature and navigation buttons from the bottom of `05notes_frame.html`. In addition, remove any other hyperlinks that join the pages together.

Finally, you need to create a new HTML document called `html_footer.html`. In this document you will place the information previously shown in the `<ADDRESS>` block of your individual pages. What you place in this document is up to you; however, you should keep in mind that it will need to fit into the small 80-pixel-high frame at the bottom of the frameset.

To give you some idea about how you might create the contents of `html_footer.html`, here is the partial HTML source used for Figure 12.13:

```
<TABLE>
<TR> <!-- Start of row one -->
<TD WIDTH="50%">
<ADDRESS>
Created by <B>Wes Tatters</B><BR>
Cornerstone Productions, Australia
Copyright (c) 1995,1996
</ADDRESS>
</TD>
<TD WIDTH="50%" ALIGN="RIGHT">
<ADDRESS>
Internet: <A HREF="mailto:wtatters@world.net">wtatters@world.net</A><BR>
Microsoft: <A HREF="mailto:wtatters@msn.com">wtatters@msn.com</A><BR>
CompuServe: <A HREF="mailto:wtatters@compuserve.com">wtatters@compuserve.com
</A><BR>
</ADDRESS>
</TD>
</TR>
</TABLE>
```

In this example, a table without borders has been used to place my name on the left side of the screen and my e-mail addresses on the right.

Naming Individual Frames

If you were to load `html_frame.html` into Navigator 2.0 at this stage, you would see a screen similar to the one shown in Figure 12.13. Some of the text sizes and spacing might be slightly different, but the general picture would be the same. If, however, you were to click any of the hyperlinks in the left frame, you would most likely get some very strange results. To be more

12

specific, Navigator 2.0 would attempt to load the contents of the file you select into the left frame, when what you really want it to do is load each document into the right frame.

To make this happen, you need to use a slight variation on the TARGET attribute discussed at the beginning of this chapter. But instead of the TARGET pointing to a new window, you want it to point to one of the frames in the current frameset.

You can achieve this by first giving each frame in your frameset a frame name, or window name. To do this, you include a NAME attribute inside the <FRAME> tag, which takes the following form:

```
<FRAME SRC="document URL" NAME="frame name">
```

Therefore, to assign a name to each of the frames in the html_frame.html document, you alter the <FRAME> tags to look like this:

```
<FRAMESET ROWS="*, 80">
    <FRAMESET COLS="30%, *">
        <FRAME SRC="html_contents_frame.html"  NAME="Contents">
        <FRAME SRC="05notes_frame.html"  NAME="Chapter">
    </FRAMESET>
    <FRAME SRC="html_footer.html"  NAME="Footer">
</FRAMESET>
```

This names the left frame "Contents", the right frame "Chapter", and the bottom frame "Footer". After this, resave the updated html_frame.html file, and you are just about finished with the exercise.

Linking Documents to Individual Frames

All that now remains are some minor alterations to html_contents_frame.html so that each chapter document is loaded into the right-hand frame of the frameset.

If you cast your mind back to the beginning of the chapter, you will recall that the TARGET attribute was used with the <A> tag to force a document to load into a specific window. This is the same attribute that is used to control which frame a document is loaded into.

For this exercise, whenever you click a hyperlink in the left frame, you want the corresponding document to be loaded into the right frame. Because you have already assigned the right frame a window name of "Chapter", to load all the documents into the right frame, all you need to do is add TARGET="Chapter" to each tag in the html_contents_frame.html document. The following HTML source demonstrates how this is done:

```
<A HREF="05notes_frame.html" TARGET="Chapter"><H3>Chapter 5</H3></A>
<DD>
<P>This chapter discusses document tags, headings, character styles
and the comment tag. </P>
<UL>
<LI><A HREF="05notes_frame.html#document_tags" TARGET="Chapter">Document tags
</A>
```

```
<LI><A HREF="05notes_frame.html#heading_tags" TARGET="Chapter">Heading tags</A>
<LI><A HREF="05notes_frame.html#paragraph_tags" TARGET="Chapter">Paragraph
Formatting tags</A>
</UL>
```

Note: If you are using the new naming system set out in this exercise, you need to change the HREF value of each <A> tag to point to the new names for each document. For example, 05notes.html becomes 05notes_frame.html.

Alternatively, because every tag in the html_contents_frame.html document points to the same frame, you could also use the <BASE TARGET="*value*"> tag. In this case, you don't need to include TARGET="Chapter" inside each <A> tag. Instead, you place the following inside the <HEAD>…</HEAD> block of the document:

```
<BASE TARGET="Chapter">
```

The only other change you need to make to html_content_frame.html is purely cosmetic. In the original document, the main heading line uses <H1>; however, this is too large a heading size for the small left frame. Therefore, you should replace it with this:

```
<H2 ALIGN="CENTER">HTML Reference Table of Contents</H2>
```

With all the changes and new documents created, you should now be able to load html_frame.html into Navigator 2.0 and view all of your HTML reference documents by selecting from the table of contents in the left frame.

Tip: To get the layout exactly right, after you have gotten all your links working properly, you might need to go back and adjust the size of the rows and columns as defined in the <FRAMESET> tags. But remember, the final appearance of a frameset is still determined by the size of the screen and the operating system used by people viewing the documents.

Magic *TARGET* Names

Netscape Communications has defined four special values that can be assigned to a TARGET attribute, two of which you have already encountered. Netscape calls these values Magic TARGET names. Table 12.2 lists the Magic TARGET names and describes their use.

12

Table 12.2. Magic TARGET names.

TARGET Name	Description
TARGET="_blank"	Forces the document referenced by the <A> tag to be loaded into a new "unnamed" window.
TARGET="_self"	Causes the document referenced by the <A> tag to be loaded into the window or frame that held the <A> tag.
TARGET="_parent"	Forces the link to load into the <FRAMESET> parent of the current document. If, however, the current document has no parent, TARGET="_self" will be used.
TARGET="_top"	Forces the link to load into the full Web browser window, replacing the current <FRAMESET> entirely. If, however, the current document is already at the top, TARGET="_self" will be used.

Summary

If your head is hurting after reading this chapter, you are probably not alone. Although the basic concepts behind the use of frames are relatively straightforward, their implementation is somewhat harder to come to grips with. As a result, the best way to learn about frames is by experimenting with them.

In this chapter you have learned how to link a document to a new or an existing window. In addition, you have learned how to create framesets and link them together by using the tags listed in Table 12.3.

Table 12.3. New tags discussed in this chapter.

Tag	Description
<BASE TARGET="window">	Sets the global link window for a document.
<FRAMESET>	Defines the basic structure of a frameset.
COLS	Defines the number of frame columns and their width in a frameset.
ROWS	Defines the number of frame rows and their height in a frameset.
<FRAME>	Defines the contents of a frame within a frameset.
SRC	The URL of the document to be displayed inside the frame.

Tag	Description
MARGINWIDTH	The size in pixels of the margin on each side of a frame.
MARGINHEIGHT	The size in pixels of the margin above and below the contents of a frame.
SCROLLING	Enables or disables the display of scroll bars for a frame. Values are YES, NO, and AUTO.
NORESIZE	Doesn't allow the user to resize frames.
<NOFRAME>	Defines text to be displayed by Web browsers that don't support the use of frames.

If you have made it this far through the book, you should give yourself a pat on the back. With the knowledge you have gained, you are now ready to place your Web pages onto the Internet itself. Tomorrow, in Day 5, you will learn about Web servers, advertising and promotion, and explore some of the hints and tips that improve the quality of a Web site.

Workshop

The first section of the Workshop lists some of the common questions people ask about the World Wide Web along with a brief answer to each. Next is a quiz about the chapter you have just read. If you have problems answering any of the questions in the quiz, you can turn to Appendix E, "Answers to Quiz Questions."

Q&A

Q Is there any limit to how many levels of <FRAMESET> tags I can nest within a single screen?

A No, there isn't a limit. Practically speaking, however, when you get below about four levels, the size of the window space available does start to become unusable.

Q What would happen if I included a reference to a frame definition document within a <FRAME> tag?

A Navigator 2.0 handles such a reference correctly, by treating the nested frame definition document as a nested <FRAMESET>. In fact, this technique is used regularly by people to reduce the complexity of nested frames.

There is, however, one limitation. You cannot include a reference to the current frame definition document in one of its own frames. This situation, called recursion, causes an infinite loop. Netscape Communications has included built-in protection to guard against this type of referencing.

12

Quiz

1. What does the TARGET attribute do when used inside an <A> tag?
2. What is the difference between the ROWS and COLS attributes of the <FRAMESET> tag?
3. What attribute is used with the <FRAME> tag to specify a margin above and below a frame?
4. Why would you use TARGET="_top" in a hyperlink?
5. What does the <NOFRAME> tag do?

Exercise

As usual, you need to create the 12note.html document for your HTML reference collection. This time, however, instead of creating a document that will be viewed on its own, integrate it with the frameset created in the exercise "Using Named Frames and Hyperlinks." To do this, add the appropriate links to html_contents_frame.html.

In addition, if you have not already updated all the other chapter documents so that they work with the new frameset version, you should do so now.

DAY 5

Going Online

13

FIVE

Installing Your Web Pages on a Web Server

This is the day of reckoning. You've put together a Web presentation with a well-organized structure, included meaningful images (and specified values for the ALT attributes), written your text with wit and care, used only relative links, and tested it extensively on your own system.

Now, on Day 5, "Going Online," it's finally time to publish your presentation, to put it all online so that other people on the Web can see it and link their pages to yours. In this chapter you'll learn nearly everything you need to know to get started publishing the work you've done:

☐ Where you can find a Web server on which to put your presentation

☐ How to install your Web presentation

☐ How to determine your URL

☐ How to test your Web pages

☐ Some hints for administering your own server

☐ How to obtain Netscape Now recognition

What Does a Web Server Do?

A Web server is a program that sits on a machine on the Internet, waiting for a Web browser to connect to it and make a request. When a request comes over the wire, the server locates and sends the file back to the browser. It's as easy as that.

Web servers and Web browsers communicate using the hypertext transfer protocol (HTTP), a special "language" created specifically for transferring hypertext documents over the Web. Because of this, Web servers are often called HTTPD servers.

Note: The D in HTTPD stands for daemon. *Daemon* is a UNIX term for a program that sits in the background and waits for requests. When it receives a request, it wakes up, processes that request, and then goes back to sleep. You don't have to be on UNIX for a program to act like a daemon, so Web servers on any platform are still called HTTPDs. Most of the time, I call them Web servers.

When a server sends a file to a browser, the server also sends information about what kind of file it is sending (for example, a GIF or JPEG file or a QuickTime movie). The browser uses that information to determine whether it can display the file itself or whether it needs to start a helper application. You can also extend the behavior of your server to include files that might not be part of the default set.

Finally, Web servers can also be set up to run scripts and programs based on information your readers provide from their browsers. For example, you could set up a Web page that asks your reader for a search string. When the browser sends back the string—as entered by the reader, using the browser—the server passes that string to a program on the server side that does the search and passes the result to the server, which in turn hands it back to the browser.

These special programs are called CGI scripts, gateway programs, or gateway scripts. They are the basis for creating interactive forms and clickable image maps (images that contain several "hotspots" and that perform different operations based on the selected location within the image). You'll learn about these scripts in Chapter 16, "Interacting with the Web Server by Using CGI," and about forms and image maps tomorrow. But for now, let's focus on getting your pages out onto the Web.

Finding a Server to Use

Before you can put your Web presentation on the World Wide Web, you'll need to find a Web server you can use. Depending on how you get your access to the Internet, this might be really easy or not quite so easy.

Using a Web Server Provided by Your School or Work

If you get your Internet connection through school or work, that organization will most likely allow you to publish Web pages on its Web server. Given that these organizations usually have fast connections to the Internet, and people to administer the site for you, this is an ideal situation.

If you're in this situation, you'll have to ask your system administrator, computer consultant, or network provider whether a Web server is available, and if so, where to put your pages so that they can be viewed by the Web community at large.

Using a Commercial Internet or Web Service

If you pay for your access to the Internet through an Internet service provider or a commercial online service, you might also be able to publish your Web pages using that service. It might, however, cost you extra to do so, and there might be restrictions on the kind of pages you can publish or whether you can run CGI scripts. Ask through your provider's help line or by seeking out groups or conferences related to Internet services to see how they have set up Web publishing.

Alternatively, several organizations have popped up in the past year that provide nothing but space on their server so that you can publish your Web pages. These services usually provide some method for transferring your files to their site, and they provide the disk space and the network connection. Generally, you are charged a flat monthly rate, with some additional cost if you use a large amount of disk space. Some services even allow gateway scripts for forms and image maps and provide consulting to help you set them up. And a few even set up their server with your own "vanity" domain name so that it looks as if you've got your own server running on the Web. These features can make commercial Web sites an especially attractive option. Appendix D, "Sources of Additional Information," includes pointers to lists of these sites.

Using Anonymous FTP or Gopher

If your service provider doesn't provide a Web server but does allow you to make files available using FTP or Gopher, you can serve HTML files to the Web using those services instead. However, as a rule, accessing Web pages using either FTP or Gopher will normally take longer than via a Web server. You'll have a different URL (starting with either `ftp://` or `gopher://` instead of `http://`), and you won't have access to all the features of a real Web site (forms, CGI scripts, image maps), but if it's all you've got, it'll work just fine. In addition, this is often a cheaper option than a dedicated Web server.

Note: With the rapid growth in popularity of the World Wide Web over the past year or so, the use of FTP or Gopher servers for Web hosting is becoming less and less popular. Frankly, if your current site cannot provide you with access to a Web server, then it's probably time to look elsewhere.

Setting Up Your Own Server

For the ultimate in Web publishing, running your own Web server is the way to go. If you run your own server, not only can you publish as much as you want to and include any kind of content, but you also can use forms, CGI scripts, image maps, and other special options that many other Web servers won't let you use.

There is, of course, a drawback. There are several, in fact. To set up your own server, not only will you need access to a computer system to run it on, but more important, you'll also need a fast full-time connection to the Internet. A part-time dialup 14,400bps or 28,800bps SLIP or PPP connection might be fine for browsing other people's Web pages, but if you are publishing information yourself, you'll want your server available all the time and you'll want the fastest connection you can possibly afford. Although you can serve pages at 14,400bps,

your server will be painfully slow to nearly all sites trying to access your information. The bare minimum is 28,800bps, but a dedicated line such as a 56,000bps or ISDN line is preferable. But, of course, those lines are considerably more expensive than the little dialup SLIP or PPP connection you get through your normal Internet provider; they can run into hundreds of dollars a month.

> **Note:** The Serial Line Internet Protocol (SLIP) and the Point-to-Point Protocol (PPP) are the two most common methods used when connecting a dialup modem to the Internet. The Integrated Services Digital Network (ISDN), on the other hand, is a high-speed 56,000bps plus digital communications system used primarily for permanent Internet connections.

In addition, you'll need the technical background to be able to administer the server. For Macintosh and Windows systems, this might not be such a big problem, but for UNIX systems, you'll need to know a good deal about UNIX and network administration, as well as how to set up and administer the server itself and keep it running all the time.

Between the system you'll need in order to serve documents, the fees for the Internet connection, the amount of knowledge you need, and the time you'll spend administering it, setting up your own server might not be a cost-effective method of publishing Web documents, to say the least. This is particularly true when Web services can give you most of what you need for a low monthly fee and none of the hassles. But running your own server does provide the most flexibility and power of all of these solutions, because you can configure everything the way you want it to be and can install and use gateway scripts for interactivity and forms.

Choosing Your Server Software

If you do decide to install your own server on your own system, you can choose from several servers for each platform. This section describes the most popular servers and their major features.

FTP and Web sites for all the servers in this section are described in Appendix D.

Servers for UNIX Systems

The Web began on UNIX systems, and even today new features are usually introduced on UNIX systems first. UNIX systems often make the best Web servers because of the advantage they have in Web technology—more tools and hints and publicly available software exist for managing Web servers on UNIX than on any other platform.

Many Web servers are publicly available for UNIX, but the two most widely used are the Web Consortium's W3C httpd Web server (known previously as the CERN HTTPD server) and NCSA's HTTPd server. Both are freeware and both serve Web files equally well. Both also provide advanced features such as forms and CGI scripts.

The W3C httpd server can also be run as a proxy; that is, it can be set up to handle outgoing Web connections from inside an Internet firewall. Some organizations set up their networks so that most of the machines are on an internal network, with only one machine actually talking to the Internet at large, to prevent (or minimize) unauthorized access on the internal network. That one machine is called a firewall, and with W3C's httpd running on it, it can pass Web information back and forth between the internal network and the Web at large.

W3C httpd servers running as proxies also have a facility for *caching*—storing frequently retrieved documents on the firewall system instead of retrieving them from the Web every time they are requested. This can significantly speed up the time it takes to access a particular document through a firewall.

NCSA's HTTPd, on the other hand, supports server-side include files, which allow documents to include other documents and be customized when a reader requests them. NCSA's server is also somewhat better supported and is more popular on the Web at large, so more tools and help are available for it than for the W3C httpd server.

At the time this book was written, the most current version of the W3C httpd server was 3.1, and the most current version of the NCSA HTTPd server was 1.5.

Note: To install either W3C's or NCSA's server to run most effectively in its default configuration, you should have root access (preferably at the system administrator level) on the system you are running on. But you can run a Web server even if you don't have root access by installing it on a port number above 1024. (See the documentation for your server for instructions on doing this.) If you decide to go this route, be sure to check with your system administrator first. Web servers can be a significant draw on system resources, and the providers of your system might not want you running a Web server at all, in which case you'll have to look for an alternative solution to serving your files.

In addition to the popular W3C httpd and NCSA HTTPd servers, Netscape Communications offers a range of server products. The Netscape servers have many extra administrative features that the freeware HTTPDs do not have, and they can handle extremely busy sites better than those servers as well. The catch, of course, is that the Netscape servers are not freeware.

The Netscape Communications Server for UNIX—currently at Version 1.12—costs $1,295, with technical support adding $495 to the bill. To try out the features offered by the Communications Server, Netscape offers a 60-day test-drive program, after which time you'll be so in love with it that you'll fork over the money.

The Netscape Commerce Server provides all the features of the Communications Server as well as software to provide encrypted connections between the server and the browser for secure transactions over the Internet. The Netscape Commerce Server for UNIX systems costs $2,995, with support costing an extra $995.

You can find out more about the Netscape servers at the Netscape home page at `http://www.netscape.com/`.

Servers for Microsoft Windows

Although the Web has been slanted toward UNIX for some time now, this situation is rapidly changing. If you use a PC running Windows, Windows for Workgroups, Windows NT, or Windows 95, that PC can easily run as a Web server.

For Windows and Windows for Workgroups, WinHTTPD is a popular server. Based on NCSA's HTTPd, WinHTTPD has been very popular and has proven to be as robust and fast as UNIX-based servers. It also provides CGI scripting capabilities through a DOS shell or a Visual Basic interface. Its current version is 1.4c. It's free for personal use, but commercial users are expected to register and pay for it (registration costs a scant $99).

With the introduction of Windows 95 a number of new Web servers have begun to appear on the market. These new servers take advantage of the 32-bit capabilities offered by Windows 95 and make for an ideal entry-level Web server system. For people interested in exploring the possibilities offered by Windows 95, a demonstration version of the Alibaba HTTP server and the Purveyor server have been included on the CD-ROM. (Note that an NT version of each is also provided.)

On the commercial front, for Windows NT and Windows 95, a 32-bit version of WinHTTPD called WebSite is provided by O'Reilly and Associates for around $379. In addition, the Netscape Communications Server is available for Windows NT, at $495, as is the Commerce Server, at $1,295. See Netscape's home page for details.

Servers for Macintosh

MacHTTP is an HTTP server for the Macintosh that is exceptionally easy to set up and use. It provides extensive CGI scripting capabilities through AppleScript. MacHTTP is shareware; you can use it for 30 days, and after that the cost is $65 for educational users and $95 for everyone else.

Organizing and Installing Your HTML Files

After you have access to a Web server of some sort, you can publish the Web presentation you've labored so hard to create. But before you actually move it into place on your server, it's best to have your files organized and to have a good idea of what goes where so that you don't lose files and your links don't break.

Probably the best way to organize each of your presentations is to include all the files for that presentation in a single directory. If you have lots of extra files—for your images, for example—you can put those in a subdirectory of that main directory. Your goal is to contain all your files in a single place instead of scattering them around on your disk. After you have your files contained, you can set all your links in your files to be relative to that directory. If you follow these hints, you stand the best chance of being able to move that directory around to different servers without breaking the links.

Web servers usually have a default HTML file that is loaded when the reader requests a URL that ends with a directory rather than a specific file. For most Web servers, this file is usually called `index.html` (`index.htm` for MS-DOS). Your home page or top-level index for each presentation should be called by this name so that the server knows which page to load as the default page. Using this default filename also allows the URL to that page to be shorter because you don't have to include the actual filename. So, for example, your URL might be `http://www.myserver.com/www/` rather than `http://www.myserver.com/www/index.html`.

Each file should also have an appropriate extension indicating what kind of file it is so that the server can map it to the appropriate file type. When you publish your files, the server uses the file extension to tell the browser what kind of file it's sending (much the way the browser used the file extension for your local files to figure out what kind of file it was).

Table 13.1 lists the common file extensions you should be using for your files and media.

Table 13.1. File types and extensions.

Format	Extension
HTML	`.html, .htm`
ASCII text	`.txt`
Java class	`.class`
JavaScript script	`.js`
PostScript	`.ps`
GIF	`.gif`

Format	Extension
JPEG	`.jpg`, `.jpeg`
AU audio	`.au`
TrueSpeech	`.dsp`
MPEG video	`.mpeg`, `.mpg`

Installing Your Files

With your files organized into a single directory, all you have to do is put them in the appropriate spot on the server. After the server can access your files, you're officially published on the Web. That's all there is to it.

But where is the appropriate spot on your server? Here's where you'll have to ask the person who runs your Web server. All servers are set up differently, and everyone has a different place for storing Web files. Usually, your server administrator will set up a directory for you to put your files in.

The W3C httpd and NCSA HTTPd UNIX-based servers can be set up so that you can store your Web files in your home directory, instead of storing them in a central location elsewhere on the system. In this case, you'll need to create that special directory and put your files there. Again, here's where you'll have to talk to the person running your Web server to find out how he has set it up.

Some Gotchas About Moving Files Between Systems

If you're using a Web server that has been set up by someone else, you'll probably have to move your Web files from your system to that person's Web server using FTP, Zmodem transfer, or some other method. Although the HTML markup within your files is completely portable, moving the actual files from platform to platform has its gotchas. In particular, be careful to carry out the following actions:

☐ Transfer binary files as binary.

Watch out for your images and other media; make sure that you send them in binary mode when you transfer them, or they might not work on the other end.

Watch out for Macintosh media—in particular, that you transfer the files as regular binary and not MacBinary. MacBinary files cannot be read on other platforms.

☐ Observe filename restrictions.

If you're moving your files to or from pre-Windows 95 MS-DOS systems, you'll have to watch out for the dreaded 8.3—the DOS rule that says filenames must be only up to eight characters long with three-character extensions. If your server is a PC and you've been writing your files on some other system, you might have to rename your files and the links to them to have the right file naming conventions. (Moving files you've created on a PC to some other system is usually not a problem.)

Also, if you're moving files from a Macintosh to other systems, be sure that your filenames do not have spaces or other funny characters in them. Keep your filenames as short as possible, use only letters and numbers, and you'll be fine.

☐ Be aware of carriage returns and line feeds.

Different systems use different methods for ending a line. The Macintosh uses carriage returns, UNIX uses line feeds, and DOS uses both. When you move files from one system to another, most of the time the end-of-line characters are converted appropriately, but sometimes they are not. This difficulty can result in your file coming out double-spaced or all on a single line on the system it was moved to.

Most of the time it does not matter because browsers ignore spurious returns or line feeds in your HTML files. The existence or absence of either is not terribly important. It might be an issue in sections of text you've marked with <PRE>; you might find that your well-formatted text that worked so well on one platform doesn't come out well-formatted after it has been moved.

Note: This is an issue only when you move files between platforms, not when you use a browser on one platform to view a file being served from another platform. The Web server and browser know enough to convert the end-of-line conventions properly.

If you do have end-of-line problems, this information might help:

☐ Many text editors enable you to save ASCII files in a format for another platform. If you know what platform you're moving to, you can prepare your files for that platform before moving them.

☐ If you're moving to a UNIX system, note that small filters for converting line feeds, called dos2unix and unix2dos, might exist on the UNIX or DOS systems.

☐ You can convert Macintosh files to UNIX-style files by using the following command line on UNIX:

```
tr '\015' '\012' < oldfile.html > newfile.html
```

oldfile.html is the original file with end-of-line problems, and *newfile.html* is the name of the new file.

What's My URL?

At this point, you have a server, your Web pages are installed and ready to go, and all that is left is to tell people that your presentation exists. All you need now is a URL.

If you're using a commercial Web server or a server that someone else administers, you might easily be able to find out what your URL is by asking the administrator. Otherwise, you'll have to figure it out yourself. Luckily, that isn't too hard.

As noted in Chapter 9, "Working with Links and URLs," a URL consists of four parts: the protocol, the hostname, the directory path, and a filename. To determine each of these parts, use the following questions:

☐ What are you using to serve the files?

If you're using a real Web server, your protocol is http:. If you're using FTP or Gopher, the protocol is ftp: or gopher:, respectively. (Isn't this easy?)

☐ What's the domain name of your server?

This is the network name of the machine your Web server is located on, typically beginning with www (for example, www.mysite.com or www.netcom.com). If it doesn't start with www (don't worry; that doesn't affect whether people can get to your files. Note that the domain name you'll use is the "fully qualified" hostname—that is, the name that people elsewhere on the Web would use to get to your Web server, which might not be the same name you use to get to your Web server. That name usually has several parts and ends with .com, .edu, or the code for your country (for example, .uk or .fr).

With some SLIP or PPP connections, you might not even have a network name, just an IP address—something like 192.123.45.67. You can use that as the network name.

If the server has been installed on a port other than 80, you'll need to know that number too.

> **Note:** The process of recognition and allocation of both Internet domain names and IP addresses is the responsibility of Internic. For more information about obtaining a domain name or IP address, point your Web browser to `http://www.internic.net/`.

☐ What's the path to your home page?

The path to your home page most often begins at the root of the directory in which Web pages are stored (part of your server configuration), which might or might not be the top level of your file system. For example, if you've put files into the directory `/home/www/files/myfiles`, your pathname in the URL might be `/myfiles`. This is a server-configuration question, so if you can't figure it out, you might have to ask your server administrator.

If your Web server has been set up so that you can use your home directory to store Web pages, you can use the UNIX convention of the tilde (~) to refer to the Web pages in your home directory. You don't have to include the name of the directory you created in the URL itself. So, for example, if you had a Web page called `home.html` stored in a directory called www—which was assigned as the Web directory by your server—and this directory was located in your home directory (myhome), the path to that file in the URL would be this:

`/~myhome/home.html`

After you know the answers to these three questions, you can construct a URL. You'll probably remember from Chapter 9 that a URL looks like this:

`protocol://machinename.com:port/path/filename.html`

You should be able to plug your values for each of those elements into the appropriate places in the URL structure. Here's an example:

`http://www.mymachine.com/www/tutorials/index.html`

> **Note:** Many HTTP servers are set up to use `index.html` as the default document to load for a directory (which is why I suggested you use that name for your home page). If your server has been configured to do this, you can omit the name of the file in your URL, making it slightly shorter to type:
>
> `http://www.mymachine.com/www/tutorials/`
>
> The Web server will append the name of the file to the end of the URL.

Test, Test, and Test Again

13

Now that your Web pages are available on the Net, you can take the opportunity to test them on as many platforms using as many browsers as you possibly can. It is only when you've seen how your documents look on different platforms that you'll realize how important it is to design documents that can look good on as many platforms and browsers as possible.

In addition, if you are designing Navigator 2.0–specific pages, spend some time using other browsers as well to make sure that the elements like <NOFRAMES> and server-pushed pages (more on these in coming chapters) work the way you intended for non-Navigator browsers.

It is also vital that you check and recheck all the hyperlinks included on your Web pages. In fact, you should aim to check all your links an average of about one every two weeks, where possible. The dynamic nature of the World Wide Web means that it is not uncommon for Web pages to move location or simply disappear. This is especially the case just after the end of the college year, when student projects are often simply removed to make room for the following year's intake of students.

Tips for Good Server Administration

If you've set up your own Web server, you can do several simple things to make that server useful on the Web and to your readers.

Alias Your Domain Name to *www.yoursystem.com*

A common convention on the Web is that the system that serves Web pages to the network has the name that begins with www. Typically, your network administrator or your network provider will create a hostname alias, called a CNAME, which points to the actual machine on the network serving Web files. You don't have to follow this convention, of course, but it is helpful for several reasons:

- ☐ It's easier to remember than some other domain name, and it's a common convention for finding the Web server for any given site. So if your primary system is mysystem.com and I want to get to your Web pages, www.mysystem.com would be the appropriate place for me to look first.

- ☐ If you change the machine on your network that is serving Web pages, you can simply reassign the alias. If you don't use an alias, all the links that point to your server will break.

Create a Webmaster Mail Alias

If the system you're using has the capability to send and receive mail, create a globally available mail alias for "webmaster" that points to your e-mail address so that if someone sends mail to webmaster@yoursite.com, that mail is sent to you. Like other administrative mail aliases, such as root (for general problems), postmaster (for e-mail problems), and Usenet (for news), the webmaster alias provides a standard contact address for problems or complaints about your Web server. (You might not want to hear about problems or complaints, but it is the polite thing to do.)

Note: If you're not too sure about how you create a webmaster mail alias, you should talk to your system administrator or refer to the documentation accompanying your mail server.

Create a Server Home Page

Your server might be home to several Web presentations, especially if you are serving many users (for example, if you've set up a Web "storefront"). In cases such as this, you should provide a sitewide home page, typically http://www.yoursite.com/index.html, that provides some general information about your site, legal notices, and perhaps an overview of the contents of your site—with links to the home pages for each presentation, of course.

The configuration file for your server software should have an entry for a site-specific home page.

Create Sitewide Administrative and Design Guidelines

If you are the Web master for a large organization, it might be helpful for you and for your organization to define who is responsible for the Web server: who is the contact for day-to-day complaints or problems, who sets up access control for users, and who answers questions about policy concerning what can appear in a public Web page on this site.

In addition, your organization might want to have some kind of creative control over the Web pages it publishes on the Web. You can use many of the hints and guidelines in this book to create suggestions for Web page style and create sample pages that your users can use as a basis for their own Web pages.

Seek Netscape Now Recognition for Your Site

If your site contains Netscape-specific features such as frames, Java, or JavaScript routines, tables, or plug-ins, you should check out a program operated by Netscape Communications called Netscape Now.

When you apply for Netscape Now recognition, you are granted the right to include either the Netscape Now logo or the Netscape 2.0 Now logo on your Web pages. By including this logo on your home page, you tell the world that your site is best viewed by Navigator 2.0 or Navigator 1.2, depending on which logo you use. (See Figure 13.1.) In addition, by making this logo a hyperlink, you provide people with an easy method of downloading a copy of the Navigator 2.0 program best suited to their needs.

To learn more about the Netscape Now program or to apply for recognition, point your Web browser to `http://home.netscape.com/comprod/mirror/netscape_now_program.html`.

Figure 13.1.

Including the Netscape Now logo on your home pages lets the world know that your page is best viewed using Netscape Web browsers.

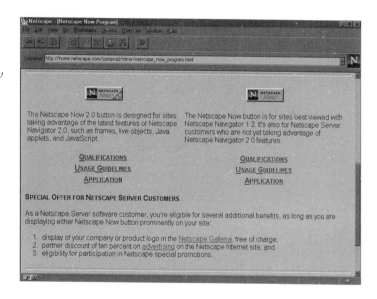

Summary

In this chapter you've reached the final point in creating a Web presentation: releasing your work to the World Wide Web through the use of a Web server, either installed by you or available from a Network provider.

From here on, everything you'll learn is icing on an already-substantial cake. You'll simply be adding more features (interactivity, forms) to the presentation you already have available on the Web.

Workshop

The first section of the Workshop lists some of the common questions people ask about the World Wide Web along with a brief answer to each. Next is a quiz about the chapter you have just read. If you have problems answering any of the questions in the quiz, you can turn to Appendix E, "Answers to Quiz Questions."

Q&A

Q **I really don't understand all this network stuff. CNAMEs? protocols? ports? domain name? Help!**

A You don't have to know any of this if you can get access to a Web server through the people who provide your usual Net access, or if you rent space on a commercial Web site. You can let someone else do all the network stuff; all you'll have to do is ensure that your documents have relative pathnames and can be moved as a group onto the server. And after they are there, you're done.

Q **How can I set up a server to do access control (to only let certain sites in) or to run as a proxy across a firewall?**

A If this were a book all about setting up Web servers, I'd have written whole chapters on these subjects. As it is, the documentation for your server should tell you how to perform each of these tasks (and the documentation for all four servers I've mentioned in this chapter is excellent, so with a little poking around, you should be able to find what you need).

Q **I'd really like to run a UNIX Web server because I'm familiar with UNIX and those servers seem to have the most features and the most flexibility. But UNIX workstations are so incredibly expensive. What can I do?**

A You can get a cheap PC (a high-end 486 or low-end Pentium) and run UNIX on it, and then use many of the UNIX-based Web servers. Several versions of UNIX for PCs exist, including Linux, BSDI, and NetBSD. I like the freeware Linux, which you can usually pick up on CD for under $20. Both W3C's httpd and NCSA's HTTPd servers run seamlessly under this version (in fact, my own Web server runs on Linux, and all the scripts you'll learn about the next couple of chapters were written on Linux).

Or simply run a server on your existing PC or Macintosh system. Although UNIX servers have the advantage of new technology appearing there first and they do tend to be the most flexible, PC- and Macintosh-based servers are catching up and have been proven to be just as robust as UNIX-based servers. There is nothing on the Web that says you have to use UNIX.

Q I created my files on a DOS system, using the `.htm` extension, like you told me to earlier in the book. Now I've published my files on a UNIX system provided by my job. The problem now is that when I try to get to my pages using my browser, I get the HTML code for those pages—not the formatted result! It all worked on my system at home...what went wrong?

A Some older servers have this problem. Your server has not been set up to believe that files with a `.htm` extension are actually HTML files, so they send them as text instead. Then, when your browser reads one of your files from a server, it uses the information the server sends it about the content of the file, not the file extension. So your server is messing everything up.

There are several ways you can fix this problem. The first is to change all the names of your files after you upload them to the UNIX system, and all the links within those files. Less hideous, but still not very useful, is the option of creating symbolic links from the `.html` files to the same names with a `.html` extension.

But by far the best way to fix this problem is to tell the administrator of your Web site to change the server configuration so that `.htm` files are sent as HTML—usually a simple step that magically causes all your files to work properly from then on. The documentation for the server will tell the administrator how to do this.

Quiz

1. Can you use an anonymous FTP server to host Web pages?
2. What are the two most popular public domain UNIX servers currently available?
3. What requirements must your site meet to achieve Netscape 2.0 Now certification?
4. What is a daemon?
5. Can you run a Web server on a computer system other than UNIX?

Exercise

If you have not already done so, now would be a good time to look around for either a Web service provided of your own or someone to provide you with a permanent Internet connection. A good place to start this exploration is the W3 Consortium site at `http://www.w3.org/`. Also, if you are looking for a Web service provider `http://www.webcom.com/` is as good a site as any to investigate first.

14

How to Tell the World You Have Arrived

The "build it, and they will come" motto from the movie *Field of Dreams* notwithstanding, people won't simply start to visit your site of their own accord after you've put it online. In fact, with more than 10 million Web pages online already, and that number set to double again in the next year, it is highly unlikely that anyone could ever just stumble across your site by accident.

As a result, to get people to visit your Web site, you need to advertise its existence in as many ways as possible. After all, the higher the visibility, the greater the prospect of your site receiving lots of *hits*.

> **Note:** *Hits* is Web-speak for the number of visits your Web site receives. It does not differentiate between people, but instead is simply a record of the number of times a copy of your Web page has been downloaded. Most Web servers provide an automatic mechanism for recording the number of hits your site receives.

In this chapter you will learn about many of the avenues available to Web publishers for the promotion of their sites, by exploring these topics:

- ☐ Getting your site listed on the major WWW directories
- ☐ How to list your site with the major WWW indexes
- ☐ Using the Usenet to announce your site
- ☐ Business cards, letterheads, and brochures
- ☐ More directories and related Web pages

WWW Site Listings

Many people, when they first start working with the World Wide Web, find it hard to understand that there are numerous Web sites out there just itching for the chance to include a hyperlink for your Web pages as part of their own list. And what they find even harder to understand is that, for the most part, no cost is involved.

There is a simple reason for the existence of so many apparently philanthropic individuals. When the World Wide Web was young and fresh, the best way for a person to promote the existence of his site was by approaching other Web developers and asking them to list his site on their pages. In return for this favor, he would also list their site on his pages. Over time, this process has been refined somewhat, but today many sites will still be only too happy to include a link to your site. In fact, don't be surprised if you occasionally receive an e-mail from someone asking to be included in your list of sites.

This cooperative nature is a strikingly unique feature of the World Wide Web. Instead of competing for visitors with other similar sites, most Web pages actually include a list of their competitors. For example, I run a film and television reviews site at http://www.webcom.com/taketwo/. At this site, you can find an interactive movie review system that enables people to submit reviews of movies and television. It is not, however, the only film and television site on the World Wide Web, so I also include a list of hundreds of related sites for people to explore.

Unfortunately, however, there is still a problem with just exchanging hyperlink references with other sites. As was originally the case, people still need to be able to locate a single site as a starting point. To this end, some sort of global Internet directory was needed. Currently, there is no single site on the World Wide Web that could be regarded as the Internet directory, but a few major directories and libraries come very close.

Yahoo

By far, the most well-known directory of Web sites is the Yahoo site (see Figure 14.1), created by David File and Jerry Yang at http://www.yahoo.com/. This site started in April 1994 as a small private list of David and Jerry's favorite Web sites. But since then, it has grown to become a highly regarded catalog and index of Web sites.

Figure 14.1.
Yahoo—one of the most popular directories on the World Wide Web.

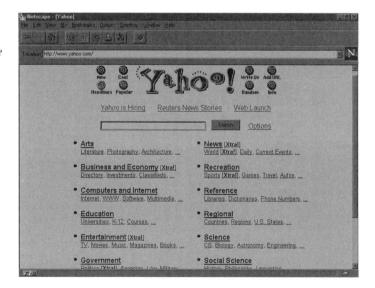

Yahoo uses an elegant multilevel catalog to organize all the sites it references. To view the contents of any level of the catalog, select the major category hyperlink that most closely represents the information you are interested in, and then follow the chain of associated pages to a list of related Web sites like the one shown in Figure 14.2. The page shown in the figure is one you should definitely take a look at. It contains a list of Announcement Services and related Web pages that can help you spread the word about your new Web site.

Figure 14.2.

The Announcement Services category contains a list of sites that can help you promote your site's existence.

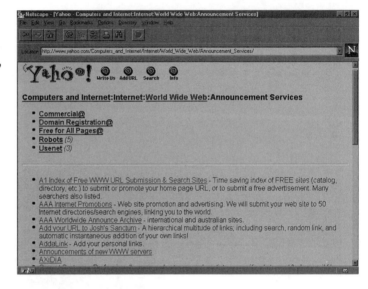

To add your site to the list maintained by Yahoo, return to the Yahoo home page at `http://www.yahoo.com/` and select the category appropriate to your site. Work your way down the catalog through any subcategories until you locate a list of sites similar to your own. On this page, click the Add URL button. Yahoo then displays a form like the one shown in Figure 14.3, where you can enter the URL and other details about your Web site.

After you submit the form, a new hyperlink is automatically added to the category you selected previously. In addition, your site is also listed in the daily and weekly Yahoo What's New list, which can be found at `http://www.yahoo/com/New/`.

Figure 14.3.

By filling out an online form, you can include a hyperlink to your site as part of the Yahoo catalog.

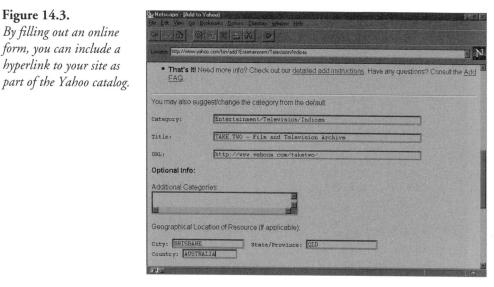

The World Wide Web Virtual Library

The World Wide Web (W3) Virtual Library, located at http://www.w3.org/pub/DataSources/bySubject/Overview.html, is another very popular online catalog. But unlike Yahoo, which is operated by a single group of people, the W3 Virtual Library is a distributed effort. As such, the contents of each separate category are maintained by different people (all volunteers) and sometimes housed on different computers all over the world.

As a result, to submit your URL for inclusion in a category of the Virtual Library, you need to send an e-mail request to the person maintaining it. To obtain a list of the e-mail address for each maintainer, point your Web browser to http://www.w3.org/pub/DataSources/bySubject/Maintainers.html.

The top-level directory (see Figure 14.4) maintained by the W3 Consortium also contains a link to the Maintainers page, along with other links that describe the submission process in greater detail. In addition, you will find information on this page that describes how people can add their own categories to the W3 Virtual Library and become maintainers themselves.

Figure 14.4.
The World Wide Web Virtual Library is a distributed virtual catalog of Web sites and services.

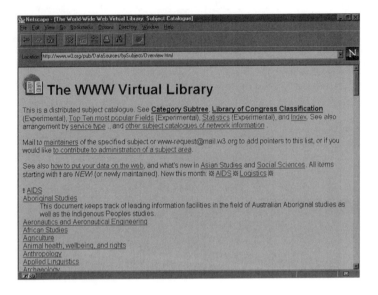

Yellow Pages Listings

Another popular method of promoting your site is by registering it with the growing number of Yellow Pages directories that have begun to spring up on the World Wide Web. These sites can best be thought of as the electronic equivalent of your local telephone Yellow Pages directory.

As a rule, Yellow Pages sites are designed specially for commercial and business Web users who want to advertise their services and expertise. For this reason, most of the Yellow Pages sites offer both free and paid advertising space, with the paid listings including graphics, corporate logos, and advanced layout features. The free listings, on the other hand, tend to be little more than a hyperlink and a short comment. When you're starting out, however, free advertising is without a doubt the best advertising. Of the Yellow Pages sites currently in operation, these are the three most popular:

- ☐ WORLDWIDE Yellow Pages
- ☐ The ISP Internet Yellow Pages
- ☐ WWW Business Yellow Pages

WORLDWIDE Yellow Pages

As the name suggests, this site aims to be a global online Yellow Pages directory. It can store Web addresses, postal information, phone numbers, and information about the category your business falls under. To check out the WORLDWIDE Yellow Pages site, use `http://www.yellow.com/`. To submit an entry to this directory, point your Web browser to `http://www.yellow.com/cgi-bin/online`, as shown in Figure 14.5.

Figure 14.5.
The Yellow Pages for the next 100 years.

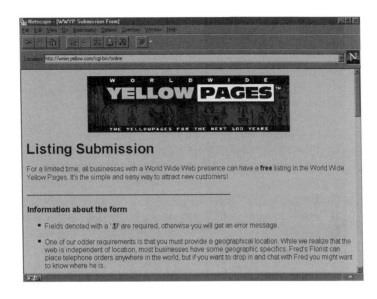

14

Note: When submitting an entry to WORLDWIDE Yellow Pages, be sure to include the geographic location of your business. This is especially important for commerce sites. After all, if your Online Pizza Delivery Service is based in downtown LA, there's not much chance of your making that "30 minutes or it's free" deadline to me, down here in Brisbane, Australia.

The ISP Internet Yellow Pages

Unlike WORLDWIDE Yellow Pages, which is designed specifically for businesses with a Web presence, the ISP Internet Yellow Pages—`http://www.index.org/`—takes a somewhat more general approach; however, it still does not accept listings for personal home pages.

To submit a site for inclusion in the ISP Internet Yellow Pages directory, point your Web browser to `http://www.index.org/submit.html`, as shown in Figure 14.6.

WWW Business Yellow Pages

The WWW Business Yellow Pages is not as large as the other two mentioned previously, but because it is free, no harm can be done by including an entry for your business site here. It is operated as a community service by the University of Houston, College of Business Administration, at `http://www.cba.uh.edu/ylowpges/`.

Figure 14.6.
The ISP Internet Yellow Pages directory is operated by a consortium of Internet service providers.

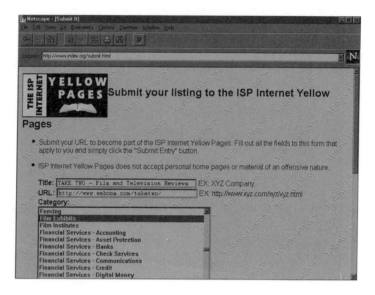

As with the other two Yellow Pages sites, if you want your site included at the WWW Business Yellow Pages, you need to submit an online form. The URL for the application form, as shown in Figure 14.7, is http://www.cba.uh.edu/cgi-bin/autosub.

Figure 14.7.
WWW Business Yellow Pages.

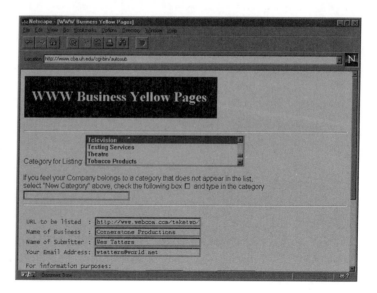

What's New Listings

A special type of Web site, called a What's New listing, was designed with one purpose in mind: to announce the arrival of new Web sites. The granddaddy of all the What's New listings is the one operated by the NCSA, creators of NCSA Mosaic. (See Figure 14.8.)

Figure 14.8.
Hundreds of new sites are listed on the NCSA What's New pages every day.

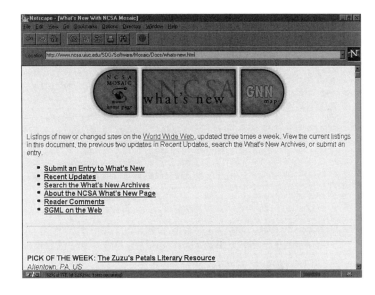

To submit your site for inclusion on the NCSA listing, follow the instructions outlined on the What's New home page at `http://www.ncsa.uiuc.edu/SDG/Software/Mosaic/Docs/whats-new.html`. Currently, you need to submit an e-mail request, but it is likely that this requirement will change in the future.

To complement the NCSA lists, various other groups, such as Netscape Communications, operate their own What's News lists as well. But unlike the NCSA site, the Netscape page does provide an online form, like the one shown in Figure 14.9. To use this form, point your Web browser to `http://home.netscape.com/escapes/submit_new.html`.

Private Directories

In addition to the broad mainstream Web directories, many private directories on the World Wide Web cater to more specific needs. Some of these directories deal with single issues, whereas others are devoted to such areas as online commerce, education, business, and entertainment.

Figure 14.9.

To make a submission for the Netscape What's New listing, you use an online form.

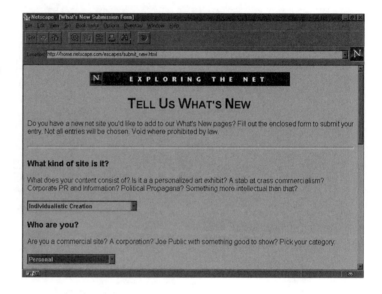

The best way to locate most of these directories is by using an Internet search tool such as the Lycos site discussed in previous chapters. Alternatively, most of these directories will already be listed in such places as Yahoo and the W3 Virtual Library, so a few minutes spent visiting relative catalogs at these sites is normally very beneficial.

The Internet Mall

For those of you who plan to operate online stores via the World Wide Web, a directory such as the Internet Mall—http://www.internet-mall.com/—which is shown in Figure 14.10, is a very good place to start. Listing your Web site on such a mall gives you instant visibility. That does not necessarily mean that people will start knocking down your doors immediately, but it does give your store a much greater chance of succeeding.

The main criteria for obtaining a listing on the Internet Mall are that your site must sell tangible products and people must be able to place an order for them online. Apart from this, only a few types of commerce are not welcome, including these:

- ☐ Multilevel marketing schemes
- ☐ Products available through dealerships
- ☐ Franchise opportunities
- ☐ Web publishing or design services
- ☐ Marketing services
- ☐ Hotels, restaurants, and nonbusiness sites

If you want to lodge a request for the inclusion of your online store at the Internet Mall, point your Web browser to `http://www.internet-mall.com/howto.htm` for more information.

Figure 14.10.
If you operate a site that provides online order capabilities, registering with the Internet Mall is a good place to start.

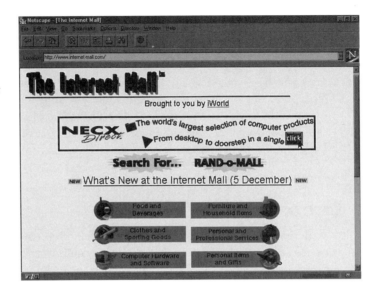

Netscape Galleria

If you operate your Web site on a Netscape Communications Web server or Netscape Commerce server, you can list your site on Netscape's own shopping mall, called the Netscape Galleria. (See Figure 14.11.)

Figure 14.11.
People who use a Netscape Web server can list their sites at the Netscape Galleria.

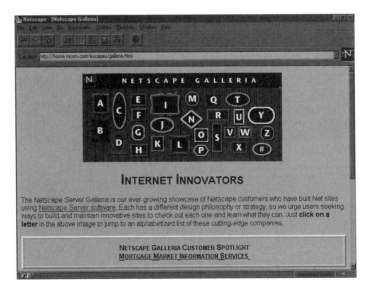

In addition, if you rent space from a Web service provider that uses either of the Netscape servers, you might also qualify for a listing. For more information, visit the Netscape Galleria at http://home.mcom.com/escapes/galleria.html.

Site Indexes

After you have your new site listed on the major directories and maybe a few smaller directories, you next need to turn your attention to the indexing and search tools, such as Lycos, WebCrawler, and InfoSeek. Unlike directories, which traditionally contain a hierarchical list of Web sites, indexes contain a database of sites that can be searched using a form. Each of these search engines provides a mechanism that enables you to submit your site for inclusion as part of its index.

Lycos

With more than 91 percent of the World Wide Web now indexing by Lycos at http://www.lycos.com/, it is without a doubt the most comprehensive index of Web pages currently available. (See Figure 14.12.) To achieve such good coverage, Lycos uses a special program called a "spider" that spends all its time exploring the World Wide Web. Each day, the Lycos spiders visit thousands of pages, recording and indexing the contents of each and following all the new hyperlinks they contain.

Figure 14.12.
If you can't find it with Lycos, it's not on the World Wide Web!

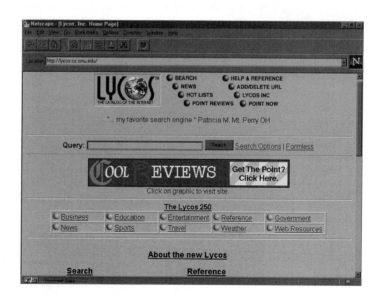

When you use such a system, if your site has been listed on just about any other Web page, chances are that it will eventually be included in the Lycos database. To bypass this hit-and-miss approach, however, you can also directly submit the URL of your home page to Lycos. When Lycos receives this URL, it sends a spider to visit your site. While the spider is there, it indexes the contents of each page and adds their location to the Lycos main database. From that moment on, whenever a person queries Lycos looking for a site similar to yours, your URL will be included in the search results.

To submit a URL to Lycos or to delete a dead site, point your Web browser to `http://www.lycos.com/register.html`.

WebCrawler

Following its recent move onto the Internet, America Online has taken over the operation of the WebCrawler indexing system located at `http://webcrawler.com/GNN/WebQuery.html`. (See Figure 14.13.) Like Lycos, the WebCrawler has created its database by crawling across the World Wide Web, exploring sites and adding them to its index.

Figure 14.13.
WebCrawler is operated by America Online.

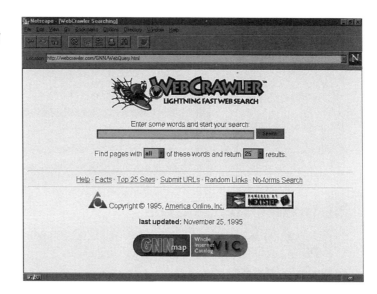

WebCrawler does not have coverage as wide as that of Lycos, with less than an estimated 40% of the World Wide Web index, but it does have the advantage of being the Internet index system of choice for more than 3.5 million America Online and Global Network Navigator (GNN) users.

The Submit URL form for WebCrawler is located at `http://webcrawler.com/WebCrawler/SubmitURLS.html`.

InfoSeek

PC Computing magazine recently voted InfoSeek (shown in Figure 14.14) the Most Valuable Internet Tool for 1995. Like Lycos and WebCrawler, InfoSeek is a Web indexing tool, but what makes it even more powerful is its capability to search through many kinds of additional services and databases in addition to the World Wide Web. Such functionality, however, does come at a cost—only the Web search engine can be used without charge.

Figure 14.14.

E-mail a request to www-request@infoseek.com to register your URL with InfoSeek.

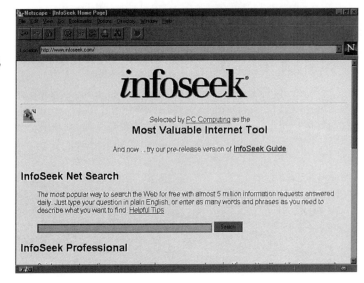

The other main difference between InfoSeek and other search tools is that you send your URL submission request via e-mail to www-request@infoseek.com.

Submission Tools

Besides the 3 search tools already covered, there are about 15 other search engines with differing capabilities, and you will need to make a separate submission to each to ensure that your site is indexed.

Instead of listing the URLs and details for each of these sites, however, this discussion will turn to two special Web pages that take much of the drudgery out of submitting Web sites to search indexes and directories.

PostMaster

The PostMaster site shown in Figure 14.15—http://www.netcreations.com/postmaster/
index.html—is an all-in-one submission page that asks you to fill out all the details required
for more than 25 Web indexes and directories, including the following:

- ☐ Yahoo, Netscape's Escapes, PowerLink
- ☐ JumpStation, Lycos, InfoSeek, WebCrawler, World Wide Web Worm
- ☐ GNN Whole Internet Catalog, World Wide Yellow Pages, EInet Galaxy
- ☐ NCSA's What's New, WhatsNewToo, Scout Report, Net-Happenings

Figure 14.15.

*After you complete the
form provided,
PostMaster automatically
submits your site details
to all the most popular
search tools and Web
directories.*

After you have completed all the details—which normally takes around 15 minutes—
clicking the Submit button at the bottom of the page results in the URL of your site and any
other required information being automatically submitted to each supported service.

Note: PostMaster also offers a commercial version of its submission system that
delivers announcements about your new site to more than 200 magazines,
journals, and other periodicals, in addition to all the sites included in the free
version. Using the commercial version, however, is an expensive exercise.

Submit It!

The Submit It! service provided by Scott Banister is a lot like PostMaster in that it helps you submit your URL to different directories and search indexes. It supports just about all the same services, but what sets it apart is the way you submit your information. Figure 14.16 shows a list of the search indexes and directories currently supported by Submit It!.

Figure 14.16.
Submit It! enables you to control which sites your URL is sent to.

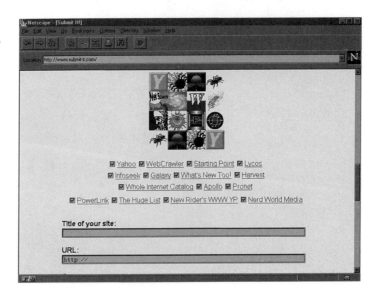

Submit It! doesn't ask you to complete one enormous page, something that many people find daunting. Instead, after you have filled out some general information, you select only the sites you want to submit an entry to and then perform each submission one site at a time.

To learn more about Submit It! point your Web browser to `http://www.submit-it.com/`.

Announce Your Site via Usenet

The World Wide Web is not the only place on the Internet that can be used to announce the launch of your new Web site. Many people use a small set of Usenet newsgroups that are designed specially for making announcements. To locate these newsgroups, look for newsgroup names that end with `.announce`. (Refer to the documentation that came with your Usenet newsreader for information about how this can be done.)

One newsgroup is even devoted just to World Wide Web–related announcements. The name of this newsgroup is `comp.infosystems.www.announce`. Provided that you have

configured Navigator 2.0 for use with Usenet, you can view articles submitted to this newsgroup—and add your own announcements—by entering the following URL into the Document URL field:

```
news:comp.infosystems.www.announce
```

This entry instructs Navigator 2.0 to open its newsgroup reader, as shown in Figure 14.17, and load all the latest WWW announcements.

Figure 14.17.
Announce your new Web site to the world via the `comp.infosystems.` `www.announce` *newsgroup.*

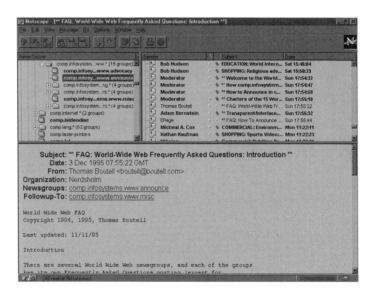

> **Note:** `comp.infosystems.www.announce` is a moderated newsgroup. As such, any submissions you make to it are approved by a moderator before they appear in the newsgroup listing. To ensure that your announcement will be approved, you should read the charter document that outlines the announcement process. You can read this document by pointing your Web browser to `http://boutell.com/` `%7Egrant/charter.html`.

Business Cards, Letterheads, and Brochures

Although the Internet is a wonderful place to promote your new Web site, there is another great advertising method that many people fail to even consider.

Most businesses spend a considerable amount of money each year producing letterheads, business cards, and other promotional material. Very few, however, consider printing their e-mail addresses and home page URLs on them. But why not? With more than 35 million people on the Internet, chances are that some of your customers are already on the Internet, or will be within a few months.

By printing your e-mail address and home page URL on all your correspondence and even promotional material, you can reach an entirely new group of potential site visitors. And who knows, maybe you'll even pick up new clients by spending time explaining to people what all your new address information means.

The bottom line with the promotion of your Web site is lateral thinking. You need to use every tool at your disposal if you want to have a successful and active site.

Other Directories and Related Web Pages

To complete this chapter, Table 14.1 lists other sites you should visit when looking to promote the arrival of a new Web site.

Note: An excellent FAQ is published regularly to `comp.infosystems.www.announce` called "FAQ: How to Announce Your New Web Site." This FAQ contains an up-to-date list of all the best and most profitable means of promoting your Web site. If you can't locate the FAQ in this newsgroup, you can view an online version at `http://ep.com/faq/webannounce.html`.

Table 14.1. Useful sites for promoting a new Web page.

URL	Description
`http://theyellowpages.com/`	This is yet another Yellow Pages site.
`http://wings.buffalo.edu/world/`	The Virtual Tourist lists Web sites by geographic location and category. (This site is undergoing changes. Watch for a new URL coming soon.)

URL	Description
`http://www.stpt.com/`	Starting Point is part of the new wave of Web directories.
`http://galaxy.einet.net/galaxy.html`	Galaxy is a directory-like system that also provides a powerful built-in search tool.
`http://www.stir.ac.uk/jsbin/jsii/`	JumpStation II is a small Lycos-like search tool based in the United Kingdom.
`http://www.nerdworld.com/users/dstein/index.html`	The Nerd World Media Internet Subject Index is another directory of Web sites.
`http://thehugelist.com/`	The Huge List. 'nuff said?
`http://www.directory.net/`	Open Market Inc. operates a commercial sites index.
`http://www.rns.com/www_index/new_site.html`	This is the Nikos search engine URL submission form.

Summary

Writing the HTML for Web documents on a new Web site is only part of the story when it comes down to being a Web publisher. You also need to promote the site after you get it online.

To help you get started in this area, this chapter introduces you to Web directories, Web search tools, and submission utilities that enable you to advertise your site on other Web pages.

Workshop

The first section of the Workshop lists some of the common questions people ask about the World Wide Web along with a brief answer to each. Next is a quiz about the chapter you have just read. If you have problems answering any of the questions in the quiz, you can turn to Appendix E, "Answers to Quiz Questions."

Q&A

Q **I've submitted my site to various directories, but I can't find it listed anywhere. Should I submit the request again?**

A No. Although most of the submission forms are automated, the physical addition of your site to most directories is a manual job. As a result, sometimes it takes a few weeks for your site to appear on the list. If your site has still not appeared after a week or so, send an e-mail query to the site's webmaster.

Quiz

1. What is the URL for the Lycos search engine?
2. What is so special about the PostMaster site?
3. What type of newsgroups would you normally use to announce the existence of your new Web site?
4. Where can the NCSA What's New site be found?
5. What requirement must you meet before your site can be listed in the Netscape Galleria?

Exercises

1. If you have not done so already, add all the hyperlinks listed in this directory to your Favorite Web Sites page. After all, for you as a Web publisher, any site that promotes the existence of your site must be a favorite!
2. By using either Submit It! or PostMaster, register your Web site with all the major search indexes and directory listings. In addition, if your have not done so already, now would be a good time to submit entries to all the What's New directories and in any relevant .announce newsgroups.

15

Developing Effective Web Pages

You won't learn about any tags in this chapter, or how to convert files from one strange file format to another. You're done with the HTML part of Web page design for the moment. In this chapter you'll get to deal with the intangibles, the things that separate your documents from those of someone who just knows the tags and can fling text and graphics around and call the result a presentation.

Armed with the information contained in this book you could go off and merrily create Web pages to your heart's content without ever reading this chapter. However, armed with both that information and what you'll learn in this chapter, you can create *better* Web pages. Do you need any more incentive to continue reading?

This chapter includes hints for creating well-written and well-designed Web pages, and it highlights dos and don'ts concerning the following items:

- ☐ How to write your Web documents so that they can be easily scanned and read
- ☐ Issues concerning design and layout of your Web pages
- ☐ When and why you should create links
- ☐ Other miscellaneous tidbits and hints

Writing for Online

Writing on the Web is no different from writing in the real world. Even though the writing you do on the Web is not sealed in hard copy, it is still "published" and is still a reflection of you and your work. In fact, because it is online, and therefore more transient to your reader, you'll have to follow the rules of good writing even more closely because your readers will be less forgiving.

Because of the vast quantities of information available on the Web, your readers are not going to have much patience if your Web page is full of spelling errors or is poorly organized. They are much more likely to give up after the first couple sentences and move on to someone else's page. After all, there are several million pages. There isn't time to waste on bad pages.

This doesn't mean that you must go out and become a professional writer to create a good Web page. But here are a few hints for making your Web page easier to read and understand.

Write Clearly and Be Brief

Unless you are writing the Great American Web Novel, your readers are not going to visit your page to linger lovingly over your words. One of the best ways you can make the writing in your Web documents effective is to write as clearly and concisely as you possibly can, present your points, and then stop. Obscuring what you want to say with extra words just makes it more difficult for the reader to figure out your point.

If you don't have a copy of Strunk and White's book *The Elements of Style*, go buy it right now and read it. Then reread it, memorize it, inhale it, sleep with it under your pillow, show it to all your friends, quote it at parties, make it your life. There is no better guide to the art of good, clear writing than that book.

Organize Your Documents for Quick Scanning

Even if you write the clearest, briefest, most scintillating prose ever seen on the Web, chances are good that your readers will not start at the top of your Web page and carefully read every word.

Scanning, in this context, is the first quick look your readers give to each page to get the gist of the content. Depending on what your users want out of your documents, they might scan the parts that jump out at them (headings, links, and other emphasized words), perhaps read a few contextual paragraphs, and then move on. By writing and organizing your documents for easy "scanability," you can help your readers get the information they need as fast as possible.

To improve the scanability of your Web documents follow these guidelines:

- ☐ Use headings to summarize topics. Note how this book has headings and subheadings. You can flip through quickly and find the portions that interest you. The same thing applies to Web pages.

- ☐ Use lists. Lists are wonderful for summarizing related items. Every time you find yourself saying something like, "Each widget has four elements," or "Use the following steps to do this," the content after that phrase should be an ordered or unordered list.

- ☐ Don't forget link menus. As a form of list, link menus have all the advantages of lists for scanability and double as excellent navigation tools.

- ☐ Where practical, use frames to keep your table of contents on the screen at all times.

- ☐ Use tables to highlight and group related blocks of text.

- ☐ Don't bury important information in text. If you have a point to make, make it close to the top of the page or at the beginning of a paragraph. Long paragraphs are harder to read and make gleaning information more difficult. The further into the paragraph you put your point, the less likely anybody will be to read it.

Figure 15.1 shows the sort of writing technique you should avoid.

Figure 15.1.

A Web page that is difficult to scan.

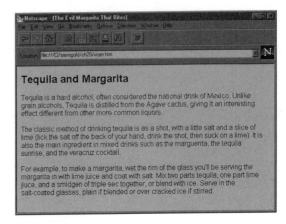

Because all the information on this page is in paragraph form, your readers must read all three paragraphs to find out what they want and where they want to go next.

How would you improve this example? Try rewriting this section so that the main points can be better extracted from the text. Consider this information:

☐ There are actually two discrete topics in those three paragraphs.

☐ The four ingredients of the drink would make an excellent list.

Figure 15.2 shows what an improved version might look like.

Figure 15.2.

An improvement on the difficult Web page.

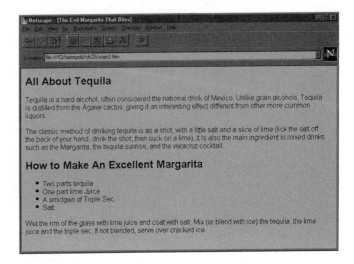

Make Each Page Stand on Its Own

Keep in mind as you write that your reader could jump into any of your Web pages from anywhere. For example, you might structure a page so that section four distinctly follows section three and has no other links to it. Then someone you don't even know might create a link to the page starting at section four. From then on, a reader could very well find himself on section four without even being aware that section three exists.

Be careful to write each page so that it stands on its own. These guidelines will help:

☐ Use descriptive titles, as I mention in Chapter 5, "Basic HTML and the World Wide Web." The title should describe the subject of the page, and also its relationship to the rest of the pages in the presentation of which it is a part.

☐ If a document depends on the one before it, provide a navigational link to the document before it (and preferably also one up to the top level).

☐ Avoid initial sentences such as "You can get around these problems by...," "After you're done with that, do...," and "The advantages to this method are..." The information referred to by "these," "that," and "this" is on some other page. If those sentences are the first thing your reader sees, he will be confused.

15

Be Careful with Emphasis

Use emphasis sparingly in your text. Paragraphs with a whole lot of **boldface** and *italic* or words in ALL CAPS are hard to read, both if you use any of them several times in a paragraph and if you emphasize long strings of text. The emphasis is best used only with small words (such as **and**, *this*, or BUT).

Link text is also a form of emphasis. Use single words or short phrases as link text. Do not use entire passages or paragraphs as links.

Figure 15.3 illustrates a particularly good example of too much emphasis obscuring the rest of the text.

Figure 15.3.
Too much emphasis.

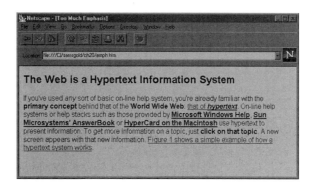

By removing some of the boldface and using less text for your links, you can considerably reduce the amount of distraction in the paragraph. Figure 15.4 shows an improved version.

Figure 15.4.
Less emphasis.

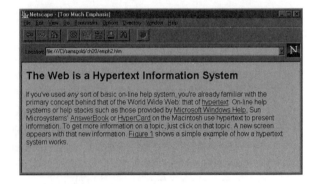

Don't Use Browser-Specific Terminology

Avoid references in your text to specific features of specific browsers. For example, don't use wording like this:

☐ *Click here.* What if your reader is using a browser without a mouse? A more generic phrase is "Select this link." (Of course, you should avoid the "here" syndrome in the first place, which neatly gets around this problem as well.)

☐ *To save this document, pull down the File menu and select Save.* Each browser has a different set of menus and different ways of accomplishing the same action. If at all possible, do not refer to specifics of browser operation in your Web pages.

☐ *Use the Back button to return to the previous page.* Again, each browser has a different set of buttons and different methods for going "back." If you want your readers to have the ability to go back to a previous page, or to any specific page, link them.

Spell Check and Proofread Your Documents

Spell checking and proofreading might seem like obvious suggestions, but given the number of documents I have seen on the Web that have obviously not had either done to them, this bears mentioning.

Designing a set of Web pages and making them available on the Web is like publishing a book, producing a magazine, or releasing a product. It is, of course, considerably easier to publish Web pages than to publish books, magazines, or other products, but just because it is easy does not mean it can be sloppy.

Thousands of people might be reading and exploring the content you provide. Spelling errors and poor grammar reflect badly on your work, on you, and on the content you are describing. Poor writing might be irritating enough that your reader won't bother to delve any deeper than your home page, even if the subject you're writing about is fascinating.

Proofread and spell check each of your Web documents. If possible, have someone else read them—other people can often pick up errors that you, the writer, can't see. Even a simple edit can greatly improve many documents and make them easier to read and navigate.

Design and Page Layout

15

Although the design capabilities of HTML and the Web are still quite limited compared with the capabilities of document presentation programs such as CorelDRAW!, PageMaker, and QuarkXPress, there's still a lot you can work with, and there are still quite a few opportunities for people without a sense of design to create something that looks simply awful.

Probably the best rule to follow at all times as far as laying out each Web page is this: Keep the design as simple as possible. Reduce the number of elements (images, headings, rule lines), and make sure that the eye is drawn to the most important parts of the page first.

Keep that cardinal rule in mind as you read the next sections, which offer some other suggestions for basic design and layout of Web pages.

Don't Overuse Images

Be careful about including lots of images on your Web page. Besides the fact that each image slows down the time it takes to load the document, including too many images on the same page can make your document look busy and cluttered and can distract the reader from the point you are trying to get across. (See Figure 15.5.)

As a basic rule, first consider why you need to use each image before you put it on the page. If it doesn't directly contribute to the content, consider leaving it off. In Figure 15.5, for example, the thick horizontal block serves no purpose that <HR> couldn't have equaled. In addition, the <HR> tag would have correctly adjusted its width to cater to wide pages.

Figure 15.5.
Too many images.

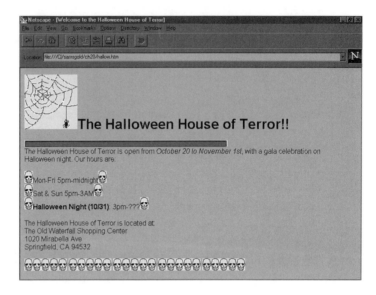

Use Alternatives to Images

Of course, as soon as I mention images, I must also mention that not all browsers can view those images. To make your documents accessible to the widest possible audience, you need to take the text-only browsers into account when you design your Web pages. Two possible solutions can help:

- [ ] Use the ALT attribute of the <IMG> tag to automatically substitute appropriate text strings for the graphics in text-only browsers. Either use a descriptive label to substitute for the default [image] that appears in the place of each inline image, or use an empty string ("") to ignore the image altogether.

- [ ] If providing a single-source page for both graphical and text-only browsers becomes too much work and the result is not turning out to be acceptable, consider creating separate pages for each: a page designed for the full-color, full-graphical browsers, and a page designed for the text-only browsers. Then provide the option of choosing one or the other from your home page.

Be Careful with Backgrounds and Link Colors

By using the Netscape extensions, you can use background colors and patterns and change the color of the text on your pages. Using this feature can be very tempting, but be very careful if you decide to do so. The ability to change the document and font colors and to provide

fancy backdrops can give you the ability to quickly and easily make your pages entirely unreadable. Here are some hints for avoiding this problem:

☐ Make sure that you have enough contrast between the background and foreground (text) colors. Low contrast can be hard to read. Also, light-colored text on a dark background is harder to read than dark text on a light background.

☐ Avoid changing link colors. Because your readers have semantic meanings attached to the default colors (blue means unfollowed, purple or red means followed), changing the colors can be very confusing.

☐ Sometimes increasing the font size of all the text in your document using <BASEFONT> can make it more readable on a background. Both the background and the bigger text will be missing in other browsers that don't support the Netscape tags.

☐ If you're using background patterns, make sure that the pattern does not interfere with the text. Some patterns might look interesting on their own but can make it difficult to read the text you put on top of them.

When in doubt, try asking a friend to look at your pages. Because you are familiar with the content and the text, you might not realize how hard your pages are to read. Someone who hasn't read them before will not have your biases and will be able to tell you that your colors are too close or that the pattern is interfering with the text. Of course, you'll have to find a friend who will be honest with you.

Use Headings as Headings

Headings are often rendered in graphical browsers in a larger or bolder font. Because of this, it's often tempting to use a heading tag to provide some sort of warning, note, or emphasis in regular text, as shown in Figure 15.6.

Figure 15.6.

The wrong way to use headings.

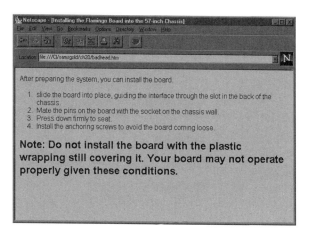

Headings work best when they're used as headings, because they stand out from the text and signal the start of a new topic. If you really want to emphasize a particular section of text, consider using rule lines and a small icon instead. Figure 15.7 shows an example of the same text in Figure 15.6 with a different kind of visual emphasis.

Figure 15.7.
An alternative to the wrong way to use headings.

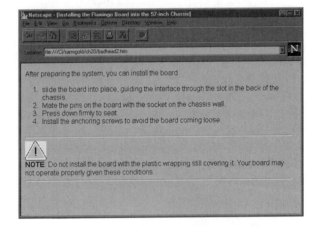

Group Related Information Visually

Grouping related information within a page is a task for both writing and design. By grouping related information under headings, as I suggested in the writing hints section, you improve the scanability of that information. Visually separating each section from the others helps make each section distinct and emphasizes how related the information is.

If a Web page contains several sections of information, find a way to separate those sections visually—for example, with a heading or a rule line <HR>. (See Figure 15.8.) As an alternative, the table options provided by Navigator 2.0 can also be used to good effect when you need to separate sections of a document.

Use a Consistent Layout

When you're reading a book or a magazine, each page and each section usually have the same layout. The page numbers are where you expect them, and the first word on each page starts in the same place.

The same sort of consistent layout works equally well in Web pages. A single "look and feel" for each page in your Web presentation is comforting to your readers. After two or three pages, they will know what the elements of each page are and where to find them. With a consistent design, your readers can find the information they need and navigate through your pages without having to stop at every page to try to find things.

Figure 15.8.
Separate sections visually.

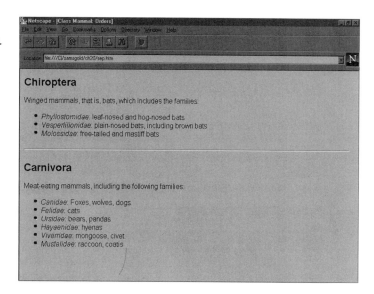

Consistent layout can include these components:

☐ Consistent page elements. If you use second-level headings (<H2>) on one page to indicate major topics, use second-level headings for major topics on all your pages. If you have a heading and a rule line at the top of your page, use that same layout on all your pages.

☐ An address or signature section at the bottom of every page. The <ADDRESS> tag is ideally suited to this purpose.

☐ Consistent forms of navigation. Put your navigation menus in the same place on every page (usually the top or the bottom of the page), and use the same number of them. If you use navigation icons, be sure to use the same icons in the same order for every page.

☐ Frames that separate the components of the page into separate windows. This could include a heading frame, a footer frame, or navigation frames, and possibly a table of contents frame.

Using Links

Without links, Web pages would be really dull, and finding anything interesting on the Web would be close to impossible. The quality of your links, in many ways, can be as important as the writing and design of your actual pages. Here's some friendly advice on creating and using links.

Use Link Menus with Descriptive Text

As I've noted in this chapter and in other parts of this book, link menus are a great way of organizing your content and the links on a page. When you organize your links into lists or other menu-like structures, your reader can scan the options for the page quickly and easily.

However, just organizing your links into menus often isn't enough. When you arrange your links into menus, make sure that you aren't too short in your descriptions. It's tempting to use menus of filenames or other marginally descriptive links in menus, as in the menu shown in Figure 15.9.

Figure 15.9.

A poor link menu.

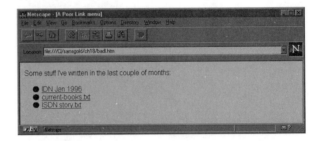

Well, that is a menu of links, and the links describe the actual document they point to, but they don't really describe the *content* of that document. How do readers know what's on the other side of that link, and how can they make a decision about whether they're interested in it from the limited information you've provided? Of these three links, only the last one (ISDN.story.txt) hints at what you will see when you jump to that file.

A better plan is either to provide some extra text describing the content of the file (see Figure 15.10) or to avoid the filenames altogether (who cares?). Just describe the contents of the files in the menu, with the appropriate text highlighted. (See Figure 15.11.)

Either of these forms is better than the first form; both give your reader more of a clue of what's on the other side of the link. Also, in Figure 15.11, an additional inline link has been added to the first menu item to point to the home page of the online magazine that published the article.

Figure 15.10.

A better link menu.

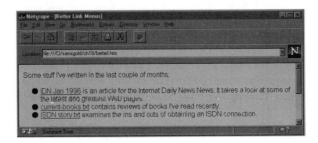

Figure 15.11.
An even better link menu.

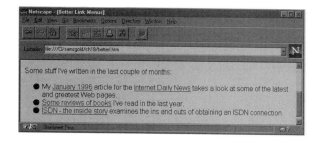

Using Links in Text

Instead of putting links on their own lines in menu form, you can put links directly into paragraphs on the page—to show a footnote-like tangent, for example, or to describe an actual cross-reference to some other document. (For example, "For more information on fainting goats, see The Fainting Goat Primer.") Also, some link menus work better with some extra text in which some of the words are highlighted as a link. Figure 15.12 shows an example of links in body text. This page is part of the Netscape Communications home page at http:
//home.netscape.com/.

Figure 15.12.
Links in text.

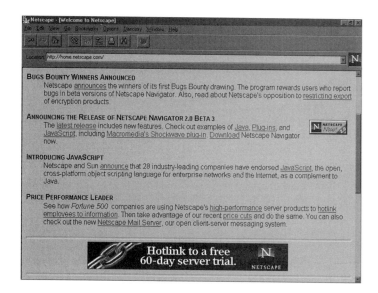

The best way to provide links in text is to first write the text without the links. Then highlight the appropriate words that point to the linked document. Make sure you don't interrupt the flow of the document when you include a link. The idea of links in text is that the text should stand on its own. That way, the links provide additional or tangential information that your readers can choose to ignore or follow based on their own whims.

Figure 15.13 shows another example of using links in text, but one in which the text itself isn't especially relevant—it's just there to support the links. If you're using text just to describe links, consider using a link menu rather than a paragraph. With a link menu, instead of having to read the entire paragraph, the readers can skim for the links that interest them.

Figure 15.13.

Links in text that don't work well.

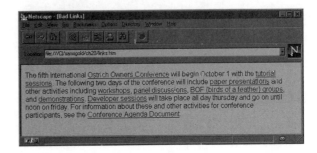

Probably the easiest way to figure out whether you're doing links within text properly is to print the formatted Web page from your browser. In hard copy, without hypertext, would the paragraph still make sense? If the page reads funny on paper, it'll read funny online as well. Some simple rephrasing of sentences can often help enormously in making the text on your pages more readable and more usable both online and when printed.

Avoid the "Here" Syndrome

As mentioned previously, a common mistake that many Web authors make in creating links in body text is using the "here" syndrome. The "here" syndrome is the tendency to create links with a single highlighted word ("here") or the words ("this link"), and to describe the link somewhere else in the text. Following are a couple examples:

```
Information about ostrich socialization is contained here.

Select this link for a tutorial on the internal combustion engine.
```

Because links are highlighted on the Web page, those links visually "pop out" more than the surrounding text (or they "draw the eye," in graphics design lingo). Your reader will see the link first, before reading the text. Try it. Figure 15.14 shows a particularly heinous example of the "here" syndrome. Close your eyes and then open them quickly, pick a "here" at random, and see how long it takes you to find out what the "here" is for.

Now try the same thing with a well-organized link menu of the same information, shown in Figure 15.15.

Figure 15.14.
A page suffering from the "here" syndrome.

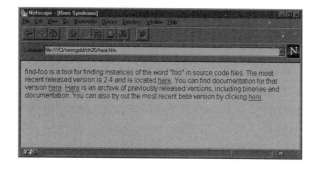

Figure 15.15.
The same page, reorganized.

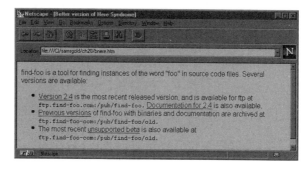

Because "here" says nothing about what the link is for, your poor reader has to search the text before and after the link to determine what is supposed to be "here." In paragraphs that have lots of "here" or other undescriptive links, it becomes difficult to match the links with what they are supposed to link to.

So rather than a link like

```
Information about ostrich socialization is contained here.
```

a much better choice of wording would be something like

```
The Palo Alto Zoo has lots of information about ostrich socialization.
```

or just

```
The Palo Alto Zoo has lots of information about ostrich socialization.
```

To Link or Not to Link

Just as with graphics, every time you create a link, consider why you are linking two documents or sections. Is the link useful? Will it give your readers more information or take them closer to their goal? Is the link relevant in some way to the current content?

Each link should serve a purpose. Link for relevant reasons. Just because you mention the word "coffee" deep in a page about some other topic, you don't have to link that word to the coffee home page. It might seem cute, but if a link has no relevance to the current content, it confuses your reader.

This section describes some of the categories of links that are useful in Web documents. If your links do not fall into one of these categories, consider why you are including them in your document.

> **Note:** Thanks to Nathan Torkington for his "Taxonomy of Tags," published on the www-talk mailing list, which inspired this section.

Explicit navigation links are links that indicate the specific paths one can take through your Web documents: forward, back, up, home. These links are often indicated by navigation icons. (See Figure 15.16.)

Figure 15.16.
Explicit navigation links.

Implicit navigation links (see Figure 15.17) are different from explicit navigation links in that the link text implies, but does not directly indicate, navigation between documents. Link menus are the best example of this; it is apparent from the highlighting of the link text that you will get more information on this topic by selecting the link, but the text itself does not necessarily say that. Note that the major difference between explicit and implicit navigation links is this: If you print a page containing both, you should no longer be able to pick out the implicit links.

Implicit navigation links can also include table-of-contents-like structures or other overviews made up entirely of links.

Figure 15.17.
Implicit navigation links.

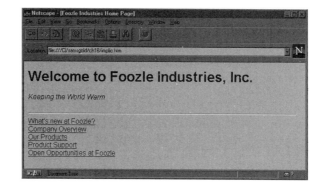

Word or *concept definitions* make excellent links, particularly if you are creating large networks of documents that include glossaries. By linking the first instance of a word to its definition, you can explain the meaning of that word to readers who don't know what it means while not distracting those who do. (See Figure 15.18.)

Figure 15.18.
Definition links.

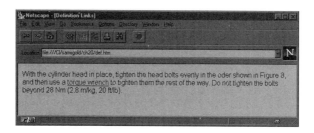

Finally, links to *tangents* and *related information* are valuable when the text content would distract from the main purpose of the document. (See Figure 15.19.) Think of tangent links as footnotes or end notes in printed text. They can refer to citations to other works, or to additional information that is interesting but not directly relevant to the point you're trying to make.

Figure 15.19.
Footnote links.

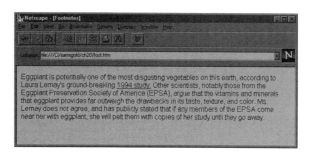

Be careful that you don't get carried away with definitions and tangent links. Link to only the first instance of a definition or tangent, and resist the urge to link every time you possibly can—for example, linking every instance of the letters WWW on your page to the WWW project home page in Switzerland. If you are linking twice or more to the same location on one page, consider removing most of the extra links. Your readers can make the effort to select one of the other links if they are interested in the information.

Other Good Habits and Hints

In this section, I've gathered several other hints and bits of advice about good habits to get into when working with groups of Web pages. These include notes on how big to make each document in your presentation and how to sign your documents.

Link Back to Home

Consider including a link back to the top level or home page on every page of your presentation. Providing this link allows readers a quick escape from the depths of your content. Using a home link is much easier than trying to navigate backward through a hierarchy, or trying to use the "back" facility of a browser.

Don't Split Topics Across Pages

Each Web document works best if it covers a single topic in its entirety. Don't split topics across pages; even if you link between them, the transition can be confusing. It will be even more confusing if someone jumps in on the second or third page and wonders what is going on.

If you think that one topic is becoming too large for a single document, consider reorganizing the content so that you can break that topic into subtopics. This technique works especially well in hierarchical organizations. It enables you to determine exactly to what level of detail each "level" of the hierarchy should go, and exactly how big and complete each page should be.

Don't Create Too Many or Too Few Documents

There are no rules about how many pages you must have in your Web presentation, or about how large each page should be. You can have one page or several thousand pages, depending on the amount of content you have and how you have organized it.

With this in mind, you might decide to go to one extreme or the other, each of which has advantages and disadvantages. For example, say you put all your content in one big document, and create links to sections within that document (as illustrated in Figure 15.20).

Figure 15.20.
One big document.

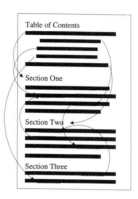

Advantages:

☐ One file is easier to maintain, and links within that file won't ever break if you move things around or rename files.

☐ This structure mirrors real-world document structure. If you are distributing documents both in hard copy and online, having a single document for both makes producing them easier.

Disadvantages:

☐ A large file takes a very long time to download, particularly over slow network connections and especially if the document includes lots of graphics.

☐ Readers must scroll a lot to find what they want. Accessing particular bits of information can become tedious. Navigating at points other than at the top or bottom becomes close to impossible.

☐ The structure is overly rigid. A single document is inherently linear. Although you can skip around within sections in the document, the structure still mirrors that of the printed page and doesn't take advantage of the flexibility of smaller documents linked in a nonlinear fashion.

Or, at the other extreme, you could create a whole bunch of little documents with links between them (as illustrated in Figure 15.21).

Figure 15.21.
Lots of little documents.

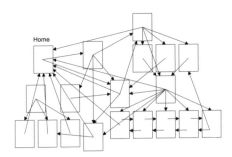

Advantages:

- ☐ Smaller documents load very quickly.
- ☐ You can often fit the entire page on one screen, so the information in that document can be scanned very easily.

Disadvantages:

- ☐ Maintaining all those links will be a nightmare. Just adding some sort of navigational structure to that many documents might create thousands of links.
- ☐ If you have too many jumps between documents, the jumps might seem jarring. Continuity is difficult when your reader spends more time jumping than actually reading.

So what is the solution? Often the content you're describing will determine the size and number of documents you need, especially if you follow the one-topic-per-page suggestion. Testing your Web pages on various platforms and network speeds will let you know whether a single document is too large. If you spend a lot of time scrolling around in the document, or if it takes more time to load than you expected, it might be too large.

Sign Your Documents

Each document should contain some sort of information at the bottom of the page that acts as the "signature." I mention this briefly in Chapter 7, "Advanced Formatting Options," as part of the description of the <ADDRESS> tag; that particular tag was intended for just this purpose.

Here is a list of some useful information to consider putting in the <ADDRESS> tag on each page:

- ☐ Contact information for the person who created this Web page or the person responsible for it, colloquially known as the "webmaster." This should include at least his or her name and preferably an e-mail address.

☐ The status of the document. Is it complete? Is it a work in progress? Is it intentionally left blank?

☐ When this document was last revised. This information is particularly important for documents that change a lot. Include a date on each document so that people know how old it is.

☐ Copyright or trademark information, if it applies.

Figure 15.22 shows a nice example of an address block.

Figure 15.22.
A sample address.

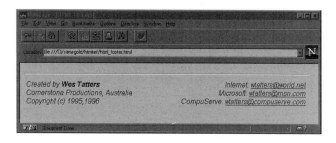

A nice touch to include on your Web page is to link a mailto URL to the text containing the e-mail address of the webmaster, like this:

```
<ADDRESS>
Wes Tatters <A HREF="mailto:wtatters@world.net">wtatters@world.net</A>
</ADDRESS>
```

This technique enables the readers of the document who have browsers that support the mailto URL to simply select the link and send mail to the relevant person responsible for the page without having to retype the address into their mail programs.

Note: This technique works only in browsers that support mailto URLs. But even in browsers that don't accept it, the link text will appear as usual, so there's no harm in including the link.

Finally, if you don't want to clutter each page with a lot of personal contact or boilerplate copyright information, a simple solution is to create a separate page for the extra information and then link the signature to that page, like this:

```
<ADDRESS>
<A HREF="copyright.html">Copyright</A> and
<A HREF="webmaster.html">contact</A> information is available.
</ADDRESS>
```

Provide Nonhypertext Versions of Hypertext Documents

Even though the Web provides a way to create documents in new and exciting ways, some readers still like to read many things offline, say, on the bus or at the breakfast table. These kinds of readers have real problems with hypertext documents, because after you start using hypertext to organize a document, it becomes difficult to be able to tell your browser to "print the whole thing"—the browser knows only the boundaries of individual pages.

If you are using the Web to publish anything that might be readable and usable outside the Web, consider also creating a single text or PostScript version. You can then make that version available as an external document for downloading. This method enables your readers both to browse the document online and, if they want, also to print it for reading offline. You can even link the location of the hard copy document to the start of the hypertext version, like this:

```
A <A HREF="ftp://myhome.com/pub/mydir/myfile.ps">PostScript version</A>
of this document is available via ftp at myhome.com in the directory
/pub/mydir/myfile.ps.
```

And, of course, a handy cross-reference for the hard copy version would be to provide the URL for the hypertext version:

```
"This document is also available in hypertext form on the World Wide Web at
the  http://myhome.com/pub/mydir/myfile.index.html."
```

Summary

The main dos and don'ts for Web page design from this chapter are summarized here:

- ☐ DO write your documents clearly and concisely.
- ☐ DO organize the text of your document so that your readers can scan for important information.
- ☐ DON'T write Web pages that are dependent on pages before or after them in the structure. DO write context-independent pages.
- ☐ DON'T overuse emphasis (boldface, italic, all caps, link text). DO use emphasis sparingly and only when absolutely necessary.
- ☐ DON'T use terminology specific to any one browser ("click here," "use the back button," and so on).
- ☐ DO spell check and proofread your documents.
- ☐ DO keep your layout simple.

- ☐ DON'T clutter the page with lots of pretty but unnecessary images.
- ☐ DO provide alternatives to images for text-only browsers.
- ☐ DO take care with Netscape's backgrounds and colored text not to make your pages flashy but unreadable.
- ☐ DON'T use heading tags to provide emphasis.
- ☐ DO group related information both semantically (through the organization of the content) and visually (through the use of headings or by separating sections with rule lines).
- ☐ DO use a consistent layout for all your pages.
- ☐ DO use link menus to organize your links for quick scanning, and DO use descriptive links.
- ☐ DON'T fall into the "here" syndrome with your links.
- ☐ DO have good reasons for using links. DON'T link to irrelevant material.
- ☐ DON'T link repeatedly to the same site on the same page.
- ☐ DO always provide a link back to your home page.
- ☐ DO match topics with pages.
- ☐ DON'T split individual topics across pages.
- ☐ DO provide a signature block or link to contact information at the bottom of each page.
- ☐ DO provide single-document, nonhypertext versions of linear documents.

Workshop

The first section of the Workshop lists some of the common questions people ask about the World Wide Web along with a brief answer to each. Next is a quiz about the chapter you have just read. If you have problems answering any of the questions in the quiz, you can turn to Appendix E, "Answers to Quiz Questions."

Q&A

Q I'm converting existing documents into Web pages. These documents are very text heavy and are intended to be read from start to finish instead of being quickly scanned. I can't restructure or redesign the content to better follow the guidelines you've suggested in this chapter—that's not my job. What can I do?

A Some content will be like this, particularly when you're converting a document written for paper to online. Ideally, you would be able to rewrite and restructure for online presentation, but realistically, you often won't be able to do anything with the content other than throw it online.

All is not lost, however. You can still improve the overall presentation of these documents by providing reasonable indexes to the content (summaries, table of contents pages, subject indexes, and so on) and by including standard navigation links back out of the text-heavy pages. In other words, you can create an easily navigable framework around the documents themselves, which can go a long way toward improving content that is otherwise difficult to read online.

Q I have a standard signature block that contains my name and e-mail address, revision information for the document, and a couple lines of copyright information that my company's lawyers insisted on. It's a little imposing, particularly on small pages, where the signature is bigger than the page itself! Is there a solution to this problem?

A If your company's lawyers agree, consider putting all your contact and copyright information on a separate page, and then linking it to every page instead of duplicating it every time. This way, your pages won't be overwhelmed by the legal stuff, and if the signature changes, you won't have to change it on every page.

Quiz

1. What is scanability?
2. Should you use browser specific terminology in a Web page?
3. Why should you include an ALT attribute for every <IMG> tag?
4. How important is spelling and proofreading?
5. What is the "here" syndrome?

Exercise

If you have managed to keep up with the pace of this book, congratulations. But really, you should consider getting a life outside the Internet. To this end, your exercise for this chapter is just that. Put this book down, get away from the front of your computer, go outside, and take a brisk walk or maybe a jog in the park.

After all, it's the end of another day's lessons and you deserve the break. Not to mention the fact that the last two days delve into some pretty heady topics and you will need to be fresh and alert to absorb all the information the final six chapters contain.

DAY

6

Developing Interactive Web Pages

16

Interacting with the Web Server by Using CGI

CGI stands for *Common Gateway Interface*, a method of running programs on the Web server based on input from a Web browser anywhere on the Net. CGI scripts are an extremely powerful feature of Web browser and server interaction that can completely change how you think of a Web presentation. CGI scripts enable your reader to interact with your Web pages—to search for an item in a database, to offer comments on what you've written, or to select several items from a form and get a customized reply in return. If you've ever come across a fill-in form or a search dialog box on the Web, you've used a CGI script. You might not have realized it at the time because most of the work happens on the Web server, behind the scenes. You see only the result.

As a Web author, you create all the sides of the CGI script: the side the reader sees, the programming on the server side to deal with the reader's input, and the result given back to the reader.

This chapter describes the following items:

- ☐ What a CGI script is and how it works
- ☐ When you should use a CGI script
- ☐ What the output of a CGI script looks like
- ☐ How to create simple scripts that execute programs
- ☐ How to create scripts that prompt the reader for a small reply
- ☐ How to create scripts that return special responses
- ☐ How to troubleshoot problems with your CGI scripts

After you have learned the basics of creating CGI scripts, you can use them to create all kinds of customized Web pages. CGI scripts are the starting point from which you can create fill-in forms and clickable image maps, which you'll learn about in the following chapters.

Note: This chapter and the next focus primarily on Web servers running on UNIX systems, and most of the examples and instructions apply only to UNIX. If you run your Web server on a system other than UNIX, the procedures you'll learn in this section for creating CGI scripts might not apply. But this chapter will at least give you an idea of how CGI works, and then you can combine that information with the documentation of CGI on your specific server.

What Is a CGI Script?

A CGI script, most simply, is a program that is run on a Web server, triggered by input from a browser. The script is usually a link between the server and some other program running on the system (for example, a database).

CGI scripts do not have to be actual script; depending on what your Web server supports, they can be compiled programs or batch files or any other executable entity. For the sake of using a simple term in this chapter, however, I'll call them scripts.

CGI is the method the W3C httpd and NCSA HTTPd Web servers on UNIX use to allow interaction between servers and programs (and specifically, between forms and programs). Other servers on other platforms might provide similar gateway capabilities, but they don't necessarily use the Common Gateway Interface to do so. The term *CGI script*, however, has come to mean any script or program that is run on the server side, so I'll use that term here.

How Do CGI Scripts Work?

CGI scripts are called by the server, based on information from the browser. Figure 16.1 shows the path of how things work among the browser, the server, and the script.

Figure 16.1.

Browser to server to script to program and back again.

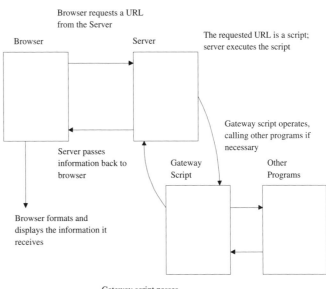

Here's a short version of what's actually going on:

1. A URL points to a CGI script the same way it points to any other document on a server. The browser requests that URL from a server just as it would any other document.

2. The server receives the request, notes that the URL points to a script (based on the location of the file or based on its extension, depending on the server), and executes that script.

3. The script performs some action based on the input, if any, from the browser. The action might include querying a database, calculating a value, or simply calling some other program on the system.

4. The script formats its result in a manner that the Web server can understand.

5. The Web server receives the result from the script and passes it back to the browser, which formats and displays it for the reader.

Got it? No? Don't be worried; it can be a confusing process. Read on, and it'll become clearer with a couple examples.

A Simple Example

Here's a simple example, with a step-by-step explanation of what's happening on all sides of the process. In your browser, you'll encounter a page that looks like the page shown in Figure 16.2.

Figure 16.2.

A page with a script link.

The link to display the date goes to a CGI script. It is embedded in the HTML code for the page just like any other link. If you were to look at the HTML code for that page, that link might look like this:

```
Instead you use this page to find out
➥ <A HREF="http://www.somesite.com/cgi-bin/getdate">today's date.</A>
```

The fact that there's a cgi-bin in the pathname is a strong hint that this is a CGI script. In many servers (the W3C httpd and NCSA HTTPd servers, in particular) cgi-bin is the only place CGI scripts can be kept.

When you select the link, your browser requests that URL from the server at the site www.somesite.com. The server receives the request and figures out from its configuration that the URL it has been given is a script called getdate. It executes that script.

The getdate script, in this case a shell script to be executed on a UNIX system, looks something like this:

```
#!/bin/sh

echo Content-type: text/plain
echo

/bin/date
```

This script does two things. First, it outputs the line Content-type: text/plain, followed by a blank line. Second, it calls the standard UNIX date program, which prints the date and time. So the complete output of the script looks something like this:

```
Content-type: text/plain

Sun Dec 10 18:45:22 AES 1995
```

What's that Content-type thing? That's a special code the Web server passes on to the browser to tell it what kind of document this is. The browser then uses that code to figure out whether it can display the document or whether it needs to load an external viewer. You'll learn specifics about this line later in this chapter.

So after the script has finished executing, the server gets the result and passes it back to the browser over the Net. The browser has been waiting patiently all this time for some kind of response. When the browser gets the input from the server, it simply displays it in a new window. (See Figure 16.3.)

That's the basic idea. Although things can get much more complicated, this interaction among browser, server, and script is at the heart of how CGI scripts work.

16

Figure 16.3.
The result of the date script.

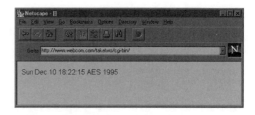

Can I Use CGI Scripts?

Before you can use CGI scripts in your Web presentations, both you and your server must meet several basic conditions. CGI scripting is an advanced Web feature and requires knowledge on your part as well as the cooperation of your Web server provider.

Make sure that you can answer all the questions in the following sections before going on.

Is Your Server Configured to Allow CGI Scripts?

To write and run CGI scripts, you need a server. Unlike with regular HTML files, you cannot write and test CGI scripts on your local system; you must go through a Web server to do so.

But even if you have a Web server, that server must be specially configured to run CGI scripts. That usually means that all your scripts will be kept in a special directory called cgi-bin. And your server provider might not let you have access to that directory for security or other reasons. Before trying out CGI scripts, ask your server administrator whether you are allowed to install and run CGI scripts, and if so, where to put them when you're done writing them. Also, you must have a real Web server to run CGI scripts—if you publish your Web pages on an FTP or a gopher server, you cannot use CGI.

If you run your own server, you'll have to specially create a cgi-bin directly and configure your server to recognize that directory as a script directory (part of your server configuration, which of course varies from server to server). The section "Setting Up CGI Capabilities on Your Server" describes how to do this. But also keep in mind the following issues that CGI scripts bring up:

☐ Each script is a program and it runs on your system when the browser requests it, using CPU time and memory during its execution. What happens to the system if dozens or hundreds or thousands of these scripts are running at the same time? Your system might not be able to handle the load, making it crash or rendering it unusable for normal work.

☐ Unless you are very careful with the CGI scripts you write, you can potentially open yourself up to someone breaking into or damaging your system by passing arguments to your CGI script that are different from those it expects.

Can You Program?

Beginner beware! To do CGI, process forms, or do any sort of interactivity on the World Wide Web, you must have a basic grasp of programming concepts and methods, and you should have some familiarity with the system on which you are working. If you don't have this background, I strongly suggest that you consult with someone who does, pick up a book in programming basics (and work through it), or take a class in programming at your local college. This book is far too small for me to explain both introductory programming and CGI programming at the same time; in this chapter in particular, I am going to assume that you can read and understand the code in these examples.

What Programming Language Should You Use?

You can use just about any programming language you are familiar with to write CGI scripts, as long as your script follows the rules in the next section, and as long as that language can run on the system your Web server runs on. Some servers, however, might support only programs written in a particular language. For example, MacHTTP uses AppleScript for its CGI scripts, and WinHTTPD uses Visual Basic. To write CGI scripts for your server, you must program in the language that server accepts.

In this chapter and throughout this book, I'll be writing these CGI scripts in two languages: the UNIX Bourne shell and the Perl language. The Bourne shell is available on nearly any UNIX system and is reasonably easy to learn, but doing anything complicated in it can be difficult. Perl, on the other hand, is freely available, but you'll have to download and compile it on your system. The language itself is extremely flexible and powerful (nearly as powerful as a programming language such as C), but it is very difficult to learn.

Setting Up CGI Capabilities on Your Server

To run any CGI scripts, whether they are simple scripts or scripts to process forms, your server needs to be set up explicitly to run them. This might mean that your scripts must be kept in a special directory or that they must have a special file extension, depending on which server you're using and how it's set up.

If you are renting space on a Web server, or if someone else is in charge of administering your Web server, you have to ask the person in charge whether CGI scripts are allowed and, if so, where to put them.

If you run your own server, read on for information about configuring and using CGI scripts.

CGI on the W3C httpd Server

To enable the use of CGI scripts in the W3C httpd server, edit your configuration file (usually `/etc/httpd.conf`), and add a line similar to the following one:

```
Exec /cgi-bin/*   /home/www/cgi-bin/*
```

The `Exec` command indicates that a directory (conventionally the directory `cgi-bin`) contains executable scripts and not regular files, and the command tries to execute those files rather than just display their text.

The first argument indicates how that directory name will appear in the URL. Here, that directory name is `cgi-bin`, and it will be the first directory name after the hostname in the URL (for example, `http://myhost.com/cgi-bin/`).

The second argument is the actual pathname of the CGI directory on your system. CGI directories are usually stored in the same directory as the rest of your Web files (in this example, in the `/home/www` directory), but they can be anywhere on the system. Once again, `cgi-bin` is the conventional directory name. Make sure that you also create that directory on your system.

> **Note:** You can have as many script directories on your system as you want. Simply include multiple `Exec` lines in your configuration file.

Finally, after you've made the appropriate changes to your configuration file, restart the server using the following command:

```
httpd -restart
```

> **Note:** If you are running your httpd server through `inetd`, you don't have to restart it.

CGI on the NCSA HTTPd Server

The NCSA HTTPd server has two methods of indicating CGI scripts: by using a special directory (as with the W3C httpd server), or by using a special extension, .cgi, which indicates that a file is a script and will be treated as a script regardless of where it is stored.

> **Note:** Allowing a file extension for scripts enables you to put them anywhere on the system. As long as your scripts have a .cgi extension, they are treated as executable scripts. Keep in mind, however, that allowing the file extension is an enormous security hole for your system, because you might not be able to keep track of what scripts are being used and what they are doing.

To set up a script directory using the NCSA HTTPd server, edit your srm.conf file (usually in the conf directory), and add a line similar to the following:

```
ScriptAlias /cgi-bin/ cgi-bin/
```

The ScriptAlias command indicates that a directory contains executable scripts and not regular files, and it tries to execute those files rather than just display their text.

The first argument indicates how the directory name will appear in the URL. Here, that directory name is cgi-bin, and it will be the first directory name after the hostname in the URL (for example, http://myhost.com/cgi-bin/). By convention, this directory name is cgi-bin.

The second argument to ScriptAlias points to the actual pathname of the CGI directory as it appears on your file system. CGI directories are usually stored in the same directory as the rest of your Web files (in this example, in the /home/www directory), but you can put them anywhere you want to. Once again, cgi-bin is the conventional directory name for CGI directories. Make sure that you also create that directory on your system.

> **Note:** You can have as many script directories on your system as you want. Simply include multiple ScriptAlias lines in your configuration file.

To allow the use of script files with a .cgi extension, edit your srm.conf file and add this line (unless it's already there, in which case you'll just have to uncomment it):

```
AddType application/x-httpd-cgi .cgi
```

16

This line uses the AddType directive to add a new kind of file that the server understands. The first argument is the MIME type of CGI scripts (here, x-httpd-cgi), and the second argument is the filename extension indicating that a file is a script.

Finally, after you've made the appropriate changes to your configuration file, you'll need to restart the server. First, find out the process ID of the server by using the ps command. For example, the command

```
ps aux ¦ grep httpd
```

might return the following line, in which the process number is 51:

```
root 51  0.0 2.4 420 372 con S 15:28 0:00 /usr/local/bin/httpd
```

When you know the process ID, you can restart the server using the following command, in which the last argument is the process ID of the server:

```
kill -1 51
```

Note: If you are running your HTTPD server through inetd, you don't have to restart it after editing the configuration files.

What if You're Not on UNIX?

If you're not on UNIX, stick around. There's still lots of general information about CGI that might apply to your server. But just for general background, here's some information about CGI on other common Web servers.

WinHTTPD for Windows includes CGI capabilities in which you manage form and CGI input through Visual Basic programs, and it includes a Visual Basic module to decode form input. Also included is a DOS CGI interface, which can be configured to handle scripts using Perl or tcl (or any other language).

WebSite, written by Robert Denny, is a 32-bit Web server that runs on Windows NT. The CGI capabilities are very similar to those of WinHTTPD.

MacHTTP has CGI capabilities in the form of AppleScript scripts. (The new version of MacHTTP will be called WebStar and is available from StarNine.) Jon Wiederspan has written an excellent tutorial on using AppleScript CGI, which is included as part of the MacHTTP documentation in the Tutorials:Extending_MacHTTP folder.

CGI Script Behavior

If you've made it this far, past all the warnings and configuration, congratulations! You are now well on the way to writings CGI scripts and creating forms and image maps for your presentations. In this section you'll learn about how your scripts should behave so that your server can talk to them and get the correct response back.

The Output Header

Your CGI scripts will generally get some sort of input from the browser by way of the server: search keys, form input, and x and y coordinates for image maps. You can do anything you want with that information in the body of your script, but the output of that script must follow a special format.

> **Note:** By "script output," I'm referring to the data your script sends back to the server. On UNIX the output is sent to the standard output. On other systems and other servers, your script output might go somewhere else; for example, you might write to a file on the disk or send the output explicitly to another program. Again, this is a case in which you should carefully examine the documentation for your server to see how CGI scripts have been implemented in that server.

16

The first thing your script should output is a special header that gives the server, and eventually the browser, information about the rest of the data your script is going to create. The header isn't actually part of the document; it's never displayed anywhere. Web servers and browsers actually send information like this back and forth all the time; you just never see it.

You can output three types of headers from scripts: Content-type, Location, and Status. Content-type is the most popular, so I'll explain it here; you'll learn about Location and Status headers later in this chapter.

A Content-type header includes the words Content-type, a special code for describing the kind of file you're sending, and a blank line, like this:

```
Content-type: text/html

#make sure you include a blank line immediately after the content-type
➡declaration
```

In this example, the contents of the data to follow are of the type text/html; in other words, it's an HTML file. Each file format you work with when you're creating Web presentations has a corresponding content-type, so you should match the format of the output of your script to the appropriate content-type. Table 16.1 shows some common formats and their equivalent content-types.

Table 16.1. Common formats and content-types.

Format	Content-Type
HTML	text/html
Text	text/plain
GIF	image/gif
JPEG	image/jpeg
PostScript	application/postscript
MPEG	video/mpeg

Note: The content-types are derived from MIME content-types. MIME is a method for sending included files in e-mail messages. A lot more content-types are available than I've listed here. In fact, if you're using the NCSA HTTPd server, the file conf/mime-types has a whole list of the content-types that the server can accept. As long as a file type is in that list, you can send that content of the file as output to your script.

Note that the content-type line *must* be followed by a blank line. The server cannot figure out where the header ends if you don't include the blank line.

The Output Data

The remainder of your script is the actual data you want to send back to the browser. The content you output in this part should match the content type you told the server you were giving it; that is, if you use a content-type of text/html, the rest of the output should be in HTML. If you use a content-type of image/gif, the remainder of the output should be a binary GIF file, and so on for all the content-types.

Exercise: Try It

This exercise is similar to the simple example from earlier in this chapter, the one that prints the date. This time, however, you'll modify the script so that it outputs an HTML document, which then is parsed and formatted by the browser.

First, determine the content-type you'll be outputting. Because this will be an HTML document, the content-type is text/html. So the first part of your script simply prints a line containing the content-type, and a blank line after that:

```
#!/bin/sh

echo Content-type: text/html
echo
```

Now, add the remainder of the script: the body of the HTML document, which you had to construct yourself from inside the script. Basically, what you're going to do here is this:

- ☐ Print the tags that make up the first part of the HTML document.
- ☐ Call the date program to add the text.
- ☐ Print the last bit of HTML tags to finish the document.

Start with the first bit of the HTML. The following commands will do this in the UNIX shell:

```
cat << EOF
<HTML><HEAD>
<TITLE>Date</TITLE>
</HEAD><BODY>
<P>The current date is: <B>
EOF
```

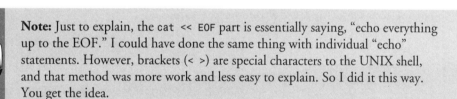

Note: Just to explain, the `cat << EOF` part is essentially saying, "echo everything up to the EOF." I could have done the same thing with individual "echo" statements. However, brackets (< >) are special characters to the UNIX shell, and that method was more work and less easy to explain. So I did it this way. You get the idea.

So now you've printed the HTML structuring commands, printed a nice sentence explaining the output, and turned on boldface. Now call the UNIX date program to output the date itself:

```
/bin/date
```

And, finally, print another block of HTML to finish the page:

```
cat << EOF
</B></BODY></HTML>
EOF
```

And that's it. If you run the program by itself from a command line, you'll get a result something like this:

```
Content-type: text/html

<HTML><HEAD>
<TITLE>Date</TITLE>
</HEAD><BODY>
<P>The current date is: <B>
Sun Dec 10 18:45:22 AES 1995
</B></P></BODY></HTML>
```

Looks like your basic HTML document, doesn't it?

Now install this script in the proper place for your server. This step will vary depending on the platform you're on and the server you're using. Most of the time, on UNIX servers, there will be a special `cgi-bin` directory for scripts. Copy the script there and make sure it's executable.

> **Note:** If you don't have access to the `cgi-bin` directory, you must ask your Web server administrator for access.

Now that you've got a script ready to go, you can call it from a browser. Assume, for the purposes of this example, that you've installed the script into a `cgi-bin` directory on a machine called `www.ostrich.com`. The URL to the script would then be this:

```
http://www.ostrich.com/cgi-bin/prettydate
```

Figure 16.4 shows the result of running the script.

Figure 16.4.
The result of running the `prettydate` script.

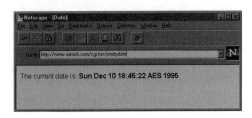

Just for reference, here's what the final script looks like:

```
#!/bin/sh

echo Content-type: text/html
echo

cat << EOF
```

```
<HTML><HEAD>
<TITLE>Date</TITLE>
</HEAD><BODY>
<P>The current date is: <B>
EOF
/bin/date
cat << EOF
</B></BODY></HTML>
EOF
```

Creating an Interactive Search

Writing a CGI script is easy if you just want to do one thing on the server and get a single result back. But what if you want to do something more complicated—such as prompt your reader for a string, search for that string in a file, and then return that result as a nice formatted page?

In this case, things get considerably more complicated, because you must somehow get input from your reader into your CGI script. There are two primary ways of doing this: through a document-based query (sometimes called an ISINDEX query) or by using a form. You'll learn more about forms in Chapter 17, "Forms and CGI"; this section explains more about the document-based query.

Note: Document-based queries, as you'll learn in this section, are the old way of getting information back to servers and to CGI scripts. Few pages use document-based queries any more, because forms have made queries much more flexible and easier to work with. If you're impatient to get on with forms, you might want to skip this section and move on to "Creating Special Script Output," later in this chapter. That section provides more information about the sorts of things you can do with CGI scripts and finishes the background you need in order to work with forms in Chapter 17.

Document-based queries were designed to get search keys from a browser and use them to make queries to databases or to search files. For this reason, document queries are good for getting small bits of information (such as single words or phrases) back from the reader.

Document-based queries work through the interaction of three things: the use of an HTML tag called <ISINDEX>, a special form of URL a browser generates, and a set of arguments to your script.

Here's what's going on at each step of the query:

1. When a reader first requests your CGI script through a URL, your script is called with no arguments. In your script, you test for the existence of arguments, and because there are none, you output a default page that prompts for the search.

   In the HTML code for the default page, you include the special <ISINDEX> HTML tag (this tag is why document-based queries are called ISINDEX queries). The <ISINDEX> tag turns on searching in the browser.

2. The reader enters a string to search for prompt and presses Enter or selects a button (depending on how searching has been implemented in the browser).

3. The browser requests the same URL to the CGI script, except this time, the URL includes the string the user specified in the search, tacked onto the end of the URL after a question mark, like this:

   ```
   http://musite.com/cgi-bin/dosearch?ostriches
   ```

   For this example, dosearch is the script and ostriches is the string the reader typed at the search prompt.

4. The server receives the URL and passes control on to the CGI script, using the part of the URL after the question mark as the argument (or arguments) to the script itself.

5. Your script is called a second time, but this time, because it was called with arguments, it performs a different operation. In this example, it searches for the argument in a file and returns an HTML page indicating whether the argument was found.

Each part of the document-based query relies on the other parts. The script provides activation of the <ISINDEX> tag, which allows the query. The browser attaches the query itself to the URL, which is then passed back to the script. The script uses it to perform the appropriate action and then output a result back to the browser.

Each part of the document-based query is described in more detail in the following sections.

The Script

In document-based queries, you base what your script does on whether the script was called with arguments, and (often) on the arguments you receive. The script will have two main results:

☐ If the script was called with no arguments, the result will be to output the HTML for a default page that prompts the user for a search string.

Keep in mind that the default page is generated by a script; it's not a plain HTML file. You cannot trigger searches in this way by using a plain HTML document.

☐ If the script was called with any arguments, your script will use the arguments to perform the search, make a test, or perform the operation it was intended to do, and then output an appropriate result.

The *<ISINDEX>* Tag

The <ISINDEX> tag is a special HTML tag used especially for document-based queries. <ISINDEX> doesn't enclose any text, nor does it have a closing tag.

So what does <ISINDEX> do? It "turns on" searching in the browser that is reading this document. Depending the browser, this task might involve enabling a search button (see Figure 16.5) or special window in the browser itself. For other browsers, it might involve including an input field on the page itself. (See Figure 16.6.) The reader can then enter a string to search for, then press Enter or click the button to submit the query to the server.

Figure 16.5.

A search prompt in the Browser window of the Macintosh browser.

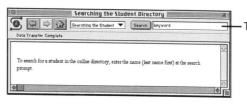

— The search prompt

Figure 16.6.

A search prompt on the page in Navigator 2.0.

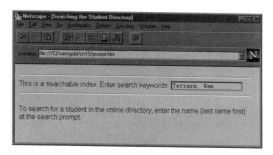

According to the HTML 2.0 specification, the <ISINDEX> tag should go inside the <HEAD> part of the HTML document (it's one of the few tags that go into <HEAD>, <TITLE> being the other obvious example). In older browsers, in which there was a single location for the search prompt, this made sense, because neither the search prompt nor the <ISINDEX> tag was actually part of the data of the document. However, because more recent browsers display the input field on the HTML page itself, it is useful to be able to put <ISINDEX> in the body of the document so that you can control where on the page the input field appears (if it's in

the <HEAD>, it'll always be the first thing on the page). Most browsers will now accept an <ISINDEX> tag anywhere in the body of an HTML document and will draw the input box wherever that tag appears.

Finally, there is a Netscape extension to the <ISINDEX> tag that enables you to define the search prompt. Again, in older browsers, the search prompt was fixed (it was usually something confusing like "This is a Searchable index. Enter keywords"). The Netscape-only PROMPT attribute to <ISINDEX> enables you to define the string that will be used to indicate the input field. For example, Figure 16.7 shows the result of this tag when used with the following HTML source:

```
<P> To search for a student in the online directory, enter the name
(last name first):
<ISINDEX PROMPT="Student's name:   ">
```

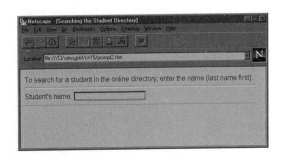

Figure 16.7.
*A Navigator 2.0 search
prompt.*

In other browsers, as with all Netscape extensions, the prompt will be ignored and the default search prompt used instead, so you might want to use only a few words in PROMPT and explain the purpose of the search field elsewhere.

The Search String and the Script's URL

When the reader presses Enter or clicks a button after entering the search string, the browser calls the URL for the same CGI script again. This time, it appends the value the reader typed into the search prompt to the end of the URL, with a question mark separating the name of the script and the argument. Because spaces and other special characters have a special meaning to URLs, if there are spaces in the search string, the browser converts them to the + character before the URL is called. Other special characters are similarly encoded.

On the server side, the server calls the script again and replaces the + in the argument list with spaces. This has the effect of calling the script with multiple arguments.

An example will make the interaction among all these parts clearer.

Exercise: Say Hello

Although document-based queries were originally intended to perform searches on databases and other documents stored on the server, you don't have to use document-based queries to actually search anything. In your CGI script, you can use the arguments passed back from the browser for any purpose you want. For example, you could use it to create a talkative browser. In this exercise, you'll do just that. In this example, the main page prompts you to say "hello" to it via the search prompt. Figure 16.8 shows that main page.

Figure 16.8.
Hello, the first page.

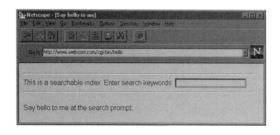

From this page, you can type `hello` and choose Search. If you were to try typing `bonjour`, the CGI script would give you the response shown in Figure 16.9.

Figure 16.9.
The first response.

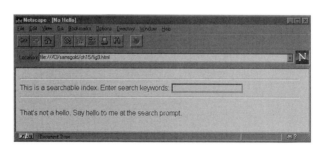

Our script is obviously not multilingual. If you gave in and tried typing `hello`, you'd get the response shown in Figure 16.10.

Figure 16.10.
Hello!

Implementing this sort of script simply involves writing the script so that it tests the argument it gets from your reader and returns the appropriate page depending on what that argument was. Next, we'll go through all the steps of writing the script so that it behaves like this.

Create the Default Page

First, you need to create the case in which the script is called with no arguments; that is, the first default page. But even before you do that, you should create the basic structure of this script. First, print the script header and the first bits of the HTML page:

```
#!/bin/sh

echo Content-type: text/html
echo

cat << EOF
<HTML><HEAD><TITLE>
EOF
```

Now you need to test whether the script was called with arguments. In Bourne shell scripts, the test looks like this:

```
if [ $# = 0 ]; then
    ...
fi
```

Put the rest of the HTML needed to create the default page inside the if…fi lines, like this:

```
if [ $# = 0 ]; then
cat << EOF
Say Hello to me</TITLE><ISINDEX></HEAD><BODY>
<P>Say hello to me at the search prompt.
EOF
fi
```

And the end of the script finishes the HTML file:

```
cat << EOF
</P></BODY></HTML>
EOF
```

So if you saved this script and ran it without arguments, you'd get the following result:

```
Content-type: text/html

<HTML><HEAD><TITLE>
Say Hello to me</TITLE><ISINDEX></HEAD><BODY>
<P>Say hello to me at the search prompt.
</P></BODY></HTML>
```

The formatting is a little funny, but HTML doesn't care about that. It will get displayed as usual.

Note the `<ISINDEX>` tag. Again, this is what activates the search feature in the browser reading this document.

Test the Arguments and Return the Appropriate Result

Now you have a basic script that works fine if there are no arguments. But when your reader types something into the search field and presses Enter (or presses the appropriate button), the script will be called again with whatever was typed as an argument. You'll have to add to your script to handle that argument.

Modifying the script to react differently if there are arguments is not that difficult; all you have to do is add an `else` to your `if`. Note, however, that in this example there can be two different results, depending on what your reader types into the search field (either the correct result, `hello`, or anything else), so just adding a single `else` isn't enough. You need to add another test to make sure that the response is `hello`. In the Bourne shell, the structure of `if`s and `else`s in this case would look like this:

```
if [ $# = 0 ]; then
    #the default page
else if [ $1 != "hello" ]; then
    #the not hello response
else
    #the hello response
fi
fi
```

All I've included here is the structure to create the appropriate branches, and the comments (the parts starting with #) to explain what parts go where. Now, finish the script by adding the HTML codes in the right slots.

16

With the structure in place, you can add the rest of the HTML code within each section. For example, for the first section (the response to anything other than `hello`), you'd use this:

```
else if [ $1 != "hello" ]; then
cat << EOF
Not Hello</TITLE><ISINDEX></HEAD><BODY>
<P>That's not a hello. Say hello to me at the search prompt.
EOF
```

Note that the `<ISINDEX>` tag is there again, because you're still expecting a response (and you want the right one this time!).

Finally, fill in the last slot with code to produce the "correct" page:

```
else
cat << EOF
How Friendly!</TITLE></HEAD><BODY>
<P>Hello to you too!
EOF
```

Here, in the final branch, you don't need an `<ISINDEX>` tag because you're done prompting for a response. All you're producing here is the congratulatory page, which is just plain old HTML.

To test it, you can call the script from the command line with the appropriate arguments. The `sayhello` script with an argument of `goodbye` results in this output:

```
Content-type: text/html

<HTML><HEAD><TITLE>
Not Hello</TITLE><ISINDEX></HEAD><BODY>
<P>That's not a hello. Say hello to me at the search prompt.
</P></BODY></HTML>
```

And an argument of `hello` prints this output:

```
Content-type: text/html

<HTML><HEAD><TITLE>
How Friendly!</TITLE></HEAD><BODY>
<P>Hello to you too!
</P></BODY></HTML>
```

For each possible response the reader gives you, there is an appropriate HTML output. You've covered all the options in separate branches.

The Complete Script

Just for reference, here's the full `sayhello` script:

```
#!/bin/sh

echo Content-type: text/html
echo
```

```
cat << EOF
<HTML><HEAD><TITLE>
EOF

if [ $# = 0 ]; then
cat << EOF
Say Hello to me</TITLE><ISINDEX></HEAD><BODY>
<P>Say hello to me at the search prompt.
EOF
else if [ $1 != "hello" ]; then
cat << EOF
Not Hello</TITLE><ISINDEX></HEAD><BODY>
<P>That's not a hello. Say hello to me at the search prompt.
EOF
else
cat << EOF
How Friendly!</TITLE></HEAD><BODY>
<P>Hello to you too!
EOF
fi
fi

cat << EOF
</P></BODY></HTML>
EOF
```

Creating Special Script Output

For most of this chapter, you've written scripts that output data, usually HTML data, that is sent to the browser for interpretation and display. But what if you don't want to send a stream of data as a result of a script's actions? What if you want to load an existing document instead? What if you just want the script to do something and not give any response to the browser?

Fear not, you can do those things. This section explains how.

Responding by Loading Another Document

In the previous sayhello example, you might have noticed that the last page you created through the script, the one that congratulated the user for saying hello, had nothing special in it that would imply that it needed to be constructed in the script. The other two branches had to be constructed by the script so that they could include the <ISINDEX> tag, but the last one was just an ordinary page.

Wouldn't it have been easier, instead of constructing the content of a regular page in the script (and having to go through all that `cat << EOF` stuff), to simply output a file that was stored on the system? Or, even better, to redirect the server to load that existing file?

What I've just described is possible with CGI scripts. To load an existing document as the output of a script, you use a line similar to this one:

```
Location: ../docs/final.html
```

The `Location` line is used in place of the normal output; that is, if you use `Location`, you do not need to use `Content-type` or include any other data in the output (and, in fact, you can't include any other data in the output). As with `Content-type`, however, you must also include a blank line after the `Location` line.

The pathname to the file can be either a full URL or a relative pathname. All relative pathnames will be relative to the location of the script itself. This one looks for the document `final.html` in a directory called `docs` one level up from the current directory:

```
else
echo Location: ../docs/final.html
echo
fi
```

If the server can find the document you've specified in the `Location` line, it retrieves it and sends it back to the browser just as the output to `Content-type` would have been sent.

> **Note:** You cannot combine `Content-type` and `Location` output. For example, if you want to output a standard page and then add custom content to the bottom of that page, you'll have to use `Content-type` and construct both parts yourself. Note that you could use script commands to open a local file and print it directly to the output—for example, use `cat filename` rather than the `cat << EOF` that the scripts in this chapter used.

So if you were using a `Location` line to output the last branch of the `sayhello` script, how would you modify the script to do so?

The script was originally written such that each branch of the `if` statement printed much the same thing. Therefore, the `Content-type` lines and the beginning and end of the HTML file were specified outside the `if` statement. Because the final branch doesn't use these, you'll have to copy them inside the branch instead. The final modified script would look like this:

```
#!/bin/sh

if [ $# = 0 ]; then
echo Content-type: text/html
```

```
echo
cat << EOF
<HTML><HEAD><TITLE>
Say Hello to me</TITLE><ISINDEX></HEAD><BODY>
<P>Say hello to me at the search prompt.
</P></BODY></HTML>
EOF
else if [ $1 != "hello" ]; then
echo Content-type: text/html
echo
cat << EOF
<HTML><HEAD><TITLE>
Not Hello</TITLE><ISINDEX></HEAD><BODY>
<P>That's not a hello. Say hello to me at the search prompt.
</P></BODY></HTML>
EOF
else
echo Location: ../docs/sayhellofinal.html
echo
fi
fi
```

No Response

Sometimes it might be appropriate for a CGI script to have no output. Sometimes you just want to take the information you get from the reader. You might not want to load a new document, either by outputting the result or by opening an existing file. The document that was on the browser's screen before should just stay there.

Fortunately, taking this action is easy. Instead of outputting a Content-type or Location header, use the following line (with a blank line after it, as always):

```
Status: 204 No Response
```

The Status header provides status codes to the server (and to the browser). The particular status of 204 is passed on to the browser, and the browser, if it can figure out what to do with it, should do nothing. Otherwise, you may see a strange message on the screen, but as a rule most of the newer browsers—including Navigator 2.0—recognize Status: 204 No Response.

You'll need no other output from your script because you don't want the browser to do anything with it—just send the one Status line followed by a blank line. Of course, your script should do something; otherwise, why bother calling the script?

16

Troubleshooting

Here are some of the most common problems with CGI scripts and how to fix them:

☐ The content of the script is being displayed, not executed.

Have you configured your server to accept CGI scripts? Are your scripts contained in the appropriate CGI directory (usually cgi-bin)? If your server allows CGI files with .cgi extensions, does your script have that extension?

☐ You get the error Error 500: Server doesn't support POST.

You'll get this error from forms that use the POST method. This error most often means that either you haven't set up CGI scripts in your server or you're trying to access a script that isn't contained in a CGI directory (see the preceding item).

It can also mean, however, that you've misspelled the path to the script itself. Check the pathname in your form, and if it's correct, make sure that your script is in the appropriate CGI directory (usually cgi-bin) and that it has a .cgi extension (if your server allows this).

☐ You get the error Document contains no data.

Make sure that you included a blank line between your headers and the data in your script.

☐ You get the error Error 500: Bad Script Request.

Make sure that your script is executable (on UNIX, make sure that you've done chmod +x to the script). You should be able to run your scripts from a command line before you try to call them from a browser.

Summary

CGI scripts, sometimes called server-side scripts or gateway scripts, make it possible for programs to be run on the server, and for HTML or other files to be generated on-the-fly.

This chapter covers the basics of how to deal with CGI scripts, knowledge that you'll use in Chapter 17 and Chapter 18, "Image Maps and Dynamic Documents," when you create forms and image maps. In particular, you have created simple scripts that run as links and you have worked with document queries using the <ISINDEX> tag.

You have also learned about the three headers you can pass back to the server from your script:

☐ Content-type: The output following this header is a file of the type specified in this header. Content-types are MIME-based forms that include such things as text/html and image/gif.

☐ Location: This header opens and sends the specified file back to the browser using either a full URL or a relative pathname.

☐ Status: An HTTP status code. Status is most generally used with 204 No Response to produce no visible output from a script.

Workshop

The first section of the Workshop lists some of the common questions people ask about the World Wide Web along with a brief answer to each. Next is a quiz about the chapter you have just read. If you have problems answering any of the questions in the quiz, you can turn to Appendix E, "Answers to Quiz Questions."

Q&A

Q What if I don't know how to program? Can I still use CGI scripts?

A If you have your access to a Web server through a commercial provider, you might be able to get help from the provider with your CGI scripts (for a fee, of course). Also, if you know even a little programming but you're unsure of what you're doing, you can make use of the many examples available for the platform and server you're working with. Usually, these examples are part of the server distribution or are at the same FTP location. See the documentation that came with your server; it often has pointers to further help. In fact, for the operation you want to accomplish, there might already be a script you can use with only slight modification. But be careful; if you don't know what you're doing, you can rapidly get in over your head.

Q My Web server has a cgi-bin directory, but I don't have access to it. So I created my own cgi-bin directory and put my script there, but calling it from my Web pages didn't work. What did I do wrong?

A Web servers must be specially configured to run CGI scripts, and that means indicating specific directories or files that are meant to be scripts. You cannot just create a directory or a file with a special extension; your server administrator must be involved. Ask him or her for help in installing your scripts.

Q Can I put the <ISINDEX> tag in any HTML document?

A Well, it's legal HTML, so yes, you can put it in any HTML document. And it will turn on the searching interface in the browser when that document is read. But nothing will happen if your readers type something into the search box; they'll get an error or nothing at all when they try to send the results of the search.

The <ISINDEX> tag makes sense only in documents generated by CGI scripts that can handle the results of the query.

Q Can I call my CGI script with command-line options?

A It depends on what you actually want to do with the command-line options. But keep in mind that the only arguments your script is ever called with are the ones appended to the URL as part of the search query. There's no way to intercept the call to your script to add command-line options.

You can, however, hard code the results of a search query in the call to your script. Remember, the browser sends the contents of the search input field to the server through the use of the URL, with the arguments appended to the end of the URL after a question mark. So you could, for example, set up a link to your script that included arguments in the URL itself and bypass the search input altogether. Experiment to see what works.

Q What if I want to do something more complicated in my search? What if I want to include a list of 10 items in the search box and have the script do something with those 10 items? That's an awful lot to include in a search box.

A Yes, that is an awful lot to include in a single string, and that's precisely why forms were created: to allow more extensive kinds of input back from the browser. If you can wait until tomorrow, you'll learn all about forms in Chapter 17.

Quiz

1. What directory are CGI scripts usually stored in?
2. What are the two most common languages used for CGI scripts?
3. What does the <ISINDEX> tag do?
4. What is the content type of a standard HTML document?
5. What status code do you need to send to a Web browser to inform it that there will be no response document sent by a CGI script?

Exercise

Since there are so many different types of Web servers and CGI scripting implementations currently available, your first task, once you decide to step into the world of CGI scripting, is to find out what is and is not supported by your Web server or Web service provider.

For today's exercise, you should either talk to your system administrator or get out the documentation that came with your Web server and start reading. The aim of these explorations is to find out about the CGI scripting capabilities available to you. Then, once you know what is available, you will need to obtain a copy of the appropriate documentation.

With your CGI scripting documentation in hand, you should then convert the examples discussed in this chapter to get a feel for the options open to you. This is important since you will need an understanding of CGI scripting to complete the next two chapters.

17

Forms and CGI

With the knowledge you gained by reading Chapter 16, "Interacting with the Web Server by Using CGI," you now have the background you need to take advantage of two of the most powerful features of Web publishing: forms and image maps. (And if you've skipped to this chapter, shame on you! Go back and read Chapter 16 now!) Forms and image maps make it possible for you to transform your Web pages from primarily text and graphics that your readers passively browse to interactive "toys," surveys, and presentations that can provide different options based on the reader's input.

In this chapter you'll learn about forms by examining some new HTML tags and by creating some new CGI scripts. Then in Chapter 18, "Image Maps and Dynamic Documents," you'll find out what image maps are all about. But, back to the current chapter for now. In this chapter you will learn about the following:

- ☐ How form-based queries are different from document-based queries, including how to handle the input you get from a form
- ☐ The basic form input elements: text fields, radio buttons, and check boxes, as well as buttons for submitting and resetting the form
- ☐ Other form elements: text areas, menus of options, hidden fields, file input fields, and password fields

Anatomy of a Form

In Chapter 16 you learned how to add simple interactivity to your Web pages using <ISINDEX> and documents that were generated exclusively from CGI scripts. Creating interactive presentations using forms is very similar (particularly on the server side), except that it's even easier.

When you created a document-based query using <ISINDEX>, the CGI script did most of the work. It generated the original HTML document and then generated a result based on the input to that same script. This made the script you had to write quite complex because you had to deal with several different branches and with generating many different HTML pages as you went along.

When you create form-based queries, you actually create two separate things: the HTML document that contains the form and the CGI script to process the input from that form.

In the HTML code for the form, which you'll learn about later in this chapter, you do two special things to link the form with the script. First, you include a pointer to the script so that the browser knows where to send the form input. Second, you attach a special name to each element in your form. That name is used with the value your reader enters so that you can tell which data goes with what part of the form.

Form Input: *GET* and *POST*

The third thing you include in the HTML code for your form is how the form input should be sent to the server. There are two choices: GET and POST, which are named after the HTTP commands your browser uses to communicate with your server.

GET is actually the method that ISINDEX searches use to pass input back to the server. The encoded input is appended onto the end of the URL and sent back to the server. In forms, however, that input is then put into an environment variable called QUERY_STRING. (An environment variable is a special storage variable maintained by your Web server and its corresponding CGI programs.)

As a result, unlike with ISINDEX searches, you don't necessarily get the input as arguments to your script. In addition, POST passes the input back to the server on a separate stream, which is then passed directly to the standard input of your CGI script. No variables or arguments are assigned.

Note: As I mentioned in Chapter 16, my discussion of CGI scripting in this book is quite UNIX specific. Your server might have a different way of managing form input, although GET and POST will still exist in some form. Check your server documentation to see how forms are handled.

When you create your HTML form, you'll have a choice of which method to use, GET or POST. So which should you use? The problem with GET is that because it assigns an environment variable to the input of your form, there are usually system-defined limits on the number of characters that variable can hold. So if you have a form with a lot of input to process, some of that input might be cut off. With POST there are no such limits. So for most forms, it makes sense to use POST most of the time. I use POST in all the examples throughout this section.

The CGI Script to Process the Form

CGI scripts to process forms are almost identical to other CGI scripts. Everything you learned in Chapter 16 about creating special headers (such as Content-type) and generating your own HTML documents still applies.

You do, however, have to watch out for a few things with CGI scripts to process forms. For example, the first problem is that you don't get your input as arguments; instead, you get it either from the QUERY_STRING environment variable (for form input sent using GET) or from the standard input (input using POST).

17

The second problem is that when the browser packages the form input for delivery to the server, it puts the form input in a special format called URL encoding. URL encoding tacks all the field names and values together, replacing spaces and special characters where necessary. Form input that has been URL encoded can end up looking kind of bizarre. Here's an example:

```
vitamin=on&svga=on&fish=on&theSex=female&theNametheName=My%20Name
```

In this example, all the field names and their corresponding values are strung together in a single line of text, with each field name/value pair separated by an & symbol. In addition, any spaces have been converted to their corresponding hex value (that is, %20). The field names themselves represent the names assigned to individual input elements on the form, such as a text box, radio button, or pick list, and the values represent the information entered into these fields by the user. (You will learn more about input elements later in the chapter.)

Because form input is passed to your script in this URL-encoded form, you must decode it before you can use it. Because decoding this information is a common task, however, lots of tools are available for the decoding task. There's no reason for you to write your own decoding program unless you want to do something very unusual. The decoding programs you can get should do a fine job, and they might consider things you haven't, such as how to avoid having your script break because someone gave your form funny input.

I've noted a few programs for decoding form input in Appendix D, "Sources of Additional Information," but the program I use for the examples in this book is called uncgi. uncgi decodes the input from a form submission for you and creates a set of environment variables. These environment variables include one for each name in the name/value pairs, with the prefix WWW_ prepended to each name. Each value in the name/value pair is then assigned to its respective environment variable. So, for example, if you had a name in a form called username, the resulting environment variable that uncgi created would be WWW_username. After you've gotten the environment variables, you can test them just as you would any other variable.

You can get the source for uncgi from `http://www.hyperion.com/~koreth/uncgi.html`. You'll need to know the location of your `cgi-bin` directory (and you'll need access to it). Compile uncgi using the instructions that come with the source, and install it in your `cgi-bin` directory—and you're ready to go.

Exercise: Tell Me Your Name

Try this simple example for a form and the script to process it. You'll find that it's easier than you think.

In this example, you'll create the form shown in Figure 17.1. This form prompts you for your name.

Figure 17.1.
The Tell Me Your
Name form.

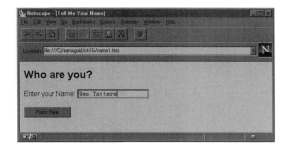

In this form, you would enter your name and click on the Press Here button, which is referred to more generally as a submit button.

> **Tip:** Most browsers provide a shortcut: if there is only one text field on the page (besides a submit button), you can just press Enter to activate the form.

> **Note:** The submit button can take many different names, as you will learn shortly. In Figure 17.1, for example, it is the button labeled Press Here.

The input is sent to the script, which sends back an HTML document that displays a hello message with your name in it. (See Figure 17.2.)

Figure 17.2.
The result of
entering a name in
the Tell Me Your
Name form.

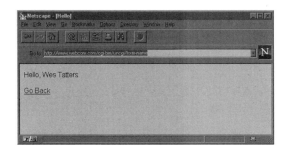

What if you didn't type anything at the Enter your Name prompt? The script would send you the response shown in Figure 17.3.

Figure 17.3.

The result if you didn't enter a name in the form.

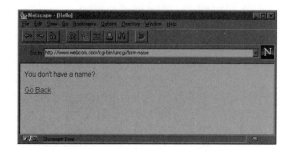

The Layout

First, you'll create the HTML page for this form. As with all HTML documents, you start with a basic framework, with just a single level-two heading that reads "Who are you?"

```
<HTML>
<HEAD>
<TITLE>Tell Me Your Name</TITLE>
</HEAD>
<BODY>
<H2>Who are you?</H2>
</BODY>
</HTML>
```

Now, add the form.

To create a form, you use the <FORM> tag to indicate that the following content is a form. <FORM> is a double-sided tag, and all the elements of the form should be included inside the opening and closing tags. You can include multiple forms in one document, but you can't nest forms—that is, you can't include a <FORM> tag inside another <FORM>.

The opening tag of the <FORM> element usually includes two attributes: METHOD and ACTION. The METHOD attribute can be either GET or POST, as I described earlier in this chapter. The default is GET, so if you want to use POST, be sure to include METHOD="POST" in your <FORM> tag.

The ACTION attribute indicates the script that will be called to process the form when it's submitted. ACTION can be indicated by a relative path or by a full URL on your server or somewhere else. For example, the following <FORM> tag would call a script called form-name in a cgi-bin directory one level up from the current directory:

```
<FORM METHOD="POST" ACTION="../cgi-bin/form-name">
</FORM>
```

If you're using uncgi to decode form input, as I am in these examples, things are slightly different. To make uncgi work properly, you call uncgi first and then append the name of the actual script as if uncgi were a directory, like this:

```
<FORM METHOD="POST" ACTION="../cgi-bin/uncgi/form-name">
</FORM>
```

And now with the form framework in place, you can add the elements of the form. Note that <FORM> doesn't specify the appearance and layout of the form; you'll have to use other HTML tags for that.

The first element inside the form is the text-entry area for the name. First, include the prompt, just as you would any other line of text in HTML:

```
<P>Enter your Name:
```

And then add the HTML code that indicates a text input field:

```
<P>Enter your Name: <INPUT NAME="theNametheName"></P>
```

The <INPUT> tag indicates a simple form element. (Several other form elements also use tags other than <INPUT>, but <INPUT> is the most common one.) <INPUT> usually takes at least two attributes: TYPE and NAME.

TYPE is the kind of form element this is. There are several choices, including text for text-entry fields, radio for radio buttons, and check for check boxes. If you leave the TYPE attribute out, as was done here, the element will be a text entry field.

The NAME element indicates the name of this element. As I noted before, your CGI script receives the input from the form as a series of name and value pairs. The value is the actual value or information your reader enters in the form's field; the name is what you call the field itself. You can put anything you want here, but as with all good programming conventions, a descriptive name would be most useful. Here I've picked the name theName. (Descriptive, yes?) You should record the names you use for each element because you'll need them when you create the script to process the form.

Now add the final form element: the submit button (or link). Most forms require the use of a submit button; however, if you have only one text field in the form, you can omit it. The form will be submitted when the reader presses Enter.

```
<P><INPUT TYPE="SUBMIT"></P>
```

You'll use the <INPUT> tag for this element as well. The TYPE attribute is set to the special type of "SUBMIT", which creates a submit button for the form. The submit button doesn't require a name because no value is attached to it.

It's good practice to always include a submit button on your form, even if there's only one text field. The presence of a submit button is so common that your readers might become confused if it's not there.

Note that each element is surround by <P> tags for document formatting, just as if this were text; form elements follow the same rules as text in terms of how your browser formats them. As with any HTML document, you'll need <P> tags to separate the elements onto different lines; otherwise, you'd end up with all the elements in the form on the same line.

17

So now you have a simple form with two elements. The final HTML code to create the form looks like this:

```
<HTML>
<HEAD>
<TITLE>Tell Me Your Name</TITLE>
</HEAD>
<BODY>
<H2>Who are you?</H2>
<FORM METHOD="POST" ACTION="../cgi-bin/uncgi/form-name">
<P>Enter your Name: <INPUT NAME="theNametheName"></P>
<P><INPUT TYPE="SUBMIT"></P>
</FORM>
</BODY>
</HTML>
```

The Script

After you have a form in an HTML document, you need a CGI script on the server side to process the form's input. As with the CGI scripts you learned about in Chapter 16, the output from your script will be passed back to the server, so everything you learned about the Content-type headers and generating HTML output applies to form scripts as well.

Note: The term *server-side* is used to refer to anything that happens on the Web server itself; while *client-side*—mentioned elsewhere—refers to anything that happens on the Web browser.

The first step in a form script usually is to decode the information that was passed to your script through the POST method. In this example, however, because you're using uncgi to decode form input, the form decoding has already been done for you. Remember how you put uncgi in the ACTION attribute of the form, followed by the name of your script? What happens there is that when the form input is submitted, the server passes that input to the uncgi program, which decodes the form input for you and then calls your script with everything already decoded. Now, at the start of your script, all the name/value pairs are there for you to use.

Moving on, print the usual CGI headers and HTML code to begin the page:

```
echo Content-type: text/html
echo
cat << EOF
    <HTML>
    <HEAD>
    <TITLE>Hello</TITLE>
    </HEAD>
    <BODY>
    <P>
EOF
```

Now comes the meat of the script. You have two branches to deal with: one to accuse the reader of not entering a name, and one to say hello when the reader enters a name.

The value of the theName element, as you named the text field in your form, is contained in the WWW_theName environment variable. Using a simple Bourne shell test (-z), you can see whether this environment variable is empty and include the appropriate response in the output:

```
if [ ! -z "$WWW_theName" ]; then
    echo "Hello, "
    echo $WWW_theName
else
    echo "You don't have a name?"
fi
```

Finally, add the last bit of HTML code to include the "go back" link. This link points back to the original form:

```
cat << EOF
    </P>
    <P><A HREF="../www/name1.html">Go Back</A><P>
    </BODY>
    </HTML>
EOF
```

Like all CGI scripts, the script to process your form must be executable and installed in your cgi-bin directory. And that's it! You have both parts, and they've been linked together so that your form input gets processed and you get a response back. You now know just about all you need to know to handle forms and their interaction with CGI scripts. That wasn't bad at all, was it?

Simple Form Layout

So now that you have the basics down, I'm sure you want to know exactly what kind of nifty interface elements you can put in a form.

In this section, you'll learn about the <INPUT> tag and the simple form elements you can create with it. You can use a few other elements for complex form input; you'll learn about those later in the chapter.

Each of the elements described in this section goes inside a <FORM>...</FORM> tag, which you learned about in the preceding exercise. In these examples, the form calls a script called test-cgi, which simply returns the values it is given.

17

The Submit Button

Each <FORM> tag block can normally have one, and only one, submit button. (You'll learn more about this later in Chapter 19, "JavaScript.") To create a submit button, use "submit" as the TYPE attribute in an <INPUT> tag:

```
<INPUT TYPE="SUBMIT">
```

You can change the label text of the button by using the VALUE attribute:

```
<INPUT TYPE="SUBMIT" VALUE="Submit Query">
```

The following input and output example shows two simple forms with submit buttons: one with a default button and one with a custom label. Figure 17.4 shows the output in Navigator 2.0:

```
<FORM METHOD=POST ACTION="../cgi-bin/uncgi/test-cgi">
<INPUT TYPE="SUBMIT">
</FORM>
<HR>
<FORM METHOD=POST ACTION="../cgi-bin/uncgi/test-cgi">
<INPUT TYPE="SUBMIT" VALUE="Press Here">
</FORM>
```

Figure 17.4.
The output in Navigator 2.0.

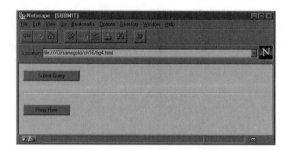

Text Input Fields

Text fields enable your reader to type text into a single-line field. For multiple-line fields, use the <TEXTAREA> element, described later in this chapter.

To create a text-entry field, you can either use TYPE="TEXT" in the <INPUT> tag or leave off the TYPE specification altogether. The default TYPE for the INPUT tag is text. You must also include a NAME attribute. NAME indicates the name of this field as passed to the script processing the form.

```
<INPUT TYPE="TEXT" NAME="myText">
```

You can also include the attributes SIZE and MAXLENGTH in the <INPUT> tag. SIZE indicates the length of the text-entry field in characters; the field is 20 characters by default. Your readers can enter as many characters as they want. The field scrolls horizontally as your reader types. Try to keep SIZE under 50 characters so that it will fit on most screens.

```
<INPUT TYPE="TEXT" NAME="longText" SIZE="50">
```

MAXLENGTH enables you to limit the number of characters your reader can type into a text field (refusing any further characters). If MAXLENGTH is less than SIZE, browsers will sometimes draw a text field as large as MAXLENGTH.

In addition to a regular text field, there are also password fields, indicated by TYPE="PASSWORD". Password text fields are identical to ordinary text fields except that all the characters typed are echoed back in the browser (masked) as asterisks or bullets. (See Figure 17.5.)

```
<INPUT TYPE="PASSWORD" NAME="passwd">
```

Figure 17.5.
Password fields show entered text as asterisks or bullets.

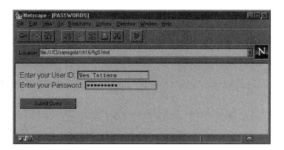

 Caution: Despite the masking of characters in the browser, password fields are not secure. The password is sent to the server in clear text; that is, anyone could intercept the password and read it. The masking is simply a convenience.

The following input and output example shows several text fields and their result in Navigator 2.0 (see Figure 17.6):

```
<FORM METHOD=POST ACTION="../cgi-bin/uncgi/test-cgi">
<P>Enter your Name: <INPUT TYPE="TEXT" NAME="theNametheName"><BR>
Enter your Age:
<INPUT TYPE="TEXT" NAME="theAge" SIZE="3" MAXLENGTH="3"><BR>
Enter your Address:
<INPUT TYPE="TEXT" NAME="theAddress" SIZE="70" ></P>
</FORM>
```

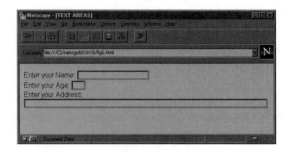

Figure 17.6.
Text fields with adjust-
able sizes in a form.

Radio Buttons

Radio buttons indicate a list of items, only one of which can be chosen. If one radio button in a list is selected, all the other radio buttons in the same list are deselected.

Radio buttons use "RADIO" for their TYPE attribute. You indicate groups of radio buttons by using the same NAME for each button in the group. In addition, each radio button in the group must have a unique VALUE attribute, indicating the selection's value:

```
<OL>
<INPUT TYPE="RADIO" NAME="theType" VALUE="animal">Animal<BR>
<INPUT TYPE="RADIO" NAME="theType" VALUE="vegetable">Vegetable<BR>
<INPUT TYPE="RADIO" NAME="theType" VALUE="mineral">Mineral<BR>
</OL>
```

You can use multiple, independent groups of radio buttons by using different names for each group:

```
<OL>
<INPUT TYPE="RADIO" NAME="theType" VALUE="animal">Animal<BR>
<OL>
<LI><INPUT TYPE="RADIO" NAME="theAnimal" VALUE="cat">Cat
<LI><INPUT TYPE="RADIO" NAME="theAnimal" VALUE="dog">Dog
<LI><INPUT TYPE="RADIO" NAME="theAnimal" VALUE="fish">fish
</OL>
<INPUT TYPE="RADIO" NAME="theType" VALUE="vegetable">Vegetable<BR>
<INPUT TYPE="RADIO" NAME="theType" VALUE="mineral">Mineral<BR>
</OL>
```

When the form is submitted, a single name/value pair for the group of buttons is passed to the script. That pair includes the NAME attribute for each group of radio buttons and the VALUE attribute of the button that is currently selected.

Here's an input and output example that shows two groups of radio buttons and shows how they look in Navigator 2.0 (see Figure 17.7):

```
<FORM METHOD=POST ACTION="../cgi-bin/uncgi/test-cgi">
<OL>
<LI><INPUT TYPE="RADIO" NAME="theType" VALUE="animal">Animal<BR>
<OL>
<LI><INPUT TYPE="RADIO" NAME="theAnimal" VALUE="cat">Cat
<LI><INPUT TYPE="RADIO" NAME="theAnimal" VALUE="dog">Dog
<LI><INPUT TYPE="RADIO" NAME="theAnimal" VALUE="fish">fish
</OL>
<LI><INPUT TYPE="RADIO" NAME="theType" VALUE="vegetable">Vegetable
<LI><INPUT TYPE="RADIO" NAME="theType" VALUE="mineral">Mineral
</OL>
</FORM>
```

Figure 17.7.
Radio buttons on a form.

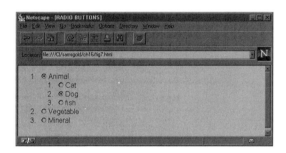

Check Boxes

Check boxes make it possible to choose multiple items in a list. Each check box can be either "on" or "off." Check boxes use "CHECKBOX" as their TYPE attribute:

```
<UL>
<LI><INPUT TYPE="CHECKBOX" NAME="red">Red
<LI><INPUT TYPE="CHECKBOX" NAME="green">Green
<LI><INPUT TYPE="CHECKBOX" NAME="blue">Blue
</UL>
```

When the form is submitted, only the name/value pairs for each selected check box are submitted (unchecked check boxes are ignored). By default, each name/value pair for a check box has a value of ON. However, you can also use the VALUE attribute to indicate the value you would rather be sent in your script:

```
<UL>
<LI><INPUT TYPE="CHECKBOX" NAME="red" VALUE="checked">Red
<LI><INPUT TYPE="CHECKBOX" NAME="green" VALUE="yes">Green
<LI><INPUT TYPE="CHECKBOX" NAME="blue" VALUE="ok">Blue
</UL>
```

In this case, the name/value pairs would return red=checked, green=yes, and blue=ok, instead of the traditional red=on, green=on, and blue=on, when the form is transmitted to a Web server.

You can also implement check box lists so that elements have the same NAME attribute, similar to radio buttons. Notice, however, that this means that your script will end up with several name/value pairs with the same name (each check box that is selected will be submitted to the script), and you'll have to take that situation into account when you process the input in your script.

Here's another input and output example, showing a series of check boxes and how they look in Navigator 2.0 (see Figure 17.8):

```
<FORM METHOD=POST ACTION="../cgi/-in/uncgi/test-cgi">
<P>Profession (choose all that apply): </P>
<UL>
<LI><INPUT TYPE="CHECKBOX" NAME="doctor">Doctor
<LI><INPUT TYPE="CHECKBOX" NAME="lawyer">Lawyer
<LI><INPUT TYPE="CHECKBOX" NAME="teacher">Teacher
<LI><INPUT TYPE="CHECKBOX" NAME="nerd">Programmer
</UL>
</FORM>
```

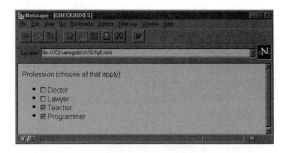

Figure 17.8.
Check boxes in a form.

Note: By default, check boxes are unchecked when they are first displayed on the screen. If you want a check box to be checked by default, include a CHECKED attribute inside the <INPUT> tag, like this:

```
<INPUT TYPE="CHECKBOX" NAME="lawyer" CHECKED>
```

HTTP File Upload

Navigator 2.0 introduces an experimental new INPUT type that provides a method for uploading files via a Web page. This new type was recently submitted for comment as [RFC1867], which can be downloaded from the InterNIC archive as ftp://ds.internic.net/ rfc/rfc1867.txt.

Note: By its nature the Internet is very much an "of the people, by the people" type of place. As a result, whenever anyone wants to change the way part of the Internet operates, everyone else on the Internet has the right to make comments or criticisms about the proposal. To streamline this process, a system called "Request for Comment" was put in place back in the very early days of the Internet. Whenever a new Request for Comment proposal (or document) is published, it is placed online in an archive maintained by the InterNIC—the Internet administrative body set up by the National Science Foundation (NSF).

When incorporated into a form, `<INPUT NAME="`*`field_name`*`" TYPE="FILE">` causes a special text field, with a BROWSE button associated with it, to be displayed on the Web page as shown in Figure 17.9. When you click this BROWSE button, Navigator 2.0 displays a File Upload dialog box, where you can select the file you want to upload.

Figure 17.9.
Navigator 2.0 introduces support for HTTP-based file uploads.

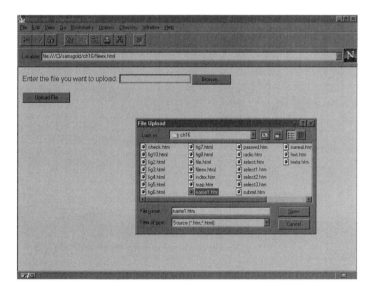

On its own, however, this new INPUT type is not enough to cause a file to be uploaded to your Web server. Unfortunately, the standard method used by Web browsers when sending the results of a form back to a Web server are not ideally suited to the transmission of large binary files. To get around this problem, a new method of encoding the information was required.

In [RFC1867], the method proposed involves the use of multipart MIME encoding, not unlike that used by many e-mail programs. To tell the form to use this new format when uploading a file, you add a new attribute to the `<FORM>` tag called `ENCTYPE`. Most current Web browsers use an `ENCTYPE` of `application/x-www-form-urlencoded` by default, but for forms that include a `TYPE="FILE"` field, you need to set `ENCTYPE` to `multipart/form-data`, as shown here in the first line of the form shown in Figure 17.9:

```
<FORM ENCTYPE="multipart/form-data" ACTION="/cgi-bin/upload_file" METHOD=POST>
```

Apart from this change to the `<FORM>` tag, the remainder of the form code remains much the same as for previous exercises. As a result, the completed form definition for Figure 17.9 looks like this:

```
<FORM ENCTYPE="multipart/form-data"
      ACTION="../cgi-bin/upload_file"
      METHOD=POST>
<P>Enter the file you want to upload:
<INPUT SIZE=20 NAME="uploadfile" TYPE="FILE"></P>
<P><INPUT TYPE="SUBMIT" VALUE="Upload File"></P>
</FORM>
```

When someone selects a file to be uploaded and clicks the Upload File (submit) button, Navigator 2.0 does not send a set of result pairs that can be decoded by scripts such as uncgi. Instead, it transmits a MIME data stream as described in [RFC1521] MIME (multipurpose Internet mail extensions) and [RFC1522] MIME, both of which are also available from the InterNIC site mentioned previously.

To decode the transmitted file, your CGI script will need to sort through the MIME data, locate any fields, and then run the file through a MIME decoder to re-create the original file.

Note: The actual steps involved in decoding a MIME stream and re-creating the uploaded file are beyond the scope of this book. If you want to learn more about the use of this experimental feature, the three Request for Comment (RFC) documents mentioned previously are a good place to start. In addition, you should get a good book on CGI scripting—preferably using Perl—although you could possibly get by with a Bourne shell script.

Setting and Resetting Default Values

Each form element can have a default value that is entered or selected when the form is viewed:

☐ For text fields, use the VALUE attribute with a string for the default value. VALUE is entered in the box automatically when the form is displayed.

☐ For check boxes and radio buttons, the attribute CHECKED selects that element by default.

In addition to the default values for each element, you can include a reset button, similar to the submit button, on your form. The Reset button clears all selections or entries your reader has made and resets them to their default values. And as with the submit button, a VALUE attribute indicates the label for the button:

```
<INPUT TYPE="RESET" VALUE="Reset Defaults">
```

Exercise: The Surrealist Census

Now it's time to tackle a more complicated example. In this example, the Surrealist Society of America has created a small census, via an interactive form on the World Wide Web. Figure 17.10 shows that census.

Figure 17.10.
The Surrealist Society's census form.

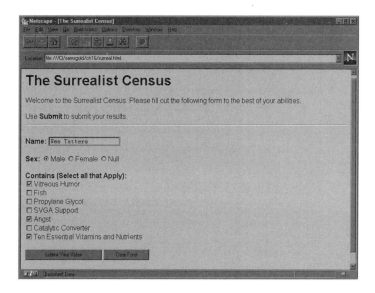

After the reader fills out the form and presses Submit Your Votes, the CGI script for the form processes the input and returns a formatted report of the votes the reader has made, as shown in Figure 17.11.

Figure 17.11.

The result of the census.

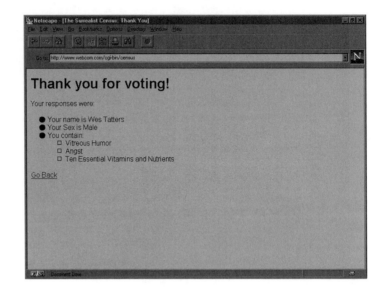

The Form

The form to create the census falls roughly into three parts: the name field, the radio buttons for sex, and the check boxes for the things your reader contains.

Start with the basic structure, as with all HTML documents. Remember, you'll call uncgi in the action as you did in the preceding example:

```
<HTML>
<HEAD>
<TITLE>The Surrealist Census</TITLE>
</HEAD>
<BODY>
<H1>The Surrealist Census</H1>
<P>Welcome to the Surrealist Census. Please fill out the following
form to the best of your abilities.</P>
<P>Use <STRONG>Submit</STRONG> to submit your results.
<HR>
<FORM METHOD="POST" ACTION="../cgi-bin/uncgi/census">

</FORM>
<HR>
</BODY>
</HTML>
```

Notice that I've included rule lines before and after the form. Because the form is a discrete element on the page, it makes sense to visually separate it from the other parts of the page. This is especially important if you have multiple forms on the same page; separating them with rule lines visually divides them.

Now add the first element for the reader's name. This is essentially the same element used in the preceding example, with the name of the element being theNametheName:

```
<P><STRONG>Name: </STRONG><INPUT TYPE="TEXT" NAME="theNametheName"></P>
```

The second part of the form is a series of radio buttons for the reader's sex. There are three: Male, Female, and Null (remember, this is the Surrealist Census). Because radio buttons are exclusive (only one can be selected at a time), you'll give all three buttons the same value for NAME (theSextheSex).

```
<P><STRONG>Sex: </STRONG>
<INPUT TYPE="RADIO" NAME="theSextheSex" VALUE="male">Male
<INPUT TYPE="RADIO" NAME="theSextheSex" VALUE="female">Female
<INPUT TYPE="RADIO" NAME="theSextheSex" VALUE="null">Null
</P>
```

Even though each <INPUT> tag is arranged on a separate line, the radio button elements are formatted on a single line. Always remember that form elements do not imply formatting; you must include other HTML tags to arrange them in the right spots.

Now add the last part of the form, the list of Contains check boxes:

```
<P><STRONG>Contains (Select all that Apply): </STRONG><BR>
<INPUT TYPE="CHECKBOX" NAME="humor">Vitreous Humor<BR>
<INPUT TYPE="CHECKBOX" NAME="fish">Fish<BR>
<INPUT TYPE="CHECKBOX" NAME="glycol">Propylene Glycol<BR>
<INPUT TYPE="CHECKBOX" NAME="svga">SVGA Support<BR>
<INPUT TYPE="CHECKBOX" NAME="angst">Angst<BR>
<INPUT TYPE="CHECKBOX" NAME="catcon">Catalytic Converter<BR>
<INPUT TYPE="CHECKBOX" NAME="vitamin">Ten Essential Vitamins and Nutrients<BR>
</P>
```

Unlike with radio buttons, any number of check boxes can be selected, so each value of NAME is unique. This fact will be important later when you write the script to process the form.

Finally, add the submit button so that the form can be submitted to the server. A nice touch is to also include a Reset Form button. Both buttons have special labels specific to this form:

```
<P><INPUT TYPE="SUBMIT" VALUE="Submit Your Votes">
<INPUT TYPE="RESET" VALUE="Clear Form"></P>
```

Whew! With all the elements in place, here's what the entire HTML file for the form looks like:

```
<HTML>
<HEAD>
<TITLE>The Surrealist Census</TITLE>
</HEAD>
<BODY>
<H1>The Surrealist Census</H1>
<P>Welcome to the Surrealist Census. Please fill out the following
form to the best of your abilities.</P>
<P>Use <STRONG>Submit</STRONG> to submit your results.</P>
<HR>
```

```
<FORM METHOD="POST" ACTION="../cgi-bin/census">
<P><STRONG>Name: </STRONG><INPUT TYPE="TEXT" NAME="theNametheName"></P>
<P><STRONG>Sex: </STRONG>
<INPUT TYPE="RADIO" NAME="theSextheSex" VALUE="male">Male
<INPUT TYPE="RADIO" NAME="theSextheSex" VALUE="female">Female
<INPUT TYPE="RADIO" NAME="theSextheSex" VALUE="null">Null
</P>
<P><STRONG>Contains (Select all that Apply): </STRONG><BR>
<INPUT TYPE="CHECKBOX" NAME="humor">Vitreous Humor<BR>
<INPUT TYPE="CHECKBOX" NAME="fish">Fish<BR>
<INPUT TYPE="CHECKBOX" NAME="glycol">Propylene Glycol<BR>
<INPUT TYPE="CHECKBOX" NAME="svga">SVGA Support<BR>
<INPUT TYPE="CHECKBOX" NAME="angst">Angst<BR>
<INPUT TYPE="CHECKBOX" NAME="catcon">Catalytic Converter<BR>
<INPUT TYPE="CHECKBOX" NAME="vitamin">Ten Essential Vitamins and Nutrients<BR>
</P>
<P><INPUT TYPE="SUBMIT" VALUE="Submit Your Votes">
<INPUT TYPE="RESET" VALUE="Clear Form"></P>
</FORM>
<HR>
</BODY></HTML>
```

The Script

And now it's time to write the script to process the form you've just created. The output of the script essentially just prints the values from the form in a nice bulleted list. This script will look very similar to the script you created in the preceding example, so you'll start with a copy of that script, modified slightly to fit the desired output:

```
#!/bin/sh

echo Content-type: text/html
echo

cat << EOF
    <HTML>
    <HEAD>
    <TITLE>The Surrealist Census: Thank You</TITLE>
    </HEAD>
    <BODY>
    <H1>Thank you for voting!</H1>
    <P>Your responses were:</P>
    <UL>
EOF

if [ ! -z "$WWW_theNametheName" ]; then
    echo "<LI>Your name is "
    echo $WWW_theNametheName
else
    echo "<LI>You don't have a name."
fi
```

That if statement should look really familiar. For the most part, it's the same as the one in the preceding exercise. Now add a bullet for the sex the reader chose. Remember, each value

of NAME in the original form is turned into an environment variable with WWW_ prepended, so the value of these radio buttons (which were named theSextheSex) will be contained in the WWW_theSextheSex variable. All the names in the form will match the variables in the script.

For the theSextheSex name/value pair, you don't have to test to see whether theSextheSex is empty; the radio button structure means that at least one value must be submitted with the form, so all you really must do for the Sex element is print the value:

```
echo "<LI>Your Sex is "
echo $WWW_theSextheSex
```

And now add the Contains elements as a nested list. Because you don't know which of the check boxes were submitted, you'll have to test all those variables (their values will be "on" if they were selected) and create output for the ones that were submitted, like this:

```
echo "<LI>You contain:"
echo "<UL>"

if [ "$WWW_humor" = "on" ]; then
echo "<LI>Vitreous Humor"
fi
if [ "$WWW_fish" = "on" ]; then
echo "<LI>Fish"
fi
```

I've only included the if statements for the first two tests here; the other five look exactly the same. You can check the script at the end of this section if you're really interested.

Finally, finish the script by printing the rest of the HTML for the page. As part of this last bit of HTML, include a link back to the form. You should always provide some way out of the HTML files you generate from forms. Although going back to some known spot (such as the home page) would make the most sense, going back to the form is better than nothing:

```
cat << EOF
    </UL></UL>
    <P><A HREF="../www/census.html">Go Back</A><P>
    </BODY>
    </HTML>
EOF
```

Here's the full script for processing the census form:

```
#!/bin/sh

echo Content-type: text/html
echo

cat << EOF
    <HTML><HEAD>
    <TITLE>The Surrealist Census: Thank You</TITLE>
    </HEAD><BODY>
    <H1>Thank you for voting!</H1>
    <P>Your responses were:</P>
    <UL>
```

17

423

```
EOF

if [ ! -z "$WWW_theNametheName" ]; then
  echo "<LI>Your name is "
  echo $WWW_theNametheName
else
  echo "<LI>You don't have a name."
fi

echo "<LI>Your Sex is "
echo $WW_theSextheSex
echo "<LI>You contain:"
echo "<UL>"

if [ "$WWW_humor" = "on" ]; then
  echo "<LI>Vitreous Humor"
fi
if [ "$WWW_fish" = "on" ]; then
  echo "<LI>Fish"
fi
if [ "$WWW_glycol" = "on" ]; then
  echo "<LI>Propylene Glycol"
fi
if [ "$WWW_svga" = "on" ]; then
  echo "<LI>SVGA Support"
fi
if [ "$WWW_angst" = "on" ]; then
  echo "<LI>Angst"
fi
if [ "$WWW_catcon" = "on" ]; then
  echo "<LI>Catalytic Converter"
fi
if [ "$WWW_vitamin" = "on" ]; then
  echo "<LI>Ten Essential Vitamins and Nutrients"
fi

cat << EOF
    </UL></UL>
    <P><A HREF="../www/Surreal.htm">Go Back</A><P>
    </BODY></HTML>
EOF
```

More Forms Layout

In addition to the <INPUT> tag with its many options, two other tags also create form elements: <SELECT>, which can create pull-down menus and scrolling lists, and <TEXTAREA>, for allowing the reader to enter long blocks of text.

This section describes these other two tags. It also explains how to create "hidden" elements—form elements that don't actually show up on the page, but exist in the form nonetheless. And it shows how forms can be used in Netscape frames.

Selections

Selections enable the reader of a form to select one or more items from a menu or a scrolling list. They're similar to radio buttons or check boxes, in a different form.

Selections are indicated by the <SELECT> tag, and individual options within the selection, by the <OPTION> tag. The <SELECT> tag also contains a NAME attribute to hold its value when the form is submitted.

<SELECT> and <OPTION> work much the way lists do, with the entire selection surrounded by the opening and closing <SELECT> tags. Each option begins with a single-sided <OPTION>, like this:

```
<P>Select a hair color:
<SELECT NAME="hcolor">
<OPTION>Black
<OPTION>Blonde
<OPTION>Brown
<OPTION>Red
<OPTION>Blue
</SELECT>
</P>
```

When the form is submitted, the value of the entire selection is the text that follows the selected <OPTION> tag—in this case, Black, Blonde, Brown, and so on. You can also use the VALUE attribute with each <OPTION> tag to indicate a different value.

Selections of this sort are generally formatted in graphical browsers as popup menus, as shown in Figure 17.12.

Figure 17.12.
Selections.

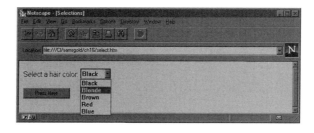

You can set the default item to be initially selected by using the SELECTED attribute, part of the OPTION tag:

```
<P>Select a hair color:
<SELECT NAME="hcolor">
<OPTION>Black
<OPTION>Blonde
<OPTION SELECTED>Brown
<OPTION>Red
<OPTION>Blue
</SELECT>
</P>
```

By default, selections act like radio buttons; that is, only one item can be selected at a time. You can change the behavior of selections to allow multiple options to be selected by using the MULTIPLE attribute, part of the <SELECTION> tag:

```
<P>Shopping List:
<SELECT NAME="shopping" MULTIPLE>
<OPTION>Butter
<OPTION>Milk
<OPTION>Flour
<OPTION>Eggs
<OPTION>Cheese
<OPTION>Beer
<OPTION>Pasta
<OPTION>Mushrooms
</SELECT></P>
```

Be careful when you use MULTIPLE in the script that will process this form. Remember that each selection list only has one possible NAME. This means that if you have multiple values in a selection list, all those values will be submitted to your script, and the program you use to decode the input might store those in some special way. For example, uncgi stores them in the same environment variable separated by pound signs.

> **Note:** Each browser determines how the reader makes multiple choices. Usually, the reader must hold down a key while making multiple selections, but that particular key might vary from browser to browser.

The optional SIZE attribute for the <SELECT> tag displays the selection as a scrolling list in graphical browsers, with the number of elements in the SIZE attribute visible on the form itself (Figure 17.13 shows an example):

```
<P>Shopping List:
<SELECT NAME="shopping" MULTIPLE SIZE="5">
<OPTION>Butter
<OPTION>Milk
<OPTION>Flour
<OPTION>Eggs
<OPTION>Cheese
<OPTION>Beer
<OPTION>Pasta
<OPTION>Mushrooms
</SELECT></P>
```

Figure 17.13.
Selections with SIZE.

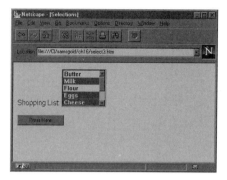

Here's an input and output example that shows a simple selection list and how it appears in Navigator 2.0 (see Figure 17.14):

```
<P>Select a hair color:
<SELECT NAME="hcolor">
<OPTION>Black
<OPTION>Blonde
<OPTION SELECTED>Brown
<OPTION>Red
<OPTION>Blue
</SELECT></P>
```

Figure 17.14.
*The output in
Navigator 2.0.*

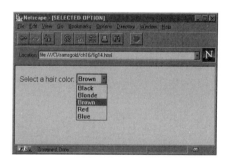

Text Areas

Text areas are input fields the reader can type in. Unlike regular text input fields (<INPUT TYPE="TEXT">), text areas can contain many lines of text, making them extremely useful for forms that require extensive input. For example, if you wanted to create a form that enabled readers to compose electronic mail, you could use a text area for the body of the message.

To include a text area element in a form, use the <TEXTAREA> tag. <TEXTAREA> includes four attributes:

☐ NAME: The name to be sent to the CGI script when the form is submitted.

☐ ROWS: The height of the text area element, in rows of text as displayed on the form.

☐ COLS: The width of the text area element in columns (characters) as displayed on the form.

☐ WRAP="OFF": Text is not automatically wrapping. Lines are sent to the Web server exactly as typed.

☐ WRAP="VIRTUAL": The display word wraps, but long lines are sent to the Web server as one line without any new-line markers.

☐ WRAP="PHYSICAL": The display word wraps, and the text is transmitted as separate lines based on the wrap points.

The TEXTAREA tag is a two-sided tag, and both sides must be used. If you have any default text you want to include in the text area, include it between the opening and closing tags. Here's an example:

```
<TEXTAREA NAME="theBody" ROWS="14" COLS="50">Enter your message here.</TEXTAREA>
```

The text in a text area is generally formatted in a fixed-width font such as Courier, but it is up to the browser to decide how to format it beyond that. Some browsers allow text wrapping in text areas; others scroll to the right. Some allow scrolling if the text area fills up, whereas others just stop accepting input.

This input/output example shows a simple text area in Navigator 2.0 (see Figure 17.15):

```
<P>Enter any Comments you have about this Web page here:
<TEXTAREA NAME="comment" ROWS="25" COLS="60">
</TEXTAREA>
</P>
```

Figure 17.15.
Output of the
<TEXTAREA> tag.

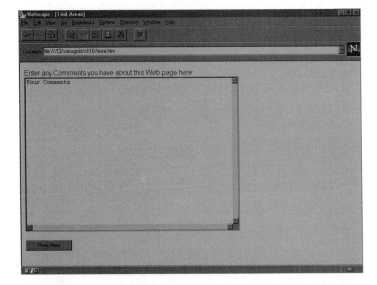

Hidden Fields

One value for the TYPE attribute of the <INPUT> tag I haven't mentioned is "hidden". Hidden fields do not appear on the actual form; they are invisible in the browser display. They will still appear in your HTML code if someone decides to look at the HTML source for your page.

Hidden input elements look like this:

```
<INPUT TYPE="HIDDEN" NAME="theNametheName" VALUE="TheValue">
```

Why would you want to create a hidden form element? If it doesn't appear onscreen and the reader can't do anything with it, what's the point?

Take a hypothetical example. You create a simple form. In the script that processes the first form, you create a second form based on the input from the first form. The script to process the second form takes the information from both of the forms and creates a reply based on that information. Figure 17.16 shows how all this flows.

Figure 17.16.
Form-to-form reply.

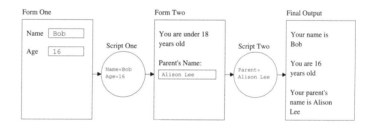

How would you pass the information from the first form to the script that processes the second form? You can take one of two actions:

- ☐ Write the information from the first form to a temporary file, and then read that file back in again when the second form starts.
- ☐ In the first script that constructs the second form, create hidden fields in the form with the appropriate information in NAME and VALUE fields. Then those names and values will be passed automatically to the second script when the reader submits the second form.

See? Hidden elements do make sense, particularly when you get involved in generating forms from forms.

Forms and Frames

With the introduction of frames in Navigator 2.0, a new attribute has become available for the `<FORM>` tag. By including a `TARGET` attribute, as shown here, you can redirect the response from a form to a separate window or frame:

```
<FORM METHOD="POST" ACTION="../cgi-bin/uncgi/census" TARGET="window_name">
```

Naming Forms

To provide a simple mechanism for handling multiple forms on a single Web page, Navigator 2.0 has introduced a naming system for forms. As a rule, you will not need to worry greatly about this new capability, unless you plan to use the JavaScript language, which is discussed in Chapter 19, "JavaScript," and Chapter 20, "Working with JavaScript."

For now, all you need to know is that each form can be assigned a name by including a `NAME` attribute in the `<FORM>` tag, as shown here:

```
<FORM METHOD="POST" ACTION="../cgi-bin/uncgi/census" NAME="form_name">
```

Summary

Forms are one of the most interesting innovations added to Web publishing in recent times. With the advent of these features, the Web changed from a publishing medium with hypertext links to a fully interactive environment with the potential for being something entirely new.

In this chapter you've learned how to lay out form elements in HTML as well as how to process the results on the server when that form is submitted. You should now know the difference between GET and POST and be able to explain why one is better.

It's been a very full chapter, so to help refresh you memory, Table 17.1 presents a summary of the tags and attributes you've learned about in this chapter.

Table 17.1. HTML tags from this chapter.

Tag	Use
`<FORM>...</FORM>`	A form. You can have multiple forms within a document, but forms cannot be nested.
`METHOD`	An attribute of the `<FORM>` tag indicating the method with which the form input is given to the script that processes the form. Possible values are GET and POST.

Tag	Use
ACTION	An attribute of the <FORM> tag indicating the script to process the form input. Contains a relative path or URL to the script.
ENCTYPE	An attribute of the <FORM> tag used to specify the multipart/form-data encoding method for HTTP-based file uploads.
TARGET	An attribute of the <FORM> tag used to specify the target window for the results of a form submission.
NAME	An attribute of the <FORM> tag used to assign a unique name to the specified form.
<INPUT>	A form element.
TYPE	An attribute of the <INPUT> tag indicating the type of form element. Possible values are SUBMIT, RESET, TEXT, RADIO, CHECKBOX, PASSWORD, FILE, and HIDDEN:
	SUBMIT creates a button to submit the form to the script that processes the input.
	RESET creates a button that resets the default values of the form, if any.
	TEXT creates a single-line text field.
	RADIO creates a radio button.
	CHECKBOX creates a check box.
	PASSWORD creates a text field that masks the characters entered by the user.
	FILE creates a text field with a BROWSE button that opens an Upload File dialog box.
	HIDDEN creates a form element that is not presented but has a name and a value that can then be passed on to the script that processes the form input.
NAME	An attribute of the <INPUT>, <SELECT>, and <TEXTAREA> tags. Indicates the name of the variable that holds the eventual value of this element, as submitted to the script.
VALUE	An attribute of the <INPUT> tag indicating the default value for the form element, if any, or the value submitted with the NAME to the script. For SUBMIT and RESET buttons, VALUE indicates the label of the button.

continues

17

Table 17.1. continued

Tag	Use
SIZE	An attribute of the <INPUT> tag used only when TYPE is TEXT. Indicates the size of the text field, in characters.
MAXLENGTH	An attribute of the <INPUT> tag used only when TYPE is TEXT. Indicates the maximum number of characters this text field will accept.
CHECKED	An attribute of the <INPUT> tag used only when TYPE is CHECKBOX or RADIO. Indicates that this element is selected by default.
<SELECT>	A menu or scrolling list of items. Individual items are indicated by the <OPTION> tag.
MULTIPLE	An attribute of the <SELECT> tag indicating that multiple items in the list can be selected.
SIZE	An attribute of the <SELECT> tag that causes the list of items to be displayed as a scrolling list with the number of items indicated by SIZE being visible.
<OPTION>	Individual items within a <SELECT> element.
SELECTED	An attribute of the <OPTION> tag indicating that this item is selected by default.
<TEXTAREA>	A text-entry field with multiple lines.
ROWS	An attribute of the <TEXTAREA> tag indicating the height of the text field, in rows.
COLS	An attribute of the <TEXTAREA> tag indicating the width of the text field, in characters.
WRAP	An attribute of the <TEXTAREA> tag that indicates how text is word wrapped in a text area field. Possible values are OFF, VIRTUAL, and PHYSICAL.

Workshop

The first section of the Workshop lists some of the common questions people ask about the World Wide Web along with a brief answer to each. Next is a quiz about the chapter you have just read. If you have problems answering any of the questions in the quiz, you can turn to Appendix E, "Answers to Quiz Questions."

Q&A

Q Is there any reason to use the GET method in my forms?

A As I noted earlier in this chapter, it's better to use POST, because processing the input from POST isn't much more complicated and enables you to create forms of any length. If you use GET, however, the input to your form will be encoded into the URL where you can see it or, more usefully, where you can save it to a regular link or put it in your hotlist. The next time you call that URL with the form input appended to it, you can bypass filling out the form and go back to that same place. You might find a use for this in your presentations.

Quiz

1. What are the two possible values of the METHOD attribute that indicate how the results of a form get sent back to a Web server?

2. How do you tell a Web browser that it should send its results to a CGI script?

3. Name four of the possible TYPE values for an <INPUT> tag.

4. What tag would you use to declare a field that is 4 rows long and 60 characters wide?

5. Why would you use a <SELECT> tag in a form?

Exercises

1. You should be very familiar with this exercise step by now, so go ahead and create the 17notes.html documents for your reference collection. (Remember to update the contents page also.)

   Make sure you include all the elements and tags listed in Table 17.1 and include a hyperlink to the Surrealist Census exercise document as well.

2. As mentioned earlier in this chapter, the CGI examples discussed in this book refer to UNIX-based Web servers. For those of you who are using Windows- or Macintosh-based systems, now would be a good time to dig out your server documentation and examine the CGI capabilities it provides.

   Also, for those of you that rent space from a Web service provider, you will need to take a look at the documentation the service provides to learn about how you can implement forms and CGI scripting of your system (if at all).

18

Image Maps and Dynamic Documents

Image Maps and Dynamic Documents

Like the forms you learned about in Chapter 17, "Forms and CGI," image maps and dynamic documents are two advanced Web capabilities that can greatly enhance the look and feel of your Web pages. In addition, like forms, in their most common format image maps and dynamic documents both require CGI scripts to function correctly.

In this chapter you will learn about image maps and dynamic documents by examining the following:

- [ ] What is an image map
- [ ] Creating server-side image maps
- [ ] Creating client-side image maps
- [ ] Supporting both types of image maps
- [ ] Creating dynamically updating documents

What Is an Image Map?

In Chapter 10, "Adding Images to Your Web Documents," you learned how to create an image that doubles as a link, simply by including the <IMG> tag inside a link (<A>) tag. In this way, the entire image becomes a link. You could click the image, the background, or the border, and you'd get the same effect.

In image maps, different parts of the image activate different links. (See Figure 18.1.) By using image maps, you can create a visual hyperlinked map that links you to pages describing the regions you click. Or you can create visual metaphors for the information you're presenting: a set of books on a shelf or a photograph in which each person in the picture is individually described.

Figure 18.1.
Image maps: different places, different links.

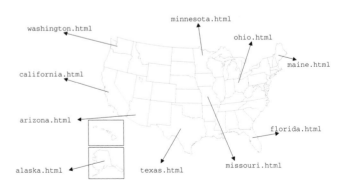

Server-Side Image Maps

Traditionally, image maps are created by using a special form of CGI script. Such image maps are referred to as *server-side image maps*.

When a browser activates a link on an image map, it calls a special image map program stored on a Web server—in much the same way that a form calls a CGI script. But instead of sending field names and values to the script, it sends the x and y coordinates of the position, on the image, where the mouse was clicked. The image map program then looks up a special map file that matches regions in the image to URLs, does some calculations to figure out which page to load, and then loads that page.

Client-Side Image Maps

Although server-side image maps have now been in common use for some time, the problems associated with them have led to the development of a new type of image map called a client-side image map. These are the main problems associated with server-side image maps:

☐ Normally, when you move your cursor over a hyperlink, the URL pointed to by the link is displayed in the Web browser's status bar. Because, however, the Web browser has no idea where the parts of a server-side image map point, all you normally see when you place your cursor over a server-side image map is a set of coordinates and no URL.

☐ There is no way to use server-side image maps with local files, because they work only with the `http:` protocol and require a dedicated Web server for much of their processing.

☐ Because a special program must be run by the server each time a user clicks a page that contains image maps, a notable degradation of server performance can occur. This often results in image maps that seem to take forever to respond to requests for a new page.

Client-side image maps, on the other hand, remove all these difficulties by removing the need for a special image map program on the server. Instead, they manage all the image map processing locally on the Web browser itself.

Note: Client-side image maps are currently supported by only a few of the very latest Web browsers, including Navigator 2.0; however, the Netscape Communications implementation has been proposed as a standard for HTML 3.0.

18

Image Maps and Text-Only Browsers

Because of the inherently graphical nature of image maps, they can work only on graphical browsers. In fact, if you try to view a document with an image map in a text-only browser such as Lynx, you don't even get an indication that the image exists. (Unless, of course, the image contains an ALT attribute.) But even with the ALT attribute, you won't be able to navigate the presentation without a graphical browser.

If you decide to create a Web page with an image map on it, it is doubly important that you also create a text-only equivalent so that readers with text-only browsers can use your page. The use of image maps can very effectively lock out readers with text-only browsers; have sympathy and allow them at least some method for viewing your content.

Creating Server-Side Image Maps

As with CGI scripts in general, each server has a different method of implementing image maps. The methods even vary among servers on the same platform. For example, the W3C httpd server and NCSA HTTPd server have incompatible methods of implementing image files. All servers, however, use the same basic ingredients for image maps:

- ☐ Special HTML code to indicate that an image is a map
- ☐ A map file on the server that indicates regions on the image and the Web pages they point to
- ☐ An image-mapping CGI script that links it all together

This section explains how to construct clickable images in general, but it focuses particularly on examples for the NCSA HTTPd and W3C httpd servers. If you need more information for your server, see the documentation that comes with that server, or get help from your Web administrator.

Getting an Image

To create an image map, you'll need an image (of course). The image that serves as the map is most useful if it has several discrete visual areas that can be individually selected; for example, images with several symbolic elements or images that can be easily broken down into polygons. Photographs make difficult image maps because their various "elements" tend to blend together or are of unusual shapes. Figures 18.2 and 18.3 show examples of good and poor images for image maps.

Figure 18.2.
A good image map.

Figure 18.3.
A not-so-good image map.

Creating a Map File

The heart of the image map structure is a map file. Creating a map file involves sketching out the regions in your image that are clickable, determining the coordinates that define those regions, and deciding on the HTML pages where they should point.

Note: The format of the map file depends on the image-mapping CGI script you're using on your server. In this section, I'll talk about image mapping on the W3C httpd and NCSA HTTPd servers and the map files they use. If you're using a different server, you might have several image-mapping programs to choose from with several map formats. Check with your Web administrator or read your server documentation carefully if you're in this situation.

You can create a map file either by sketching regions and noting the coordinates or by using an image map–making program. The latter method is easier, because the program will automatically generate a map file based on the images you draw with the mouse.

The mapedit and MapThis programs for Windows and WebMap for the Macintosh can all help you create map files in W3C httpd or NCSA HTTPd format. In addition, the latest version of MapThis (Version 1.20) also includes support for the creation of client-side image map definitions, as well. (Refer to the documentation included on the CD-ROM for more information about how these programs are used.)

Alternatively, if you use a UNIX-based system there is a version of mapedit available via FTP. (See Appendix D, "Sources of Additional Information," for a full list of related FTP sites.) If you need your map file in a different format, you can always write a map file yourself. Do this by first making a sketch of the regions you want to make active on your image (for example, as in Figure 18.4).

Figure 18.4.

Sketching mappable regions.

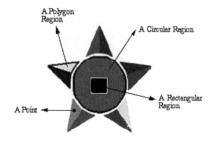

You next need to determine the coordinates for the endpoints of those regions. (See Figure 18.5.) Most image-editing programs have an option that displays the coordinates of the current mouse position. Use this feature to note the appropriate coordinates. (All the mapping programs mentioned previously will create a map file for you, but for now, following the steps manually will help you better understand the processes involved.)

For circle regions, note the coordinates of the center point and the radius, in pixels. For rectangle regions, note the upper-left and lower-right corners. For polygon regions, note the coordinates of each corner. For point regions, note the coordinates of the point.

Note: The 0,0 origin is in the upper-left corner of the image, and positive Y is down.

Figure 18.5.

Getting the coordinates.

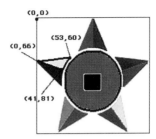

You're more than halfway there. The next step is to come up with a set of URLs to link for each region or point that is selected. You can have multiple regions pointing to the same URL, but each region must have only one link.

With all your regions, coordinates, and URLs noted, you can now write a map file for your server. Map files for W3C httpd look something like this:

```
default URL
circle (x,y) radius URL
rectangle (x,y) (x,y) URL
polygon (x1,y1) (x2,y2) ... (xN,yN) URL
```

NCSA HTTPd image map files are roughly the same as those for W3C httpd image map files, but the elements are in a different order. NCSA HTTPd map files look like this:

```
default URL
circle URL x,y radius
rect URL x,y x,y
poly URL x1,y1 x2,y2 ... xN,yN
point URL x,y
```

The map files for your particular image map program for your server might look different from this, but the essential parts are there. Substitute the values for the coordinates you noted previously in each of the x or y positions (or *x1*, *y1*, and so on). Note that you must include the parentheses in the W3C httpd file, and the *radius* (in the circle line) is the radius for the circle region.

The URLs you specify for either format must be either full URLs (starting with `http` or `ftp` or some other protocol) or the full pathnames to the files you are linking, that is, everything you could include after the hostname in a URL. You cannot specify relative pathnames in the image map file.

Here's a sample of a W3C httpd map file:

```
circle (10,15) 20 /www/mapping.html
circle (346,23) 59 /www/mapping.html
polygon (192,3) (192,170) (115,217) /www/test/orange.html
rectangle (57,57) (100,210) /www/pencil.html
default /www/nopage.html
```

> **Note:** W3C httpd's map files do not include individual points.

Here's a sample of an NCSA HTTPd map file:

```
circle /www/mapping.html 10,15 20
circle /www/mapping.html 346,23 59
poly /www/test/orange.html 192,3 192,170 115,217
rect /www/pencil.html 57,57 100,210
point /www/pencil.html 100,100
point /www/orange.html 200,200
```

Points in NCSA HTTPd maps enable you to specify that a given mouse click, if it doesn't land directly on a region, will activate the nearest point. Points are useful for photographs or other images with nondiscrete elements, or for a finer granularity than just "everything not in a region."

The order of regions in the map file is relevant; the further up a region is in the file, the higher precedence it has for mouse clicks. If part of the region that occurs on overlapping regions is selected, the first region listed in the map file is the one that is activated.

Finally, both map files include a "default" region, with no coordinates, just a URL. The default is used when a mouse click that is not inside a region is selected; it provides a catch-all for the parts of the image that do not point to a specific link. (Note that if you use an NCSA HTTPd map file and you include default, you shouldn't include any points. The existence of point elements precludes that of default.)

Installing the Map File and the Image Map CGI Program

Creating the image map file is the hardest part of making an image map. The only thing left to do is to store the map file in a central location on your server. After that, just hook up the image on your Web page to the image-mapping CGI program and to the map file.

Save your map file with a descriptive name (say, myimage.map). Where you store the map file isn't important, but I like to put my map files in a directory called maps at the top level of my Web files (the same level as the cgi-bin directory).

Finally, you'll need your image map program installed in your cgi-bin directory. For the W3C httpd server that program is called htimage and for the NCSA HTTPd server it's called imagemap.

Note: Be careful with the NCSA HTTPd server and the imagemap program. Older versions of imagemap were more difficult to work with and required an extra configuration file; the program that comes with the 1.5 version of the server works much better. If you aren't running the most recent version of NCSA HTTPd's server, you can get it from `http://hoohoo.ncsa.uiuc.edu/docs/setup/OneStep.html` and the latest version of the imagemap script from `http://hoohoo.ncsa.uiuc.edu/docs/tutorials/imagemap.txt`.

Linking It All Together

So now you have an image, a map file, and an image map CGI program. All that's left is to hook it all up. In your HTML document that contains the image map, you'll use the `<A>` and `<IMG>` tags together to create the effect of the clickable image. Here's one for the W3C httpd htimage program:

```
<A HREF="../cgi-bin/htimage/maps/myimage.map">
<IMG SRC="image.gif" ISMAP>
</A>
```

Notice several things about this link. First, the link to the image map script (`htimage`) is indicated the way you would expect, but then the path to the map file is appended onto the end of it. The path to the map file should be a full pathname from the root of your Web directory (everything after the hostname in your URL), in this case `/maps/myimage.map`.

The second part of the map is the `ISMAP` attribute to the `<IMG>` tag. This is a simple attribute that indicates to the browser and the server to send individual mouse-click coordinates to the CGI script for processing.

Here's one for the NCSA httpd server. It's identical to the preceding example, except the name of the image map program is different:

```
<A HREF="../cgi-bin/imagemap/maps/myimage.map">
<IMG SRC="image.gif" ISMAP>
</A>
```

And now try it out! Load your HTML file in the browser (it'll have to be installed on your server), and try clicking the image map. You should be able to select various bits of the image by using the mouse and have the coordinates sent as part of the URL to the image-mapping script, which in turn uses the map file to find an appropriate action for each region.

18

Note: If you're running the NCSA HTTPd server and you don't have the newest version of imagemap, you will get the error `Cannot Open Configuration file` when you try to select portions of your image. If you get these errors, check with your Web administrator.

▼ Exercise: A Clickable Bookshelf

Image maps can get pretty hairy. The map files are prone to error if you don't have your areas clearly outlined and everything installed in the right place. In this exercise, you'll take a simple image and create an entry for both the W3C httpd and NCSA HTTPd map files. This entry will define a clickable area on an image so that you can get a feel for what the map files look like and how to create them.

The image you'll use here is a simple color rendering of some books. (See Figure 18.6.) You can't see the colors here, but from left to right, they are red, blue, yellow, and green.

Figure 18.6.
*The bookshelf
image.*

First, you'll define the regions that will be clickable on this image. Because of the angular nature of the books, it's most appropriate to create polygon-shaped regions. Figure 18.7 shows an example of the sort of region it makes sense to create on the image. This one is for the leftmost (red) book. You can define similar regions for each book in the stack. (Draw on the figure here in the book, if you want to. I won't mind.)

With an idea of the areas for each region, now find the coordinates of the corners. You can use a mapping program such as mapedit or WebMap, or you can do it by hand. I used Adobe Photoshop to find the coordinates using the Info window and came up with the coordinates shown in Figure 18.8. If you had the file, you could also find coordinates for each polygon region on each book as well.

Figure 18.7.
*The bookshelf with
an area defined.*

Figure 18.8.
*The bookshelf with
coordinates.*

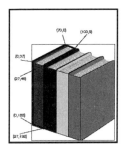

With regions and a list of coordinates, all you need now are Web pages to jump to when the appropriate book is selected. These can be any documents, or they can be scripts; anything you can call from a browser you can use as a jump destination. For this example, I've created a document called `redbook.html` in my Web directory (`/www` from the top of the Web root). This is the page we'll define as the endpoint of the jump when the red book is selected.

All that's left is to create the entry in the map file for this area with the coordinates and the file to link. In the W3C httpd map file, it would look like this:

```
polygon (70,0) (0,37) (0,183) (27,192) (27,48) (103,9) /www/redbook.html
```

And for an NCSA HTTPd map file, the same information looks like this:

```
poly /www/redbook.html 70,0 0,37 0,183 27,192 27,48 103,9
```

Note that the URLs in the map file must be absolute pathnames from the top of the Web root (not from the top of the file system). They cannot be relative URLs from the map file; image maps don't work like that. In this case, my www directory is at the Web root, and the `redbook.html` file is in that directory, so the URL for the purposes of the map file is `/www/redbook.html`.

18

Now that you've done it for the red book, you can create identical entries for the other books in the image (blue, yellow, and green). Don't forget to include a default line in the map file to map mouse clicks that don't hit any books (here, a file called `notabook.html`):

```
default /www/notabook.html
```

Now save your map file to your map directory (or wherever you keep your maps), and create a Web page with the books on it, with the `ISMAP` attribute to the image map and the link to the image-mapping CGI program. Here I've used the NCSA HTTPd server with its `imagemap` script:

```
<A HREF="../cgi-bin/imagemap/maps/bookncsa.map">
<IMG SRC="images/books.gif" ISMAP>
</A>
```

And that's it. With everything connected, clicking the image on each book should load the page for that part of the image.

Creating Client-Side Image Maps

When creating a client-side image map, you need to take a slightly different approach to defining the mapping coordinates than you did for a server-side image map. Unlike a server-side image map, which uses a separate file to store the coordinates and references for each hyperlink, a client-side image map stores all the mapping information as part of an HTML document.

The *<MAP>* and *<AREA>* Tags

To include the mapping information with an HTML document, you use the new double-sided `<MAP>` tag, which looks like this:

```
<MAP NAME="mapname"> coordinates and links  </MAP>
```

The value assigned to the `NAME` attribute can be any valid link name—along the same lines as the rules for anchor names. This is the name that will be used later to associate the image map with its corresponding coordinates and hyperlink references.

Between the `<MAP>` and the `</MAP>` tags, you enter the mapping coordinates for each clickable area in the image map, using the same values and links that you determined in the preceding section. This time, however, the coordinates are defined inside yet another new tag—the `<AREA>` tag. For example, to define the polygon area from the exercise "A Clickable Bookshelf," you would write this:

```
<AREA SHAPE="POLY" COORDS="70,0, 0,37, 0,183, 27,192, 27,48, 103,9" HREF="/www/
➡redbook.html">
```

The type of shape to be used for the region is declared by the SHAPE attribute, which currently supports the values RECT, POLY, and CIRCLE. For each shape, you then need to define a set of coordinates using the COORDS attribute. The forms taken by the COORDS attribute for the POLY, RECT, and CIRCLE regions are as shown next:

```
<AREA SHAPE="POLY" COORDS="x1,y1,x2,y2,x3,y3,…,xN,yN" HREF="URL">
```

In this form, each x,y combination represents a point on the polygon, with 0,0 starting at the upper-left corner, and 80,100 being right 80 pixels and down 100 pixels.

```
<AREA SHAPE="RECT" COORDS="x1,y1,x2,y2" HREF="URL">
```

In this form, x1,y1 is the upper-left corner of the rectangle, and x2,y2 is the lower-right corner.

```
<AREA SHAPE="CIRCLE" COORDS="x,y,radius" HREF="URL">
```

In this form, x,y represents the center of a circular region of size radius.

The last attribute you need to define for each <AREA> tag is the HREF attribute. HREF can be assigned any URL you would usually associate with an <A> link, including relative links—something that tends to break some server-side image maps. In addition, you can assign HREF a value of "NOHREF" to define regions of the image that don't contain links to a new page.

> **Note:** When using client-side image maps with frames, you can also include the TARGET attribute inside an <AREA> tag to control the window where the new document will be opened, as in this example:
>
> ```
> <AREA SHAPE="RECT" COORDS="x1,y1,x2,y2" HREF="URL" TARGET="window_name">.
> ```

The *USEMAP* Attribute

After your image map has been defined, the last step in the process is to actually place the physical image on your Web page. To do this, you use a special form of the <IMG> tag that includes a new attribute called USEMAP. When included with an <IMG> tag, USEMAP takes this form:

```
<IMG SRC="image.gif" USEMAP="#mapname">
```

In this form, the value mapname is the name of a map defined by the <MAP NAME="mapname"> tag.

18

Note: Unlike with server-side image maps, you do not need to enclose the `<IMG>` tag inside an `<A>` tag. Instead, the USEMAP attribute tells the Web browser that the `<IMG>` contains a clickable image map.

Tip: The value assigned to USEMAP is a standard URL. This is why *mapname* has a pound (#) symbol in front of it. This tells Navigator 2.0 to look for *mapname* in the current Web document by using relative URL addressing. As a result, if you have a very complex image map, it can be stored in a separate HTML file and referenced by using absolute addressing.

Exercise: The Clickable Bookshelf Exercise Revisited

To conclude this discussion of image maps, take a look at how the image map example discussed in the preceding exercise would be written using client-side image maps.

First, you need to define the `<MAP>` tag and its associated `<AREA>` tag like this:

```
<MAP NAME="books">
<AREA SHAPE="POLY" COORDS="70,0, 0,37, 0,183, 27,192, 27,48, 103,9" HREF="/www/
➥redbook.html">
</MAP>
```

Then, define an `<IMG>` that references this map with USEMAP:

```
<IMG SRC="images/books.gif" USEMAP="#books">
```

Finally, put the whole lot together and test it, as shown in Figure 18.9:

```
<HTML><HEAD>
<TITLE>The Virtual Bookshelf</TITLE>
</HEAD><BODY>
<H1>The Virtual Bookshelf</H1>
<P>Please select a book:</P>
<IMG SRC="images/books.gif" USEMAP="#books">
<MAP NAME="books">
<AREA SHAPE="POLY" COORDS="70,0, 0,37, 0,183, 27,192, 27,48, 103,9"
➥HREF="/www/redbook.html" >
</MAP>
</BODY>
</HTML>
```

Figure 18.9.
The finished image map.

Building Web Pages That Support Both Types of Image Map

The main problem associated with using client-side image maps is that like many of the other new features discussed in this book, they are currently supported only by Navigator 2.0. For this reason, Netscape has created a special form of the client-side image map that is backward-compatible with the older server-side image maps.

To create an image map that uses client-side support if available, but falls back to server-side support when needed, take a standard server-side definition:

```
<A HREF="../cgi-bin/htimage/maps/myimage.map">
<IMG SRC="image.gif" ISMAP>
</A>
```

And include the client-side image map details as part of the `<IMG SRC="image.gif" ISMAP>` text, like this:

```
<A HREF="../cgi-bin/htimage/maps/myimage.map">
<IMG SRC="image.gif" USEMAP="#books" ISMAP>
</A>
```

You will, of course, need to have installed the `myimage.map` file on your server, and to have included the "books" `<MAP>` tag definition somewhere in your HTML document.

18

Dynamic Documents

To complete this chapter, we'll briefly look at one final option available to users of Navigator 1.1 or later Netscape Web browsers. As a rule, the World Wide Web is driven by user interaction. When you click a hyperlink or enter a URL, the appropriate Web page is retrieved and displayed. After this happens, your Web browser just sits and waits for your next request—that was, at least, until the release of Navigator 1.1.

When Netscape Communications introduced Version 1.1, it announced the inclusion of two special mechanisms that let Web pages update themselves automatically, under the control of either the server or the Web browser. In each case, there is no need for any interaction on the part of the user. Instead, new pages, or parts of pages, are sent to the Web browser automatically.

These are the two mechanisms in question:

☐ Server push—With this method, a Web server can be set to send blocks of data regularly to a Web browser. The Web server does this by maintaining the connection between the Web browser and itself after the first page of information is transmitted. After this connection has been established, the Web server can send additional information at any stage, which might be an entirely new page or even a single image when it chooses.

☐ Client pull—With client pull, when a server sends a page of data to a browser, it includes a special directive that tells the browser where or when to load another page of information. This directive could be an instruction to reload the current page or an entirely different page.

▼ Exercise: Server Push

To send a continuous stream of information to a Web browser by using server push, you need to use CGI scripts similar to those created in Chapter 16, "Interacting with the Web Server by Using CGI." However, instead of starting each Web page you compose by using these scripts with `Content-type: text/html`, for server push, you need to use a new content type called `multipart/x-mixed-replace`.

To find out more about how server push works, look at how you would convert the time and date generator created in Chapter 16's "Try It" exercise into a continually updating Web page that refreshes the time every 10 seconds. If you don't recall back that far (yes, I realize this has been a long day), here is the source code from the original example:

```
#!/bin/sh

echo Content-type: text/html
echo
```

```
cat << EOF
<HTML>
<HEAD>
<TITLE>Date</TITLE>
</HEAD>
<BODY>
<P>The current date is: <B>
EOF
/bin/date
cat << EOF
</B>
</BODY>
</HTML>
EOF
```

When you run this script, a Web page is created that tells you the current date and time. But now you want to convert this script into a server push system that updates the page regularly.

First up, you need to tell the Web browser to start a server push session. To do this, at the start of the new script, write this:

```
#!/bin/sh

echo "Content-type: multipart/x-mixed-replace;boundary=MyBoundaryMarker"
echo
echo "--MyBoundaryMarker"
```

The Content-type: multipart/x-mixed-replace; statement on the first echo line informs the Web browser that the following information is part of a multipart stream of data. In addition, boundary=MyBoundaryMarker defines some random text that will be used by the script to indicate when the current block of information is complete, at which stage the browser can display it. As a result, to ensure that the first two echo statements are properly received, on the fourth line, the first echo "--MyBoundaryMarker" statement is sent to reset the browser.

You now want to create a loop in the script that sends the information contained in the script created in the "Try It" exercise regularly. You achieve this task by using a shell statement called a while do loop. When coded into the script, it looks like this:

```
while true
do
```

Following the do statement, you include the script statements to draw the required Web page:

```
echo Content-type: text/html
echo

cat << EOF
<HTML><HEAD>
<TITLE>Date</TITLE>
</HEAD><BODY>
<P>The current date is: <B>
EOF
```

18

```
/bin/date
cat << EOF
</B></BODY></HTML>
EOF

echo "--MyBoundaryMarker"
```

Following the body of the script, you need to include a new `echo "--MyBoundaryMarker"` statement to tell the Web browser that the current page is finished and can now be displayed.

At this stage, you want to tell the script to pause for a short while before sending a fresh page to the browser. You can achieve this action by using `sleep 10`, which tells the script to pause for 10 seconds. Then after the `sleep` statement, close the `while do` loop with a `done` statement. The `done` statement tells the script to look back to the preceding `do` statement and work through all the instructions again.

The Completed Script

When the parts are combined, the resulting script looks like this:

```
#!/bin/sh

echo "Content-type: multipart/x-mixed-replace;boundary=MyBoundaryMarker"
echo
echo "--MyBoundaryMarker"

while true
do
echo Content-type: text/html
echo

cat << EOF
<HTML><HEAD>
<TITLE>Date</TITLE>
</HEAD><BODY>
<P>The current date is: <B>
EOF
/bin/date
cat << EOF
</B></BODY></HTML>
EOF

echo "--MyBoundaryMarker"
sleep 10
done
```

If you save this script in the `cgi-bin` directory on your Web server and call it by using a Netscape Navigator Web browser, you will see a Web page that updates every 10 seconds to display a new date and time.

Client Pull

The HTML 3.0 specification introduces a new element called a `<META>` tag. This tag is designed to give you control over some of the many messages and instructions that are exchanged between a Web browser and Web server during the course of their operation. These messages are called HTTP response headers, and by using the `<META>` tag, you can simulate these headers in your HTML documents. For the most part, the use of such instructions is well beyond the scope of even the most advanced Web designers; however, one particular instruction does come in handy under certain circumstances.

For example, if you were to type the statement

```
<META HTTP-EQUIV="Refresh" CONTENT="10; URL=doc2.html">
```

inside the `<HEAD>...</HEAD>` block of an HTML document called `doc1.html`, when you loaded `doc1.html` into Navigator 1.1 or later, after 10 seconds the Web browser would automatically load `doc2.html` over `doc1.html`. This is the mechanism known as client pull.

Basically, what client pull enables you to do is include an instruction, as part of a Web page, that tells the Web browser to load a second page at some specified time after the original document finishes loading. Like server push, the client pull mechanism is currently supported by a limited number of HTML 3.0–based Web browsers. This can, however, make it a useful tool.

For example, by creating a generic home page that gives people the option of viewing either Netscape-ready pages or more generic pages, you provide the entire Web community with access to the information your site contains. But, because the Netscape browser supports client pull, it makes sense to remove the need for selecting the Netscape version of your home page altogether, and instead add a `<META>` tag with `CONTENT="0;` to your home page. This method simply pushes people with Netscape browsers to a new page. If you want to, you can still include the hyperlink as an option, but in most cases, the `CONTENT="0;` forces the client pull mechanism to activate faster than a person could select a hyperlink.

18

Playing Music with Client Pull

Since the client pull mechanism can be use to retrieve any type of file, some Web publishers have begun to use it to add background music to their Web pages. For example, by including the following as a part of the <HEAD> block on a Web page:

```
<META HTTP-EQUIV="Refresh" CONTENT="10; URL=sound.au">
```

a sound file called sound.au could be made to play whenever anyone loaded your Web page. In fact, any type of file can be sent using this mechanism. As a result, you could send an entire WAV file or maybe a MIDI-compatible music file. However, there are some limitations with this system. People viewing your page will need to have a compatible helper application installed on their systems or they may wind up with pages full of hieroglyphics.

Note: Microsoft recently introduced a new <BGSOUND> tag for the Internet Explorer Web browser, which plays background music or a sound file for a Web page. It is likely that in the future this tag may be more widely adopted by other Web browsers such as Navigator 2.0.

Summary

In this chapter you've learned how to add image maps to your Web pages and what dynamic documents are. You should now know the difference between a W3C httpd server image map, an NCSA HTTPd image map, and a client-side image map; how to create them; and how to connect clickable images, map files, and CGI scripts on the appropriate servers. In addition, you've learned about the <META> and how server push and client pull systems can be implemented.

Again, it's been a very full chapter, so to help refresh your memory, Table 18.1 presents a summary of the tags and attributes you've learned about in this chapter.

Table 18.1. HTML tags from this chapter.

Tag	Use
<MAP>	Defines a map for a client-side image map.
NAME	An attribute of the <MAP> tag used to define the map's name.
USEMAP	An attribute of the <IMG> tag used to associate an image with a client-side image map specified by <MAP NAME="*mapname*">.
<AREA>	The individual regions within a <MAP> element.

Tag	Use
TYPE	An attribute of the <AREA> tag indicating the type of region. Possible values are RECT, POLY, and CIRCLE.
COORDS	An attribute of the <AREA> tag indicating the point bounding the region.
HREF	An attribute of the <AREA> tag indicating the URL of the region.
<META>	Use to simulate HTTP header response messages in an HTML document.
HTTP-EQUIV	An attribute of the <META> tag indicating the header response to simulate.
CONTENT	An attribute of the <META> tag used to specify the value assigned to a header response.

In a sense, with the completion of this chapter you now have all the knowledge you need to create exciting and dynamic Web sites that take advantage of all the best features that the World Wide Web has to offer. If you were to put this book down now, your Web sites would still be as exciting and dynamic as the bounds of your creative talent.

But there's more. With the introduction of Navigator 2.0, two exciting new possibilities have been opened up to Web publishers—JavaScript, the scripting language built into Navigator 2.0, and Java, the Internet language developed by Sun Microsystems. In the final day's lessons you will be introduced to some of the amazing possibilities offered by these new services.

Workshop

The first section of the Workshop lists some of the common questions people ask about the World Wide Web along with a brief answer to each. Next is a quiz about the chapter you have just read. If you have problems answering any of the questions in the quiz, you can turn to Appendix E, "Answers to Quiz Questions."

Q&A

Q My image maps aren't working. What's wrong?

A Here are a couple things you can look for:

☐ Make sure that the URLs in your map file are absolute pathnames from the top of your root Web directory to the location of the file where you want to link. You cannot use relative pathnames in the map file. If absolute paths aren't working, try full URLs (starting with http).

18

☐ Make sure that when you append the path of the map file to the image map script (htimage or imagemap), you also use an absolute pathname (as it appears in your URL).

☐ If you're using an NCSA HTTPd server, make sure that you're using the newest version of imagemap. Requests to the new imagemap script should not look for configuration files.

Q I saw an example of a form that used an <INPUT> with TYPE="IMAGE". It looked like another way to do image maps. Is it?

A You're right, it is precisely another way to do image maps. Using this form, instead of using ISMAP in your image with a link, you would create a form with the ACTION pointing to your image-mapping script, and you'd use an input tag similar to the following one:

```
<INPUT TYPE="image" NAME="point" SRC="myimage.gif">
```

In that form, you wouldn't need a submit button. Clicking the image would "submit" the form.

So why didn't I describe this in the chapter? Netscape has introduced client-side image maps to serve a similar purpose.

Quiz

1. What is the main difference between a client-side and server-side image map?
2. What attribute do you need to include in an <IMG> tag for it to be treated as a server-side image map?
3. What is a <MAP> tag used for?
4. How do you associate an <IMG> tag with a client-side image map?
5. What is client pull?

Exercises

1. Yep, it's that time again. Create the 18notes.html documents for your reference collection. (Remember to update the contents page also.) Make sure you include all of the elements and tags listed in Table 18.1.

2. And finally, this is not so much an exercise as a debriefing. It is now time to take what you have learned in this book and put it to some practical use.

   If you have not as yet obtained access to a Web site of your own, you should start investigating the options available. Then, once you have a site, start Web publishing. When you get your site up and running, drop me a line via e-mail to

(wtatters@world.net) and let me know your URL so that I can add it to a list of sites created by people who have read this book.

To view the list, point your Web browser to `http://www.webcom.com/taketwo/sites.shtml`.

18

DAY 7

Programming with Java and JavaScript

JavaScript

JavaScript

When I first started putting this book together, Netscape Communications had just announced the introduction of a proprietary scripting language for Navigator 2.0. This language, called LiveScript, allowed the embedding of small programs in an HTML document to control various actions related to a Web page. The language was a scaled-down, noncompiled version of the powerful Java programming language, developed by Sun Microsystems for Internet and World Wide Web programming. (To learn more about Java, see Chapter 21, "Java.")

The fact that this language was proprietary, however, led to a very slow uptake in interest and usage. Unlike most of the current Netscape extensions—which will probably eventually be incorporated into the HTML 3.0 specification—the nature of LiveScript meant that it was unlikely to ever be supported by other Web browsers. As a result, Web pages that took advantage of LiveScript were definitely in the category of "Netscape Navigator Only" pages and, it seemed, would be so for a long time.

Then, suddenly, LiveScript was no more, and in its place a new scripting language called JavaScript appeared. In reality, the two languages are basically identical. However, JavaScript has the backing and support of not only Netscape Communications, but also Sun Microsystems, America Online, Apple Computers, Borland International, MacroMedia, Paper Software, Silicon Graphics, the Santa Cruz Operation, and Toshiba Corporation, just to mention a few of the companies that stand behind the endorsement of JavaScript as the new open Internet scripting language standard.

In this chapter you will learn about the basics of JavaScript by exploring the following topics:

- [ ] What JavaScript is
- [ ] Why you would want to use JavaScript
- [ ] The <SCRIPT> tag
- [ ] Basic commands and language structure
- [ ] Basic JavaScript programming

Note: As this book goes to press, JavaScript is still very much in a state of flux, with changes and modifications being made weekly to both the specification and the available features. For this reason, the best place to learn about all the latest features and capabilities provided by JavaScript is on the Netscape Communications home page at `http://home.netscape.com/comprod/products/navigator/version_2.0/script/script_info/index.html`.

Note: All the JavaScript examples in this book require the use of Netscape Navigator 2.0b5 or later. If you are not currently using the latest version of Navigator, you will need to upgrade your system before proceeding.

Introducing JavaScript

According to the press release made jointly by Netscape Communications and Sun Microsystems, "JavaScript is an easy-to-use object scripting language designed for creating live online applications that link together objects and resources on both clients and servers. JavaScript is designed for use by HTML page authors and enterprise application developers to dynamically script the behavior of objects running on either a client or server."

What Is JavaScript?

Put into simple English, what this means is that by using JavaScript, you can add functionality to your Web pages, which in the past would have demanded access to complex CGI-based programs on a Web server. In many ways, JavaScript is a lot like Visual Basic— the user-friendly programming language developed by Microsoft—in that people with little or no programming knowledge can use JavaScript. These novices can quickly and easily create complex Web-based applications without having to deal with all the background complexities such activities involve.

What makes JavaScript so different, however, is the unique way it integrates itself with the World Wide Web. Instead of being stored as a separate file—like a CGI script—JavaScript code is included as part of a standard HTML document, just like any other HTML tags and elements. In addition, unlike CGI scripts, which run on a Web server, JavaScript scripts are run by the Web browser itself. Thus they are portable across any Web browser that includes JavaScript support, regardless of the computer type or operating system.

Note: In the future, it is likely that a server-side version of JavaScript will be released as a replacement for the popular Perl and Bourne shell scripts currently used for CGI, making JavaScript both the server and the client scripting language of choice.

Why Would I Want to Use JavaScript?

The answer to this question depends, to a certain extent, on exactly what capabilities are eventually included as part of the JavaScript language. It is likely, however, that scripts written using JavaScript will eventually be able to control all aspects of a Web page or Web form, and to communicate directly with plug-ins displayed on a Web page and also with compiled Java applets. In fact, Paper Software—the developers of the WebFX VRML plug-in—has already indicated that it is actively working on such technology for future versions of WebFX. By using these capabilities, you will eventually be able to create fully interactive 3D virtual worlds on the World Wide Web that can be modified and controlled by Java applets (more on these in Chapter 21) and JavaScript scripts.

But apart from such future possibilities, what JavaScript enables you to do now is perform many simple (and not so simple) programming tasks at the Web browser (or client) end of the system, instead of relying on CGI scripts at the Web server end. In addition, JavaScript enables you to control with far greater efficiency the validation of information entered by users on forms and other data-entry screens. And finally, when integrated with frames, JavaScript brings a wide variety of new document presentation options to the Web publishing domain.

Ease of Use

Unlike Java, JavaScript is designed for nonprogrammers. As such, it is relatively easy to use and is far less pedantic about details such as the declaration of variable types. In addition, you do not need to compile JavaScript code before it can be used—something you need to do with most other languages, including Java.

Increasing Server Efficiency

As more and more people begin to flood the World Wide Web, many popular Web sites are rapidly being pushed to the limit of their current processing capabilities. As a result, Web operators are continually looking for ways to reduce the processing requirements for their systems—to ward off the need for expensive computer upgrades. This was one of the main reasons for the development of client-side image maps like those discussed in Chapter 18, "Image Maps and Dynamic Documents."

With the introduction of JavaScript, some exciting new performance options are now available to Web publishers. For example, say you have created a form that people use to enter their billing details for your online ordering system. When this form is submitted, the first thing your CGI script needs to do with it is validate the information provided and make sure that all the appropriate fields have been filled out correctly. You need to check that a name and address have been entered, that a billing method has been selected, that credit card details have been completed—and the list goes on.

But what happens if your CGI script discovers that some information is missing? In this case, you need to alert the user that there are problems with the submission and then ask him to edit the details and resubmit the completed form. This entire process is very resource intensive. First, the Web server needs to allocate a dedicated resource to perform all the validation and checks, and second, when there are errors, two additional data transmissions must be handled by the server—one to alert the user of errors and one to receive the updated information.

On the other hand, by moving all the validation and checking procedures to the Web browser—through the use of JavaScript—you remove the need for any additional transactions, because only one "valid" transaction will ever be transmitted back to the server. In addition, because the Web server does not need to perform any validations of its own, there is a considerable reduction in the amount of server hardware and processor resources required to submit a complex form.

JavaScript and Web Service Providers

With an increasing number of Web service providers severely limiting the availability of CGI script support for security reasons, JavaScript offers an excellent method of regaining much of the missing CGI functionality. It moves tasks that would previously have been performed by a server-side CGI script onto the Web browser.

Most Web service providers usually furnish some form of basic CGI script, which can take a form submitted by a user and perform basic processing operations such as saving it to disk or mailing it to the site's owner. When it comes to more complex forms, however, in the past the only alternatives were to find another service provider or set up your own Web server. But now, with JavaScript, this no longer need be the case.

By using a Web service provider's basic form-processing CGI scripts with JavaScript routines buried in the Web page itself, there are very few form-based activities that cannot be duplicated on even the most restrictive and security-conscious Web service provider's site. In addition, after the full integration of Java, JavaScript, and plug-ins has been achieved, you will be able to do things on a Web page that would never have been considered possible previously with even the most capable CGI script.

Submitting Forms Without CGI

The ACTION attribute of the <FORM> tag has traditionally been associated with a CGI script located on a Web server. But, in fact, any URL can be assigned to the ACTION attribute. Doing so, however, has little value unless the resource associated with the URL can process the contents of the form in some way.

That said, there is one type of URL—apart from a CGI script—that can process the results of a form in a meaningful way—mailto:. For example, if you included the following <FORM> tag on a page, clicking the submit button would e-mail the contents of the form to my e-mail address:

```
<FORM METHOD="POST" ACTION="mailto:wtatters@world.net">
```

In the past, however, using ACTION in such a way could be relied on only when the contents of the form were not vital, because there was no way to validate the information. But by using JavaScript, you can now validate the data before it is e-mailed and even perform basic calculations or other processing.

Note: Using the ACTION="mailto:*email_address*" option only works if the Web user has properly configured his or her Web browser to send e-mail. If this has not been done, no e-mail message will be transmitted.

The *javascript:* Protocol

To complement the use of the mailto: protocol within the ACTION attribute, a new URL and protocol specifically for JavaScript has also been introduced. This new URL takes the following form:

```
javascript:function()
```

where *function()* can be replaced by any of the functions and methods you will learn about later in this chapter. This new URL can be used in place of any of the previously discussed URLs: inside <FORM> tags, <A> tags, and even inside the <AREA> tag of a client-side image map.

Note: At the time of this writing, some elements of the javascript: URL were still under development. Refer to the JavaScript documentation provided by Netscape Communications for the most up-to-date information.

The *<SCRIPT>* Tag

To accommodate the inclusion of JavaScript programs in a normal HTML document, Netscape has proposed the introduction of a new <SCRIPT> tag. By placing a <SCRIPT> tag in a document, you tell Navigator 2.0 to treat any lines of text following the tag as script rather

than as content for the Web page. This action then continues until a corresponding </SCRIPT> tag is encountered, at which point the Web browser reverts to its usual mode of operation—treating text as Web content.

When used in a document, every script tag must include a LANGUAGE attribute to declare the scripting language to be used. Currently, the two possible values for this attribute are LANGUAGE="LiveScript" and LANGUAGE="JavaScript". As a rule, however, you should always use the JavaScript option because LiveScript is included only for legacy scripts, and it is doubtful whether it will be supported in future Netscape Navigator releases.

The Structure of a JavaScript Script

When you include any JavaScript code in an HTML document, apart from using the <SCRIPT> tag, you should also follow a few other conventions:

- [ ] As a rule, the <SCRIPT> tag should be placed inside the <HEAD> and </HEAD> tags at the start of your document and not inside the <BODY> tags. This is not a hard and fast requirement (as you will learn later), but it is a standard you should adopt whenever possible. Basically, since the code for your scripts is not to be displayed on the Web page itself, it should not be included in the <BODY> section, but instead in the <HEAD> section with all the other control and information tags such as <TITLE> and <META>.

- [ ] Because Web browsers that are not JavaScript aware will attempt to treat your JavaScript code as part of the contents of your Web page, it is vitally important that you surround your entire JavaScript code with a <!-- comment tag -->. Doing this will ensure that non-JavaScript–aware browsers can at least display your page correctly, if not make it work properly.

- [ ] Unlike HTML, which uses the <!-- comment tag -->, comments inside JavaScript code use the // symbol. Any line of JavaScript code that starts with this symbol will be treated as a comment and ignored.

Taking these three points into consideration, the basic structure for including JavaScript code inside an HTML document looks like this:

```
<HEAD>
<TITLE>Test script</TITLE>
<SCRIPT LANGUAGE="JavaScript">
<!-- Use the start of a comment tag to hide the JavaScript code
  Your JavaScript code goes here
// close the comment tag on the line immediately before the </SCRIPT> tag --!>
</SCRIPT>
</HEAD>
<BODY>
   Your Web document goes here
</BODY>
</HTML>
```

The *SRC* Attribute

Besides the LANGUAGE attribute, the <SCRIPT> tag can also include an SRC attribute. Doing this allows a JavaScript script stored in a separate file to be included as part of the current Web page. This is a handy option if you have several Web pages that all use the same JavaScript code and you don't want to type the scripts separately into each page.

When used like this, the <SCRIPT> tag takes the following form:

```
<SCRIPT LANGUAGE="JavaScript" SRC="http://script.js">
```

In this form, *script* can be any relative or absolute URL, and .js is the file extension for a JavaScript file.

 Note: At the time this book went to press, the SRC attribute was not fully implemented, and it now appears that it will not be operational before the official release of Navigator 2.0.

Basic Commands and Language Structure

At its heart, JavaScript uses an object-oriented approach to computer programming. This basically means that all the elements on a Web page are treated as objects that are grouped together to form a completed structure.

Using this structure, all the elements of a single Web page are said to be contained within a base object container called a window. Inside the window *object* are a set of smaller containers (or objects) that hold information about the various elements of a Web browser page. These are some of the main objects:

location	Inside the location object is information about the location of the current Web document, including its URL and separate components such as the protocol, domain name, path, and port.
history	The history object holds a record of all the sites a Web browser has visited during the current session, and it also gives you access to built-in functions that enable you to change the contents of the current window.

document

The document object contains the complete details of the current Web document. This includes all the forms, form elements, links, and anchors. In addition, it provides many types of functions that enable you to programmatically alter the contents of items such as text boxes, radio buttons, and other form elements.

19

Properties and Methods

Within each object container there are two main types of resources you can access.

The first type is called properties. Properties are basically variables that hold a value associated with the object you are interested in. For example, within the document object, there is a property called title that contains the title of the current document as described by the <TITLE> tag.

In JavaScript you could obtain the value of this property by using the statement document.title. The first part of the statement tells JavaScript which object you want to work with, and the second part—following the dot—represents the physical property itself.

In addition to properties, most objects also have special functions associated with them called methods. *Methods* are basically programming commands that are directly related to a particular object. For example, the document object has a method associated with it that enables you to write text directly onto a Web page. This method takes the following form:

```
document.write( "Hello world") ;
```

As is the case for properties, you describe a method by first declaring the object it is associated with, followed by a dot, and then indicating the method itself. In this example, the method must be assigned a value by including the relevant information inside the parentheses (()) that follow the method name. It is important to realize, however, that the parentheses must be included even if no values are assigned to the method, as is the case for the toString() method of the location object. This method is used to convert the current document's URL into a form suitable for use with other methods such as document.write().

By combining these methods and the document.title property mentioned previously into an HTML document like the following one, you would produce the results shown in Figure 19.1:

```
<HTML>
<HEAD>
<TITLE>Test JavaScript</TITLE>
<SCRIPT LANGUAGE="JavaScript">
document.write( document.title + "<BR>" ) ;
document.write( location.toString() ) ;
</SCRIPT>
</HEAD>
</HTML>
```

Figure 19.1.
*The results of your first
JavaScript script.*

Note: The online JavaScript documentation provided by Netscape Communications covers in detail all the properties and methods associated with each object recognized by JavaScript.

Caution: Method, property, function, and variable names in JavaScript are all case specific. If you are having problems getting the script for Figure 19.1 to work, make sure you have written `location.toString()` and not `location.tostring()`.

Events and JavaScript

Although implementing methods such as `document.write()` to create Web pages might have some uses, the real power behind JavaScript lies in its capability to respond to events generated by a Web page.

Events are actions that occur on a Web page, normally when a user interacts with the page in some way. For example, when a person enters a value into a text box on a form, or clicks a submit button, a series of events are triggered inside the Web browser, all of which can be intercepted by JavaScript programs, usually in the form of functions.

Functions

Functions are very similar to methods. The difference, however, is that whereas methods are associated with a specific object, functions are standalone routines that operate outside the

bounds of an object. To define a function for the current Web page, you would write something like this:

```
<SCRIPT LANGUAGE="JavaScript">

function functionName( operands ) {
  The actions to be performed by your function go here
}
</SCRIPT>
```

functionName is any unique name you choose, and *operands* is a list of any values you want sent to the function. Following the function definition and inside the set of braces ({ }), you include the list of instructions you want the function to perform. These could be a set of calculations, validation tests for a form, or just about anything else you can think of.

> **Note:** JavaScript also includes a set of built-in objects and functions that enable you to perform mathematical operations, string manipulation, and date and time calculations. For a full list of built-in functions, refer to the online JavaScript documentation.

Assigning Functions to Events

After you have your functions defined, the next thing you need to do is assign them to the various events you want trapped. You do this by assigning what are called *event handlers* to the various elements of a Web page or form. Currently, you can set the following event handlers:

onFocus	Whenever a user enters a specified field
onBlur	Whenever a user leaves a specified field
onSelect	Whenever a user selects the contents of a specified field
onChange	Whenever a user changes the contents of a specified field
onClick	Whenever a user clicks a specified button
onMouseOver	Whenever a user places the mouse cursor over a specified field
onSubmit	Whenever a user submits a specified form
onLoad	Whenever a Web page is loaded or reloaded
onUnload	Whenever the current Web page is changed

To specify functions that should be associated with any of these events, all you need to do is include the appropriate event handler as an attribute of the field you want to control. For example, take a standard form with a couple text fields and a submit button, as shown here:

```
<FORM METHOD="POST" SRC="../cgi-bin/form">
<INPUT TYPE="TEXT" NAME="username">
<INPUT TYPE="TEXT" NAME="emailAddress">
<INPUT TYPE="SUBMIT">
</FORM>
```

By adding onSubmit="return checkform(this)" to the <FORM> tag, the function called checkform() will be run before Navigator 2.0 submits the form. In checkform(), you can do any checks you want and, if there are any problems, halt the form submission and ask the user to fix them. The this parameter, inside the parentheses (()), is used to tell the checkform() function which form object is associated with the <FORM> tag. (Note that you'll learn more on this in Chapter 20, "Working with JavaScript.")

In addition, you can do checking field by field, by including either onChange or onBlur event handlers in each <INPUT> tag. Because the onBlur handler is called each time a person leaves a field, it is ideal for input validation.

You can also include onClick events in buttons, such as the submit button, which will be activated whenever the user clicks the specified button. For example, <INPUT TYPE="SUMBIT" onClick="processclick()"> would launch a function called processclick() whenever the submit button was clicked.

Note: JavaScript introduces a new <INPUT> type called button, which simply places a button on the Web page.

Variables

In addition to properties, JavaScript also enables you to assign or retrieve values from what are called variables. A *variable* is basically a user-defined container that can hold a number, some text, or an object. But unlike most high-level languages that force you to limit the contents of each variable to a specific type, in JavaScript variables are said to be loosely typed language. This means that you don't need to specify the type of information a variable contains when the variable is created. In fact, the same variable can be assigned to data of different types, depending on your requirements.

To declare a variable for a JavaScript program, you would write this:

```
var variablename = value ;
```

In this form, *variablename* is any unique name you choose. The equal (=) sign following the *variablename* is called an assignment operator. It tells JavaScript to assign whatever is on the right side of the = sign—*value*—as the contents of the variable. This *value* can be a text string, a number, a property, the results of a function, an array, a date, or even another variable. Here's an example:

```
var name = "Wes Tatters" ;
var age = 30 ;
var title = document.title ;
var documenturl = location.toString() ;
var myarray = new Array(10);
var todaysdate = new Date();
var myname = anothername ;
```

Note: Variable names (and function names) can consist of the letters a through z, the numbers 0 through 9, and the underscore (_) symbol. But the name cannot start with a number.

Tip: If you declare a variable inside a function, you will be able to access the contents of that variable only from inside the function itself. This is said to be the scope of the variable. On the other hand, if you declare a variable inside a <SCRIPT> block, but not inside any functions, you can access the contents of the variable anywhere inside the current Web page.

Operators and Expressions

After a variable has been defined, you can work with its contents, or alter them, by using *operators*. Table 19.1 lists some of the more popular operators provided by JavaScript and includes an example that demonstrates the use of each. (As before, for a full list of all the supported operators, refer to the online JavaScript documentation.)

Note: The examples shown in the second column of Table 19.1 are called expressions. Basically, an *expression* is any valid set of variables, operators, and expressions that evaluate to a single value. For example, b + c evaluates to a single value, which is assigned to a.

Table 19.1. JavaScript operators and expressions.

Operator	Example	Description
+	a = b + c	Add variables b and c, and assign the result to variable a.
-	a = b - c	Subtract the value of variable c from variable b, and assign the result to variable a.
*	a = b * c	Multiply variable b by variable c, and assign the result to variable a.
/	a = b / c	Divide variable b by variable c, and assign the result to variable a.
%	a = b % c	Obtain the modulus of variable b when it is divided by variable c, and assign the result to variable a. (Note: modulus is a function that returns the remainder.)
++	a = ++b	Increment variable b by 1, and assign the result to variable a.
- -	a = - -b	Decrement variable b by 1, and assign the result to variable a.

There is also a special set of operators that combine the assignment function (=) and an operator into a single function. Such operators are called *assignment operators*. Table 19.2 lists the assignment operators provided by JavaScript.

Table 19.2 JavaScript assignment operators.

Assignment Operator	Example	Description
+=	a += b	This is equivalent to the statement a = a + b.
-=	a -= b	This is equivalent to the statement a = a - b.
*=	a *= b	This is equivalent to the statement a = a * b.
/=	a /= b	This is equivalent to the statement a = a / b.
/=	a %= b	This is equivalent to the statement a = a % b.

> **Note:** The + and += operators can be used with string variables as well as numeric variables. When they're used with strings, the result of a = "text" + " and more text" is a variable containing "text and more text".

Basic JavaScript Programming

To tie together all the event handlers, methods, parameters, functions, variables, and operators, JavaScript includes a simple set of programming statements that are similar to those provided by Java and BASIC.

If you have any programming experience at all, spending a few minutes browsing through the list of supported statements discussed in Netscape Communications's online documentation will set you well on your way toward creating your first JavaScript programs. But for those of you who don't have the experience, the following section includes a quick crash course on basic programming.

What Is a Program?

Regardless of what language you use, a program is simply a set of instructions that describe to a computer some action, or group of actions, you want it to perform. In the most basic case, this set of instructions starts at the beginning of a list of code and works through each instruction in the list one at a time, until it reaches the end:

```
<SCRIPT LANGUAGE="JavaScript">
// start of program - NOTE: lines that start with '//' are treated as comments
document.write( "step one") ;
document.write( "step two") ;
// end of program
</SCRIPT>
```

It is rare, however, that you will ever want a program to proceed straight through a list of steps—especially in JavaScript—because it would be easier to write the messages on the screen using HTML than to code them by using JavaScript. For this reason, most programming languages include a basic set of instructions that enable you to control the flow of the instructions.

The *if* Statement

The first such instruction is called the if statement. Basically, it enables you to perform tests inside program code, to determine which parts of the program should be run under any given

situation. For example, assume that you have a Web form that asks whether a person is male or female. In such cases, you might want to respond to the person using a specific response, based on the indicated sex:

```
if ( form.theSex.value == "male" ) {
    document.write("Thank you for your response, Sir" ) ;
}
if ( form.theSex.value == "female") {
    document.write("Thank you for your response, Madam" ) ;
}
```

If this piece of code were run and the property form.theSex.value had been assigned a value of "male", the first document.write() method would have been called. If it had been assigned a value of "female", the second statement would have been displayed. For the moment, don't worry about how the value form.theSex.value was assigned; you will learn more about that issue in Chapter 20.

The block of code next to the if statement performs a comparison between the property form.theSex.value and the word "male". This comparison is controlled by what are called *comparison operators*. In this case, a test for equivalence was performed as signified by the == symbol. Table 19.3 lists the comparison operators currently recognized by JavaScript.

Table 19.3 JavaScript comparison operators.

Operator	Operator Description	Notes
==	Equal	a == b: tests to see if a equals b.
!=	Not equal	a != b: tests to see if a does not equal b.
<	Less than	a < b: tests to see if a is less than b.
<=	Less than or equal to	a <= b: tests to see if a is less than or equal to b.
>=	Greater than or equal to	a >= b: tests to see if a is greater than or equal to b.
>	Greater than	a > b: tests to see if a is greater that b.

The *if...else* Statement

The preceding example could have also been written in a slightly different way, by using a different version of the if statement that incorporates an else statement:

```
if ( form.theSex.value == "male" ) {
   document.write("Thank you for your response, Sir" ) ;
}
else {
   document.write("Thank you for your response, Madam" ) ;
}
```

In this example, because there is no need for a second if test—because a person can be only male or female—the else statement was used to tell the program to display the second message if the first test failed.

 Note: In both of the preceding examples, any number of statements could be assigned to each outcome by including each statement inside the appropriate set of braces.

Looping Statements

On occasion, you will want a group of statements to run multiple times rather than just once. Two looping statements are supported by JavaScript to carry out this task. The first kind of statement, called a for loop, is ideal for situations in which you want a group of instructions to occur a specified number of times. And the second kind, the while loop, is better suited to situations in which the number of loops required is to be determined by an outside source.

for Loops

The basic structure of a for loop is this:

```
for (var count = 1; count <= 10; ++count ) {
  your statements go here
}
```

In this example, a variable called count is declared and set to a value of 1. Then a test is made to see whether the value of count is less than or equal to 10. If it is, all the statements inside the braces ({}) following the for statement are executed once. Then the value of count is incremented by 1 by the statement ++count, and the count <= 10 test is performed again. If the result is still true, all the instructions inside the braces are executed again. This process keeps going until the value of count is greater than 10, at which point the for loop ends.

while **Loops**

The basic structure of a while loop is this:

```
while ( contition ) {
  your statements go here
}
```

Unlike the for loop, which has a built-in increment mechanism, the only test required for a while loop is a true result from the condition test following the while statement. This test could be an equivalence test, as in a == b, or any of the other tests mentioned previously for the if statement.

As long as this condition tests true, the statements inside the braces following the while loop will continue to run forever—or at least until you close your Web browser.

Caution: When using while loops, you need to avoid creating endless loops. (Such a loop is known as an *infinite loop*.) If you do manage to create an endless loop, about the only option you have to halt the loop is to shut down the Web browser.

Learn More About Programming in JavaScript

The list of statements, functions, and options included in this chapter represents only part of the potential offered by JavaScript. And in fact, as we go to press, many new statements and functions are being added weekly.

For this reason, I cannot overemphasize the importance of the online documentation provided by Netscape Communications. (See Figure 19.2.) Currently, it is the only full documentation for the JavaScript language. In addition, as the JavaScript language matures between now and the rumored release of Navigator 2.1 (yes, folks, it's already being planned), all the latest JavaScript enhancements and features will be documented at http:// home.netscape.com/comprod/products/navigator/version_2.0/script/script_info/ index.html first.

Figure 19.2.

The online JavaScript documentation at Netscape Communications is the best source of up-to-date information on JavaScript.

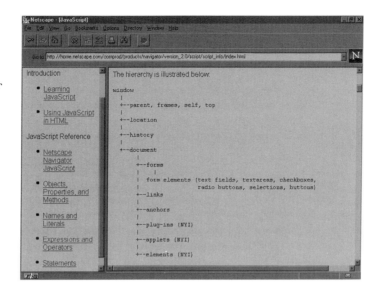

Summary

JavaScript offers HTML publishers the ability to include simple programs or scripts in a Web page without having to deal with the many difficulties usually associated with programming in high-level languages such as Java or C++.

In this chapter you have learned about the <SCRIPT> tag and how it is used to embed JavaScript programs into an HTML document. In addition, you have explored the basic structure of the JavaScript language and some of the statements and functions it offers.

With this knowledge under your belt, in the next chapter you will explore some real-world examples of JavaScript and learn more about JavaScript programming.

Workshop

The first section of the Workshop lists some of the common questions people ask about the World Wide Web along with a brief answer to each. Next is a quiz about the chapter you have just read. If you have problems answering any of the questions in the quiz, you can turn to Appendix E, "Answers to Quiz Questions."

Q&A

Q **If JavaScript is being proposed as an Internet standard, does that mean it will run on any Web browser?**

A Yes and no. If and when it is approved as an Internet standard, it will then be up to Web browser developers to integrate support for JavaScript into their browsers. Until this occurs, only Navigator 2.0 will fully support JavaScript, and the indications are that even Navigator might not support all the proposed features until the release of Version 2.1—sometime around the middle of 1996.

Q **In Java and C++, I used to define variables with statements such as `int`, `char`, and `string`. Why can't I do this in JavaScript?**

A Because you can't. As I mentioned previously, JavaScript is a very loosely typed language. This means that all variables can take any form and can even be changed on-the-fly. As a result, the type of value assigned to a variable determines its type.

Quiz

1. What are the two attributes that can be assigned to a `<SCRIPT>` tag?

2. What does the += assignment operator do?

3. When is the `onBlur` event triggered?

4. Why do you need to surround the contents of a `<SCRIPT>` tag with a `<!-- comment -->` tag?

5. Is `document.write()` an example of a property or a method?

Exercises

1. Create a `19notes.html` document for your HTML reference library and include a description of the `<SCRIPT>` tag. You might also want to include notes about the various topics discussed in this chapter, but a better approach would be to include a hyperlink to the online documentation discussed previously.

2. Your second task is to actually read through the online documentation provided by Netscape. Doing so will help you understand what is happening in Chapter 20 as you create some JavaScript scripts of your own.

20

Working with JavaScript

Now that you have some understanding of what JavaScript is all about, it's time to take a look at some practical applications of the possibilities JavaScript offers.

In this chapter you will learn how to complete the following tasks:

- ☐ Create a random link generator
- ☐ Validate the contents of a form
- ☐ Create a Web tour guide by using frames
- ☐ Build a "WebTop" calculator

Creating a Random Link Generator

A random link generator is basically a hyperlink that takes you to different locations every time you click it. In the past, the only way to implement such a link was through the use of a CGI, but with JavaScript, all the previous server-side processing can now be performed by the Web browser itself.

In the sections that follow, you will learn how to create three different random link generators. The first uses an inline <SCRIPT> tag and a single function, the second uses event handlers, and the third examines the use of arrays within a script.

Note: An inline <SCRIPT> tag is one that is embedded in the <BODY> section of an HTML document rather than in the <HEAD> section, as is the more common practice.

▼ Exercise: The Inline Random Link Generator

Because the JavaScript code for this generator will be incorporated in a standard HTML document, open the text editor or HTML editor you normally use for designing Web pages, and create a new file called random.html.

In this new file, create a basic document framework like the following one. You should recognize all the elements of this document from previous chapters, including the <A>...</A> tag combinations on the third-from-last line. If you were to run this document as it is, you would see a result like the one shown in Figure 20.1:

```
<HTML>
<HEAD>
<TITLE>Random Link Generator</TITLE>
</HEAD>
<BODY>
<H1>My random link generator</H1>
Click <A HREF="dummy.html">here</A> to visit a randomly selected site
from my list of favorites.
</BODY>
```

20

Figure 20.1.
*Clicking the hyperlink
loads a document
called* dummy.html.

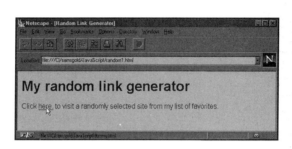

Now it's time to add some JavaScript code to turn the hyperlink into a random link generator.
First, add a <SCRIPT> tag to the <HEAD> section immediately after the <TITLE> tag block:

```
<TITLE>Random Link Generator</TITLE>
<SCRIPT LANGUAGE="JavaScript">
<!-- the contents of the script need to be hidden from other browsers
  the JavaScript code goes here.
// End of script -->
</SCRIPT>
</HEAD>
```

The next step involves adding the code that generates the random links, based on a list of your
favorite sites. Now would be a good time to dig out that list of favorite sites you used in
Chapter 6, "Linking Web Pages Together." Inside the <SCRIPT> tag—and comment tag—
you will create a function called picklink(). So you first define the framework for a function
like this:

```
function picklink() {
  your JavaScript code goes here.
}
```

And finally, here's the code that actually makes the picklink() function work:

```
function picklink() {

var linknumber = 4 ;
var linktext = "nolink.html" ;

var randomnumber = Math.random() ;
var linkselect = Math.round( (linknumber-1) * randomnumber) + 1 ;
```

```
if ( linkselect == 1 )
    { linktext="http://www.netscape.com/" }
if ( linkselect == 2 )
    { linktext="http://www.webcom.com/taketwo/" }
if ( linkselect == 3 )
    { linktext="http://java.sun.com/" }
if ( linkselect == 4 )
    { linktext="http://www.realaudio.com/" }

document.write('<A HREF="' + linktext + '">here.</A>') ;

}
```

To help you understand what this code is doing, we'll examine it section by section. The first two lines following the function definition declare some work variables for the function: `linknumber` tells the function how many links it has to choose from when selecting a random link, and `linktext` is a work variable used to hold the value of the URL for the selected random link.

The next line—`var randomnumber = Math.random() ;`—declares a variable called `randomnumber` and assigns a randomly selected decimal value between 0 and 1 to it by calling a special built-in function named `Math.random()`. The next line then takes the `randomnumber` variable and uses it to create a second number called `linkselect`, which will contain an *integer* between 1 and the value set in `linknumber`. (An integer is any whole number that does not contain any decimals; 1, 2, and 10 are integers; 1.3, 2.356, and 10.9999 are called *decimal* or *floating point* numbers.)

Note: The `Math.random()` function is still under development as this book goes to press and is currently only functional on the UNIX version of Navigator 2.1. If it does not make the final release of 2.0, you will need to use the replacement `random()` function shown here. This function is based loosely on one developed by Bob Jamison (`rjamison@gothamcity.jsc.nasa.gov`):

```
function random() {
    var curdate = new Date()
    var work = curdate.getTime() + curdate.getDate()
    return ( (work * 29 + 1) % 1024 ) / 1024
}
```

Simply add this function before the `// End of script -->` line and replace the `Math.random()` statement with `random()`. See the copy of this example on the CD-ROM for more information.

The set of `if` statements that follows then checks the randomly selected value assigned to `linkselect` and, when a match is found, assigns a URL to the variable `linktext`. You can add any number of URLs you like here, but remember that you need to alter the value of `linknumber` so that it reflects how many links you have defined.

After you have a URL assigned to `linktext`, the final step in the process is to create the physical hyperlink by using a `document.write()` method. You do this by writing this line:

```
document.write('<A HREF="' + linktext + '">here.</A>') ;
```

The value inside the parentheses takes advantage of JavaScript's capability to add strings of text together. In this case, `'<A HREF="'`, the value of `linktext`, and `'">here.</A>'` are added together to create a properly formed link tag.

With the function definition complete, all that now remains to be done is to replace the original `<A HREF=` tag from the basic framework with the new hyperlink created by `picklink()`. This can be done in various ways, but the simplest method is by embedding a call to `picklink()` inside the body of your document, as shown here:

```
Click <SCRIPT LANGUAGE="JavaScript">picklink()</SCRIPT>
 to visit a randomly selected site from my list of favorites.
```

> **Note:** Some JavaScript purists may argue that you should include `<SCRIPT>` blocks only in the `<HEAD>` section of an HTML document, and for the most part they are correct. But to demonstrate how inline script calls work and for the purposes of this exercise, the rules sometimes need to be broken. In the following exercise, however, you will learn about a mechanism that allows a random link generator to be created without the use of inline `<SCRIPT>` tags.

The Completed Document

For those of you who are keying in each exercise as you go along, here is the completed HTML document:

```
<HTML>
<HEAD>
<TITLE>Random Link Generator</TITLE>
<SCRIPT LANGUAGE="JavaScript">
<!-- the contents of the script need to be hidden from other browsers
function picklink() {
var linknumber = 4 ;
var linktext = "nolink.html" ;
var randomnumber = Math.random() ;
var linkselect = Math.round( (linknumber-1) * randomnumber) + 1 ;
// Add as many links as you want here
if ( linkselect == 1 )
   { linktext="http://www.netscape.com/" }
if ( linkselect == 2 )
   { linktext="http://www.webcom.com/taketwo/" }
if ( linkselect == 3 )
   { linktext="http://java.sun.com/" }
if ( linkselect == 4 )
   { linktext="http://www.realaudio.com/" }
```

485

```
// Remember to alter linknumber so it reflects the number of links you define
document.write('<A HREF="' + linktext + '">here</A>') ;
}
// End of script -->
</SCRIPT>
<BODY>
<H1>My random link generator</H1>
Click <SCRIPT LANGUAGE="JavaScript">picklink()</SCRIPT>
 to visit a randomly selected site from my list of favorites.
</BODY>
```

Exercise: A Random Link Generator Using an Event Handler

Besides being bad style-wise, using inline <SCRIPT> tags can cause unpredictable problems when images are displayed on a page. To avoid such difficulties, the safest way to work with scripts is to use them only in the <HEAD> block, where at all practical.

But this situation poses a problem for your random link generator, which needs to alter the value of a hyperlink each time it is used. If you can't include <SCRIPT> tags in the <BODY> of a document, how can the link be randomly selected?

Whenever you click a hyperlink, a button, or any form element, Navigator 2.0 generates an event signal that can be trapped by one of the event handlers mentioned in Chapter 19, "JavaScript." By taking advantage of this fact, and the fact that each link in a document is actually stored as an object that can be referenced by JavaScript, you will find it surprisingly easy to alter your existing script to avoid the need for an inline <SCRIPT> tag.

First, look at the changes that need to be made in the body of the document to accommodate the use of an event handler. In this exercise, the inline <SCRIPT> tag is replaced by a normal <A> tag, as shown here:

```
Click <A HREF="dummy.html">here</A> To visit a randomly selected site
from my list of favorites.
```

After this is done, you need to associate an onClick event handler with the hyperlink by including the handler as an attribute of the <A> tag. When onClick is used as an attribute, the value assigned to it must represent a valid JavaScript instruction or function call. For this exercise, you want to call the picklink() function created previously and make the URL it selects overwrite the default URL defined in the <A> tag as HREF="dummy.html".

This job is easy to do because each hyperlink is actually stored as an object of type link, and the link type contains the same properties as the location object mentioned in Chapter 19. As a result, all you need to do is assign a new value to the HREF property of the hyperlink, in the onClick event handler, as shown here:

```
Click <A HREF="dummy.html" onClick="this.href=picklink()">here</A>
 To visit a randomly selected site from my list of favorites.
```

> **Note:** The this statement is a special value that tells JavaScript to reference the current object without having to worry about its exact name or location. In this example, this points to the link object associated with the hyperlink, and this.href indicates the href property of this object. Therefore, by assigning a new value to this.href, you change the destination URL of the hyperlink.

20

With the onClick handler set up, all you need to alter in the picklink() function is the document.write() method. Because you are no longer physically writing anything onto the Web page, the document.write() function needs to be removed. But in its place, you need some way for the value of linkselect to be sent back to the this.href property.

You achieve this by using the return statement, which sends a value back from a function call, as shown here:

```
return linkselect ;
```

In the picklink() function, you need to replace

```
document.write('<A HREF="' + linktext + '">here</A>')
```

with this new statement.

The Completed Exercise

If you examine the completed text for this new HTML document, you will notice that there is very little difference between it and the preceding exercise, except for the removal of the inline <SCRIPT> tag and the replacement of document.write() with a return statement:

```
<HTML>
<HEAD>
<TITLE>Random Link Generator with events</TITLE>
<SCRIPT LANGUAGE="JavaScript">
<!-- the contents of the script need to be hidden from other browsers
function picklink() {
var linknumber = 4 ;
var linktext = "nolink.html" ;
var randomnumber = Math.random() ;
var linkselect = Math.round( (linknumber-1) * randomnumber) + 1 ;
if ( linkselect == 1 )
   { linktext="http://www.netscape.com/" }
if ( linkselect == 2 )
   { linktext="http://www.webcom.com/taketwo/" }
if ( linkselect == 3 )
   { linktext="http://java.sun.com/" }
if ( linkselect == 4 )
   { linktext="http://www.realaudio.com/" }
```

```
return linktext;
}
// End of script -->
</SCRIPT>
<BODY>
<H1>My random link generator</H1>
Click <A HREF="dummy.html" onClick="this.href=picklink()">here</A>
 to visit a randomly selected site from my list of favorites.
</BODY>
```

> **Note:** Again, please note that if you encounter any error messages when trying to use the built-in `Math.random()` function, you may need to use the replacement `random()` function discussed previously.

Exercise: A Random Link Generator Using an Array

The only problem with the preceding example is the need to keep adding additional `if` tests for each new link you want to include in your random list of favorites. To get around this difficulty, and to streamline the appearance of the script considerably, JavaScript provides a mechanism that enables you to create lists of variables—or what are called arrays.

An array is a list of variables that are all referenced by the same variable name. For example, an array called `mylinks[]` could be used to contain a list of all the links used by the `picklink()` function. The value of each link in the list is then referenced by the placement of a numeric value inside the square brackets (`[]`): the first variable can be found with `mylinks[1]`, the second with `mylinks[2]`, and so on.

> **Note:** Arrays in JavaScript operate somewhat differently from arrays that you might have encountered in other high-level languages such as C++. In reality, the arrays used in this example are objects, but JavaScript enables you to treat them like arrays. Refer to the JavaScript documentation provided by Netscape Communications for more information about the use of arrays.

To take advantage of the possibilities offered by arrays, you first need to create a small function known as a *constructor method*. This function is needed because arrays are really objects. The online JavaScript documentation listed in the preceding note provides additional information about how such a constructor should look. The `MakeArray()` constructor is based on a function created by Brenden Eich—the programmer at Netscape Communications responsible for the creation of JavaScript. Here is the `MakeArray()` function:

```
function MakeArray(n) {
// Initial concept Brenden Eich - Netscape Communications
   this.length = n;
   for (var i = 1; i <= n; i++)
      { this[i] = 0 }
   return this
   }
```

You need to include this function in your JavaScript code whenever you want to use arrays in a program. After the MakeArray() function has been defined, you can create the mylinks[] array discussed previously by writing

```
mylinks = new MakeArray( value )
```

in which *value* is the number of elements to be declared in the array.

> **Note:** As of 2.0b5, a built-in array constructor was included as a part of the JavaScript language. To use this constructor instead of MakeArray(), you would write mylinks = new Array(value). However, at this stage using the Array() function is somewhat problematic since it does not write the number of elements created for the array into element zero—mylinks[0]—as the MakeArray() constructor does.

You can then fill the mylinks[] array with values by simply assigning them as you would any other variable. Here's an example of an array with five elements with a URL assigned to each:

```
<SCRIPT LANGUAGE="JavaScript">
<!-- the contents of the script need to be hidden from other browsers

mylinks = new MakeArray( 5 ) ;

mylinks[1] = "http://www.netscape.com/" ;
mylinks[2] = "http://www.webcom.com/taketwo/" ;
mylinks[3] = "http://java.sun.com/" ;
mylinks[4] = "http://www.realaudio.com/" ;
mylinks[5] = "http://www.worlds.com/" ;
```

Now that you have a list of URLs defined, you'll modify the original picklink() function so that it selects a link by choosing from those included in the array, instead of by using if tests. Here is the new code:

```
function picklink() {
   linknumber = mylinks[0] ;
   randomnumber = Math.random() ;
   linkselect = Math.round( (linknumber-1) * randomnumber ) + 1 ;
   return mylinks[ linkselect ] ;
}
```

The first change you need to make deals with the value assigned to linknumber. In the previous examples, you set this value manually, but now you need to set it to the number of

elements in the `mylink[]` array. You do this by using the value stored automatically by the `MakeArray()` constructor in `mylinks[0]`. This element contains the number of elements in the array.

You should also have noticed that all the `if` tests from the earlier exercise have been removed, and a single `return mylinks[ linkselect ]` statement has been put in their place. This statement causes the value assigned to the element referenced by `mylinks[ linkselect ]` to be returned, `linkselect` being a random number between 1 and the value of `linknumber`.

It is important to note that you can consolidate the `picklink()` function even further by removing all the work variables and simply performing all the math inside the `return` statement, as shown here:

```
function picklink() {
    return mylinks[ ( Math.round( ( mylinks[0] - 1) * Math.random() ) + 1 ) ] ;
}
```

The Completed Random Link Script with an Array

Finally, incorporate all these changes into the document created in the earlier exercise, remembering to include the `MakeArray()` constructor function. If you are a little lost at this stage, you can use the following completed HTML document as a guide:

```
<HTML>
<HEAD>

<TITLE>Random Link Generator with an Array</TITLE>

<SCRIPT LANGUAGE="JavaScript">
<!-- the contents of the script need to be hidden from other browsers

mylinks = new MakeArray( 5 );

mylinks[1] = "http://www.netscape.com/" ;
mylinks[2] = "http://www.webcom.com/taketwo/" ;
mylinks[3] = "http://java.sun.com/" ;
mylinks[4] = "http://www.realaudio.com/" ;
mylinks[5] = "http://www.worlds.com/" ;

function picklink() {
    return mylinks[ ( Math.round( ( mylinks[0] - 1) * Math.random() ) + 1 ) ] ;
}

function MakeArray( n ) {
// Initial concept Brenden Eich - Netscape Communications
    this.length = n;
    for (var i = 1; i <= n; i++)
        { this[i] = 0 }
    return this ;
    }
```

```
// End of script -->
</SCRIPT>

<BODY>
<H1>My random link generator</H1>
Click <A HREF="dummy.html" onClick="this.href=picklink()">here</A>
 to visit a randomly selected site from my list of favorites.
</BODY>
```

Note: To add new links to your list, simply increase the `value` assigned by `new MakeArray( value )`, and add the new links to the list following the array elements already defined.

Exercise: Form Validation

In the second exercise in Chapter 17, "Forms and CGI," you created a form called The Surrealist Census, shown in Figure 20.2. When this form was submitted, the CGI script displayed a new Web page that listed the entries you selected.

Figure 20.2.

The Surrealist Census form from an exercise in Chapter 17.

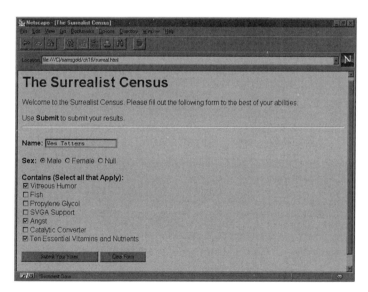

What the CGI script did not do, however, was check that you had entered values into all the fields—apart from telling you if you had not entered a name. All of this checking could be done with CGI scripts, but instead, take a look at how the Surrealist Census would be validated with JavaScript.

Whenever you click the submit button of a form, two events are triggered by Navigator 2.0: an onClick event and an onSubmit event. First, we'll look at the onSubmit event.

The onSubmit event is assigned as an attribute of the <FORM> tag, as shown here:

```
<FORM METHOD="POST"
      ACTION="../Web/cgi-bin/uncgi/census"
      onSubmit="return checkform( this )"
      NAME="surrealform" >
```

In this example, the value assigned to onSubmit is a call to a function named checkform()—which will be examined soon. But first, the return statement at the beginning of the onSubmit field and the this statement inside the checkform() function's parentheses need some further explanation.

First, the this statement. Whenever you call a function, you can send it a list of variables or objects or both. You do this by including them inside the function's parentheses. In the preceding example, the statement this is used to pass a reference to the form object associated with the current form.

Second, the return statement. This statement is used to transmit a value back to the internal Navigator 2.0 routine that called the onSubmit event handler. For example, if the checkform() function returns a value of false—after evaluating the form—the submission process will be halted by the return command transmitting this false value back to Navigator 2.0. If the return command was not included, the false value could be sent back to Navigator 2.0, and the submission process would occur even if problems were detected by the checkform() function.

And finally, the form has also been assigned a name using the NAME attribute. Doing so gives you a simple method of referencing the form inside a JavaScript script. Although naming the Surrealist Census form is not a necessary step to complete this particular example, it will become a regular feature of later examples so you should get used to seeing it now.

The Validation Script

As you have done before, define a <SCRIPT> tag inside the <HEAD> block and declare checkform() as a function. But this time, you also need to define a variable to receive the form object sent by the calling function, as mentioned previously. The code for the function declaration looks like this:

```
<SCRIPT>
<!-- start script here
function checkform( thisform ) {
```

In this example, the object representing the current form is assigned the name thisform by the checkform(thisform) statement. Through thisform, you can address all the fields, radio

buttons, check boxes, and buttons on the current form by treating each as a sub-object of
`thisform`.

The first test you want to make is whether a name has been entered in the Name: text box.
If you look at the `<INPUT>` tag for this field, you will recall that it was assigned a `NAME` attribute
of `theName`, as shown here:

```
<INPUT TYPE="TEXT" NAME="theName">
```

This is the name you use to reference the field as a sub-object of `thisform`. As a result, the field
`theName` can be referenced as `thisform.theName` and its contents as `thisform.theName.value`.

20

By using this information and an `if` test, it is a simple process to test the contents of `theName`
to see whether a name has been entered, by writing this:

```
if ( thisform.theName.value == null |¦ thisform.theName.value == "" ) {
    alert ("Please enter your name") ;
    thisform.theName.focus() ;
    thisform.theName.select() ;
    return false ;
}
```

> **Note:** The ¦¦ symbol shown in the `if` test of the previous example tells
> JavaScript to perform the actions enclosed by the braces if either of the two tests
> is true. As a result, the ¦¦ symbol is commonly known as the `OR` operator.

In the first line, `thisform.theName.value` is tested to see whether it contains a `null` value, or
whether it is empty (`""`). When a field is first created and contains no information at all, it
is said to contain a `null`, which is different from it being empty or containing just spaces.
If either of these situations is true, an `alert()` message is displayed, the cursor is repositioned
in the field by `thisform.theName.focus()`, the field is then highlighted by using
`thisform.theName.select()`, and the function is terminated by a `return` statement that is
assigned a value of `false`.

If a name has been entered, you next need to test whether a sex has been selected. You do this
by checking the value of `theName`. Because all the elements in a radio button set have the same
name, however, you need to treat them as an array. As a result, you can test the status value
of the first radio button by using `testform.theSex[0].status`, the second radio button by
using `testform.theSex[1].status`, and so on. If a radio button element is selected, the status
returns a value of `true`; otherwise, it returns a value of `false`.

To test that one of the `theSex` radio buttons has been selected, declare a new variable called
`selected` and give it a value of `false`. Now loop through all the elements using a `for` loop,

and if the `status` of any radio button is `true`, set `selected = true`. Finally, after you have finished the loop, if `selected` still equals `false`, display an `alert()` message and exit the function by calling `return false`. The code required to perform these tests is shown here:

```
var selected = false ;
for ( var i = 0; i <= 2 ; ++i ) {
   if ( testform.theSex[i].status == true )
      { selected = true }
   }
if ( selected == false ) {
   alert ("Please choose your sex") ;
   return false ;
}
```

Finally, if both of the tests pass successfully, call `return` with a value of `true` to tell Navigator 2.0 that it can proceed with the submission of the form:

```
   return true
}
```

The Completed Surrealist Census with JavaScript Validation

When the script discussed previously is integrated with the original Surrealist Census HTML document from the exercise "The Surrealist Census," the result is a Web form that tests its contents before they are transmitted to the CGI script for further processing. With this method, no data is sent to the CGI script until everything is correct, and if there is a problem, Navigator 2.0 takes care of informing the user of the difficulty. (See Figure 20.3.)

Figure 20.3.
If you don't enter your name, JavaScript will halt the submission process and ask you to type one.

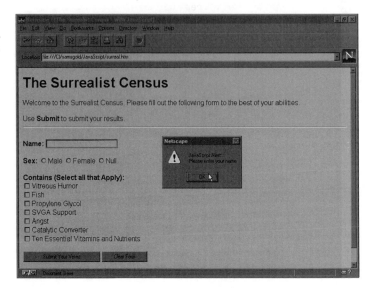

So that you don't need to flip back to the exercise in Chapter 17 to obtain the HTML source used when creating the form, here is the completed form with the full JavaScript code:

```html
<HTML>
<HEAD>
<TITLE>The Surrealist Census - With JavaScript</TITLE>
<SCRIPT LANGUAGE="JavaScript">
<!-- start script here
function checkform( thisform ) {
    if (thisform.theName.value == null || thisform.theName.value == "" ) {
        alert ("Please enter your name") ;
        thisform.theName.focus() ;
        thisform.theName.select() ;
        return false ;
    }
    var selected = false ;
    for ( var i = 0; i <= 2 ; ++i ) {
        if ( thisform.theSex[i].status == true )
            { selected = true }
        }
    if ( selected == false ) {
        alert ("Please choose your sex") ;
        return false ;
    }
    return true
}
// End of script -->
</SCRIPT>
</HEAD>

<BODY>
<H1>The Surrealist Census</H1>
<P>Welcome to the Surrealist Census. Please fill out the following
form to the best of your abilities.</P>
<P>Use <STRONG>Submit</STRONG> to submit your results.
<HR>
<FORM METHOD="POST"
      ACTION="../cgi-bin/uncgi/census"
      onSubmit="return checkform( this )" >
<P>
<STRONG>Name: </STRONG>
<INPUT TYPE="TEXT" NAME="theName">
</P>
<P>
<STRONG>Sex: </STRONG>
<INPUT TYPE="RADIO" NAME="theSex" VALUE="male">Male
<INPUT TYPE="RADIO" NAME="theSex" VALUE="female">Female
<INPUT TYPE="RADIO" NAME="theSex" VALUE="null">Null
</P>
<P>
<STRONG>Contains (Select all that Apply): </STRONG><BR>
<INPUT TYPE="CHECKBOX" NAME="humor">Vitreous Humor<BR>
<INPUT TYPE="CHECKBOX" NAME="fish">Fish<BR>
<INPUT TYPE="CHECKBOX" NAME="glycol">Propylene Glycol<BR>
<INPUT TYPE="CHECKBOX" NAME="svga">SVGA Support<BR>
```

```
<INPUT TYPE="CHECKBOX" NAME="angst">Angst<BR>
<INPUT TYPE="CHECKBOX" NAME="catcon">Catalytic Converter<BR>
<INPUT TYPE="CHECKBOX" NAME="vitamin">Ten Essential Vitamins and Nutrients<BR>
</P>
<P>
<INPUT TYPE="SUBMIT" VALUE="Submit Your Votes" >
<INPUT TYPE="RESET" VALUE="Clear Form" ></P>
</FORM>
<HR>
</BODY>
</HTML>
```

Exercise: Creating a Web Tour Guide

One of the more interesting possibilities offered by JavaScript is introduced through its capability to programmatically control the contents of a frame or frames. In the following exercise, you will learn how to use this capability to create a Web tour guide like the one shown in Figure 20.4.

Figure 20.4.

JavaScript can be used to control the presentation of pages inside a frame or frames.

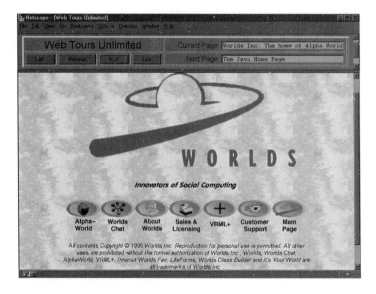

The top frame of Figure 20.4 contains buttons that enable people to take a guided tour of the World Wide Web by clicking the displayed navigation buttons. Whenever a navigation button is clicked, a new Web page is displayed in the frame at the bottom of the screen. At the same time, a description of the page currently being viewed is constantly displayed in the text box on the right of the screen, with a second text box below it showing the next destination of the tour.

The Tour Frameset

Before examining the JavaScript code, you first need to create a frameset document to describe the layout of the frames. Name this document `tourframe.html`, and add the following HTML code to it:

```
<HTML>
<HEAD>
<TITLE>Web Tours Unlimited</TITLE>
</HEAD>
<FRAMESET ROWS="20%, *">
<FRAME SRC="tourscript.html" NAME="tourtop">
<FRAME SRC="tourstart.html" NAME="tourbottom">
</FRAMESET>
```

The main difference you will probably notice between this example and the frameset examples included in Chapter 12, "Linked Windows and Frames," is the inclusion of a NAME attribute for each `<FRAME>` tag. Naming each frame gives you an easy method of addressing each frame from inside JavaScript.

The *tourstart.html* Document

When the Web tour first starts, the frameset needs to display a default page in the bottom frame. Create another new document, and name it `tourstart.html`. In this document, include the following text:

```
<HTML>
<HEAD>
<TITLE>Web Tours Unlimited</TITLE>
</HEAD>
<BODY>
<P><I>This tour is best viewed by first turning off your Web browser's
Toolbar and Location or Document URL line. </I></P>
Click start to begin the tour...
</BODY>
```

> **Tip:** If you had not wanted to display any information in the bottom frame, you could have made use of a special protocol in the `<FRAME>` tag called `about:blank`. In this case the frame definition would have looked like this:
>
> ```
> <FRAME SRC="about:blank" NAME="tourbottom">
> ```
>
> This tells Navigator 2.0 to display a blank page in much the same way as the `dummy.html` files used in Chapter 12.

The Form Details

The top frame of the frameset contains the `tourscript.html` document that looks after all the magic that makes the Web tour work. Before looking at the JavaScript itself, you'll create the table and form layout. To start, enter this basic HTML structural code:

```
<HTML>
<HEAD>
<TITLE> Web Tours Unlimited</TITLE>
</HEAD>
<BODY
BACKGROUND="http://home.netscape.com/assist/net_sites/bg/paper/peach_paper.gif"
BGCOLOR="PINK" >
```

Next, you need to define the `<FORM>` tag and `<TABLE>` definition that holds all the buttons and fields for the tour navigator. The table consists of five columns on two rows, and on the top row the first cell spans four columns. In addition, the form is assigned the name `tourform` by using the `NAME` attribute. Here is the basic structure for such a table:

```
<FORM NAME="tourform">
<TABLE WIDTH="100%" BORDER="3">
<TR> <!-- Start of row one -->
  <TD ALIGN="CENTER" COLSPAN=4> <BR> </TD>
  <TD ALIGN="RIGHT"> <BR> </TD>
</TR>
<TR ALIGN="CENTER">  <!-- Start of row two -->
  <TD WIDTH="10%"> <BR> </TD>
  <TD WIDTH="10%"> <BR> </TD>
  <TD WIDTH="10%"> <BR> </TD>
  <TD WIDTH="10%"> <BR> </TD>
  <TD ALIGN="RIGHT" WIDTH="*"> <BR> </TR>
</TABLE>
</FORM>
</BODY>
```

After you have defined and tested this basic layout—remembering to test it within the frameset as well— you are ready to add the buttons and other elements of the form, as shown here:

```
<FORM NAME="tourform">
<TABLE WIDTH="100%" BORDER="3">
<TR> <!-- Start of row one -->
  <TD ALIGN="CENTER"COLSPAN=4> <FONT SIZE=5>Web Tours Unlimited</FONT> </TD>
  <TD ALIGN="RIGHT">Current Page:
  <INPUT TYPE="text" NAME="currenturl" VALUE="Start Tour" SIZE=35></TD>
</TR>
<TR ALIGN="CENTER">  <!-- Start of row two -->
  <TD WIDTH="10%"><INPUT TYPE="button" VALUE="  Start  " onClick="firstlink()">
  </TD>
  <TD WIDTH="10%"><INPUT TYPE="button" VALUE="Previous" onClick="prevlink()">
  </TD>
  <TD WIDTH="10%"><INPUT TYPE="button" VALUE="  Next  " onClick="nextlink()">
  </TD>
```

```
    <TD WIDTH="10%"><INPUT TYPE="button" VALUE="  Last  " onClick="lastlink()">
    </TD>
    <TD ALIGN="RIGHT" WIDTH="*">Next Page:
    <INPUT TYPE="text" NAME="nexturl" VALUE="Start Tour" SIZE=35>
    </TR>
</TABLE>
</FORM>
</BODY>
```

At this stage, the only difference between this form and any of the other forms you have encountered previously is the addition of onClick handlers for each of the buttons. The button labeled Start calls a function named firstlink(). The one labeled Previous calls the prevlink() function. The nextlink() function is assigned to the button labeled Next. And finally, the button labeled Last calls the function lastlink().

The Script

With the <FORM> and <TABLE> blocks defined and tested, we'll return to the <HEAD> block and the <SCRIPT> definition. The first part of the script is very similar to the random links script in the earlier exercise called "A Random Link Generator Using an Event Handler." An array called mylinks[] is first defined with five elements, but this time, an additional array called mylinksnote[] is also declared with five elements, as shown here:

```
<SCRIPT LANGUAGE="JavaScript">
<!-- the contents of the script need to be hidden from other browsers
mylinks = new MakeArray(5);
mylinksnote = new MakeArray(5);
```

After the two arrays have been declared, they are loaded with a URL and corresponding description, like the ones shown next. You can include your own links or use these. Also, you can include extra links by increasing the value assigned in the new MakeArray(value) statement:

```
mylinks[1] = "http://www.netscape.com/" ;
mylinksnote[1] = "Netscape Communications" ;
mylinks[2] = "http://www.webcom.com/taketwo/" ;
mylinksnote[2] = "Take TWO home Page" ;
mylinks[3] = "http://www.worlds.net/" ;
mylinksnote[3] = "Worlds Inc: The home of Alpha World" ;
mylinks[4] = "http://java.sun.com/" ;
mylinksnote[4] = "The Java Home Page" ;
mylinks[5] = "http://www.realaudio.com/" ;
mylinksnote[5] = "RealAudio Home Page" ;
```

Finally, after all the URLs and descriptions have been defined, you need to declare a global work variable called currentlink. This variable will be used to keep track of the current location of the Web tour. You declare this variable by writing this:

```
var currentlink = 0;
```

The Navigation Functions

When you click any of the navigation buttons, its onClick handler calls a corresponding function.

The first of these functions is firstlink(). When firstlink() is called, the value of currentlink is set to 1, and a function named updatepage() is called. The code for the firstlink() function is as follows:

```
function firstlink() {
   currentlink = 1;
   updatepage() ;
}
```

> **Note:** As you will learn soon, updatepage() is what actually looks after the loading of each new page into the bottom form. In addition, it ensures that the correct notes are displayed in the Current Page and Next Page fields.

When the prevlink() function is called, the value of currentlink is decremented by 1 and a check is made to see whether the start of the tour has been reached. If this is the case, an alert message is displayed; otherwise, the updatepage() function is called to display the previous page of the tour.

The code required to perform these functions is shown here:

```
function prevlink() {
   if ( --currentlink < 1 ) {
      currentlink = 1 ;
      alert("Already at start of tour")
      }
   else {
       updatepage() ;
   }
}
```

When the nextlink() function is called, the value of currentlink is incremented by 1, and a check is made to see whether the end of the tour has been reached. If this is the case, an alert message is displayed; otherwise, the updatepage() function is called to display the next page of the tour.

The code required to perform these functions is shown here:

```
function nextlink() {
   if ( ++currentlink > mylinks[0] ) {
      currentlink = mylinks[0] ;
      alert("The tour is over")
   }
```

```
    else {
        updatepage() ;
    }
}
```

When the `lastlink()` function is called, the value of `currentlink` is set equal to the value of `mylinks[0]`, and then the `updatepage()` function is called to display the last page of the tour.

The code required to perform these functions is shown here:

```
function lastlink() {
    currentlink = mylinks[0] ;
    updatepage() ;
}
```

The *updatepage()* Function

As mentioned previously, the `updatepage()` function actually looks after the task of updating the contents of the bottom frame. It does this by setting the `location` property of the bottom frame. The `location` property contains the URL of the current document, displayed in either a frame or a main Web browser window. By altering the contents of this property, a new URL can be assigned to a frame or Web browser window. Doing so causes a new Web document to be loaded in place of the current one.

The `location` property of a frame can be addressed by using the statement `parent.frames[0].location`, which indicates the `location` property of the first frame of the current Web window, and `parent.frames[1].location`, the `location` property of second frame. Alternatively, you can also address a frame using the name assigned to it using the NAME attribute of its `<FRAME>` tag, which in the case of the bottom frame in this example is `tourbottom`. As a result, the bottom frame's `location` property can also be addressed by using `parent.tourbottom.location`.

Therefore, if you want to change the contents of the bottom frame to the URL pointed to by `mylinks[ currentlink ]`, you need to do only this:

```
function updatepage() {
    parent.tourbottom.location = mylinks[ currentlink ] ;
```

or alternatively this:

```
function updatepage() {
    parent.frames[1].location = mylinks[ currentlink ] ;
```

The `updatepage()` function also updates the contents of the `currenturl` and `nexturl` text fields by explicitly addressing them. You can access the contents of any field in a form by using the following:

```
document.forms[0].fieldname.value
```

where *fieldname* is replaced by the name of the field as defined by the forms `<INPUT>` tags, and `forms[0]` is the first form of the current Web document. As a result, the contents of the

currenturl and nexturl text fields can be found with `document.forms[0].currenturl.value` and `document.forms[0].nexturl.value`, respectively.

Alternatively, you can make use of the name assigned to the form by its NAME attribute, as discussed previously. In this case, you could use `document.tourform.currenturl.value` and `document.tourform.nexturl.value`.

Using this information, the code required to maintain the correct values for the currenturl and nexturl text fields is shown here:

```
document.tourform.currenturl.value = mylinksnote[ currentlink] ;
if (currentlink == mylinks[ 0 ] {
    document.tourform.nexturl.value = "Tour End"
    }
else {
    document.tourform.nexturl.value = mylinksnote[ currentlink + 1 ]
}
```

The Completed *tourscript.html* Document

To complete this exercise, listed after the note is the full text of the tourscript.html document, with the MakeArray() function added to permit the creation of mylinks[] and mylinksnote[]:

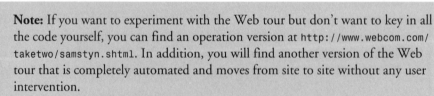

Note: If you want to experiment with the Web tour but don't want to key in all the code yourself, you can find an operation version at http://www.webcom.com/ taketwo/samstyn.shtml. In addition, you will find another version of the Web tour that is completely automated and moves from site to site without any user intervention.

```
<HTML>
<HEAD>
<SCRIPT LANGUAGE="JavaScript">
<!-- the contents of the script need to be hidden from other browsers
mylinks = new MakeArray(5);
mylinksnote = new MakeArray(5);
mylinks[1] = "http://www.netscape.com/" ;
mylinksnote[1] = "Netscape Communications" ;
mylinks[2] = "http://www.webcom.com/taketwo/" ;
mylinksnote[2] = "Take TWO home Page" ;
mylinks[3] = "http://www.worlds.net/" ;
mylinksnote[3] = "Worlds Inc: The home of Alpha World" ;
mylinks[4] = "http://java.sun.com/" ;
mylinksnote[4] = "The Java Home Page" ;
mylinks[5] = "http://www.realaudio.com/" ;
mylinksnote[5] = "RealAudio Home Page" ;
var currentlink = 0;
```

```
// Functions start here ---------------------------------------------
function firstlink() {
   currentlink = 1;
   updatepage() ;
}
function prevlink() {
  if ( --currentlink < 1 ) {
     currentlink = 1 ;
     alert("Already at start of tour")
  }
  else {
     updatepage() ;
  }
}
function nextlink() {
   if ( ++currentlink > mylinks[0] ) {
     currentlink = mylinks[0] ;
     alert("The tour is over")
   }
   else {
     updatepage() ;
   }
}
function lastlink() {
   currentlink = mylinks[0] ;
   updatepage() ;
}
function updatepage() {
   parent.tourbottom.location = mylinks[ currentlink ] ;
   document.tourform.currenturl.value = mylinksnote[ currentlink] ;
   if (currentlink == mylinks[ 0 ] ) {
      document.tourform.nexturl.value = "Tour End"
   }
   else {
      document.tourform.nexturl.value = mylinksnote[ currentlink + 1 ]
   }
}
function MakeArray( n ) {
// Initial concept Brenden Eich - Netscape Communications
   this.length = n;
   for (var i = 1; i <= n; i++)
      { this[i] = 0 }
   return this ;
   }
// End of script -->
</SCRIPT>

<BODY
 BACKGROUND="http://home.netscape.com/assist/net_sites/bg/paper/peach_paper.gif"
 BGCOLOR="PINK"
>
<FORM NAME="tourform">
<TABLE WIDTH="100%" BORDER="3">
<TR> <!-- start of row one -->
  <TD ALIGN="CENTER"COLSPAN=4>
  <FONT SIZE=5>Web Tours Unlimited</FONT>
```

```
   </TD>
   <TD ALIGN="RIGHT">Current Page:
   <INPUT TYPE="text" NAME="currenturl" VALUE="Start Tour" SIZE=35>
   </TD>
</TR> <!-- start of row two -->
<TR ALIGN="CENTER">
   <TD WIDTH="10%"><INPUT TYPE="button" VALUE=" Start   " onClick="firstlink()">
   </TD>
   <TD WIDTH="10%"><INPUT TYPE="button" VALUE="Previous" onClick="prevlink()">
   </TD>
   <TD WIDTH="10%"><INPUT TYPE="button" VALUE="  Next   " onClick="nextlink()">
   </TD>
   <TD WIDTH="10%"><INPUT TYPE="button" VALUE="  Last   " onClick="lastlink()">
   </TD>
   <TD ALIGN="RIGHT" WIDTH="*">Next Page:
   <INPUT TYPE="text" NAME="nexturl" VALUE="Start Tour" SIZE=35>
   </TR>
</TABLE>
</FORM>
</BODY>
```

The "Webtop" Calculator

The "Webtop" calculator, shown in Figure 20.5, is an example of what is possible with JavaScript and a little bit of ingenuity. In the following pages, you will find the HTML source code used to create this calculator. But for those of you who don't want to key in all the code yourself, a copy is available online at http://www.webcom.com/taketwo/samstyn.shtml.

Figure 20.5.
The "Webtop" calculator,
compliments of
JavaScript.

The "Webtop" JavaScript Code

First, you need to create the JavaScript for the "WebTop" calculator:

```
<HTML>
<HEAD>
<TITLE>The JavaScript Desktop Calculator</TITLE>
<SCRIPT LANGUAGE="LiveScript">
<!-- the contents of the script need to be hidden from other browsers
//These variables are the control registers for the calculator.
var register1 = 0      // The last value entered into the calculator
var register2 = 0      // Work variable when doing calculations
var operator1 = " "    // Last operator button selected
var operator2 = " "    // Last operator button selected - resets onClick
var memory1   = 0      // Value stored in memory

//This function maintains the contents of the calculator display window.
function setdisplay(form, value, opvalue ) {
   form.display.value = value ;
   form.display.focus() ;
   form.display.select() ;
   operator2 = opvalue ;
}

//This function is called whenever a number button is pushed
function numpush(input, character) {
 with input {    // all properties in the with block default to input object
   var testnum = checknum (value)
   if (testnum == false ¦¦ value == null ¦¦ value == "0" ¦¦ operator2 != " " ) {
      value = character ;
   }
   else {
      value += character ;
   }
 }
 operator2 = " " ;
}

//This function is called when the CE (Cancel Entry) button is pushed
function cepush( form ) {
   setdisplay( form, 0 , " " ) ;
}

//This function is called when the C (Cancel) button is pushed
function cancelpush(form) {
   register1 = 0 ;
   operator1 = " " ;
   setdisplay( form, 0 , "=" ) ;
}

//This function is called by mempush() when MC (memory cancel) is pushed
function mcpush(form) {
   form.memoryon.status = false ;
   memory1 = 0 ;
}
```

20

505

```
//This function is called by the onLoad event handler to reset the calculator
function reset( form ) {
   mcpush( form ) ;
   cancelpush( form ) ;
// form.memoryon.deselect() ;
}

//This function is called when an operator button is pushed. + - * / =
function oppush(form, opvalue) {
  if ( !checknum( form.display.value ) ) {
     cepush( form ) ;
     return ;
  }
//Check to see if calculation is needed
  if ( operator1 != " " ) {
     eqpush( form ) ;
  }
  register2 = parseFloat( form.display.value ) ;
  operator1 = opvalue ;
  register1 = register2 ;
  setdisplay( form, register1, opvalue ) ;
}

//This button is called by oppush() when an equals calculation is required
function eqpush(form) {
   if ( !checknum( form.display.value ) ) {
      cepush( form ) ;
      return ;
   }
   register2 = parseFloat( form.display.value ) ;
   if ( operator1 == "/" && register2 == 0 ) {
      alert("Divide by zero not permitted") ;
      cancelpush( form ) ;
      return ;
   }

// Perform calculations based on last operator set.
   if (operator1 == " ") {
      register1 = register2 ;
   }
   if (operator1 == "+") {
      register1 += register2 ;
   }
   if (operator1 == "-") {
      register1 -= register2 ;
   }
   if (operator1 == "*") {
      register1 *= register2 ;
   }
   if (operator1 == "/") {
      register1 /= register2 ;
   }
   setdisplay( form, register1 , " " ) ;
}
```

```
//This function is called when the +/- button is pushed
function signpush(input) {
    if (input.value.substring(0, 1) == "-") {
        input.value = input.value.substring(1, input.value.length)
    }
    else {
        input.value = "-" + input.value
    }
}

//This function is called when a memory button is pushed
function mempush(form, opvalue) {
    register2 = parseFloat( form.display.value ) ;
    if ( opvalue == "MC" ) {
        mcpush( form ) ;
    }
    if ( opvalue == "M+" ) {
        memory1 += register2 ;
    }
    if ( opvalue == "M-" ) {
        memory1 -= register2 ;
    }
    if ( opvalue == "MR" && memory1 != 0 ) {
        register2 = memory1 ;
    }
// Turn the memory checkbox on or off by setting its status
    if ( memory1 != 0 ) {
        form.memoryon.status = true ;
    }
    else {
        form.memoryon.status = false ;
    }
    setdisplay( form, register2 , opvalue ) ;
 }

//This function is used to check that form.display.value is a number
function checknum(str) {
    for (var i = 0; i < str.length; i++) {
        var ch = str.substring(i, i + 1)
        if ( ( ch < "0" ¦¦ ch > "9" ) && ch !="." && ch != "-" ) {
            alert("Please enter numbers only.") ;
            return false ;
        }
    }
    return true ;
}
// done hiding from browsers -->
</SCRIPT>
</HEAD>
```

The "Webtop" HTML Source Code

And now you need to define the HTML source code for the form and table that tie everything together:

```html
<BODY>
<H1 ALIGN=CENTER>The Java Script Desktop Calculator</H1>
<HR>
<FORM METHOD="POST" onLoad=reset( this )>  <!--  reset when form is loaded -->
<DIV ALIGN=CENTER >
<TABLE BORDER="5">

<!--  ROW 1    -->
<TR>
 <TD ALIGN="RIGHT" COLSPAN=4>
  <INPUT NAME="display" VALUE="0" ALIGN="RIGHT"> </TD>
 <TD ALIGN="CENTER" >
  Mem<INPUT TYPE="checkbox" NAME="memoryon" SIZE=3> </TD>
</TR>

<!--  ROW 2    -->
<TR ALIGN=CENTER>
 <TD><INPUT TYPE="button" VALUE=" 7 "
  onClick="numpush(this.form.display, '7')"> </TD>
 <TD><INPUT TYPE="button" VALUE=" 8 "
  onClick="numpush(this.form.display, '8')"> </TD>
 <TD><INPUT TYPE="button" VALUE=" 9 "
  onClick="numpush(this.form.display, '9')"> </TD>
 <TD><INPUT TYPE="button" VALUE=" + "
  onClick="oppush(this.form, '+')"> </TD>
 <TD><INPUT TYPE="button" VALUE=" MR "
  onClick="mempush(this.form, 'MR')"> </TD>
</TR>

<!--  ROW 3    -->
<TR ALIGN=CENTER>
 <TD><INPUT TYPE="button" VALUE=" 4 "
  onClick="numpush(this.form.display, '4')"> </TD>
 <TD><INPUT TYPE="button" VALUE=" 5 "
  onClick="numpush(this.form.display, '5')"> </TD>
 <TD><INPUT TYPE="button" VALUE=" 6 "
  onClick="numpush(this.form.display, '6')"> </TD>
 <TD><INPUT TYPE="button" VALUE=" - "
  onClick="oppush(this.form,'-')"> </TD>
 <TD><INPUT TYPE="button" VALUE=" M+ "
  onClick="mempush(this.form, 'M+')"> </TD>
</TR>

<!--  ROW 4    -->
<TR ALIGN=CENTER>
 <TD><INPUT TYPE="button" VALUE=" 1 "
  onClick="numpush(this.form.display, '1')"> </TD>
 <TD><INPUT TYPE="button" VALUE=" 2 "
  onClick="numpush(this.form.display, '2')"> </TD>
 <TD><INPUT TYPE="button" VALUE=" 3 "
```

```
  onClick="numpush(this.form.display, '3')"> </TD>
 <TD><INPUT TYPE="button" VALUE=" * "
  onClick="oppush(this.form, '*')"> </TD>
 <TD><INPUT TYPE="button" VALUE=" M- "
  onClick="mempush(this.form, 'M-')"> </TD>
</TR>

<!-- ROW 5   -->
<TR ALIGN=CENTER>
 <TD><INPUT TYPE="button" VALUE=" 0 "
  onClick="numpush(this.form.display, '0')"> </TD>
 <TD><INPUT TYPE="button" VALUE=" . "
  onClick="numpush(this.form.display, '.')"> </TD>
 <TD><INPUT TYPE="button" VALUE="+/-"
  onClick="signpush(this.form.display, '+-')"> </TD>
 <TD><INPUT TYPE="button" VALUE=" / "
  onClick="oppush(this.form, '/')"> </TD>
 <TD><INPUT TYPE="button" VALUE=" MC "
  onClick="mempush( this.form, 'MC' )"> </TD>
</TR>

<!-- ROW 6   -->
<TR ALIGN=CENTER>
 <TD COLSPAN=3><INPUT TYPE="button" VALUE="      =      "
   onClick="oppush(this.form, '=')"> </TD>
 <!-- COLSPAN -->
 <!-- COLSPAN -->
 <TD><INPUT TYPE="button" VALUE=" CE "
  onClick="cepush(this.form)"> </TD>
 <TD><INPUT TYPE="button" VALUE=" C "
  onClick="cancelpush(this.form)"> </TD>
</TR>
</TABLE>
</FORM>
</BODY>
</HTML>
```

Summary

JavaScript offers many exciting new possibilities for Web developers. In this chapter you have been given the opportunity to explore four possible applications of JavaScript.

But JavaScript is not the only way to write code for Web pages. Java—the big brother of JavaScript—adds even greater flexibility and capabilities to the Web publication environment. In the final chapter of this book, you will learn about how Java works and how it differs from other languages, including JavaScript.

Workshop

The first section of the Workshop lists some of the common questions people ask about the World Wide Web along with a brief answer to each. Next is a quiz about the chapter you have just read. If you have problems answering any of the questions in the quiz, you can turn to Appendix E, "Answers to Quiz Questions."

Q&A

Q Is there actually any difference between JavaScript and LiveScript?

A Yes there is, and as the JavaScript standard develops, the differences will increase considerably. For example, LiveScript is not case-sensitive, whereas JavaScript is case-sensitive. Currently, LiveScript code runs on Navigator 2.0, but you should make the effort to update any old code to JavaScript as soon as possible.

Q What about communicating with Java and plug-ins? I recall you mentioning it, so how do we do it?

A At this stage, some of the proposed JavaScript functions are not implemented in Navigator 2.0. Some might in fact be added before 2.0 goes into final release, but others, such as plug-in communications, might have to wait until Navigator 2.1. To find out what is and is not currently supported, check out the online documentation mentioned in Chapter 19.

Quiz

1. What does the `math.random()` function do?
2. When validating a form, how do you prevent the form from being submitted if there is an error?
3. What does the property `parent.frames[1].location` describe about a frame document?
4. How do you create an array in JavaScript?
5. What tag would you include an `onSubmit` handler in?

Exercise

If you're not already exercised out for this chapter, go back to `19notes.html` and add a set of hyperlinks to each HTML document created in this chapter.

You might also want to visit `http://www.webcom.com/taketwo/samstyn.shtml` and add links to each JavaScript demo maintained by this site.

21

Java

In the preceding two chapters, you learned about how scripting languages such as JavaScript can enhance the functionality of your Web pages, but for all its capabilities, JavaScript is still very much bound by the existing features of your Web browser. As the name in fact suggests, JavaScript is designed not as a programming language, but instead as a scripting language that enables you to control elements on your Web pages.

If, on the other hand, you are looking for a means to add new functionality to the World Wide Web, what you need to do is turn to Java itself—the language on which JavaScript is based. In this chapter you will learn about Java by examining the following topics:

☐   What is Java all about?

☐   Programming with Java

☐   Including Java applets on your Web pages

What Is Java All About?

Java was originally developed by a small, advanced projects team at Sun Microsystems, as part of a somewhat misdirected attempt to move into the mainstream consumer market. In its early days, Java—originally named OAK, reputedly after the tree outside its creator James Gosling's office window—was designed as the programming language for an interactive controller called a Portable Data Assistant (PDA).

What made this device unique was the fact that the technology it encompassed could be embedded into nearly any type of electronic consumer product. And by doing so—due to its built-in graphical user interface and of course OAK—the device could be programmed to perform any operation desired. For example, if used with a VCR, it could replace all the buttons and dials with a simple-to-use graphical display and touch screen that guided people through the steps required to set the time and program their favorite shows. At the lofty heights envisioned by the special projects team, there was no consumer product that could not benefit in some way from the PDA. It has been rumored that there was even a suggestion at one stage that an electric toaster with an infrared receiver could be programmed to deliver the perfect golden-brown piece of toast.

Unfortunately, this wonderful device somehow got lost in the hype surrounding the information superhighway. In its place, the special projects team, which by this stage was known as FirstPerson Inc., set its sights on the interactive set-top television market and the plans of companies such as TimeWarner who were considering such devices as a means of delivering Video on Demand and other interactive services through cable.

After many months of negotiations, however, the team was unable to close any deals with even one potential customer, and as a result, the future of FirstPerson and all the devices it had developed hung in the balance. Eventually, all of these projects were abandoned, but there was one resource whose potential had not been fully explored. This resource was the OAK language that had been at the heart of all the devices created by FirstPerson.

Programming the World Wide Web

By the time the activities of FirstPerson were being wound up, the Internet, and more specifically the World Wide Web, was rapidly becoming part of everyday life for companies such as Sun. It was at this time that Bill Joy—one of Sun's cofounders— realized that OAK was an ideal language for the Internet and the World Wide Web.

As a result, after some prodding, James Gosling and Patrick Naughton, who was the catalyst for the original FirstPerson project, began to form OAK into the ultimate Internet development environment. Then, as if to signal the final death of FirstPerson, OAK was renamed Java, and the language now found in Navigator 2.0 was born.

The Java Language

But enough history. What exactly is Java, and why would you want to use it?

At its heart, Java is an object-orientated programming language similar to C++. Unlike C++, however, Java was designed with one unique capability. In the Internet world, there are various computer platforms, all of which use different operating systems and require programs written in languages such as C++ to be specially crafted to suit their individual needs. As a result, you cannot simply take a C++ program written for a Macintosh computer and run it on your Windows 95–based PC.

Java, on the other hand, was designed so that you can do just that—write a program once and have it run on many different computer platforms. To achieve this goal, Java programs are compiled into what is called an *architecture-neutral byte-code*. What this basically means is that the programs are platform nonspecific. When in this architecture-neutral form, Java programs can be run on any computer platform that supports what is called a Java runtime.

Currently, Java runtime modules are available for Windows 95, Windows NT, and a small number of UNIX-based X Window systems, including HP-UX, SGI IRIX, SunOS 4.1, and Sun Solaris 2.3 or 2.4. But with the introduction of Navigator 2.0, this base is set to grow rapidly to include the Apple Macintosh and most of the other UNIX derivatives.

Distributed Programming

The second major feature of Java is the one that makes it such a viable tool for use with the World Wide Web. To use the technical definition, Java is a distributed language.

What this really means is that through the Internet, Java programs can be transferred from computer system to computer system without any intervention by the user or, because of its application-neutral technology, any concern about the type of computer system it is being sent to.

When this capability is incorporated into a Web browser such as Navigator 2.0, the true power of Java becomes apparent. Take, for example, the c|net home page shown in Figure 21.1. The small window at the top of this page titled "c|net news-top stories" contains a window a lot like a ticker tape display. In this window, headlines for all the latest-breaking Internet news are scrolled across the window from right to left.

Figure 21.1.

c\net uses Java to create its online ticker tape displays.

You might have noticed, however, that there has been no mention throughout this book of such a feature in HTML. That's because currently there is no such capability. So how does c|net make this magic work? Or more important, how do you make it work on your Web browser?

Note: The Microsoft Web browser Internet Explorer does include an extension to HTML that adds an element called <MARQUE>. This element creates a scrolling area on a Web page, but it lacks many of the features available when you code such a window in Java.

To add the ticker tape display to their Web pages, the developers at c|net wrote a small Java program. This program draws the ticker tape window on the Web page and looks after scrolling the messages. On its own such a feat is not that amazing because you have already seen how Navigator 2.0 uses plug-ins to add functionality to a Web page.

What places Java in a world all its own, however, is that unlike the plug-ins you have already seen—which must be installed on a user's computer before they can be displayed on Web pages that support them—when a Java program or *applet* is included as part of a Web page, the applet is automatically transferred and installed on the computer in question, without any user intervention.

What Can Java Be Used For?

Basically, there is very little limitation to the possible applications for Java applets and Java-based applications. To this extent, Sun has even created a Web browser called HotJava that was written entirely using the Java language.

> **Note:** Java programs generally fall into one of two specific categories: *Java applets*, which are designed to be embedded inside a Web page, and *Java applications*, which are standalone Java programs. These programs are fully self-contained and don't run within a Web browser at all.

In fact, about the only real limitation imposed by Java is the imaginations of Web developers. And if the crop of Java applets that have sprung up since the launch of Navigator 2.0 is any indication, some very imaginative minds are at play on the World Wide Web.

Blue Skies Weather Underground

Take, for example, the Blue Skies Weather Underground, operated by the University of Michigan. (See Figure 21.2.) This site represents one of the best current examples of the incredible interactive capabilities that Java brings to the World Wide Web. The weather maps and the various gadgets surrounding it in Figure 21.2 are all part of a single Java applet, which enables you to view the current weather report for major cities by highlighting them with the cursor. In addition, by clicking various regions of the map, you can zoom in for a close-up look at individual weather patterns, or alternatively, you can view a movie of the weather pattern for the past 24 hours.

What makes this service so amazing is that it all happens within one easy-to-use screen. Without Java, you would probably need many hundreds of separate Web pages to create a similar service, and even with all these pages, you would still not be able to easily duplicate some features, including the line-drawn U.S. maps over the satellite images that are created on-the-fly by Java itself.

Figure 21.2.

View the latest weather maps for the mainland United States by using Java and Blue Skies.

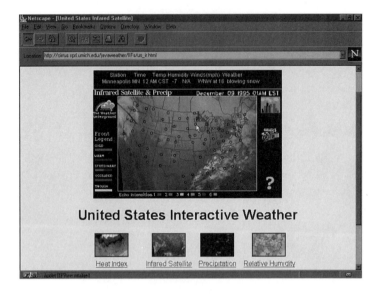

To experiment with the features offered by the Blue Skies service, point your Web browser to http://cirrus.sprl.umich.edu/javaweather/.

Gamelan

To give yourself an even better idea of the possibilities offered by Java, point your Web browser to http://www.gamelan.com/, as shown in Figure 21.3. This site contains the most up-to-date directory of sites using Java. It also includes a large collection of applets that demonstrate the wide variety of reasons people are starting to incorporate Java into their Web pages—here are a few examples:

- ☐ Online games
- ☐ Enhanced graphics, including multicolored and animated text
- ☐ Interaction with 3D tools such as VRML
- ☐ Simulations
- ☐ Spreadsheets and advanced mathematical calculations
- ☐ Real-time information retrieval

Figure 21.3.

Gamelan is regarded as the repository for Java applets.

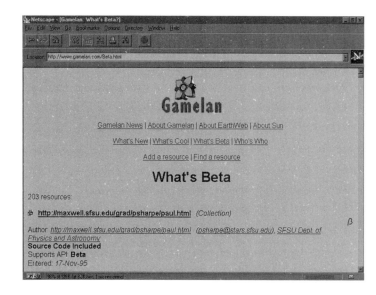

Netscape and Sun

Apart from Gamelan, both Netscape and Sun also operate their own directories of Java applets along with a wide variety of related information. To visit the Netscape directory shown in Figure 21.4, use `http://home.netscape.com/comprod/products/navigator/version_2.0/java_applets/index.html`. This index contains pointers to all the latest Netscape-related Java information, along with some of the more popular Java applets.

Figure 21.4.

Netscape is another good source of information about Java and its capabilities.

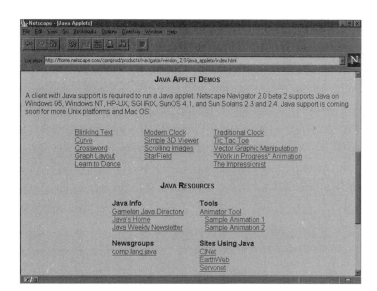

To provide even more information about Java, Sun has set up an entire Web site devoted just to the subject, as shown in Figure 21.5. This site contains up-to-the-minute details covering all aspects of Java development and usage, and it is also the primary source for Java development tools and documentation.

Figure 21.5.

http://java.sun.com/ is the home of Java.

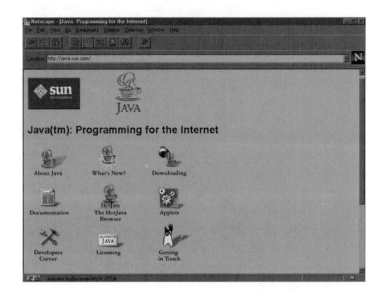

Programming with Java

Due to the size and complexity of the issues involved in using a programming language like Java to its fullest advantage, dealing with all the intricacies of Java programming is beyond the scope of this book. Therefore, instead of dealing with the actual programming techniques involved, in this section you will work through the creation of a simple ticker tape display like the one shown previously in Figure 21.1. In this way, you'll get a better idea of what Java is all about.

For those of you who are keen to learn more about the internals of Java, a copy of the complete Java documentation written by Sun Microsystems has been included on the CD-ROM accompanying this book. To view this documentation you will first need to install a copy of the Adobe Acrobat reader—also available on the CD-ROM in both Macintosh and Windows versions.

Note: For a full discussion of Java programming, refer to *Presenting Java* and *Teach Yourself Java Programming*, also by Sams.net Publishing.

The Java Developers Kit (JDK)

But first, before you begin creating your own Java applets, you must get a copy of the current version of the Java Developers Kit, known currently as the Java 1.0 JDK. This kit contains all the tools required to compile Java applets, the most up-to-date libraries (called *classes*), a standalone applet viewer to test your applets without the need for Navigator 2.0, and a debugging utility to help in locating problems in your Java code.

Note: In object-oriented terms, the class is the basic structural framework for all program design. A class is a bit like a library of prebuilt instructions, or a template that you can enhance to create new classes and entire applications. Although it is not vitally important that you understand all the concepts surrounding object-orientated design and development as you start to use Java, you might find it very handy to get a good book on the subject.

One such book is *Object-Orientated Analysis and Design with Applications*, by Grady Booch, Published by Benjamin/Cummings Publishing Company. Alternatively, you might check out *An Introduction to Object-Oriented Programming*, by Timothy Budd, Published by Addison-Wesley Publishing Company. Or you can read *Object-Oriented Technology: A Manager's Guide*, by David A. Taylor, Ph.D., published by Servio Corporation.

21

To get a copy of the JDK for your particular computer system, point your Web browser to `http://java.sun.com/JDK-1.0/index.html`, as shown in Figure 21.6. Sun currently provides JDKs for Windows 95, Windows NT, and SPARC/Solaris 2.3, 2.4, or 2.5 systems. JDKs for other systems, including the Apple Macintosh, are expected in the near future.

Note: An alternative method for compiling Java applets is provided by the Black Star Public Java Compiler—`http://mars.blackstar.com/`. This site operates a Web page where you can submit Java programs for compilation. For any serious use, however, you really do need to install the JDK on your local computer.

Figure 21.6.

To create Java applets, you must install a copy of the Java Developers Kit on your computer.

Exercise: Creating a Ticker Tape Applet

After you have downloaded the appropriate JDK, you need to unpack the archive file as described on the JDK Web pages or in the documentation included with the JDK archive. Then you should be ready to start building your first Java applet.

You can write Java programs by using a simple text editor, or alternatively, you might want to use a program editor of some sort. It really does not matter what you use, because Java source code is plain text.

Under Windows 95, however, I currently use a program called PFE (shown in Figure 21.7), which can be obtained from `http://www.lancs.ac.uk/people/cpaap/pfe/`. The one advantage of using a program like this over using a normal text editor is that you can perform actions such as compiling your code from inside the editor itself instead of having to starting a separate MS-DOS shell.

After choosing your editor, create a new directory to hold your Java applets. Start the editor and create a new file called `Ticker.java`. (Be sure to include the capital *T* because Java is case-sensitive.)

Figure 21.7.
Program editors can control repetitive tasks such as compiling your Java code.

Java Framework

At its heart, Java is an object-orientated language. As a result, when you are working with Java applets, you are really adding functionality to the basic applet framework defined in the JDK. For this reason, the basic structure of all Java applets looks almost identical.

The basic framework for the Ticker Tape applet looks like this:

```
/* Exercise - Ticker.class */
import java.applet.*;
import java.awt.* ;
public class Ticker extends Applet implements Runnable {
    Additional functionality goes in here.
}
```

The first line is simply a comment line that describes the name of the Java applet. Any text enclosed between a /* symbol and a corresponding */ symbol is treated as a comment and is ignored by the compiler.

The next two lines of code—the ones starting with `import`—are used to tell the compiler about any additional class libraries that will be used by your applet. All applets need to use routines from the `java.applet.*` library, and to display information onscreen you also need routines from the Advanced Windows Toolkit, as defined by `java.awt.*`.

The fourth line of text is the one that does all the work of defining your new class as an applet. In this line, you declare the name for your new class—`public class Ticker`. You tell the system which existing class it is based on—`extends applet`. And because the Ticker Tape applet will need to run continually, you define a special package called Runnable by using `implements Runnable`.

Caution: Make sure that you type the word `Ticker` in exactly the same way as you did when naming the `Ticker.java` text file. If the two names are not identical (case-wise), Java will report an error when you attempt to compile the program.

Declaring Variables

Immediately after the class definition, you first need to define some variables for the applet to use. Like most object-oriented languages, Java is a typed language. As a result, you must declare the type of information that a variable will hold before it can be used.

To declare all the variables that will be accessible to the entire class, make the following entry after the class declaration:

```
public class Ticker extends Applet implements Runnable {
    Thread tkthread = null;      /* Thread handle needed for  multitasking */
    String tktext = "Exercise - ticker tape";          /* Default text    */
    int tkspd = 1;             /* The default scroll speed  (slowest is 1 ) */
    String tkfname = "TimesRoman";                /* The default font name   */
    int tkfsz = 12;                         /* The default font size    */
    Font tkfont = null;            /* Font handle for graphics library   */
    String tkdirection = "Left";        /* The default scroll direction   */
    Dimension tksize = null              /* Window dimension handle   */
    int tktextwth = 0;                         /* Text width value   */
    int tktexthgt = 0;                         /* Text height value   */
    int tkpos = -63000;                    /* Scroll position    */
```

The *init()* Method

Inside every class, there can be any number of different routines called *methods*. These methods are used to control specific actions that can be taken by a class.

For every class, the first method called when the class is run (or instantiated) is the `init()` method. This method is used to set up default information for the class and to load variables like those just defined with working values. In the base applet class, an `init()` method is declared already; however, because you want to add additional functionality to the applet class, you need to override the base `init()` method with a new one of your own.

To define the `init()` method for Ticker and set up all the control variables, you write the following code:

Note: The comment lines included in this code are not required to make Ticker operate. They simply explain what each line does. If you are following along with this exercise, you need not include all the comments. Also, you might find it easier to refer to the completed example at the end of the exercise, which has all the comments removed.

Alternatively, you can download the complete source for this exercise from
http://www.webcom.com/taketwo/samstyn.shtml.

```
/* Declare the init() method    */
public void init() {

/* Declare a working variable for this method only              */
   String getval = null;

/* Retrieve the text to be displayed by Ticker                  */
/* as defined in the HTML document                              */
   getval = getParameter("tktext");
/* If no text is defined, revert to the default message         */
   tktext = (getval == null ) ? tktext : getval;

/* Retrieve the scroll speed for Ticker                         */
/*as defined in the HTML document                               */
   getval = getParameter("tkspd");
/* If no speed is defined, revert to the default speed        */
   tkspd = (getval == null ) ? tkspd : (Integer.valueOf(getval).intValue());

/* Retrieve the font for Ticker */
/* as defined in the HTML document                              */
    getval = getParameter("tkfname");
/* If no font is defined, revert to the default font          */
   tkfname = (getval == null) ? tkfname : getval ;

/* Retrieve the font size for Ticker   */
/* as defined in the HTML document     */
   getval = getParameter("tkfsz");
/* If no font size is defined, revert to the default size       */
   tkfsz = (getval == null ) ? tkfsz : (Integer.valueOf(getval).intValue());

/* Create a font class based on the font name and font size     */
   tkfont = new java.awt.Font( tkfname, Font.PLAIN, tkfsz ) ;

/* Check to see if the Reverse parameter has been set.          */
/* If not, set tkdirection to Left                              */
/* and tkpos to a large negative number                       */
/* Otherwise, set tkdirection to Right                          */
/* and tkpos to a large positive number.                     */
   getval = getParameter("tkreverse");

   tkdirection = "Left";
   tkpos = -63000 ;
```

```
    if ( getval != null ) {
        if ( getval.equalsIgnoreCase( "Yes") ) {
            tkdirection = "Right";
            tkpos  = 63000;
            }
        }

/* Set the background color for the applet window to white          */
    this.setBackground( Color.white )

}
```

> **Caution:** Be sure to include all the opening ({) and closing (}) brackets where listed. These curly brackets, or braces, are used by Java to indicate the start and finish of blocks of code, and without them, Java will get very confused indeed.

The *start()* and *stop()* Methods

The start() and stop() methods are called when a class is first started and when the class is stopped, as the names suggest.

In this exercise, the start() method needs to be overridden to define Ticker as a self-contained task, one that operates independently of all other activities on your computer. This action allows your operating system to better share its resources among all the programs that are currently running. If this is not done, there is a danger that a routine like Ticker could have a serious impact on the performance of other programs.

However, after you do define Ticker as a task, or thread of its own, you need a way to stop it from running when the applet is no longer needed. To do this, in the stop() method, you include a specific call to the thread to halt its execution.

The code required to perform the start and stop tasks is shown here:

```
/* Declare the start() method                                     */
public void start() {

/* Define a new Thread for this task                              */
    tkthread = new Thread(this);
/* start Ticker running as an independent task                    */
    tkthread.start();
}

/* Declare the stop() method                                      */
    public void stop() {

/* stop the Ticker thread running                                 */
    tkthread.stop();
}
```

The *run()* Method

In the class definition at the start this exercise, you might recall the statement `implements Runnable`. What this statement actually does is define a template for a special method that gets called after the applet has been loaded, and following the `init()` and `start()` methods. If you have any computer programming experience, you'll find that the `run()` method is a bit like a `main()` subroutine.

For everyone else, at this stage all you really need to understand is that this method contains a loop of code that causes the Java screen to be continually redrawn. Each time it gets redrawn, the text in the Ticker window is moved a step to either the left or the right.

The code for the `run()` method looks like this:

```
/* Declare the run() method                                      */
public void run() {
/* Set the multitasking priority of Ticker to the lowest value   */
    Thread.currentThread().setPriority(Thread.MIN_PRIORITY);

/* Create an infinite loop that continually repaints the Java screen   */
    while (true) {

/* Send Ticker to sleep so that other programs can get some work done   */
        try {Thread.sleep( 10 ); } catch (InterruptedException e) {}

/* Whenever Ticker wakes up, repaint the contents of the Java applet window */
        repaint();
        }
    }
```

The *paint()* Method

The final method for this exercise is the `paint()` method. Whenever the `repaint()` statement in the `run()` method is reached—each time through the `while` loop—the `paint()` method is the main method that gets run. The `paint()` method is where all the tricky stuff happens to make the text scroll across the screen.

In Java terms, the `paint()` method is where you draw information onto the Java *canvas*, which is a fancy name for the drawing area of a Java applet. The `paint()` method for Ticker looks like this:

```
/* Declare the paint method                                      */
/* Unlike the other methods, this one receives some information from the   */
/* calling routine. This information is assigned to a graphics    */
/* class called tk.                                               */
public void paint(Graphics tk) {

/* Get the size of the Java canvas                                */
/* and assign it to a dimension class called tksize.              */
    tksize = size();
```

```
/* Set the font to use to the one defined in the init() method,         */
/* and then get its specs                                               */

    tk.setFont(tkfont);
    FontMetrics tkfm = tk.getFontMetrics();

/* Calculate the height in pixels of the text,                          */
/* the first time through the paint method                              */
/* After this, use the previously calculated value.                     */
    tktexthgt = ( tktexthgt==0 ) ? tkfm.getHeight() : tktexthgt;

/* Calculate the width in pixels of the text message                    */
/* the first time through the paint method                              */
/* After this, use the previously calculated value                      */
    tktextwth = ( tktextwth==0 ) ? tkfm.stringWidth( tktext ) : tktextwth;

/* If the scroll direction is set to Left,                              */
/* use the first set of calculations to determine the                   */
/* new location for the text in this pass through paint().              */
/* Otherwise, use the set of calculations following the else statement. */
    if (tkdirection=="Left") {
        tkpos = ( tkpos <= tktextwth * -1 ) ? tksize.width : tkpos - tkspd;
        }
    else{
        tkpos = ( tkpos > tksize.width ) ? 0 - tktextwth : tkpos + tkspd;
        }
/* Set the text color to black                                          */
    tk.setColor(Color.black);
/* Draw the message in its new position on the Java canvas              */
    tk.drawString( tktext, tkpos, ( tksize.height + tktexthgt ) / 2 );
    }
```

Putting It All Together

As promised earlier, here is the completed Ticker applet, ready to be compiled. All the comments except the one on the first line have been removed, and any unnecessary line spacing is gone as well. The indentations, however, have been left in as a guide to how the various components are related. When you write Java code, using indentation to indicate the separate blocks of text is a very good way of cross-checking that no { or } symbols have been left out:

```
/* Exercise - Ticker.class */
import java.applet.*;
import java.awt.* ;

public class Ticker extends Applet implements Runnable {
    Thread tkthread = null;
    String tktext = "Exercise - ticker tape";
    int tkspd = 1;
    String tkfname = "TimesRoman";
    int tkfsz = 12;
    Font tkfont = null;
    String tkdirection = "Left";
    Dimension tksize = null;
    int tktextwth = 0;
```

```java
        int tktexthgt = 0;
        int tkpos = -63000;

public void init() {
    String getval = null;
    getval = getParameter("tktext");
    tktext = (getval == null ) ? tktext : getval;
    getval = getParameter("tkspd");
    tkspd = (getval == null ) ? tkspd : (Integer.valueOf(getval).intValue());
    getval = getParameter("tkfname");
    tkfname = (getval == null) ? tkfname : getval ;
    getval = getParameter("tkfsz");
    tkfsz = (getval == null ) ? tkfsz : (Integer.valueOf(getval).intValue());
    tkfont = new java.awt.Font( tkfname, Font.PLAIN, tkfsz ) ;
    getval = getParameter("tkreverse");
    tkdirection = "Left";
    tkpos  =  -63000 ;
    if ( getval != null ) {
        if ( getval.equalsIgnoreCase( "Yes") ) {
            tkdirection = "Right";
            tkpos  = 63000;
            }
        }
    this.setBackground( Color.white );
    }

public void start() {
    tkthread = new Thread(this);
    tkthread.start();
    }

public void stop() {
    tkthread.stop();
    }

public void run() {
    Thread.currentThread().setPriority(Thread.MIN_PRIORITY);
    while (true) {
      try {Thread.sleep( 10 ); } catch (InterruptedException e){}
      repaint();
      }
    }

public void paint(Graphics tk) {
    tksize = size();
    tk.setFont(tkfont);
    FontMetrics tkfm = tk.getFontMetrics();
    tktexthgt = ( tktexthgt==0 ) ? tkfm.getHeight() : tktexthgt;
    tktextwth = ( tktextwth==0 ) ? tkfm.stringWidth( tktext ) : tktextwth;
    if (tkdirection=="Left") {
        tkpos = ( tkpos <= tktextwth * -1 ) ? tksize.width : tkpos - tkspd;
    }
    else{
        tkpos = ( tkpos > tksize.width ) ? 0 - tktextwth : tkpos + tkspd;
    }
```

```
      tk.setColor(Color.black);
      tk.drawString( tktext, tkpos, ( tksize.height + tktexthgt ) / 2 );
      }
}
```

Compiling *Ticker.java*

After you have entered the code for `Ticker.java` into your text editor and saved a copy onto your hard drive, the next step in the process is compiling it into Java Byte code.

To do this from either the DOS prompt or the UNIX command line, enter this:

```
javac Ticket.java
```

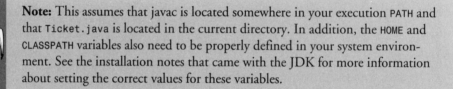

> **Note:** This assumes that javac is located somewhere in your execution PATH and that `Ticket.java` is located in the current directory. In addition, the HOME and CLASSPATH variables also need to be properly defined in your system environment. See the installation notes that came with the JDK for more information about setting the correct values for these variables.

If everything goes as planned, after a few seconds—or minutes, depending on the speed of your computer—your cursor will return to the command line, and a new file called `Ticker.class` will have been created in the current directory.

On the other hand, if the javac compiler detects any errors, you will see something that looks a bit like this:

```
C:\samsgold\java>javac Ticker.java
Ticker.java:15: ';' expected.
        Dimension tksize = null
                               ^
Ticker.java:49: ';' expected.
        this.setBackground( Color.white )
                                         ^
2 errors
```

The number following the colon indicates the line where the problem occurred, and the message after the number indicates the reason for the error. On the following line, the source for the problem line is displayed with a caret (^) indicating the fault's position in the line.

If you did receive any errors, go back and re-edit `Ticker.java` to fix the problems, and then try recompiling the applet. When you have a "good" compile of `Ticker.class`, you are ready to add the applet to your Web pages.

Learning More About Java

The fact that Java is a language that until very recently was somewhat unstable, to say the least, has made the job of writing a definitive text covering all the features of Java something akin to hitting a moving target. Luckily, however, things are now starting to change, following the freeze of the Java specification at Version 1.0, in part, to synchronize with the release of Navigator 2.0 the documentation and specifications for Java are now reasonably stable.

As a result of this stabilization, some very good tutorial documents, including the entire Java 1.0 API specification, are available online from Sun's Java Web site. To view any of this documentation or download a copy in either postscript or HTML form, point your Web browser to `http://java.sun.com/doc/programmer.html`, as shown in Figure 21.8.

Figure 21.8.

`http://java.sun.com/doc/programmer.html` is a very good source of information about writing Java applets and applications.

Including Java Applets on Your Web Pages

After you have your new applet compiled, the next thing you will want to do is include it on a Web page to test it. In the final section of this chapter, you will learn how to include the Ticker Tape applet on a Web page and how to include prebuilt applets written by other people, as well.

21

The *<APPLET>* Tag

When the <APPLET> tag is used on a Web page that is to be viewed using Navigator 2.0, it takes the following form:

```
<APPLET CODE="name.class" WIDTH=pixels HEIGHT=pixels></APPLET>
```

In the CODE attribute, you place the name of the Java class to be run, and in the WIDTH and HEIGHT attributes, you *must* declare the width and height of the drawing area (or canvas) to be used by the applet. In the current version of Navigator 2.0, if you do not include the WIDTH and HEIGHT attributes, the applet will not appear on the Web page at all.

Based on this information, you could include the Ticker Tape applet in a Web page by writing this:

```
<APPLET CODE="Ticker.class" WIDTH=400 HEIGHT=75></APPLET>
```

In this basic form, when you loaded the Web page, the Ticker applet would be displayed by using the default values set in the init() method discussed previously.

Note: So that your Web browser can locate the applet code, place the Ticker.class file in the same directory as the Web page.

The *<PARAM>* Tag

In the init() method of Ticker.class, several calls were made to a method called getParameter(). What this call actually does is interrogate the <APPLET> tag, looking for parameters that match the name declared in the getParameter() call, as shown here:

```
getval = getParameter("tktext");
tktext = (getval == null ) ? tktext : getval;
```

In this example, getParameter("tktext") tells Java to look for a parameter called tktext between the <APPLET> and </APPLET> tags. If such a value is located, the text associated with the parameter, rather than the default message text, is scrolled through the ticker tape window.

To define tktext as a parameter inside the <APPLET> tags, you use the <PARAM> tag, which takes the following form:

```
<PARAM NAME="tktext" VALUE="Exercise - Scroll this text in the Ticker Tape
➥window">
```

When used inside the <PARAM> tag, the NAME attribute is assigned the parameter name, and the VALUE attribute is assigned the information to be passed to the applet.

If you take a closer look at the `init()` code, you'll see four other parameters that can also be set for `Ticker.class`:

NAME="tkspd"—Sets the scroll speed; 1 is the slowest value.

NAME="tkfname"—Sets the font name; Times Roman is the default.

NAME="tkfsz"—Sets the font size; 12 point is the default.

NAME="tkreverse"—Reverses the scroll direction.

By combining these attributes, you can tailor the appearance of the ticker tape window in various ways. For example, when the attributes are used as shown in the following HTML source, the result is a Web page like the one shown in Figure 21.9:

```
<HTML>
<HEAD>
<TITLE>Exercise - Ticker.class</TITLE>
</HEAD>
<BODY>
<H1>Ticker Tape Java Exercise</H1>
<HR>
<P ALIGN=CENTER>
<APPLET CODE="Ticker.class" width=400 height=50>
<PARAM NAME="tktext"
       VALUE="Exercise - Scroll this text in the Ticker Tape window">
<PARAM NAME="tkspd"    VALUE="1">
<PARAM NAME="tkfname"   VALUE="Arial">
<PARAM NAME="tkfsz"     VALUE="28">
<PARAM NAME="tkreverse" VALUE="Yes">
</APPLET>
</P>
<HR>
</BODY>
</HTML>
```

Figure 21.9.
Ticker.class adds a scrolling ticker tape window to your Web pages.

Building on the Ticker Example

With a little extra work, you can add many other features to `Ticker.class`, if you want to. These could include parameters to control the color of the text or background, the capability to display text from a separate HTML document in the ticker tape window, or even fancy borders like those in the ticker tape window shown in Figure 21.1, at the start of this chapter.

You might be surprised to hear that some good examples of enhanced Ticker Tape classes are already available for download from sites on the World Wide Web—saving you the hassle of coding all these features yourself. To locate most of these sites, take a look at the Gamelan directory mentioned previously—`http://www.gamelan.com/`.

Note: Many of the Java classes currently available include source code you can freely use in your own applets. Before using anyone else's code, however, check the copyright requirements the author expects you to meet. Some authors ask for mention and possibly a hyperlink to their site, whereas others expect nothing.

Using Prebuilt Java Applets

If you're starting to feel as though this Java thing is a bit beyond you—maybe the preceding pages look more like a Chinese lottery ticket to you than a computer program—or you just feel as though you don't have the time to spend learning all its intricacies, you might be interested in an alternative method of using Java. This method provides many of the benefits without most of the programming hassles.

The distributed nature of Java means that it is possible to incorporate Java applets that have been developed by other people into your Web pages. In addition, in some cases you don't even need a copy of the Java class on your own computer; you only need to know where it is located.

For example, an enhanced version of the Ticker Tape class you learned about previously is stored on my Web site at `http://www.webcom.com/taketwo/TickerT.class`. To use this class in your own Web pages, you have two options. You can download the class by using FTP and install it at your own Web site. Or you can simply include the location of the class as part of your `<APPLET>` tag. If used in this second form, the `<APPLET>` tag will look something like this:

```
<APPLET CODE="TickerT.class" CODEBASE="http://www.webcom.com/taketwo/"
➥HEIGHT="30" WIDTH="400" >
```

The difference between this example and previous ones is in the inclusion of the CODEBASE attribute, which contains a URL that describes the location of the directory where the Ticker.class file is located.

Note: To find out about the latest features of TickerT.class, point your Web browser to http://www.webcom.com/taketwo/TickerT.shtml. This page contains information about the supported parameters and describes how you can download the file yourself. All I ask is that if you do decide to use this applet on your Web pages, please include a link to my home page at http://www.webcom.com/taketwo/, as described previously.

A quick exploration of the Gamelan site will reveal various other sites that also offer classes you can incorporate into your own Web pages. Take, for example, the J_tools site shown in Figure 21.10. This collection includes applets that display animated bullets, multicolored wavy text, and different types of horizontal rules. To find out more about how you can use these applets in your own pages, take a look at http://www.crl.com/~integris/j_tools.htm.

21

Figure 21.10.

J_tools is a collection of Java applets that enable you to display animated bullets, text, and rules on your Web pages.

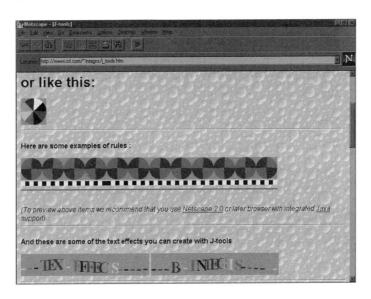

 A copy of the J_tools applet class has been included on the CD-ROM that accompanies this book, along with a collection of sample applets for you to experiment with. The applets (some with source code) are in zip files to preserve the long filename structure Java uses. The following list indicates who created each applet and describes what the applet does:

- ☐ Jumping Frog applet

  Filename: `Frogjump.zip`

  Ruault Charles-Edouard, Association Decouvertes, Paris, France

- ☐ Stock Trace applet

  Filename: `Stock.zip`

  Christian Dreke, University of Virginia Networks Laboratory, Charlottesville, Virginia

- ☐ Chernobyl Reactor applet

  Filename: `NPlant.zip`

  Henrik Eriksson, Ph.D., Linköping University, Sweden

- ☐ Server Socket example applet

  Filename: `Server.zip`

  Mike Fletcher, Bell South Wireless, Atlanta, Georgia

- ☐ Clock and GoURL applets

  Filenames: `Clock.zip` and `GoURL.zip`

  Nils Hedström, Linköping University, Sweden

- ☐ Curve applet

  Filename: `Curve.zip`

  Michael Heinrichs, Burnaby, BC, Canada

- ☐ Learn to Dance applet

  Filename: `Dance.zip`

  Georg Hebmann, University of Hamburg, Germany

- ☐ J-Tools applet

  Filename: `J-tools.zip`

  Gene Leybzon, Integris, Clayton, Missouri

- ☐ Documentation, Form, Jline, Pointer, Ticker, and WAIS interface applets

  Filename: `tw.zip`

  Thomas Wendt, University of Kessel, Germany

☐ Collections (a collection of functions and utilities)

Filename: `Collect.zip`

Doug Lea, SUNY at Oswego, New York

Summary

As you have discovered in this chapter, Java has the potential to change forever the face of Web publishing, but at the same time, its capabilities require some effort to come to grips with. At the same time, Java applets are remarkably easy to incorporate into your Web pages. All it takes is an `<APPLET>` tag and a few corresponding `<PARAM>` tags.

To learn more about what Java has to offer, point your Web browser to `http://java.sun.com/` and join the journey into the next generation of Web publishing.

Workshop

21

The first section of the Workshop lists some of the common questions people ask about the World Wide Web along with a brief answer to each. Next is a quiz about the chapter you have just read. If you have problems answering any of the questions in the quiz, you can turn to Appendix E, "Answers to Quiz Questions."

Q&A

Q I keep getting errors when I try to test an applet locally by using Navigator 2.0, yet it compiled correctly and works fine across the Internet. What am I doing wrong?

A Some early versions of Navigator 2.0 contain a bug that prevents them from reloading applets. The only way to fix this problem is by exiting Navigator 2.0 and restarting it.

Q People keep telling me that I should not use Java because it is supported only by Navigator 2.0 and HotJava. It this true?

A Some people will keep living in the dark ages, it seems. The reality, however, is that all the major Web developers have indicated that they intend to include Java support in future versions of their Web browsers, and this includes even Microsoft, which in the past has not been keen on the Java concept.

As a result, Java is set to become the true standard for Internet programming. So there is absolutely no reason not to include Java applets in your Web pages.

Quiz

1. What is the name of the company responsible for the creation of Java?
2. To include a Java applet inside a Web page, which tag must you use?
3. Why would you use the CODEBASE attribute in an <APPLET> tag?
4. What is the <PARAM> tag used for?
5. What is the name of the Java applet method that is used to initialize a new class?

Exercise

As usual, your task today is to create the 21notes.html document for your HTML reference collection. Include a demonstration of the Ticker.class applet either by downloading the file yourself or by using the CODEBASE attribute. Also, don't forget to update html_contents_frame.html to include a link to the new document.

In 21notes.html, also include a list of all the Java sites mentioned in this chapter, along with a hyperlink for each.

Appendixes

A

Summary of HTML Commands

This appendix is a reference to the HTML tags you can use in your documents, according to the HTML 2.0 specifications. In addition, tags defined in both the HTML 3.0 and Netscape Navigator 2.0 specifications are listed. Tags supported by HTML 3.0 and Navigator 2.0 are listed as (HTML 3.0), while tags that are currently only available in Navigator 2.0 are listed as (NHTML). There are also a couple tags listed that Navigator 2.0 does not "yet" support; these are listed as (HTML 3.0 only).

Note: A few of the tags in this section have not been described in the body of the book. If a tag is mentioned here that you haven't seen before, don't worry about it; that means that the tag is not in active use or is for use by HTML-generating and HTML-reading tools, and not for general use in HTML documents.

HTML Tags

Comments

`<!--...-->`

Any text enclosed within a comment tag is completely ignored by the Web browser. This includes tags, elements, and entities.

`<!DOCTYPE HTML PUBLIC "-//Netscape Comm. Corp.//DTD HTML//EN">`

Used with HTML document validation systems such as Halsoft at `http://www.halsoft.com/html-val-svc/` to indicate the level of HTML support included in a document. If included in a document, this tag must be placed on the very first line, before the `<HTML>` tag.

`<!DOCTYPE HTML PUBLIC "-//Netscape Comm. Corp. Strict//DTD HTML//EN">`

Used to indicate a more strict set of compliance tests for validation systems such as Halsoft. For more information, visit the Halsoft site listed previously. This site contains

both the document validation system and a range of files covering *document type definitions* (DTD) and HTML standards.

Structure Tags

<HTML>...</HTML>

Encloses the entire HTML document.

Can Include: <HEAD> <BODY> <FRAMESET>

<HEAD>...</HEAD>

Encloses the head of the HTML document.

Can Include: <TITLE> <ISINDEX> <BASE> <NEXTID> <LINK> <META> <SCRIPT>

Allowed Inside: <HTML>

<BODY>...</BODY>

Encloses the body (text and tags) of the HTML document.

Attributes:

BACKGROUND="…"	(HTML 3.0) The name or URL for an image to tile on the page background
BGCOLOR="…"	(NHTML) The color of the page background
TEXT="…"	(NHTML) The color of the page's text
LINK="…"	(NHTML) The color of unfollowed links
ALINK="…"	(NHTML) The color of activated links
VLINK="…"	(NHTML) The color of followed links

Can Include: <H1> <H2> <H3> <H4> <H5> <H6> <P> <OL> <UL> <DIR> <MENU> <DL> <PRE> <BLOCKQUOTE> <FORM> <ISINDEX> <HR> <ADDRESS> <TABLE> <SCRIPT> <APPLET> <EMBED>

Allowed Inside: <HTML>

Tags That Can Be Included Inside the <HEAD> Block

<TITLE>...</TITLE>

Indicates the title of the document.

Allowed Inside: <HEAD>

<BASE>

Defines base values for the current document.

Attributes:

HREF="..."	Overrides the base URL of the current document
TARGET="..."	Defines a default target window for all links in the current document

Allowed Inside: <HEAD>

<ISINDEX>

Indicates that this document is a gateway script that allows searches.

Attributes:

PROMPT="..."	(HTML 3.0) The prompt for the search field

Allowed Inside: <BLOCKQUOTE> <BODY> <DD> <FORM> <HEAD> <LI> <TABLE>

<LINK>

Indicates the relationship between this document and some other document. Generally used only by HTML-generating tools.

Attributes:

HREF="..."	The URL of the referenced HTML document
REL="..."	The forward relationship
REV="..."	A reverse relationship, usually the mailto: address of the document's author
URN="..."	Universal resource number

TITLE="…"   The link's title

METHODS="…"   Supported public methods of the object

Allowed Inside: <HEAD>

<META>

Used to simulate HTTP response header messages in an HTML document.

Attributes:

HTTP-EQUIV="…"   HTTP response header name

CONTENT="…"   Value assigned to the response header

NAME="…"   Meta information name

Allowed Inside: <HEAD>

<NEXTID>

Indicates the "next" document to this one (as might be defined by a tool to manage HTML documents in series).

Attributes:

N="…"

Allowed Inside: <HEAD>

Headings

All heading tags have the following characteristics:

Attributes:

ALIGN="CENTER"   (HTML 3.0) Centers the heading

ALIGN="LEFT"   (HTML 3.0) Left justifies the heading

ALIGN="RIGHT"   (HTML 3.0) Right justifies the heading

ALIGN="JUSTIFY"   (HTML 3.0 only) Block justifies the heading where possible

Can Include: <A> <IMG>
 <BIG> <B> <BLINK> <I> <SMALL> <SUB> <SUP> <TT> <CITE> <CODE> <DFN> <EM> <KBD> <SAMP> <STRONG> <VAR>

Allowed Inside: <BLOCKQUOTE> <BODY> <FORM>

\<H1\>...\</H1\>
A first-level heading.

\<H2\>...\</H2\>
A second-level heading.

\<H3\>...\</H3\>
A third-level heading.

\<H4\>...\</H4\>
A fourth-level heading.

\<H5\>...\</H5\>
A fifth-level heading.

\<H6\>...\</H6\>
A sixth-level heading.

Paragraphs

\<P\>...\</P\>
A plain paragraph. The closing tag (`</P>`) is optional.

Attributes:

`ALIGN="CENTER"`	(HTML 3.0) Centers the paragraph
`ALIGN="LEFT"`	(HTML 3.0) Left justifies the paragraph
`ALIGN="RIGHT"`	(HTML 3.0) Right justifies the paragraph
`ALIGN="JUSTIFY"`	(HTML 3.0 only) Block justifies the paragraph where possible

Can Include: `<A>` `<IMG>` `<BR>` `<BIG>` `<B>` `<BLINK>` `<I>` `<SMALL>` `<SUB>` `<SUP>` `<TT>` `<CITE>` `<CODE>` `<DFN>` `<EM>` `<KBD>` `<SAMP>` `<STRONG>` `<VAR>`

Allowed Inside: `<BLOCKQUOTE>` `<BODY>` `<DD>` `<FORM>` `<LI>` `<TABLE>`

<DIV>...</DIV>

Declare a block of text, but unlike the <P> tag, the <DIV> tag does not add a trailing double-line space.

Attributes:

ALIGN="CENTER"	(HTML 3.0) Centers the text defined by the division
ALIGN="LEFT"	(HTML 3.0) Left justifies the text defined by the division
ALIGN="RIGHT"	(HTML 3.0) Right justifies the text defined by the division
ALIGN="JUSTIFY"	(HTML 3.0 only) Block justifies the text defined by the division where possible

Can Include: <A> <IMG>
 <BIG> <B> <BLINK> <I> <SMALL> <SUB> <SUP> <TT> <CITE> <CODE> <DFN> <EM> <KBD> <SAMP> <STRONG> <VAR> <TABLE>

Allowed Inside: <BLOCKQUOTE> <BODY> <DD> <FORM> <LI> <TABLE>

Links

<A>...</A>

With the HREF attribute, creates a hyperlink to another document or anchor; with the NAME attribute, creates an anchor that can be linked to.

Attributes:

HREF="..."	The URL pointed to by a link
TARGET="..."	The target window for the new document
NAME="..."	The anchor name for a reference anchor

Can Include: <IMG>
 <BIG> <B> <BLINK> <I> <SMALL> <SUB> <SUP> <TT> <CITE> <CODE> <DFN> <EM> <KBD> <SAMP> <STRONG> <VAR> <TABLE>

Allowed Inside: <ADDRESS> <BIG> <B> <BLINK> <I> <SMALL> <SUB> <SUP> <TT> <CITE> <CODE> <DFN> <EM> <KBD> <SAMP> <STRONG> <VAR> <BLOCKQUOTE> <DD> <FORM> <LI> <TABLE>

Lists

<OL>...</OL>

An ordered (numbered) list.

Attributes:

> TYPE="..."   (NHTML) The type of numerals to label the list with. Possible values are A, a, I, i, and 1.

> START="..."   (NHTML) The value to start this list with.

Can Include: <LI>

Allowed Inside: <BLOCKQUOTE> <BODY> <DD> <FORM> <LI> <TABLE>

<UL>...</UL>

An unordered (bulleted) list.

Attributes:

> TYPE="..."   (NHTML) the bullet dingbat to use to mark list items. Possible values are DISC, CIRCLE, and SQUARE.

Can Include: <LI>

Allowed Inside: <BLOCKQUOTE> <BODY> <DD> <FORM> <LI> <TABLE>

<MENU>...</MENU>

A menu list of items. (Note: Removed from the HTML 3.0 specifications.)

Can Include: <LI>

Allowed Inside: <BLOCKQUOTE> <BODY> <DD> <FORM> <LI> <TABLE>

<DIR>...</DIR>

A directory listing; items are generally smaller than 20 characters. (Note: No longer supported in the HTML 3.0 specifications.)

Can Include: <LI>

Allowed Inside: <BLOCKQUOTE> <BODY> <DD> <FORM> <LI> <TABLE>

<LI>

A list item for use with <OL>, <UL>, <MENU>, or <DIR>.

Attributes:

TYPE="…"   (NHTML) The type of bullet or number that labels this item. Possible values are DISC, CIRCLE, SQUARE, A, a, I, i, and 1.

VALUE="…"   (NHTML) The numeric value this list item should have (affects this item and all below it in <OL> lists).

Can Include: <A> <IMG>
 <BIG> <B> <BLINK> <I> <SMALL> <SUB> <SUP> <TT> <CITE> <CODE> <DFN> <EM> <KBD> <SAMP> <STRONG> <VAR> <P> <DIV> <OL> <UL> <DIR> <MENU> <DL> <PRE> <BLOCKQUOTE>

Allowed Inside: <DIR> <MENU> <OL> <UL>

<DL>…</DL>

A definition or glossary list. The COMPACT attribute specifies a formatting that takes less whitespace to present.

Attributes: COMPACT

Can Include: <DT> <DD>

Allowed Inside: <BLOCKQUOTE> <BODY> <DD> <FORM> <LI> <TABLE>

<DT>

A definition term, as part of a definition list.

Can Include: <A> <IMG>
 <BIG> <B> <BLINK> <I> <SMALL> <SUB> <SUP> <TT> <CITE> <CODE> <DFN> <EM> <KBD> <SAMP> <STRONG> <VAR>

Allowed Inside: <DL>

<DD>

The corresponding definition to a definition term, as part of a definition list.

Can Include: <A> <IMG>
 <BIG> <B> <BLINK> <I> <SMALL> <SUB> <SUP> <TT> <CITE> <CODE> <DFN> <EM> <KBD> <SAMP> <STRONG> <VAR> <P> <OL> <UL> <DIR> <MENU> <DL> <PRE> <BLOCKQUOTE> <FORM> <ISINDEX> <TABLE>

Allowed Inside: <DL>

Character Formatting

All the character formatting tags have these features:

Can Include: <A> <IMG>
 <BIG> <B> <BLINK> <I> <SMALL> <SUB> <SUP> <TT> <CITE> <CODE> <DFN> <EM> <KBD> <SAMP> <STRONG> <VAR>

Allowed Inside: <A> <ADDRESS> <BIG> <B> <BLINK> <I> <SMALL> <SUB> <SUP> <TT> <CITE> <CODE> <DFN> <EM> <KBD> <SAMP> <STRONG> <VAR> <DD> <DT> <H1> <H2> <H3> <H4> <H5> <H6> <LI> <P> <PRE> <TABLE>

<BIG>...</BIG>

Big text: Text uses larger font than standard text.

<B>...</B>

Bold: Bold text.

<BLINK>...</BLINK>

Blinking: Blinking text.

<I>...</I>

Italic: Italic text.

<SMALL>...</SMALL>

Small text: Text uses smaller font than standard text.

_{...}

Subscript: Text is subscripted.

^{...}

Superscript: Text is superscripted.

<TT>...</TT>

Typewriter: Text uses monospaced typewriter font.

<CITE>...</CITE>

Citation: For quotes and references.

<CODE>...</CODE>

Program code: For computer program source code.

<DFN>...</DFN>

Defined: For word definitions.

<EM>...</EM>

Emphasis: When italic emphasis is required.

<KBD>...</KBD>

Keyboard: When showing text people need to type in.

<SAMP>...</SAMP>

Sample: For examples.

<STRONG>...</STRONG>

Strong: When bold text is required.

<VAR>...</VAR>

Variable: For names of program variables.

Other Text Layout Elements

<HR>

A horizontal rule line.

Attributes:

SIZE="…"	(NHTML) The thickness of the rule, in pixels.
WIDTH="…"	(NHTML) The width of the rule, in pixels.
ALIGN="…"	(NHTML) How the rule line will be aligned on the page. Possible values are LEFT, RIGHT, and CENTER.
NOSHADE="…"	(NHTML) Causes the rule line to be drawn as a solid color with no shading.

Allowed Inside: <BLOCKQUOTE> <BODY> <FORM> <PRE> <TABLE>

*
*

A line break.

Attributes:

> CLEAR="…"   (HTML 3.0) causes the text to stop flowing around any images. Possible values are RIGHT, LEFT, and ALL.

Allowed Inside: <ADDRESS> <BIG> <B> <BLINK> <I> <SMALL> <SUB> <SUP> <TT> <CITE> <CODE> <DFN> <EM> <KBD> <SAMP> <STRONG> <VAR> <DD> <DT> <H1> <H2> <H3> <H4> <H5> <H6> <LI> <P> <PRE> <TABLE>

<NOBR>…</NOBR> **(NHTML)**

Causes the enclosed text not to wrap at the edge of the page.

Allowed Inside: <A> <ADDRESS> <BIG> <B> <BLINK> <I> <SMALL> <SUB> <SUP> <TT> <CITE> <CODE> <DFN> <EM> <KBD> <SAMP> <STRONG> <VAR> <DD> <DT> <H1> <H2> <H3> <H4> <H5> <H6> <LI> <P> <PRE> <TABLE>

<WBR> **(NHTML)**

Wrap the text at this point only if necessary.

Allowed Inside: <A> <ADDRESS> <BIG> <B> <BLINK> <I> <SMALL> <SUB> <SUP> <TT> <CITE> <CODE> <DFN> <EM> <KBD> <SAMP> <STRONG> <VAR> <DD> <DT> <H1> <H2> <H3> <H4> <H5> <H6> <LI> <P> <PRE> <TABLE>

<BLOCKQUOTE>… </BLOCKQUOTE>

Used for long quotations or citations.

Can Include: <BLOCKQUOTE> <IMG> <H1> <H2> <H3> <H4> <H5> <H6> <P> <OL> <UL> <DIR> <MENU> <DL> <PRE> <FORM> <ISINDEX> <HR> <ADDRESS> <TABLE>

Allowed Inside: <BLOCKQUOTE> <BODY> <DD> <FORM> <LI> <TABLE>

<CENTER>…</CENTER>

All the content enclosed within these tags is centered. This tag is being phased out in favor of <P ALIGN="CENTER"> and <DIV ALIGN="CENTER">.

Can Include: <A> <IMG> <ADDRESS> <BIG> <B> <BLINK> <I> <SMALL> <SUB> <SUP> <TT> <CITE> <CODE> <DFN> <EM> <KBD> <SAMP> <STRONG> <VAR> <DD> <DT> <H1> <H2> <H3> <H4> <H5> <H6> <LI> <P> <PRE> <TABLE>

Allowed Inside: <BLOCKQUOTE> <BODY> <DD> <FORM> <LI> <TABLE>

<ADDRESS>...</ADDRESS>

Used for signatures or general information about a document's author.

Can Include: `<A>` `<IMG>` `<BIG>` `<B>` `<BLINK>` `<I>` `<SMALL>` `<SUB>` `<SUP>` `<TT>` `<CITE>` `<CODE>` `<DFN>` `<EM>` `<KBD>` `<SAMP>` `<STRONG>` `<VAR>` `<DD>` `<DT>` `<H1>` `<H2>` `<H3>` `<H4>` `<H5>` `<H6>` `<LI>` `<P>` `<PRE>` `<TABLE>`

Allowed Inside: `<BLOCKQUOTE>` `<BODY>` `<FORM>`

Font Sizes (NHTML)

<FONT>...</FONT>

Changes the size or color of the font for the enclosed text.

Attributes:

`SIZE="…"` The size of the font, from 1 to 7. Default is 3. Can also be specified as a value relative to the current size, for example, +2.

`COLOR="…"` The color of the font. See Appendix C, "Colors by Name and Hex Value," for more information.

Can Include: `<A>` `<IMG>` `<BIG>` `<B>` `<BLINK>` `<I>` `<SMALL>` `<SUB>` `<SUP>` `<TT>` `<CITE>` `<CODE>` `<DFN>` `<EM>` `<KBD>` `<SAMP>` `<STRONG>` `<VAR>` `<DD>` `<DT>` `<LI>` `<P>` `<PRE>` `<TABLE>`

Allowed Inside: `<A>` `<ADDRESS>` `<BIG>` `<B>` `<BLINK>` `<I>` `<SMALL>` `<SUB>` `<SUP>` `<TT>` `<CITE>` `<CODE>` `<DFN>` `<EM>` `<KBD>` `<SAMP>` `<STRONG>` `<VAR>` `<DD>` `<DT>` `<H1>` `<H2>` `<H3>` `<H4>` `<H5>` `<H6>` `<LI>` `<P>` `<PRE>` `<TABLE>`

<BASEFONT>

Sets the default size of the font for the current page.

Attributes:

`SIZE="…"` The default size of the font, from 1 to 7. Default is 3.

Allowed Inside: `<A>` `<ADDRESS>` `<BIG>` `<B>` `<BLINK>` `<I>` `<SMALL>` `<SUB>` `<SUP>` `<TT>` `<CITE>` `<CODE>` `<DFN>` `<EM>` `<KBD>` `<SAMP>` `<STRONG>` `<VAR>` `<DD>` `<DT>` `<LI>` `<P>` `<PRE>` `<TABLE>`

Images

<IMG>
Inserts an inline image into the document.

Attributes:

ISMAP	This image is a clickable image map.
SRC="…"	The URL of the image.
ALT="…"	A text string that will be displayed in browsers that cannot support images.
ALIGN="…"	Determines the alignment of the given image. If LEFT or RIGHT (HTML 3.0, NHTML), the image is aligned to the left or right column, and all following text flows beside that image. All other values such as TOP, MIDDLE, BOTTOM, or (NHTML) TEXTTOP, ABSMIDDLE, BASELINE, and ABSBOTTOM, determine the vertical alignment of this image with other items in the same line.
VSPACE="…"	The space between the image and the text above or below it.
HSPACE="…"	The space between the image and the text to its left or right.
WIDTH="…"	(HTML 3.0) The width, in pixels, of the image. If WIDTH is not the actual width, the image is scaled to fit.
HEIGHT="…"	(HTML 3.0) The width, in pixels, of the image. If HEIGHT is not the actual height, the image is scaled to fit.
BORDER="…"	(NHTML) Draws a border of the specified value in pixels to be drawn around the image. In the case of images that are also links, BORDER changes the size of the default link border.
LOWSRC="…"	(NHTML) The path or URL of an image that will be loaded first, before the image specified in SRC. The value of LOWSRC is usually a smaller or lower-resolution version of the actual image.
USEMAP="…"	(NHTML) Used to associate an image with a client-side image map specified by <MAP NAME=mapname>.

Allowed Inside: <A> <ADDRESS> <BIG> <B> <BLINK> <I> <SMALL> <SUB> <SUP> <TT> <CITE> <CODE> <DFN> <EM> <KBD> <SAMP> <STRONG> <VAR> <DD> <DT> <H1> <H2> <H3> <H4> <H5> <H6> <LI> <P> <PRE> <TABLE>

<MAP>...</MAP>

Defines a map for a client-side image map.

Attributes:

> NAME="…"   Used to define the map's name.

Can Include: <AREA>

Allowed Inside: <BODY>

<AREA>...</AREA>

Defines a clickable region for a client-side image map.

Attributes:

> TYPE="…"   Used to indicate the type of region bounded by the <AREA> tag. Possible values are RECT, POLY, and CIRCLE.
>
> COORDS="…"   This attribute describes the points bounding the region described by the <AREA> tag.
>
> HREF="…"   The URL to load when the region bounded by the <AREA> tag is clicked on.

Allowed Inside: <MAP>

Forms

<FORM>...</FORM>

Indicates a form.

Attributes:

> ACTION="…"   The URL of the script to process this form input.
>
> METHOD="…"   How the form input will be sent to the gateway on the server side. Possible values are GET and POST.
>
> ENCTYPE="…"   The only values currently supported are application/x-www-form-urlencoded and multipart/form-data (NHTML).
>
> TARGET="…"   (NHTML) The target window for response following form submission.

Can Include: <H1> <H2> <H3> <H4> <H5> <H6> <P> <OL> <UL> <DIR> <MENU> <DL> <PRE> <BLOCKQUOTE> <ISINDEX> <HR> <ADDRESS> <INPUT> <SELECT> <TEXTAREA> <TABLE>

Allowed Inside: <BLOCKQUOTE> <BODY> <DD> <LI>

<INPUT>

An input widget for a form.

Attributes:

TYPE="…"	The type for this input widget. Possible values are CHECKBOX, FILE (NHTML), HIDDEN, PASSWORD, RADIO, RESET, SUBMIT, TEXT, or IMAGE (HTML 3.0 only).
NAME="…"	The name of this item, as passed to the gateway script as part of a name/value pair.
VALUE="…"	For a text or hidden widget, the default value; for a check box or radio button, the value to be submitted with the form; for reset or submit buttons, the label for the button itself.
SRC="…"	The source file for an image.
CHECKED	For check boxes and radio buttons, indicates that the widget is checked.
SIZE="…"	The size, in characters, of a text widget.
MAXLENGTH="…"	The maximum number of characters that can be entered into a text widget.
ALIGN="…"	For images in forms, determines how the text and image will align (same as with the <IMG> tag).

Allowed Inside: <FORM>

<TEXTAREA>...</TEXTAREA>

Indicates a multiline text entry widget.

Attributes:

NAME="…"	The name to be passed to the gateway script as part of the name/value pair.
ROWS="…"	The number of rows this text area displays.
COLS="…"	The number of columns (characters) this text area displays.
WRAP="OFF"	Wrapping doesn't happen. Lines are sent exactly as typed.

WRAP="VIRTUAL"	The display word wraps, but long lines are sent as one line without new lines.
WRAP="PHYSICAL"	The display word wraps, and the text is transmitted at all wrap points.

Allowed Inside: <FORM>

<SELECT>...</SELECT>

Creates a menu or scrolling list of possible items.

Attributes:

NAME="..."	The name that is passed to the gateway script as part of the name/value pair.
SIZE="..."	The number of elements to display. If SIZE is indicated, the selection becomes a scrolling list. If no SIZE is given, the selection is a popup menu.
MULTIPLE	Allows multiple selections from the list.

Can Include: <OPTION>

Allowed Inside: <FORM>

<OPTION>

Indicates a possible item within a <SELECT> widget.

Attributes:

SELECTED	With this attribute included, the <OPTION> will be selected by default in the list.
VALUE="..."	The value to submit if this <OPTION> is selected when the form is submitted.

Allowed Inside: <SELECT>

Tables (HTML 3.0)

<TABLE>...</TABLE>

Creates a table, which can contain a caption (<CAPTION>) and any number of rows (<TR>).

Attributes:

BORDER="…"	Indicates whether the table should be drawn with or without a border. In Netscape, BORDER can also have a value indicating the width of the border.
CELLSPACING="…"	(NHTML) The amount of space between the cells in the table.
CELLPADDING="…"	(NHTML) The amount of space between the edges of the cell and its contents.
WIDTH="…"	(NHTML) The width of the table on the page, in either exact pixel values or as a percentage of page width.
ALIGN="…"	Determines the alignment of the given table. If LEFT or RIGHT (HTML 3.0, NHTML), the image is aligned to the left or right column, and all following text flows beside that image. If CENTER, the table is aligned with the center of the page (HTML 3.0 only).

Can Include: <CAPTION> <TR>

Allowed Inside: <BLOCKQUOTE> <BODY> <DD> <LI> <TABLE>

<CAPTION>...</CAPTION>

The caption for the table.

Attributes:

ALIGN="…"	The position of the caption. Possible values are TOP and BOTTOM.

<TR>...</TR>

Defines a table row, containing headings and data (<TR> and <TH> tags).

Attributes:

ALIGN="…"	The horizontal alignment of the contents of the cells within this row. Possible values are LEFT, RIGHT, and CENTER.
VALIGN="…"	The vertical alignment of the contents of the cells within this row. Possible values are TOP, MIDDLE, BOTTOM, and BASELINE (NHTML).

Can Include: <TH> TD>

Allowed Inside: <TABLE>

\<TH>...\</TH>

Defines a table heading cell.

Attributes:

ALIGN="..."	The horizontal alignment of the contents of the cell. Possible values are LEFT, RIGHT, and CENTER.
VALIGN="..."	The vertical alignment of the contents of the cell. Possible values are TOP, MIDDLE, BOTTOM, and BASELINE (NHTML).
ROWSPAN="..."	The number of rows this cell will span.
COLSPAN="..."	The number of columns this cell will span.
NOWRAP	Do not automatically wrap the contents of this cell.
WIDTH="..."	(NHTML) The width of this column of cells, in exact pixel values or as a percentage of the table width.

Can Include: \<H1> \<H2> \<H3> \<H4> \<H5> \<H6> \<P> \<OL> \<UL> \<DIR> \<MENU> \<DL> \<PRE> \<BLOCKQUOTE> \<FORM> \<ISINDEX> \<HR> \<ADDRESS> \<TABLE>

Allowed Inside: \<TR>

\<TD>...\</TD>

Defines a table data cell.

Attributes:

ALIGN="..."	The horizontal alignment of the contents of the cell. Possible values are LEFT, RIGHT, and CENTER.
VALIGN="..."	The vertical alignment of the contents of the cell. Possible values are TOP, MIDDLE, BOTTOM, and BASELINE (NHTML).
ROWSPAN="..."	The number of rows this cell will span.
COLSPAN="..."	The number of columns this cell will span.
NOWRAP	Do not automatically wrap the contents of this cell.
WIDTH="..."	(NHTML) The width of this column of cells, in exact pixel values or as a percentage of the table width.

Can Include: \<H1> \<H2> \<H3> \<H4> \<H5> \<H6> \<P> \<OL> \<UL> \<DIR> \<MENU> \<DL> \<PRE> \<BLOCKQUOTE> \<FORM> \<ISINDEX> \<HR> \<ADDRESS>

Allowed Inside: \<TR>

Frame Tags

<FRAMESET>…</FRAMESET> (NHTML)

Encloses a frameset definition in an HTML document.

Attributes:

COLS="…" (NHTML) Defines the number of frame columns and their width in a frameset.

ROWS="…" (NHTML) Defines the number of frame rows and their height in a frameset.

Can Include: <FRAME> <NOFRAMES>

Allowed Inside: <HTML>

<FRAME> (NHTML)

Used to define the contents of a frame within a frameset.

Attributes:

SRC="…" The URL of the document to be displayed inside the frame.

MARGINWIDTH="…" The size in pixels of the margin on each side of a frame.

MARGINHEIGHT="…" The size in pixels of the margin above and below the contents of a frame.

SCROLLING="…" Enable or disable the display of scrollbars for a frame. Values are YES, NO, and AUTO.

NORESIZE Don't allow the user to resize frames.

Allowed Inside: <FRAMESET>

<NOFRAMES>…</NOFRAMES> (NHTML)

Used to define a block of text that will be displayed by Web browsers that don't support frames.

Allowed Inside: <FRAMESET>

Can Include: <A> <IMG> <ADDRESS> <BIG> <B> <BLINK> <I> <SMALL> <SUB> <SUP> <TT> <CITE> <CODE> <DFN> <EM> <KBD> <SAMP> <STRONG> <VAR> <DD> <DT> <H1> <H2> <H3> <H4> <H5> <H6> <LI> <P> <PRE> <TABLE>

Programming Tags

<SCRIPT>...</SCRIPT>

Encloses a JavaScript or LiveScript program definition and related functions.

Attributes:

LANGUAGE="..."	Either JavaScript or LiveScript
SRC="..."	The URL of a JavaScript program stored in a separate file

Allowed Inside: <HEAD> <BODY>

<APPLET>...</APPLET> (NHTML)

Used to incorporate a Java applet into a Web page.

Attributes:

CODE="..."	The name of the Java class to be included
CODEBASE="..."	The URL of the directory where the Java class is stored if it is not located in the same directory as the HTML document
WIDTH="..."	The width in pixels of the area taken up by the applet
HEIGHT="..."	The height in pixels of the area taken up by the applet

Can Include: <PARAM>

Allowed Inside: <BODY>

<PARAM> (NHTML)

Used to define values (or parameter) to be passed to the Java applet.

Attributes:

NAME="..."	The name of the parameter to be passed to the Java class
VALUE="..."	The value of the parameter

Allowed Inside: <APPLET>

<EMBED> (NHTML)

Used to embed files supported by plug-ins. Netscape calls such files *live objects.*

Attributes:

SRC="..."	A URL that describes the location and filename to be handled by a plug-in. The file extension specified in this attribute determines which plug-in module is loaded.
WIDTH="..."	The width in pixels of the area taken up by the live object.
HEIGHT="..."	The height in pixels of the area taken up by the live object.
Plug-in specific	Each individual plug-in defines its own list of attributes. Refer to the appropriate documentation for additional information.

Allowed Inside: <BODY> <TABLE>

<NOEMBED>...</NOEMBED> (NHTML)

Used to define a block of text that will be displayed by Web browsers that don't support plug-ins.

Allowed Inside: <BODY>

Can Include: <A> <IMG> <ADDRESS> <BIG> <B> <BLINK> <I> <SMALL> <SUB> <SUP> <TT> <CITE> <CODE> <DFN> <EM> <KBD> <SAMP> <STRONG> <VAR> <DD> <DT> <H1> <H2> <H3> <H4> <H5> <H6> <LI> <P> <PRE> <TABLE>

B

Character Entities

Character Entities

Table B.1 contains the possible numeric and character entities for the ISO-Latin-1 (ISO8859-1) character set. Where possible, the character is shown.

Note: Not all browsers can display all characters, and some browsers may even display characters different from those that appear in the table. Newer browsers seem to have a better track record for handling character entities, but be sure to test your HTML files extensively with multiple browsers if you intend to use these entities.

Table B.1. The ISO-Latin-1 character set.

Character	Numeric Entity	Hex Value	Character Entity (if any)	Description
	&#00;-&#08;	00-08		Unused
	&#09;	09		Horizontal tab
	&#10;	0A		Line feed
	&#11;-&#31;	0B-1F		Unused
	&#32;	20		Space
!	&#33;	21		Exclamation point
"	&#34;	22	&quot;	Quotation mark
#	&#35;	23		Number sign
$	&#36;	24		Dollar sign
%	&#37;	25		Percent sign
&	&#38;	26	&amp;	Ampersand
'	&#39;	27		Apostrophe
(	&#40;	28		Left parenthesis
)	&#41;	29		Right parenthesis
*	&#42;	2A		Asterisk
+	&#43;	2B		Plus sign
,	&#44;	2C		Comma
-	&#45;	2D		Hyphen
.	&#46;	2E		Period (full stop)
/	&#47;	2F		Solidus (forward slash)

Numeric Character	Hex Entity	Character Value	Entity (if any)	Description
0–9	0–9	30-39		Digits 0–9
:	&#58;	3A		Colon
;	&#59;	3B		Semicolon
<	&#60;	3C	&lt;	Less than
=	&#61;	3D		Equals sign
>	&#62;	3E	&gt;	Greater than
?	&#63;	3F		Question mark
@	&#64;	40		Commercial at
A–Z	A–Z	41-5A		Letters A–Z
[	&#91;	5B		Left square bracket
\	&#92;	5C		Reverse solidus (back slash)
]	&#93;	5D		Right square bracket
^	&#94;	5E		Caret
—	&#95;	5F		Horizontal bar
`	&#96;	60		Grave accent
a–z	a–z	61-7A		Letters a–z
{	&#123;	7B		Left curly brace
|	|	7C		Vertical bar
}	&#125;	7D		Right curly brace
~	&#126;	7E		Tilde
	&#127;–	7F-A0		Unused
¡	&#161;	A1		Inverted exclamation point
¢	&#162;	A2		Cent sign
£	&#163;	A3		Pound sterling
¤	&#164;	A4		General currency sign
¥	&#165;	A5		Yen sign
¦	&#166;	A6		Broken vertical bar

Table B.1. continued

Character	Numeric Entity	Hex Value	Character Entity (if any)	Description
§	&#167;	A7		Section sign
¨	&#168;	A8		Umlaut (dieresis)
©	&#169;	A9	© (NHTML)	Copyright symbol
ª	&#170;	AA		Feminine ordinal
«	&#171;	AB		Left angle quote, guillemot left
¬	&#172;	AC		Not sign
-	&#173;	AD		Soft hyphen
®	&#174;	AE	® (HHTM)	Registered trademark
¯	&#175;	AF		Macron accent
°	&#176;	B0		Degree sign
±	&#177;	B1		Plus or minus
²	&#178;	B2		Superscript two
³	&#179;	B3		Superscript three
´	&#180;	B4		Acute accent
µ	&#181;	B5		Micro sign
¶	&#182;	B6		Paragraph sign
·	&#183;	B7		Middle dot
¸	&#184;	B8		Cedilla
¹	&#185;	B9		Superscript one
º	&#186;	BA		Masculine ordinal
»	&#187;	BB		Right angle quote, guillemot right
¼	&#188;	BC		Fraction one-fourth
½	&#189;	BD		Fraction one-half
¾	&#190;	BE		Fraction three-fourths
¿	&#191;	BF		Inverted question mark

Character	Numeric Entity	Hex Value	Character Entity (if any)	Description
À	&#192;	C0	&Agrave;	Capital A, grave accent
Á	&#193;	C1	&Aacute;	Capital A, acute accent
Â	&#194;	C2	&Acirc;	Capital A, circumflex accent
Ã	&#195;	C3	&Atilde;	Capital A, tilde
Ä	&#196;	C4	&Auml;	Capital A, dieresis or umlaut mark
Å	&#197;	C5	&Aring;	Capital A, ring
Æ	&#198;	C6	&AElig;	Capital AE dipthong (ligature)
Ç	&#199;	C7	&Ccedil;	Capital C, cedilla
È	&#200;	C8	&Egrave;	Capital E, grave accent
É	&#201;	C9	&Eacute;	Capital E, acute accent
Ê	&#202;	CA	&Ecirc;	Capital E, circumflex accent
Ë	&#203;	CB	&Euml;	Capital E, dieresis or umlaut mark
Ì	&#204;	CC	&Igrave;	Capital I, grave accent
Í	&#205;	CD	&Iacute;	Capital I, acute accent
Î	&#206;	CE	&Icirc;	Capital I, circumflex accent
Ï	&#207;	CF	&Iuml;	Capital I, dieresis or umlaut mark

continues

Table B.1. continued

Character	Numeric Entity	Hex Value	Character Entity (if any)	Description
Ð	&#208;	D0	&ETH;	Capital Eth, Icelandic
Ñ	&#209;	D1	&Ntilde;	Capital N, tilde
Ò	&#210;	D2	&Ograve;	Capital O, grave accent
Ó	&#211;	D3	&Oacute;	Capital O, acute accent
Ô	&#212;	D4	&Ocirc;	Capital O, circumflex accent
Õ	&#213;	D5	&Otilde;	Capital O, tilde
Ö	&#214;	D6	&Ouml;	Capital O, dieresis or umlaut mark
×	&#215;	D7		Multiply sign
Ø	&#216;	D8	&Oslash;	Capital O, slash
Ù	&#217;	D9	&Ugrave;	Capital U, grave accent
Ú	&#218;	DA	&Uacute;	Capital U, acute accent
Û	&#219;	DB	&Ucirc;	Capital U, circumflex accent
Ü	&#220;	DC	&Uuml;	Capital U, dieresis or umlaut mark
Ý	&#221;	DD	&Yacute;	Capital Y, acute accent
	&#222;	DE	&THORN;	Capital THORN, Icelandic
	&#223;	DF	&szlig;	Small sharp s, German (sz ligature)
à	&#224;	E0	&agrave;	Small a, grave accent

Character	Numeric Entity	Hex Value	Character Entity (if any)	Description
á	&#225;	E1	&aacute;	Small a, acute accent
â	&#226;	E2	&acirc;	Small a, circumflex accent
ã	&#227;	E3	&atilde;	Small a, tilde
ä	&#228;	E4	&aauml;	Small a, dieresis or umlaut mark
å	&#229;	E5	&aring;	Small a, ring
æ	&#230;	E6	&aelig;	Small ae dipthong (ligature)
ç	&#231;	E7	&ccedil;	Small c, cedilla
è	&#232;	E8	&egrave;	Small e, grave accent
é	&#233;	E9	&eacute;	Small e, acute accent
ê	&#234;	EA	&ecirc;	Small e, circumflex accent
ë	&#235;	EB	&euml;	Small e, dieresis or umlaut mark
ì	&#236;	EC	&igrave;	Small i, grave accent
í	&#237;	ED	&iacute;	Small i, acute accent
î	&#238;	EE	&icirc;	Small i, circumflex accent
ï	&#239;	EF	&iuml;	Small i, dieresis or umlaut mark
ð	&#240;	F0	&eth;	Small eth, Icelandic

continues

Table B.1. continued

Character	Numeric Entity	Hex Value	Character Entity (if any)	Description
ñ	&#241;	F1	&ntilde;	Small n, tilde
ò	&#242;	F2	&ograve;	Small o, grave accent
ó	&#243;	F3	&oacute;	Small o, acute accent
ô	&#244;	F4	&ocirc;	Small o, circumflex accent
õ	&#245;	F5	&otilde;	Small o, tilde
ö	&#246;	F6	&ouml;	Small o, dieresis or umlaut mark
÷	&#247;	F7		Division sign
ø	&#248;	F8	&oslash;	Small o, slash
ù	&#249;	F9	&ugrave;	Small u, grave accent
ú	&#250;	FA	&uacute;	Small u, acute accent
û	&#251;	FB	&ucirc;	Small u, circumflex accent
ü	&#252;	FC	&uuml;	Small u, dieresis or umlaut mark
ý	&#253;	FD	&yacute;	Small y, acute accent
	&#254;	FE	&thorn;	Small thorn, Icelandic
ÿ	&#255;	FF	&yuml;	Small y, dieresis or umlaut mark

C

Colors by Name and Hex Value

Table C.1 contains a list of all the color names recognized by Navigator 2.0 and also includes their corresponding hex triplet values. To see all these colors correctly, you will need to have a 256-color or better video card and the appropriate video drivers installed. Also, depending on the operating system and computer platform you are running, some colors may not appear exactly as you expect them to.

Table C.1. Color values and hex triplet equivalents.

Color Name	Hex Triplet
ALICEBLUE	#A0CE00
ANTIQUEWHITE	#FAEBD7
AQUA	#00FFFF
AQUAMARINE	#7FFFD4
AZURE	#F0FFFF
BEIGE	#F5F5DC
BISQUE	#FFE4C4
BLACK	#000000
BLANCHEDALMOND	#FFEBCD
BLUE	#0000FF
BLUEVIOLET	#8A2BE2
BROWN	#A52A2A
BURLYWOOD	#DEB887
CADETBLUE	#5F9EA0
CHARTREUSE	#7FFF00
CHOCOLATE	#D2691E
CORAL	#FF7F50
CORNFLOWERBLUE	#6495ED
CORNSILK	#FFF8DC
CRIMSON	#DC143C
CYAN	#00FFFF
DARKBLUE	#00008B
DARKCYAN	#008B8B
DARKGOLDENROD	#B8860B
DARKGRAY	#A9A9A9

Color Name	Hex Triplet
DARKGREEN	#006400
DARKKHAKI	#BDB76B
DARKMAGENTA	#8B008B
DARKOLIVEGREEN	#556B2F
DARKORANGE	#FF8C00
DARKORCHID	#9932CC
DARKRED	#8B0000
DARKSALMON	#E9967A
DARKSEAGREEN	#8FBC8F
DARKSLATEBLUE	#483D8B
DARKSLATEGRAY	#2F4F4F
DARKTURQUOISE	#00CED1
DARKVIOLET	#9400D3
DEEPPINK	#FF1493
DEEPSKYBLUE	#00BFFF
DIMGRAY	#696969
DODGERBLUE	#1E90FF
FIREBRICK	#B22222
FLORALWHITE	#FFFAF0
FORESTGREEN	#228B22
FUCHSIA	#FF00FF
GAINSBORO	#DCDCDC
GHOSTWHITE	#F8F8FF
GOLD	#FFD700
GOLDENROD	#DAA520
GRAY	#808080
GREEN	#008000
GREENYELLOW	#ADFF2F
HONEYDEW	#F0FFF0
HOTPINK	#FF69B4

continues

Table C.1. continued

Color Name	Hex Triplet
INDIANRED	#CD5C5C
INDIGO	#4B0082
IVORY	#FFFFF0
KHAKI	#F0E68C
LAVENDER	#E6E6FA
LAVENDERBLUSH	#FFF0F5
LEMONCHIFFON	#FFFACD
LIGHTBLUE	#ADD8E6
LIGHTCORAL	#F08080
LIGHTCYAN	#E0FFFF
LIGHTGOLDENRODYELLOW	#FAFAD2
LIGHTGREEN	#90EE90
LIGHTGREY	#D3D3D3
LIGHTPINK	#FFB6C1
LIGHTSALMON	#FFA07A
LIGHTSEAGREEN	#20B2AA
LIGHTSKYBLUE	#87CEFA
LIGHTSLATEGRAY	#778899
LIGHTSTEELBLUE	#B0C4DE
LIGHTYELLOW	#FFFFE0
LIME	#00FF00
LIMEGREEN	#32CD32
LINEN	#FAF0E6
MAGENTA	#FF00FF
MAROON	#800000
MEDIUMAQUAMARINE	#66CDAA
MEDIUMBLUE	#0000CD
MEDIUMORCHID	#BA55D3
MEDIUMPURPLE	#9370DB
MEDIUMSEAGREEN	#3CB371

Color Name	Hex Triplet
MEDIUMSLATEBLUE	#7B68EE
MEDIUMSPRINGGREEN	#00FA9A
MEDIUMTURQUOISE	#48D1CC
MEDIUMVIOLETRED	#C71585
MIDNIGHTBLUE	#191970
MINTCREAM	#F5FFFA
MISTYROSE	#FFE4E1
NAVAJOWHITE	#FFDEAD
NAVY	#000080
OLDLACE	#FDF5E6
OLIVE	#808000
OLIVEDRAB	#6B8E23
ORANGE	#FFA500
ORANGERED	#FF4500
ORCHID	#DA70D6
PALEGOLDENROD	#EEE8AA
PALEGREEN	#98FB98
PALETURQUOISE	#AFEEEE
PALEVIOLETRED	#DB7093
PAPAYAWHIP	#FFEFD5
PEACHPUFF	#FFDAB9
PERU	#CD853F
PINK	#FFC0CB
PLUM	#DDA0DD
POWDERBLUE	#B0E0E6
PURPLE	#800080
RED	#FF0000
ROSYBROWN	#BC8F8F
ROYALBLUE	#4169E1
SADDLEBROWN	#8B4513

continues

Table C.1. continued

Color Name	Hex Triplet
SALMON	#FA8072
SANDYBROWN	#F4A460
SEAGREEN	#2E8B57
SEASHELL	#FFF5EE
SIENNA	#A0522D
SILVER	#C0C0C0
SKYBLUE	#87CEEB
SLATEBLUE	#6A5ACD
SLATEGRAY	#708090
SNOW	#FFFAFA
SPRINGGREEN	#00FF7F
STEELBLUE	#4682B4
TAN	#D2B48C
TEAL	#008080
THISTLE	#D8BFD8
TOMATO	#FF6347
TURQUOISE	#40E0D0
VIOLET	#EE82EE
WHEAT	#F5DEB3
WHITE	#FFFFFF
WHITESMOKE	#F5F5F5
YELLOW	#FFFF00
YELLOWGREEN	#9ACD32

D

Sources of Additional Information

Haven't had enough yet? In this appendix you'll find the URLs for all kinds of information about the World Wide Web, HTML, developing Web presentations, and locations of tools to help you write HTML documents. With this list you should be able to find just about anything you need on the Web.

> **Note:** Some of the URLs in this section refer to FTP sites. Some of these sites may be very busy during business hours, and you may not be able to immediately access the files. Try again during non-prime hours.
>
> Also, some of these sites, for mysterious reasons, may be accessible through an FTP program, but not through Web browsers. If you are consistently getting refused from these sites using a browser, and you have access to an FTP program, try that program instead.

Collections of HTML and WWW Development Information

Yahoo's WWW section
Linkname: Computers: World Wide Web
```
http://www.yahoo.com/Computers/World_Wide_Web/
```

The Virtual Library
Linkname: The Web Developer's Virtual Library
```
http://WWW.Stars.com/
```

The HTML FAQ
```
http://www.umcc.umich.edu/~ec/www/html_faq.html
```

The Developer's JumpStation
Linkname: OneWorld/SingNet WWW & HTML Developer's JumpStation
```
http://oneworld.wa.com/htmldev/devpage/dev-page.html
```

The Repository
Linkname: Subjective Electronic Information Repository
```
http://cbl.leeds.ac.uk/nikos/doc/repository.html
```

The home of the WWW Consortium
Linkname: The World Wide Web Organization
`http://www.w3.org/`

Netscape's HTML assistance pages
Linkname: Creating Net Sites
`http://home.mcom.com/assist/net_sites/index.html`

The Spider's Web pages on the Web
Linkname: (BOBAWORLD) World Wide Web
`http://gagme.wwa.com/~boba/web.html`

The HTML Writer's Guild
Linkname: The HTML Writer's Guide Website
`http://www.mindspring.com/guild/`

Web Directories

ALIWEB, a great Web index
Linkname: ALIWEB
`http://web.nexor.co.uk/public/aliweb/aliweb.html`

An index of indexes
Linkname: Web Indexes
`http://www.biotech.washington.edu/WebCrawler/WebIndexes.html`

Galaxy
Linkname: TradeWave Galaxy
`http://www.einet.net/galaxy.html`

Point
Linkname: Point Communications Corporation
`http://www.pointcom.com/`

W3 Virtual Library
Linkname: The World-Wide Web Virtual Library: Subject Catalogue
`http://www.w3.org/hypertext/DataSources/bySubject/Overview.html`

Yahoo (my favorite index)
Linkname: Yahoo: A Guide to WWW
```
http://www.yahoo.com/
```

Web Search Tools

CUSI
Linkname: CUSI (Configurable Unified Search Interface)
```
http://Web.nexor.co.uk/susi/cusi.html
```

excite
Linkname: excite Netsearch
```
http://www.excite.com/
```

InfoSeek
Linkname: InfoSeek Net Search
```
http://www2.infoseek.com
```

Lycos
Linkname: The Lycos Home Page: Hunting WWW Information
```
http://www.lycos.com/
```

WebCrawler
Linkname: The WebCrawler
```
http://webcrawler.cs.washington.edu/WebCrawler/
```

Browsers

A general list
Linkname: WWW Client Software products
```
http://www.w3.org/hypertext/WWW/Clients.html
```

Netscape (Windows, Windows 95, Mac, X)
Linkname: Download Netscape Software
```
http://home.netscape.com/comprod/mirror/index.html
```

Microsoft Internet Explorer 2.0 (Windows 95)
Linkname: Download Microsoft Internet Explorer 2.0
```
http://www.msn.com/ie/ie.htm
```

NCSA Mosaic (X, Windows, Mac)
Linkname: NCSA Mosaic Home Page
```
http://www.ncsa.uiuc.edu/SDG/Software/Mosaic/NCSAMosaicHome.html
```

Lynx (UNIX and DOS)
Linkname: About Lynx
```
http://www.cc.ukans.edu/about_lynx/
```

WinWeb (Windows)
Linkname: EINet WinWeb
```
http://www.einet.net/EINet/WinWeb/WinWebHome.html
```

MacWeb (Macintosh)
Linkname: EINet MacWeb
```
http://www.einet.net/EINet/MacWeb/MacWebHome.html
```

Arena (X)
Linkname: Welcome to Arena
```
http://info.cern.ch/hypertext/WWW/Arena/
```

Emacs-W3 (for Emacs)
Linkname: The Emacs World Wide Web Browser
```
http://www.cs.indiana.edu/elisp/w3/docs.html
```

NetCruiser
Linkname: NetCruiser HomePort
```
http://www.netcom.com/netcom/cruiser.html
```

Web Explorer (OS/2 Warp)
```
ftp://ftp.ibm.net/pub/WebExplorer/
```

Cello (Windows)
Linkname: FAQ FOR CELLO (PART 1)
```
http://www.law.cornell.edu/cello/cellofaq.html
```

Specifications for HTML, HTTP, and URLs

The HTML Level 2 specification
Linkname: HTML Specification Review Materials

`http://www.w3.org/hypertext/WWW/MarkUp/html-spec/index.html`

The HTML+ 3.0 draft specification
Linkname: HTML+ (Hypertext markup format)

`http://www.hpl.hp.co.uk/people/dsr/html/CoverPage.html`

The HTTP specification
Linkname: HTTP: A protocol for networked information

`http://info.cern.ch/hypertext/WWW/Protocols/HTTP/HTTP2.html`

Netscape's extensions to HTML 2.0
Linkname: Extensions to HTML

`http://home.netscape.com/assist/net_sites/html_extensions.html`

Netscape's extensions to HTML 3.0
Linkname: Extensions to HTML

`http://home.netscape.com/assist/net_sites/html_extensions_3.html`

Mosaic tables
Linkname: HTML Tables in NCSA Mosaic

`http://www.ncsa.uiuc.edu/SDG/Software/XMosaic/table-spec.html`

Pointers to URL, URN, and URI information and specifications
Linkname: UR* and The Names and Addresses of WWW objects

`http://www.w3.org/hypertext/WWW/Addressing/Addressing.html`

Java and JavaScript

The Sun Microsystems Java home page
Linkname: Java: Programming for the Internet

`http://java.sun.com/`

A Java applet directory
Linkname: Gamalan

```
http://www.gamelan.com/
```

Yahoo Java directory
Linkname: Yahoo—Computers and Internet:Languages:Java

```
http://www.yahoo.com/Computers_and_Internet/Languages/Java/
```

Netscape information about Java
Linkname: Java applets

```
http://home.netscape.com/comprod/products/navigator/version_2.0/
java_applets/index.html
```

Netscape information about JavaScript
Linkname: JavaScript

```
http://home.netscape.com/comprod/products/navigator/version_2.0/script/
index.html
```

Tools for Images

Some good information about transparent GIFs
Linkname: Transparent Background Images

```
http://melmac.harris-atd.com/transparent_images.html
```

giftrans
Linkname: source for giftrans

```
ftp://ftp.rz.uni-karlsruhe.de/pub/net/www/tools/giftrans.c
```

LView Pro for Windows (at the OAK Simtel Mirror)

```
ftp://oak.oakland.edu/SimTel/win3/graphics/lviewp1b.zip
```

LView Pro for Windows 95 (at the OAK Simtel Mirror)

```
ftp://oak.oakland.edu/SimTel/win3/graphics/lviewp1c.zip
```

Graphic Converter for Macintosh (at the HyperArchive sumex-aim Mirror)

```
URL:http://hyperarchive.lcs.mit.edu/HyperArchive/Archive/grf/util/graphic-
converter-212.hqx
```

GIF Converter for Macintosh (at the HyperArchive sumex-aim Mirror)

```
http://hyperarchive.lcs.mit.edu/HyperArchive/Archive/grf/util/
gif-converter-237.hqx
```

Transparency (Macintosh)

```
ftp:// med.cornell.edu/pub/aarong/transparency
http://hyperarchive.lcs.mit.edu/HyperArchive/Archive/grf/util/
transparency-10b4.hqx
```

GIFTool (Unix)

```
http://www.homepages.com/tools/
```

Sound and Video

SOX (UNIX and DOS sound Converter)

```
http://www.spies.com/Sox/
```

WAVany (Windows sound converter)

```
ftp://oak.oakland.edu/SimTel/win3/sound/wvany10.zip
```

WHAM (Windows sound converter)

```
ftp://gatekeeper.dec.com/pub/micro/msdos/win3/sounds/wham133.zip
```

SoundAPP (Macintosh sound converter)

```
http://hyperarchive.lcs.mit.edu/HyperArchive/Archive/snd/util/
sound-app-151.hqx
```

FastPlayer (Macintosh QuickTime player and "flattener")

```
ftp://ftp.ncsa.uiuc.edu/Mosaic/Mac/Helpers/fast-player-110.hqx
```

QFlat (Windows QuickTime "flattener")

```
ftp://venice.tcp.com/pub/anime-manga/software/viewers/qtflat.zip
```

Sparkle (MPEG player and converter for Macintosh)

```
http://hyperarchive.lcs.mit.edu/HyperArchive/Archive/gst/mov/
sparkle-243a.hqx
```

XingCD (AVI to MPEG converter)

Send mail to xing@xingtech.com or call 805/473-0145

AVI-Quick (Macintosh converter for AVI to QuickTime)

```
http://hyperarchive.lcs.mit.edu/HyperArchive/Archive/gst/mov/
avi-to-qt-converter.hqx
```

SmartCap (Windows QuickTime and AVI Converter)

```
ftp://ftp.intel.com/pub/IAL/Indeo_video/smartc.exe
```

The MPEG FAQ

Linkname: MPEG Moving Picture Expert Group FAQ

```
http://www.crs4.it/~luigi/MPEG/mpegfaq.html
```

Information on making MPEG movies

Linkname: How to make MPEG movies

```
http://www.arc.umn.edu/GVL/Software/mpeg.html
```

Servers

W3C httpd

Linkname: W3C httpd Server User Guide

```
http://www.w3.org/httpd_3.0/
```

NCSA HTTPd

Linkname: NCSA HTTPd Overview

```
http://hoohoo.ncsa.uiuc.edu/docs/Overview.html
```

NCSA HTTPd for Windows

Linkname: NCSA HTTPd for Windows

```
http://www.city.net/win-httpd/
```

MacHTTP

Linkname: MacHTTP Info

```
http://www.biap.com/
```

Web Providers

An index from HyperNews

Linkname: Leasing a Server

```
http://union.ncsa.uiuc.edu/HyperNews/get/www/leasing.html
```

Gateway Scripts and the Common Gateway Interface (CGI)

Yahoo's CGI List
Linkname: Yahoo—Computers and Internet:Internet:World Wide Web:CGI—Common Gateway Interface
```
http://www.yahoo.com/Computers_and_Internet/Internet/World_Wide_Web/
CGI___Common_Gateway_Interface/The original NCSA CGI documentation
```

Linkname: The Common Gateway Interface
```
http://hoohoo.ncsa.uiuc.edu/cgi/
```

The spec for CGI
Linkname: The Common Gateway Interface Specification
```
http://hoohoo.ncsa.uiuc.edu/cgi/interface.html
```

Information about CGI in W3C httpd
Linkname: CGI/1.1 script support of the W3C httpd server
```
http://www.w3.org/pub/WWW/Daemon/User/CGI/Overview.html
```

A library of C programs to help with CGI development
Linkname: EIT's CGI Library
```
http://wsk.eit.com/wsk/dist/doc/libcgi/libcgi.html
```

An index to HTML-related programs written in Perl
Linkname: Index of Perl/HTML archives
```
http://www.seas.upenn.edu/~mengwong/perlhtml.html
```

An archive of CGI Programs at NCSA
Linkname: CGI sample scripts
```
ftp://ftp.ncsa.uiuc.edu/Web/httpd/Unix/ncsa_httpd/cgi
```

Un-CGI, a program to decode form input
Linkname: Un-CGI Version 1.2
```
http://www.hyperion.com/~koreth/uncgi.html
```

Forms and Image Maps

The original NCSA forms documentation
Linkname: The Common Gateway Interface: FORMS

`http://hoohoo.ncsa.uiuc.edu/cgi/forms.html`

Mosaic form support documentation
Linkname: Mosaic for X Version 2.0 Fill-Out Form Support

`http://www.ncsa.uiuc.edu/SDG/Software/Mosaic/Docs/fill-out-forms/`
`overview.html`

Image maps in W3C httpd
Linkname: Clickable image support in the server

`http://www.w3.org/pub/WWW/Daemon/User/CGI/HTImageDoc.html`

Image maps in NCSA
Linkname: Graphical Information Map Tutorial

`http://wintermute.ncsa.uiuc.edu:8080/map-tutorial/image-maps.html`

Some Perl scripts to manage forms
Linkname: CGI Form Handling in Perl

`http://www.bio.cam.ac.uk/web/form.html`

Mapedit: A tool for Windows and X11 for creating Imagemap map files
Linkname: mapedit 1.1.2

`http://sunsite.unc.edu/boutell/mapedit/mapedit.html`

WebMap (Macintosh map creator)

`http://hyperarchive.lcs.mit.edu/HyperArchive/Archive/text/html/`
`web-map-101.hqx`

HTML Editors and Converters

A list of converters and editors, updated regularly
Linkname: Tools for WWW Providers

`http://www.w3.org/hypertext/WWW/Tools/`

A better list of converters
Linkname: Computers:World Wide Web:HTML Converters
`http://www.yahoo.com/Computers/World_Wide_Web/HTML_Converters/`

A great list of editors
Linkname: Computers:World Wide Web:HTML Editors
`http://www.yahoo.com/Computers/World_Wide_Web/HTML_Editors/`

Other

Tim Berners-Lee's style guide
Linkname: Style Guide for Online Hypertext
`http://www.w3.org/hypertext/WWW/Provider/Style/Overview.html`

The Yale HyperText Style Guide
Linkname: Yale C/AIM WWW Style Manual
`http://info.med.yale.edu/caim/StyleManual_Top.HTML`

Some good information on registering and publicizing your Web page
Linkname: A guide to publishing on the World Wide Web
`http://www.cl.cam.ac.uk/users/gdr11/publish.html`

E

Answers to Quiz Questions

This appendix contains a list of answers for all of the quiz questions from the end of each chapter. It does not, however, contain solutions to all the additional exercises, since that would probably add an extra 50 pages to the book—and I'm trying to save a few thousand trees. If you take a look at `http://www.webcom.com/taketwo/samstyn.shtml`, you will find most of the exercises and a number of examples of Java applets and JavaScript routines.

Chapter 1, "Welcome to the World Wide Web"

1. The first Web browser was created at CERN.
2. HTML stands for hypertext markup language.
3. The World Wide Web has the following:

   Multiple protocol support

   Hypertext-based information access

   Distributed information

   A graphical interface

   Multimedia capabilities

   Interactive access

   Dynamic updating

   Cross-platform support

4. A URL is a universal resource locator.
5. Tim Berners-Lee is the father of the World Wide Web.
6. A hyperlink is an image or block of text embedded in a Web page, which when clicked causes a new file, document, or resource to be loaded.
7. I have been told that the answer is possibly 42. But really, I just wanted to see who was actually doing the quiz. Any teacher will tell you that tests and quizzes are an important part of the learning process.
8. Everyone and yet no one truly owns the World Wide Web; different companies and organizations own Web sites and servers, but the World Wide Web itself is public domain.

Chapter 2, "Getting to Know the Netscape Navigator"

1. Navigator 2.0 runs on Windows 3.1, Windows 95, Apple Macintosh, and a range of X11-based UNIX systems, including some Linux versions.

2. Select the Auto Load Images item on the Options menu to disable or enable the automatic displaying of inline images when a new Web page is loaded.

3. Yes, you can use Navigator 2.0 to receive e-mail messages.

4. You will probably need to define proxies for your Web browser if you connect to the Internet via a firewall.

5. No, you cannot run the 32-bit version of Navigator 2.0 under Windows 3.11, even if you do have a copy of WIN32s.

Chapter 4, "Before You Start"

1. Just about all Web browsers can display GIF images inline. In addition, Navigator 2.0 can also display JPEG images inline.

2. Currently, Navigator 2.0 is the only Web browser that supports the use of frames.

3. Inline multimedia is displayed as part of a Web page using a plug-in, while external multimedia must be displayed by a separate helper application.

4. Even the smallest business can take advantage of the World Wide Web for online commerce.

5. Forms are used to collect responses from Web users.

Chapter 5, "Basic HTML and the World Wide Web"

1. `<H6>` is the tag used to define the smallest possible heading on a Web page.

2. Currently, Navigator 2.0 supports `ALIGN="LEFT"`, `ALIGN="RIGHT"`, and `ALIGN="CENTER"` inside a paragraph `<P>` tag.

3. All heading tags include support for the `ALIGN` attribute. Therefore, yes, you can center text in a heading using `<H1 ALIGN="CENTER">`.

4. The `<CITE>` tag is appropriate when formatting text for a quotation.

5. A `<!-- comment -->` tag can extend over any number of lines.

Chapter 6, "Linking Web Pages Together"

1. The HREF attribute is used by the <A> tag to describe the location of the file pointed to by a hyperlink.

2. You need to use absolute addressing when referencing a Web document stored on a remote Web server.

3. The ../ symbol references the directory one level above the current base directory.

4. If a Web server or other resource is not located on its default port, you may need to assign a port number to the URL to address the server correctly.

5. You can display hotspot text using any of the physical or logical character styles.

Chapter 7, "Advanced Formatting Options"

1. The <OL> and <LI> tags are used when creating an ordered list.

2. The <DD> defines the "definition" component of a glossary or definition list.

3. The four attributes recognized by the <HR> tag are SIZE, WIDTH, ALIGN, and NOSHADE.

4. The <ADDRESS> tag is commonly used to sign Web pages.

5. The color green is represented by "#00FF00".

6. The five color attributes used by the <BODY> tag are BGCOLOR, TEXT, LINK, ALINK, and VLINK.

7. There are seven possible font sizes supported by <FONT SIZE="?">.

8. To include an ampersand (&) symbol in a Web page use &.

Chapter 8, "Adding Tables to Web Pages"

1. The <TH>…</TH> tag block is used to indicate a heading cell.

2. The VALIGN attribute can be set to TOP, CENTER, BOTTOM, or BASELINE.

3. <CAPTION ALIGN="BOTTOM"> defines a caption that is printed below a table.

4. <TABLE BORDER=value> is used to alter the size of the border around a table.

5. The ROWSPAN attribute is used to define data cells that span two or more rows of a table.

Chapter 9, "Working with Links and URLs"

1. `<A NAME="anchorname">` is a reference anchor.
2. The # symbol is used in a URL to point to an anchor reference (for example, `<A HREF="#anchorname">`).
3. The ftp: protocol is used to download a file located on an anonymous FTP server.
4. The snews: protocol is used for URLs that point to secure news servers.
5. The https: protocol is used for URLs that exchange transactions via a secure Web server.

Chapter 10, "Adding Images to Your Web Documents"

1. Using Navigator 2.0, JPEG images can be used inline. However, not all Web browsers currently support this format.
2. The HEIGHT attribute and its partner the WIDTH attribute tell the Web browser how much space an image will require. Including these attributes allows the Web browser to render the entire page before all the images are downloaded.
3. The ALIGN attribute of the <IMG> tag can be assigned a value of TOP, TEXTTOP, MIDDLE, ABSMIDDLE, BASELINE, BOTTOM, or ABSBOTTOM.
4. The BACKGROUND attribute of the <BODY> tag lets you assign a background image to a Web page.
5. To create an image hyperlink, embed an <IMG> tag inside the body of an <A>…</A> tag block (for example, `<A HREF="file.html"><IMG SRC="image.gif"></A>`).

Chapter 11, "Using External Media and Plug-Ins"

1. .jpg is the three-letter file extension for a JPEG file.
2. You could use MPEG, QuickTime, or Video for Windows to include a video clip as part of a Web page. Alternatively, if you have your own Web server you could also use VDOLive.

3. The <EMBED> tag is used to include a plug-in element on a Web page.

4. .dsp is the file extension for a TrueSpeech file.

5. AU is the audio file format currently supported by just about all Web browsers.

Chapter 12, "Linked Windows and Frames"

1. The TARGET attribute in an <A> tag is used to indicate the window or frame where the document should be loaded.

2. The ROWS attribute declares a frameset that is split into a number of rows, while the COLS attribute declares a frameset that is split into a number of columns.

3. The MARGINHEIGHT attribute is used to specify a margin above and below a frame.

4. TARGET="_top" loads the new document over the frameset, replacing it entirely.

5. The contents of a <NOFRAME> tag are only displayed on Web browsers that don't support frames.

Chapter 13, "Installing Your Web Pages on a Web Server"

1. You can use an anonymous FTP server to host Web pages, but you will not be able to make use of advanced features such as forms, server-side image maps, and CGI scripting. In addition, there are some performance problems associated with accessing an FTP site, which can make the download times for your Web pages unacceptable to most users.

2. The W3C httpd web server and the NCSA HTTPd server are the two most commonly used Web servers on UNIX systems.

3. To achieve Netscape 2.0 Now certification your Web site needs to contain Netscape-specific features such as frames, Java, or JavaScript routines, tables, or plug-ins. In addition, you must make application to Netscape Communications before you can include the Netscape 2.0 Now logo on your Web pages.

4. *Daemon* is a UNIX term for a program that sits in the background and waits for requests. When it receives a request, it wakes up, processes that request, and then goes back to sleep.

5. There are Web servers available for Windows 3.1, Windows 95, Windows NT, Apple Macintosh, and a wide variety of UNIX-based computer systems.

Chapter 14, "How to Tell the World You Have Arrived"

1. The URL for Lycos is `http://www.lycos.com/`.

2. The Postmaster site can automatically submit your site details to 25 of the most popular Web directories and indexes.

3. The `comp.infosystems.www.announce` newsgroup and any other newsgroups ending in `.announce` are often suitable for announcing the existence of new Web sites.

4. The NCSA What's New site can be found at `http://www.ncsa.uiuc.edu/SDG/Software/Mosaic/Docs/whats-new.html`.

5. To have your site listed in Netscape's Galleria, it must be housed on either a Netscape Commerce server or a Netscape Communications server.

Chapter 15, "Developing Effective Web Pages"

1. Scanability is the ease with which a person can locate information on your Web pages. A page with few headings and jumbled links is a lot harder to scan than one that is well organized with headers and appropriate links.

2. Unless your pages are Navigator 2.0 specific, you should avoid any browser-specific references such as "select the File menu and choose the Open File item." In addition, even if your site is Navigator 2.0 specific, you should still avoid such references when possible.

3. Every `<IMG>` tag should include an `ALT` attribute to cater to people with text-only browsers and those with slower modems that require the automatic displaying of inline images to be disabled.

4. If you want people to come back to your site in the future, proofreading and correct spelling are very important. While you can't judge a book by its cover, bad spelling and grammar will turn many people off returning to a site.

5. The "here" syndrome refers to the habit of including links on a Web page with `here` as the hotspot text. Other common offenders are the `this` and `this link` hyperlinks.

Chapter 16, "Interacting with the Web Server by Using CGI"

1. CGI scripts are usually stored in a /cgi-bin/ directory.

2. Perl and Bourne shell scripts are the two most commonly used languages for CGI scripts.

3. The <ISINDEX> tag "turns on" searching in the browser that is reading this document. Depending on the browser, this may involve enabling a search button or special window in the browser itself. For other browsers, it may involve including an input field on the page itself. The reader can then enter a string to search for, and then press Enter or click on the button to submit the query to the server.

4. The content type of a standard HTML document is Content-type: text/html.

5. Send "Status: 204 No Response" to a Web browser to inform it that there will be no response document sent by a CGI script.

Chapter 17, "Forms and CGI"

1. GET is the older of the two possible transmission methods, and POST is the more popular current method.

2. The ACTION attribute of the <FORM> tag is used to indicate the location of the CGI script to be run when a form is submitted.

3. Currently, the possible TYPE values for an <INPUT> tag are CHECKBOX, FILE, HIDDEN, PASSWORD, RADIO, RESET, SUBMIT, TEXT, and IMAGE.

4. The <TEXTAREA> tag would be used to declare a field that is 4 rows long and 60 characters wide (for example, <TEXTAREA NAME="theBody" ROWS="4" COLS="60">Enter your message here.</TEXTAREA>).

5. The <SELECT> tag enables the reader of a form to select one or more items from a menu or scrolling list.

Chapter 18, "Image Maps and Dynamic Documents"

1. All the processing for a server-side image map occurs on a remote Web server, while for a client-side image map all the processing occurs inside the Web browser.

2. The ISMAP attribute is used in an `<IMG>` tag to indicate that the image should be treated as a server-side image map.

3. The `<MAP>` tag is used to define the layout of a client-side image map.

4. The USEMAP attribute is used to associate an `<IMG>` tag with a client-side image map.

5. Client pull is a mechanism that lets a Web browser automatically request a new Web page after a specified amount of time.

Chapter 19, "JavaScript"

1. Only the LANGUAGE and SRC attributes are currently recognized by the `<SCRIPT>` tag.

2. The `+=` assignment operator adds the value on its right-hand side to the value stored on its left. For example a `+= b` is equivalent to a `= a + b`.

3. An onBlur event is triggered whenever a person leaves a specified input field.

4. If you don't surround the contents of a `<SCRIPT>` tag with a `<!-- comment -->` tag, Web browsers that don't understand the concept of JavaScript will attempt to display your code as part of the Web page.

5. `document.write()` is an example of a method.

Chapter 20, "Working with JavaScript"

1. The `math.random()` function generates a random decimal number between 0 and 1.

2. To prevent a form from being submitted if there is an error, return a value of `false` to the onSubmit handler (for example, `onSubmit="return checkform()"`, where `checkform()` includes a `return false` statement following the detection of any errors).

3. `parent.frames[1].location` describes the URL of the document currently displayed in the second frame of the current Web browser window.

4. The statement `var myarray = new Array(10)` will create an array called `myarray[]` with 10 elements.

5. The onSubmit handler can only be included inside a `<FORM>` tag and not in an `<INPUT TYPE="submit">` tag as could possibly be assumed.

Chapter 21, "Java"

1. Java was developed by Sun Microsystems.

2. The <APPLET> tag is used to include a Java applet inside a Web page.

3. The CODEBASE attribute lets you indicate that the applet referenced by the <APPLET> tag is stored in a different directory than the one where the HTML document was located.

4. The <PARAM> tag lets you declare parameters in a Web document that need to be passed to the Java applet.

5. The init() method is the first method called when a new class object is created. In this method you should include any code needed to initialize (or reset) the properties of a class.

F

Glossary

Glossary

This glossary contains a short description of many terms that you will find mentioned in Request for Comment documents, World Wide Web pages, Internet-related magazines, and trade and public newspapers or journals. Although this list is reasonably comprehensive, the Internet has a propensity for creating new words and jargon faster than just about any other area of life.

As a result, if you come across a term or piece of Internet jargon not covered here, there are a number of resources on the World Wide Web that may be able to offer you further assistance, including:

- Collaborative Virtual HyperGlossary:

  `http://www.cryst.bbk.ac.uk/glossary/index.html`

- WorldCom Network Services—Telecommunications Glossary:

  `http://www.wiltel.com/glossary/glossary.html`

- The Glossary of Internet Terms:

  `http://www.matisse.net/files/glossary.html`

- The Definitions and Acronyms Glossary:

  `http://www.itsi.disa.mil/cfs/glossary.html`

- A Glossary of World Wide Web Terms and Acronyms:

  `http://www.ncsa.uiuc.edu/SDG/Software/Mosaic/Glossary/index.html`

You may also want to obtain a copy of FYI18—the Internet Users' Glossary from InterNIC. This document is maintained by the User Glossary Working Group of the User Services Area of the Internet Engineering Task Force (IETF) and is the basis on which parts of the glossary that follows was based. Where a definition is based on this FYI or other sources, the reference appears after the definition, such as [FYI18], which stands for "For Your Information" document 18.

Note: Copies of For Your Information (FYI) and Request for Comment (RFC) documents can be obtained from `http://www.internic.net/`. Some definitions in this glossary include references to such documents (for example, [FYI14], [RFC18]).

A

address   There are many types of addresses to be found on the Internet: e-mail addresses, IP addresses, domain names, and URLs.

address resolution   When you type a domain name into an address field, it needs to be converted to an IP address before it can be used by programs communicating via the Internet. This process is called address resolution. *See also* domain name system.

alias   Many e-mail clients allow you to define aliases or single words that represent much longer e-mail addresses. The Eudora e-mail client refers to these aliases as *nicknames.*

anonymous FTP   Using anonymous FTP, a person can retrieve files from an FTP server without the need for an account at the site that operates it.

applet   A small program embedded into a Web page using the Java programming language.

application   Any computer program that can be run locally on a user's system or remotely using telnet.

Archie   A client/server application that allows you to search FTP sites for specific files.

archive   A single file that usually contains one or more other files in a compressed format (for example, .ZIP, .ARC, .Z).

archive site   Any machine that permits access to its files by the use of anonymous FTP.

article   Any message sent to a Usenet newsgroup.

B

bandwidth   Technically, the difference in Hertz (Hz) between the highest and lowest frequencies of a transmission channel. As typically used, the amount of data that can be sent through a given communications circuit. [FYI18]

BBS   *See* bulletin board system.

BFN   Bye for now.

binary   A base 2 numbering system that is the foundation of all computer operations.

binary file   Any file containing data stored in machine-readable format. *See also* text file.

BinHex   The Macintosh-based program that converts binary files into ASCII text files. Once a file is encoded into this format, you can send it using e-mail. BinHex is similar to MIME and uuencode, but is not directly compatible with either system.

bounce   When you send e-mail to an address that doesn't exist, the message is bounced back to you.

BRB   Be right back.

BTW   By the way.

bulletin board system   Any computer system operated for the purpose of the public exchange of electronic messages and files. BBSs, as a rule, are not directly connected to the Internet, but instead use the FIDOnet network.

C

CERN   Conseil European pour la Recherche Nucleaire (the European Laboratory for Particle Physics). CERN was responsible for the development of the World Wide Web under the direction of Tim Berners-Lee.

channel (IRC)   When using IRC, each of the discussion areas or rooms are called channels.

client   A computer system or process that requests a service of another computer system or process. A workstation requesting the contents of a file from a file server is a client of the file server. [RFC18]

client/server   The term used to describe the process used by many Internet services. FTP, Usenet, and WWW are all examples of client/server systems.

CU later   See you later.

cyberspace   A term coined by the novelist William Gibson to describe the electronic world he created for his series of cyberpunk novels—*Neuromancer, Count Zero,* and *Mona Lisa Overdrive*. The name has also become a popular method of describing the Internet to newbies.

D

decode   *See* uudecode.

decrypt   To convert an encrypted file back into a readable format. To do this, you need to know either the original key that the file was encrypted with or its secret key (if the file was encrypted using a public key system).

dial-up network   Any network that allows access using dial-up modems. To connect to the Internet using a dial-up network, you usually need access to either a PPP or SLIP terminal server.

distributed database A collection of several different data repositories that looks like a single database to the user. A prime example in the Internet is the domain name system. [FYI18]

domain name system This system provides the mechanism that allows domain names to be converted into IP addresses.

E

EFF Electronic Frontier Foundation. This was formed to address the many legal issues facing people when dealing with electronic communications using computers.

e-mail Electronic mail. The term used to describe the electronic exchange of messages via computers and typically across the Internet.

e-mail address The address used to describe the location of the intended recipient of an e-mail message. This address takes the form `userid@domain.name`.

encode *See* uuencode.

encrypt To convert a file into a seemingly scrambled format to ensure its secure transmission across the Internet. The file must then be decrypted before it can be read by anyone at the receiving end.

F

FAQ Frequently Asked Questions. Documents published on many sites and servers that contain a list of questions and answers relating to the service on which they are contained.

finger A small program used to display information about a person logged onto the Internet.

flame A strongly worded message sent in response to an article posted on a Usenet newsgroup or in a mailing list.

flame war A stream of responses and counter-flames triggered by a flame.

`file:` A URL protocol that defines a file which can be downloaded via FTP.

fragmentation The IP process in which a packet is broken into smaller pieces to fit the requirements of a physical network over which the packet must pass. [FYI18]

FTP File Transfer Protocol or File Transfer Program. A system that allows files to be transferred from one computer to another via the Internet.

FWIW For what it's worth.

FYI For Your Information documents are maintained by the InterNIC and contain useful information about the Internet and its operation.

G

<G> A grin emoticon. Also <g>, <grin>, <bg> (big grin), and <vbg> (very big grin).

gateway A communications tool used to exchange information between different computer networks and protocols.

GD&RFC Grinning, ducking, and running for cover.

GIF Graphics Interchange Format. A graphics format used to store photographic-quality images. Due to legal issues surrounding the use of this image format, it is rapidly being replaced by JPEG as the format of choice.

gopher A text-based predecessor to the World Wide Web that is still in use on many systems.

gopher: The URL header that defines a link to a gopher site.

H

hacker Any person who has a detailed understanding of computer systems and networks. In recent years this term has also come to refer to people who attempt to break into computer systems, although the term "cracker" more correctly applies to such people.

hardware Any physical components of a computer system, including CPUs, keyboards, hard drives, monitors, and printers.

host A term used to refer to any computer that allows people to connect to the Internet. The new GNN Internet service is a form of host computer system.

host name The domain name of a host computer system. Netscape Communications's host name is netscape.com.

HTML Hypertext markup language. The language used to define pages that can be displayed by World Wide Web navigators.

http: The URL protocol entry that identifies a document as a WWW page.

I

IAB Internet Architecture Board. It oversees the Internet Engineering Task Force and the Internet Research Task Force.

IETF   Internet Engineering Task Force. It is the technical body formed by the IAB to develop protocols and design strategies for the Internet.

IMHO   In my humble opinion.

Internet Protocol   The Internet Protocol is defined in RFC 791 as the network layer for the TCP/IP protocol suite.

Internet registry   The registry operated by InterNIC that is responsible for the allocation of IP addresses and the registration of domain names.

IP address   The individual address assigned to every computer connected to the Internet that distinguishes it from every other machine. This address is usually represented as a dotted quad—four numbers separated by a dot, as in 192.190.215.5, which represents the IP address of my Internet host at `world.net`.

IRC   Internet Relay Chat. The CB radio of the Internet world.

IRTF   Internet Research Task Force. It is charted by the IAB to examine the future of the Internet and discuss the long-term implications of services such as Internet radio and the possibility of video on demand.

ISDN   Integrated Services Digital Network. An emerging technology that is beginning to be offered by the telephone carriers of the world. ISDN combines voice and digital network services in a single medium, making it possible to offer customers digital data services as well as voice connections through a single "wire." The standards that define ISDN are specified by CCITT. [RFC1208]

J

Java   The platform-independent Internet programming language created by Sun Microsystems.

JavaScript   A Java-like scripting language created by Netscape Communications.

JPEG   A graphics image format developed by the Joint Photographics Experts Group. JPEG is rapidly replacing the older GIF format because of its ability to store pictures in a highly compressed format.

JPG   The file extension used by JPEG format files.

K

K12   A collection of newsgroups, IRC channels, and WWW pages devoted to discussions by students and educators. There are topics in these areas ranging from kindergarten to grade 12.

Kermit   An early file transfer protocol that is still in use on some systems. Unlike FTP, Kermit is not a network transfer protocol, but a computer-to-computer protocol.

L

LAN   Local area network. A popular method of connecting computers in a network that are situated in the same physical location.

LISTSERV   The mailing list management software supported by BITNET.

lurker   A person who reads messages posted to newsgroups and mailing lists but does not post any responses. As a rule, newbies are encouraged to lurk for a while before participating to get a feel for the style of messages and the nature of the conversations.

M

mail gateway   A gateway that permits two separate networks to exchange e-mail.

mailing list   A form of distributed messaging system that forwards a copy of every message it receives to all participants in the mailing lists. The two most common mailing list managers are Listserv and Majordomo.

mail server   An Internet site that acts as a post office for a number of users by collecting and distributing their electronic mail.

`mailto:`   The WWW URL header that defines an e-mail address.

Majordomo   The mailing list manager designed for UNIX-based computer systems that is based on the popular Perl scripting language.

Martian packets   A humorous term applied to packets that turn up unexpectedly on the wrong network because of bogus routing entries. Also used as a name for a packet that has an altogether bogus (non-registered or ill-formed) Internet address. [RFC1208]

MIME   Multipurpose Internet mail extension. It is regarded by many as the replacement for the tiring uuencode format, which sometimes cannot properly encode files related to multimedia-based activities (such as compressed video and audio).

moderator   The term used to refer to the person who moderates or determines which messages are distributed to all the recipients of a mailing list or newsgroup.

MOO   *See* MUD.

MUD   Multiuser dungeon. An interactive, text-based role-playing games that can be played across the Internet.

N

Netiquette   A pun on "etiquette," referring to proper behavior on a network. [FYI18]

network   A collection of computers connected for the purpose of realtime data transfers. The Internet is considered to be a network of networks.

newbie   A term used to describe new Internet users.

newsfeed   In the Internet world, this refers to sites that provide access to Usenet traffic, while in the commercial world it refers to services that provide access to news from organizations such as the Associated Press and CNN.

newsreader   A client program that can access articles stored in newsgroups on a Usenet server.

NIC   Network Information Center. The most well known of these is the InterNIC site at `ds.internic.net`.

NNTP   Network News Transfer Protocol—This protocol allows Usenet servers to exchange newsgroup articles using the Internet instead of the older UUCP process.

NSF   National Science Foundation. The government agencies that administer the NSFNET, which for a long time was regarded as the primary backbone of the Internet.

O

OCLC   Online Computer Library Catalog. A nonprofit membership organization offering computer-based services to libraries, educational organizations, and their users. The OCLC library information network connects more than 10,000 libraries worldwide. Libraries use the OCLC system for cataloging, interlibrary loan, collection development, bibliographic verification, and reference searching. [OCLC]

P

packet   The smallest unit of data sent across a network. A generic term used to describe a unit of data at all levels of the protocol stack, but it is most correctly used to describe application data units. [FYI18]

PING   A small program used to test your Internet host's ability to reach another point on the Internet. Usually, it also reports the amount of time taken for a message to traverse the Internet.

POP3   The standard e-mail post office protocol that allows users to retrieve messages from their mailbox on an Internet mail server.

Q

QuickTime QuickTime is a movie file format developed by Apple Computers for playing realtime multimedia movies on a desktop computer. Versions of QuickTime are available for both Macintosh- and Windows-based computer systems.

quotes A symbol such as > used in newsgroup articles and e-mail messages, to indicate a quote from a previously received message.

R

RFC Request for Comment. These documents are an integral part of life on the Internet. Now numbering in the thousands, these documents describe all the protocols used by the Internet and discuss all natures of Internet usage. The informational RFCs are also known as FYIs, and those that contain published standards are STDs.

ROTFL Rolling on the floor laughing.

route The path a packet of information takes as it travels from one host to another.

RTFM Read the *[censored]* manual. (I'll let you work out what the F stands for. Some people say it could be "fabulous," but somehow I doubt it <G>.)

S

script A small—normally uncompiled—program that controls the operation of a larger program. JavaScript is an example of a scripting language. It can be used to control the operation of a Web page.

server Any computer that provides services to the Internet community. FTP sites, WWW hosts, and Usenet providers are all examples of servers. To access the information contained on a server, you need to have a complementary client program running on your local system.

signature The tag line that is appended to the end of messages by e-mail clients and Usenet newsreaders. These lines often contain quotes and information about the message's sender.

smileys :-) and all his friends.

snail mail A derogatory term used for mail sent through the postal service that reflects the amount of time taken for the mail to be delivered.

sneaker mail The process of delivering mail by hand. Computer programs distributed this way are often said to have used sneakernet.

spider   A small, eight-legged animal. Also a small computer program developed for the Lycos search engine, which roams the World Wide Web looking for new Web sites.

STD   Request for Comments documents containing official Internet standards. As in [STD01].

StuffIt   A file compression and archive format used by Macintosh computers.

T

T1   A high-speed digital connection that can transmit data at speeds up to 1.544Mb per second.

T3   A high-speed digital connection that can transmit data at speeds up to 44.746Mb per second.

TCP/IP   The suite of protocols that allows computers to communicate with each other using the Internet.

telnet   The standard communications protocol used for remote terminal logins across the Internet.

terminal emulator   A computer program that emulates a terminal.

text file   A file containing only the characters that can be read by a text editor. They are often referred to as ASCII text files.

TTFN   Ta ta for now. A common way to sign off services such as IRC.

U

UNIX   The operating system developed by AT&T Bell Labs. Most Internet servers are UNIX based. One of the main features of the UNIX operating system is its ability to handle many tasks at once. This is called multitasking.

URL   Uniform Resource Locator. This is the common method used by the World Wide Web to describe the location of a document by defining its type, site, and directory path, along with its name.

Usenet   A collection of thousands of topically named newsgroups, the computers that run the protocols, and the people who read and submit Usenet news. Not all Internet hosts subscribe to Usenet, and not all Usenet hosts are on the Internet. [FYI18]

UUCP   UNIX-to-UNIX Copy. This program was originally the primary method of distributing articles published in Usenet newsgroups. It has now been replaced for the most part by NNTP.

uudecode   The UNIX program used to convert binary files encoded as ASCII text files back to binary files.

uuencode   The UNIX program that converts binary files into ASCII text files. Once a file is encoded into this format, you can send it using e-mail.

V

virus   A small program that is capable of replicating itself on computer after computer in much the same way as a virus infects humans. Some computer viruses are harmless, but others are malicious and have been known to destroy hard drives and wipe out files.

virtual reality   VR is the latest catch phrase of the computer industry. It refers to computer programs that create virtual worlds where people can interact in a variety of ways. MUDs, and their counterparts, MOOs, are often referred to as text-based virtual reality environments.

VRML   A new markup language that lets people navigate around the Internet as though it were a 3-D world. When used in conjunction with a WWW browser, VRML turns the WWW into a visual cyberspace.

W

W3   *See* World Wide Web.

WAIS   Wide Area Information Servers let you search thousands of documents stored on computers all over the Internet.

wais: The URL protocol for WAIS servers. In recent years the use of this protocol has fallen into disuse, in favor of gateways like WAISgate at `http://www.wais.com/`.

Web   A common method of referring to the World Wide Web.

worm   A lot like a computer virus. The main difference is that worms are designed primarily to work in network environments like the Internet. Not all worms are malicious; some often perform useful tasks such as roaming the World Wide Web looking for new home pages to add to indexes.

WWW   *See* World Wide Web.

World Wide Web   A navigator program that allows you to explore the Internet using a graphical point-and-click interface based on the popular hypertext system.

X

X Window   A UNIX-based environment popular with users of Sun workstations that fully supports the TCP/IP protocol as an integral part of its working environment.

X.500   A directory standard that one day may result in the creation of the ultimate White Pages for the Internet.

Y

Yahoo   One of the most well-known WWW directories. It can be found at `http://www.yahoo.com/`.

YFNSA   Your friendly neighborhood system administrator.

YMMV   Your mileage may vary. A popular automotive term that is now used on the Internet with reference to Internet bandwidth and the performance of a TCP/IP connection.

Z

ZIP   ZIP is a file compression format developed by PKWARE. ZIP is by far the most popular compression format used by PC-based computer systems.

ZOO   Like ZIP, ZOO is also a file compression and archive system. You most often encounter files compressed into a ZOO archive on UNIX-based computer systems.

INDEX

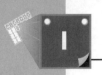

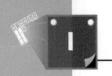

Add to Your Sams.net Library Today
with the Best Books for Internet Technologies

ISBN	Quantity	Description of Item	Unit Cost	Total Cost
1-57521-007-X		Netscape Unleashed	$49.99	
1-57521-041-X		The Internet Unleashed, 1996	$49.99	
1-57521-040-1		The World Wide Web Unleashed, 1996	$49.99	
0-672-30745-6		HTML and CGI Unleashed	$39.99	
1-57521-039-8		Presenting Java	$25.00	
1-57521-030-4		Teach Yourself Java in 21 Days	$39.99	
1-57521-004-5		The Internet Business Guide, Second Edition	$25.00	
0-672-30595-X		Education on the Internet	$25.00	
0-672-30718-9		Navigating the Internet, Third Edition	$22.50	
1-57521-064-9		Teach Yourself Web Publishing with HTML, 3.0 in a Week, Second Edition	$29.99	
1-57521-005-3		Teach Yourself More Web Publishing with HTML in a Week	$29.99	
1-57521-010-X		Pug-n-Play Netscape for Windows	$29.99	
0-672-30723-5		Secrets of the Mud Wizards	$25.00	
		Shipping and Handling: See information below.		
		TOTAL		

Shipping and Handling: $4.00 for the first book, and $1.75 for each additional book. If you need to have it NOW, we can ship product to you in 24 hours for an additional charge of approximately $18.00, and you will receive your item overnight or in two days. Overseas shipping and handling adds $2.00. Prices subject to change. Call between 9:00 a.m. and 5:00 p.m. EST for availability and pricing information on latest editions.

201 W. 103rd Street, Indianapolis, Indiana 46290

1-800-428-5331 — Orders   1-800-835-3202 — FAX   1-800-858-7674 — Customer Service

Book ISBN 1-57521-068-1

Must See CD.

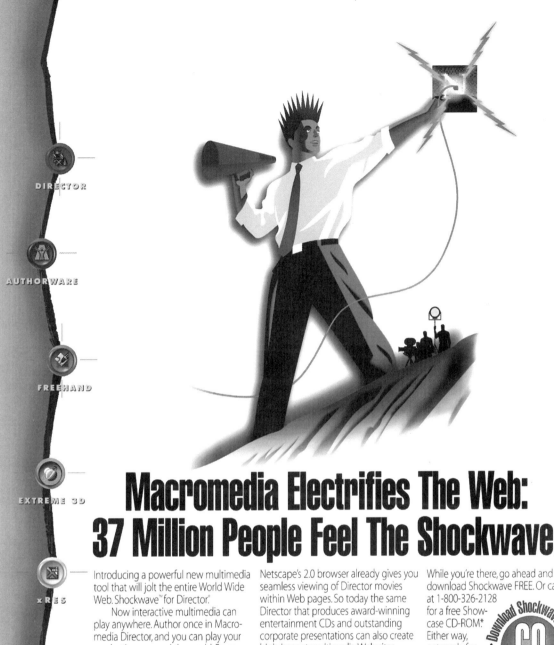

Macromedia Electrifies The Web:
37 Million People Feel The Shockwave.

DIRECTOR

AUTHORWARE

FREEHAND

EXTREME 3D

xRES

SOUNDEDIT 16

FONTOGRAPHER

Introducing a powerful new multimedia tool that will jolt the entire World Wide Web. Shockwave™ for Director.®

Now interactive multimedia can play anywhere. Author once in Macromedia Director, and you can play your productions around the world. From a Power Mac™ in Manhattan to a Windows® 95 PC in Perth. And now on the Web thanks to Shockwave. In fact,

Netscape's 2.0 browser already gives you seamless viewing of Director movies within Web pages. So today the same Director that produces award-winning entertainment CDs and outstanding corporate presentations can also create high-impact multimedia Web sites–with Shockwave. To learn more about Macromedia Director, check out our Web site at http://www.macromedia.com/

While you're there, go ahead and download Shockwave FREE. Or call us at 1-800-326-2128 for a free Show-case CD-ROM.* Either way, get ready for a shocking development on the Web.

GO · Download Shockwave Free · http://www.macromedia.com

MACROMEDIA®
Tools To Power Your Ideas™

Teach Yourself the Internet in a Week, Second Edition

— *Neil Randall*

The combination of a structured, step-by-step approach and the excitement of exploring the world of the Internet make this tutorial and reference perfect for any user wanting to master the Net. Efficiently exploring the basics of the Internet, *Teach Yourself the Internet* takes users to the farthest reaches of the Internet with hands-on exercises and detailed instructions. Completely updated to cover Netscape, Internet Works, and Microsoft's Internet Assistant.

Price: $25.00 USA/$34.99 CDN   User Level: Beginner-Inter
ISBN: 0-672-30735-9   622 pages

Tricks of the Internet Gurus

— *Various Internet Gurus*

This is a best-selling title that focuses on tips and techniques that allow the reader to more effectively use the resources of the Internet. A must-have for the power Internet user, *Tricks of the Internet Gurus* offers tips, strategies, and techniques for optimizing use of the Internet. Features interviews with various Internet leaders.

Price: $35.00 USA/$47.95 CDN   User Level: Inter-Advanced
ISBN: 0-672-30599-2   809 pages

Teach Yourself More Web Publishing with HTML in a Week

— *Laura Lemay*

This is ideal for those people who are ready for more advanced World Wide Web home page design! The sequel to *Teach Yourself Web Publishing with HTML*, *Teach Yourself More* explores the process of creating and maintaining Web presentations, including setting up tools and converters for verifying and testing pages. Teaches advanced HTML techniques and tricks in a clear, step-by-step manner with many practical examples. Highlights the Netscape extensions and HTML 3.0.

Price: $29.99 USA/$39.99 CDN   User Level: Inter-Advanced
ISBN: 1-57521-005-3   480 pages

The Internet Business Guide, Second Edition

— *Rosalind Resnick & Dave Taylor*

Updated and revised, this guide will inform and educate anyone on how they can use the Internet to increase profit, reach a broader market, track down business leads, and access critical information. Updated to cover digital cash, Web cybermalls, secure Web servers, and setting up your business on the Web, *The Internet Business Guide* includes profiles of entrepreneurs' successes (and failures) on the Internet. Improve your business by using the Internet to market products and services, make contacts with colleagues, cut costs, and improve customer service.

Price: $25.00 USA/$39.99 CDN   User Level: All Levels
ISBN: 1-57521-004-5   470 pages

Netscape Unleashed

— Dick Oliver, et. al.

This book provides a complete, detailed, and fully fleshed-out overview of the Netscape products—the hottest technologies on the Web today. Through case studies and examples of how individuals, businesses, and institutions are using the Netscape products for Web development, *Netscape Unleashed* gives a full description of the evolution of Netscape from its inception to today, and its cutting-edge developments with Netscape Gold, LiveWire, Netscape Navigator 2.0, Java and JavaScript, Macromedia, VRML, plug-ins, Adobe Acrobat, HTML 3.0 and beyond, security, and Intranet systems.

Price: $45.00 USA/$61.95 CDN   User Level: All Levels
ISBN: 1-57521-007-X   800 pages

Teach Yourself CGI Scripting with Perl in a Week

— Eric Herrmann

This book is a step-by-step tutorial of how to create, use, and maintain Common Gateway Interfaces (CGIs). It describes effective ways of using CGI as an integral part of Web development. Adds interactivity and flexibility to the information that can be provided through your Web site. Includes PERL 4.0 and 5.0, CGI libraries, and other applications to create databases, dynamic interactivity, and other enticing page effects.

Price: $39.99 USA/$53.99 CDN   User Level: Inter-Advanced
ISBN: 1-57521-009-6   500 pages

Teach Yourself Java in 21 Days

— Laura Lemay and Charles Perkins

This is the complete tutorial guide to the most exciting technology to hit the Internet in years—Java! A detailed guide to developing applications with the hot new Java language from Sun Microsystems, *Teach Yourself Java in 21 Days* shows readers how to program using Java and develop applications (applets) using the Java language. With coverage of Java implementation in Netscape Navigator and Hot Java, along with the Java Development Kit, including the compiler and debugger for Java, *Teach Yourself Java* is a must have!

Price: $39.99 USA/$53.99 CDN   User Level: Inter-Advanced
ISBN: 1-57521-030-4   600 pages

Presenting Java

— John December

Presenting Java gives you a first look at how Java is transforming static Web pages into living, interactive applications. Java opens up a world of possibilities previously unavailable on the Web. You'll find out how Java is being used to create animations, computer simulations, interactive games, teaching tools, spreadsheets, and a variety of other applications. Whether you're a new user, a project planner, or a developer, *Presenting Java* provides an efficient, quick introduction to the basic concepts and technical details that make Java the hottest new Web technology of the year!

Price: $25.00 USA/$34.95 CDN   User Level: All Levels
ISBN: 1-57521-039-8   207 pages

Education on the Internet

— Jill H. Ellsworth, Ph.D.

This tutorial and reference describes Internet basics and shows teachers, students, and parents how to find and use the educational resources available on the Internet. It includes Internet 101, which explains what the Internet is, how to get connected, and how to use its tools for learning and teaching. Readers learn how to use the Internet to research topics, explore museums of art, master a foreign language, and develop new and fresh curriculum plans.

Price: $25.00 USA/$34.95 CDN   User Level: All Levels
ISBN: 0-672-30595-X   591 pages

The Internet Unleashed 1996

— Barron, Ellsworth, Savetz, et al

The Internet Unleashed 1996 is the complete reference to get new users up and running on the Internet while providing the consummate reference manual for the experienced user. Designed to grow as the knowledge of the reader grows, *The Internet Unleashed 1996* provides the reader with an encyclopedia of information on how to take advantage of all the Net has to offer for business, education, research, and government. The companion CD-ROM contains more than 100 tools and applications to make the most of your time on the Internet. The only book that includes the experience of more than 40 of the world's top Internet experts, this new edition is updated with expanded coverage of Web publishing, Internet business, Internet multimedia and virtual reality, Internet security, Java, and more!

Price: $49.99 USA/$67.99 CDN   User Level: All Levels
ISBN: 1-57521-041-X   1,456 pages

World Wide Web Unleashed 1996

— December and Randall

The World Wide Web Unleashed 1996 is designed to be the only book a reader will need to experience the wonders and resources of the Web. The companion CD-ROM contains more than 100 tools and applications to make the most of your time on the Internet. It shows readers how to explore the Web's amazing world of electronic art museums, online magazines, virtual malls, and video music libraries, while giving readers complete coverage of Web page design, creation, and maintenance, plus coverage of new Web technologies such as Java, VRML, CGI, and multimedia!

Price: $49.99 USA/$67.99 CDN   User Level: All Levels
ISBN: 1-57521-040-1   1,440 pages

Teach Yourself Web Publishing with HTML in 14 Days, Premier Edition

— Laura Lemay

This book teaches everything about publishing on the Web. In addition to its exhaustive coverage of HTML, it also gives readers hands-on practice with more complicated subjects such as CGI, tables, forms, multimedia programming, testing, maintenance, and much more. The CD-ROM is Mac and PC compatible and includes a variety of applications that help readers create Web pages using graphics and templates.

Price: $39.99 USA/$53.99 CDN   User Level: All Levels
ISBN: 1-57521-014-2   804 pages

Teach Yourself Web Publishing with HTML 3.0 in a Week, Second Edition

— *Laura Lemay*

Ideal for those people who are interested in the Internet and the World Wide Web—the Internet's hottest topic! This updated and revised edition teaches readers how to use HTML (Hypertext Markup Language) version 3.0 to create Web pages that can be viewed by nearly 30 million users. It explores the process of creating and maintaining Web presentations, including setting up tools and converters for verifying and testing pages. The new edition highlights the new features of HTML—such as tables and Netscape and Microsoft Explorer extensions. Provides the latest information on working with images, sound files, and video, and teaches advanced HTML techniques and tricks in a clear, step-by-step manner with many practical examples of HTML pages.

Price: $25.00 USA/$34.95 CDN   User Level: Beginner-Inter
ISBN: 1-57521-064-9   518 pages

Web Page Construction Kit (Software)

Create your own exciting World Wide Web pages with the software and expert guidance in this kit! Includes HTML Assistant Pro Lite, the acclaimed point-and-click Web page editor. Simply highlight text in HTML Assistant Pro Lite and click on the appropriate button to add headlines, graphics, special formatting, links, etc. No programming skills needed! Using your favorite Web browser, you can test your work quickly and easily—without leaving the editor. A unique catalog feature enables you to keep track of interesting Web sites and easily add their HTML links to your pages. Assistant's user-defined toolkit also enables you to add new HTML formatting styles as they are defined. Includes the #1 best-selling Internet book, *Teach Yourself Web Publishing with HTML 3.0 in a Week, Second Edition,* and a library of professionally designed Web page templates, graphics, buttons, bullets, lines, and icons to rev up your new pages!

PC Computing magazine says, "If you're looking for the easiest route to Web publishing, HTML Assistant is your best choice!"

Price: $39.95 US/$46.99 CAN   User Level: Beginner-Inter
ISBN: 1-57521-000-2   518 pages

HTML & CGI Unleashed

— *John December & Marc Ginsburg*

This book is for professional developers who have a basic understanding of programming and need a detailed guide. Provides a complete, detailed reference to developing Web information systems. Covers the full range of languages—HTML, CGI, Perl C, editing and conversion programs, and more—and how to create commercial-grade Web Applications. Perfect for the developer who will be designing, creating, and maintaining a Web presence for a company or large institution.

Price: $39.99 USA/$53.99 CDN   User Level: Inter-Advanced
ISBN: 0-672-30745-6   830 pages

Web Site Construction Kit for Windows NT

— *Christopher Brown and Scott Zimmerman*

The Web Site Construction Kit for Windows NT has everything you need to set up, develop, and maintain a Web site with Windows NT— including the server on the CD! It teaches the ins and outs of planning, installing, configuring, and administering a Windows NT–based Web site for an organization, and it includes detailed instructions on how to use the software on the CD-ROM to develop the Web site's content—HTML pages, CGI scripts, image maps, and so forth.

Price: $49.99 USA/$67.99 CDN   User Level: All Levels
ISBN: 1-57521-047-9   430 pages

What's on the Disc

The companion CD-ROM contains many of the shareware programs mentioned in the book, as well as dozens of useful third-party tools and utilities.

Windows 3.1 or NT Installation Instructions

1. Insert the CD-ROM disc into your CD-ROM drive.

2. From File Manager or Program Manager, choose Run from the File menu.

3. Type *<drive>*INSTALL and press Enter, where *<drive>* corresponds to the drive letter of your CD-ROM. For example, if your CD-ROM is drive D:, type D:INSTALL and press Enter.

4. Follow the onscreen instructions in the installation program. Files will be installed to a directory named \TYNET unless you choose a different directory during installation.

INSTALL creates a Windows Program Manager group called Teach Yourself Netscape Pub. This group contains icons for exploring the CD-ROM. A Guide to the CD-ROM program starts automatically once installation has been completed.

Windows 95 Installation Instructions

1. If Windows 95 is installed on your computer and you have the AutoPlay feature enabled, the Guide to the CD-ROM program starts automatically whenever you insert the disc into your CD-ROM drive.

Note: The Guide to the CD-ROM program requires at least 256 colors. For best results, set your monitor to display between 256 and 64,000 colors. A screen resolution of 640×480 pixels is also recommended. If necessary, adjust your monitor settings before using the CD-ROM.

Macintosh Installation Instructions

1. Insert the CD-ROM disc into your CD-ROM drive.
2. When an icon for the CD appears on your desktop, open the disc by double-clicking on its icon.
3. Double-click on the icon named Guide to the CD-ROM, and follow the directions that appear.

Technical Support from Macmillan

We can't help you with Windows or Macintosh problems or software from third parties, but we can assist you if a problem arises with the CD-ROM itself. Here's how you get that help:

E-mail support: Send e-mail to support@mcp.com.

CompuServe: GO SAMS to reach the Macmillan Computer Publishing forum. Leave us a message, addressed to SYSOP. If you want the message to be private, address it to *SYSOP.

Telephone: (317) 581-3833

Fax: (317) 581-4773

Mail: Macmillan Computer Publishing
Attention: Support Department
201 West 103rd Street
Indianapolis, IN 46290-1093

Here's how to reach us on the Internet:

World Wide Web (*The Macmillan Information SuperLibrary*)

http://www.mcp.com/samsnet

Internet FTP

ftp.mcp.com (/pub/samsnet)